Social Isolation in Modern Society

Social contacts are of utmost importance for the personal and communal well-being of people. Social contacts constitute an elementary human need, are a considerable source of support and prove necessary for the integration and mutual commitment of people in society. Due to processes of individualization and social fragmentation in modern western societies, social contacts have come under increasing pressure. Individuals are finding it increasingly hard to develop and maintain a meaningful personal network, and more and more people can be characterized as socially isolated, experiencing feelings of loneliness or not participating in society.

Although social isolation has serious repercussions on people and communities, knowledge about this phenomenon remains rather limited. *Social Isolation in Modern Society* is the first multidisciplinary study to look at this issue. The book integrates relevant research traditions in the social sciences, bringing together sociological theories of social networks and psychological theories of feelings of loneliness. Both traditions are embedded in research, with the results of a large-scale empirical study being used to describe the extent, nature and divergent manifestations of social isolation. A new typology of social contacts is developed in order to take into account the number of network members and the quality of social contacts measured in terms of feelings of loneliness. The book provides a clear insight into personal, social and socio-economic causes and the consequences of social isolation and contains concrete policy recommendations.

Roelof Hortulanus is a senior lecturer in urban sociology in the Interdisciplinary Social Science Department at Utrecht University, the Netherlands. **Anja Machielse** is a lecturer in philosophy in the Interdisciplinary Social Science Department at Utrecht University. **Ludwien Meeuwesen** is an associate professor in psychology in the Interdisciplinary Social Science Department at Utrecht University.

Routledge advances in sociology

This series aims to present cutting-edge developments and debates within the field of sociology. It will provide a broad range of case studies and the latest theoretical perspectives, while covering a variety of topics, theories and issues from around the world. It is not confined to any particular school of thought.

1 **Virtual Globalization**
   Virtual spaces/tourist spaces
   Edited by David Holmes

2 **The Criminal Spectre in Law, Literature and Aesthetics**
   Peter Hutchings

3 **Immigrants and National Identity in Europe**
   Anna Triandafyllidou

4 **Constructing Risk and Safety in Technological Practice**
   Edited by Jane Summerton and Boel Berner

5 **Europeanisation, National Identities and Migration**
   Changes in boundary constructions between Western and Eastern Europe
   Willfried Spohn and Anna Triandafyllidou

6 **Language, Identity and Conflict**
   A comparative study of language in ethnic conflict in Europe and Eurasia
   Diarmait Mac Giolla Chríost

7 **Immigrant Life in the US**
   Multi-disciplinary perspectives
   Edited by Donna R. Gabaccia and Colin Wayne Leach

8   Rave Culture and Religion
Edited by Graham St John

9   Creation and Returns of Social Capital
A new research program
Edited by Henk Flap and Beate Völker

10 Self-Care
Embodiment, personal autonomy and the shaping of health consciousness
Christopher Ziguras

11 Mechanisms of Cooperation
Werner Raub and Jeroen Weesie

12 After the Bell – Educational Success, Public Policy and Family Background
Edited by Dalton Conley and Karen Albright

13 Youth Crime and Youth Culture in the Inner City
Bill Sanders

14 Emotions and Social Movements
Edited by Helena Flam and Debra King

15 Globalization, Uncertainty and Youth in Society
Edited by Hans-Peter Blossfeld, Erik Klijzing, Melinda Mills and Karin Kurz

16 Love, Heterosexuality and Society
Paul Johnson

17 Agricultural Governance
Globalization and the new politics of regulation
Edited by Vaughan Higgins and Geoffrey Lawrence

18 Challenging Hegemonic Masculinity
Richard Howson

19 Social Isolation in Modern Society
Roelof Hortulanus, Anja Machielse and Ludwien Meeuwesen

Social Isolation in Modern Society

Roelof Hortulanus, Anja Machielse
and Ludwien Meeuwesen

LONDON AND NEW YORK

First published 2006
by Routledge
2 Park Square, Milton Park, Abingdon, Oxon OX14 4RN

Simultaneously published in the USA and Canada
by Routledge
270 Madison Ave, New York, NY 10016

Routledge is an imprint of the Taylor & Francis Group

Transferred to Digital Printing 2009

© 2006 Roelof Hortulanus, Anja Machielse and Ludwien Meeuwesen

Typeset in Garamond by Wearset Ltd, Boldon, Tyne and Wear

All rights reserved. No part of this book may be reprinted or reproduced or utilized in any form or by any electronic, mechanical, or other means, now known or hereafter invented, including photocopying and recording, or in any information storage or retrieval system, without permission in writing from the publishers.

British Library Cataloguing in Publication Data
A catalogue record for this book is available from the British Library

Library of Congress Cataloging in Publication Data
A catalog record for this book has been requested

ISBN10: 0-415-36768-9 (hbk)
ISBN10: 0-415-54388-6 (pbk)

ISBN13: 978-0-415-36768-4 (hbk)
ISBN13: 978-0-415-54388-0 (pbk)

Contents

List of figures xii
List of tables xiii
Preface xvii

PART I
Social isolation 1

1 **The issue of social isolation** 3
   ROELOF HORTULANUS AND ANJA MACHIELSE

   1.1 *Social isolation: manifestations? 3*
   1.2 *Social isolation: a phenomenon of our times? 4*
   1.3 *Social isolation: how does it happen? 5*
   1.4 *Social isolation: private matter or societal problem? 6*
   1.5 *Social isolation: a theme for social policy? 7*
   1.6 *Research aim 8*
   1.7 *Method 9*
   1.8 *Structure of the book 11*

2 **Theories on social contacts and social isolation** 13
   ANJA MACHIELSE

   2.1 *Introduction 13*
   2.2 *The importance of social relationships 14*
   2.3 *Changes in the social environment 22*
   2.4 *Social isolation as an issue for social sciences 24*
   2.5 *Theoretical approaches to social isolation 29*
   2.6 *Summary and conclusions 34*

3 A typology of social contacts   37
   LUDWIEN MEEUWESEN

   3.1   Introduction 37
   3.2   Definition of social isolation 37
   3.3   Towards a typology of social contacts 39
   3.4   Measures 41
   3.5   Network size 44
   3.6   Loneliness 45
   3.7   Social contacts typology 45
   3.8   Network support functions and typology 47
   3.9   Giving and receiving support 49
   3.10 Changes in network size 50
   3.11 Sources of protection 53
   3.12 Risk factors 55
   3.13 Discussion 57

PART II
Personal and social factors   61

4 Life events and social isolation   63
   LUDWIEN MEEUWESEN

   4.1   Introduction 63
   4.2   Definitions of life events 63
   4.3   Life events and the social contacts typology 65
   4.4   Hassles and uplifts 71
   4.5   Important events and social support 72
   4.6   The effects of important life events 74
   4.7   Consolation and protection 75
   4.8   Risk factors 76
   4.9   Discussion 78

5 Personal competences and social isolation   81
   LUDWIEN MEEUWESEN

   5.1   Introduction 81
   5.2   Personality, socialization and personal competences 82
   5.3   Measures 87
   5.4   Personal competences and social isolation 88
   5.5   Personal competences at the item level 89
   5.6   Socialization and contact typology 91

5.7   Personal competences and life events 92
5.8   Social responsibility 93
5.9   Risk factors and personal competences 97
5.10 Discussion 98

6 Health and social isolation

LUDWIEN MEEUWESEN

6.1   Introduction 100
6.2   Explanatory models for health 101
6.3   Coping and health 102
6.4   Social support and health 103
6.5   Operationalization of health indicators 104
6.6   Report mark on health 106
6.7   Physical vulnerability 107
6.8   Mental vulnerability 108
6.9   Depression 109
6.10 Inter-relatedness 112
6.11 Conclusions 114

7 Social isolation: formal and informal support

ANJA MACHIELSE

7.1   Introduction 115
7.2   Relevant concepts and definitions 115
7.3   Use of facilities and informal support 119
7.4   Use of facilities and vulnerability 122
7.5   Vulnerability and the personal network 125
7.6   Use of facilities by the vulnerable in relation to the social contacts typology 128
7.7   Views on the dependency on facilities 132
7.8   Summary and conclusions 134

8 Societal participation and social isolation

ROELOF HORTULANUS

8.1   Introduction 137
8.2   A measure for societal participation 138
8.3   Societal participation: a breeding ground for significant personal networks? 146
8.4   Societal participation and significant personal networks: not the same meaning for everyone 151
8.5   Conclusions 154

x   Contents

9   Social environment and social isolation   156
ROELOF HORTULANUS

9.1   Introduction   156
9.2   Functions of the social environment   158
9.3   The many faces of environmental isolation   160
9.4   Environmental and social isolation   170
9.5   Conclusions   174

PART III
Comparisons and differentiation   177

10   Social isolation in city and countryside   179
ANJA MACHIELSE

10.1   Introduction   179
10.2   Relevant concepts and definitions   179
10.3   Population composition in urban and rural areas   182
10.4   Personal networks   184
10.5   Societal participation   187
10.6   The social environment   192
10.7   Summary and conclusions   198

11   Social isolation: a combined analysis   201
LUDWIEN MEEUWESEN

11.1   Introduction   201
11.2   The typology of social contacts   201
11.3   Summary of the research results   203
11.4   Effects of individual, social-environmental, societal and background factors on the social contacts typology   209
11.5   Consequences of social isolation   214

12   The social contact typology: a further subgroup profiling   217
ROELOF HORTULANUS

12.1   Personal competences and societal participation as causes of social isolation   217
12.2   Societal and individual well-being as products of social isolation   225
12.3   Conclusions   229

PART IV
Reflections 231

13 Research on social isolation into perspective 233
LUDWIEN MEEUWESEN, ANJA MACHIELSE AND ROELOF HORTULANUS

13.1 Introduction 233
13.2 Reflection on method 233
13.3 Theoretical reflection 237

14 Towards a new policy vision on social isolation 246
ROELOF HORTULANUS

14.1 Introduction 246
14.2 Social isolation: private problem or societal issue? 247
14.3 A new policy vision 249
14.4 New intervention strategies 253
14.5 Conclusions 256

Appendices 258
References 266
Author index 278
Subject index 281

Figures

3.1	Network size	44
3.2	Loneliness	45
3.3	A typology of social contacts	46
4.1	Number of life events related to the typology of social contacts	66
4.2	Percentage of 'no support after important event' and reason for it	73
4.3	Sources of comfort, percentages	76
5.1	Personal coping strategies	86
5.2	Social typology and personal competences	89
5.3	Motivations to offer support to friends or acquaintances, related to the social typology, percentages	95
6.1	Social typology and physical status	107
6.2	Social typology and mental status	108
6.3	Scores on the Zung depression scale, percentages	110
6.4	Social typology and degree of depression	110
8.1	Societal participation	142
9.1	Desired and actual contacts in the neighbourhood	161
9.2	Availability of support from family/friends within walking distance	163
9.3	Report mark of the neighbourhood	164
12.1	Dissatisfaction with societal well-being according to eight subcategories of personal competences, percentages	225
12.2	Dissatisfaction with societal well-being according to eight subcategories of societal participation, percentages	226
12.3	Dissatisfaction with individual well-being according to eight subcategories of personal competences, percentages	227
12.4	Dissatisfaction with individual well-being according to eight subcategories of societal participation, percentages	228
13.1	Explanatory model for the emergence of social isolation	243

Tables

3.1	Combination of network size and feelings of loneliness	39
3.2	Social typology and percentage of respondents who have nobody to ask for support	48
3.3	Received support and given support in relation to the typology of social contacts	49
3.4	Changes in network size in the past five years, percentages	51
3.5	Sources of protection against isolation, in percentages	53
3.6	Blessed with a rich social life, in percentages	54
3.7	The four main aspects of a rich social life, in percentages	55
3.8	Percentages within risk factors of the four categories of social contacts	56
4.1	Percentage ($\geq$10 per cent) of positive life events	67
4.2	Percentage ($\geq$10 per cent) of negative life events	68
4.3	Percentage ($\geq$10 per cent) of negative life events, significant	69
4.4	The mentioning of personal and social events, and respondents' evaluation (in percentages)	70
4.5	Effects of a major life event on feelings of loneliness	74
4.6	Persons who offer comfort (>5 per cent)	75
5.1	Personal competences at an item level, in percentages	90
5.2	Assessment of offering support, percentages of positive answers	96
6.1	Zung depression items, percentage of respondents with confirmative answers	111
7.1	Use of professional facilities (in the last year) in percentages	119
7.2	Use of professional facilities by the four groups of the typology, in percentages	122
7.3	Individual problem accumulation and use of professional facilities, in percentages	124
7.4	Social contacts typology of persons with a varying degree of physical, mental and financial vulnerability, in percentages	127
7.5	Use of professional facilities by the vulnerable per group, in percentages	130

7.6	Professional facilities and informal support among the vulnerable, in percentages	131
7.7	Importance of professional facilities for users, in percentages	132
7.8	Share of people that give negative assessments on dependency on institutions per contact group, in percentages	133
8.1	Relation between income and societal activities, in percentages	139
8.2	Relation of the labour situation with societal activities, in percentages	140
8.3	Relation between education and societal activities, in percentages	141
8.4	Relation between educational level and societal participation, in percentages	143
8.5	Relation of socio-economic status and societal participation, in percentages	143
8.6	Other occupations according to societal participation, in percentages	144
8.7	Satisfaction with societal well-being according to societal participation, in percentages	145
8.8	Societal exclusion according to societal participation, in percentages	145
8.9	Degree of societal participation and social contact typology, in percentages	147
8.10	Social contact typology according to feelings of exclusion due to inability to be societally useful, in percentages	147
8.11	Support received and given according to societal participation, in percentages	148
8.12	Network composition according to societal participation, in percentages	148
8.13	Protective factors according to societal participation, in percentages	149
8.14	Changes in contacts and degree of societal participation, in percentages	150
8.15	Reasons for fewer contacts and societal participation, in percentages	150
8.16	Reasons for more contacts and societal participation, in percentages	151
8.17	Age and degree of societal participation, in percentages	152
8.18	Age and social contact typology, in percentages	153
8.19	Marital status and degree of societal participation, in percentages	154
8.20	Marital status and social contact typology, in percentages	154
9.1	Neighbourhood homogeneity according to desire for contacts and actual contacts, in percentages	167

Tables xv

9.2	Existence/lack of neighbourhood-bound network (practical and/or emotional) according to neighbourhood homogeneity, in percentages	168
9.3	Neighbourhood appreciation according to neighbourhood homogeneity, in percentages	169
9.4	Social contact typology according to environmental isolation (combination of desire for contacts/actual contacts), in percentages	172
9.5	Social contact typology according to environmental isolation (neighbourhood-bound support network), in percentages	172
9.6	Social contact typology according to environmental isolation (neighbourhood report mark), in percentages	172
9.7	Social contact typology according to environmental isolation (combination of desire for contacts/actual contacts) in very heterogeneous neighbourhoods, in percentages	173
9.8	Social contact typology according to environmental isolation (combination of desire for contacts/actual contacts) in very homogeneous neighbourhoods, in percentages	173
10.1	Number of respondents who cannot count on anyone for specific forms of support in city and countryside, in percentages	184
10.2	Share of family members in city and countryside, in percentages	186
10.3	Social typology for city and countryside, in percentages	187
10.4	Use of facilities in city and countryside, in percentages	191
10.5	Statements about contacts in the neighbourhood in city and countryside, in percentages	193
10.6	Views on neighbourhood residents in city and countryside, in percentages	195
10.7	Indicators for a positive attitude towards the social environment, in city and countryside, in percentages	196
10.8	Local social orientation in city and countryside, in percentages	197
10.9	The social contact typology and local orientation, in percentages	197
11.1	Multinomial logistic regression (for the social contacts typology), with eight background factors	210
11.2	Multinomial logistic regression (for the social contacts typology), with eight personal factors	211
11.3	Multinomial logistic regression (for the social contacts typology), with eight social-environmental factors	211
11.4	Multinomial logistic regression (for the social contacts typology), with seven personal factors	212
11.5	Multinomial logistic regression (for the social contacts typology), with all the relevant factors (demographic, personal, societal and social-spatial)	213

12.1	Further profiling of the social typology according to personal competencies, in percentages	218
12.2	Further profiling of the social typology according to societal participation, in percentages	218
12.3	Further subgroup typification of the social contract typology and personal competencies	221
12.4	Further subgroup typification of the social contact typology and societal participation	223
12.5	Social contact typology and personal competencies with societal participation, in percentages	224

Preface

Nowadays, social scientists and social politicians pay more and more attention to private living conditions – such as health, education and the upbringing of our children – as a breeding ground for individual well-being. This also applies to people's private social network. It seems a paradox, but in a society that emphasizes self reliance and individual responsibility, people with an extended personal network are far better off than those who live in social isolation. However, there are reasons to believe that in modern society, more and more people become socially isolated.

Still policy interventions are not pointed at disfunctioning or absent private social networks. It seems social isolation is supposed to be a consequence of other living problems instead of regarding it as a serious problem in itself and as a cause of other problems.

Social isolation does not only evoke professional interest. Everybody is familiar with examples of socially isolated people in their own environment. At the same time, the availability of an extended personal network is an obvious fact for most of us. This, especially, is the harrowing aspect of social isolation. In our view social isolation is an important concern for our society: for individual citizens, for social organizations and for our social policy. We hope our broad statement of affairs may function as a 'X-ray' of a core aspect of our social well being and the social quality of our society.

The research project that forms the basis of this book gave us the opportunity to elaborate on the issues mentioned above. Many issues were discussed in more than 3,000 face to face interviews. The richness of the data made it possible to give an idea about the scope and several forms of social isolation, to go into the relations between the functioning of someone's personal network and other important aspects of personal and societal functioning, such as life events, personal competencies, health, participation, neighbourhood conditions and so on. With all this, *Social Isolation in Modern Society* may stimulate further research and theoretical thinking, and the development of adequate intervention strategies to prevent social isolation.

This English edition is a shortened and updated version of the Dutch edition *Sociaal isolement: Een studie over sociale contacten en sociaal isolement in*

Nederland, which appeared two years ago. This edition has benefited from Ruth Rose, for the translation into English, Gerty Lensvelt-Mulders, for assistance in additional statistical analysis and Petra Nesselaar-Hofland for electronic editing.

Roelof Hortulanus
Anja Machielse
Ludwien Meeuwesen
Utrecht, March 2005

Part I
Social isolation

1 The issue of social isolation

Roelof Hortulanus and Anja Machielse

1.1 Social isolation: manifestations?

Often we hear news reports that a person has been found dead at home. The longer the death remained unnoticed, the more attention such a report gets. The typical questions that journalists pose to neighbours are: 'Did you know the deceased? Did you not notice that he had not gone outside for quite a while?' This type of news leaves us feeling uncomfortable. It raises questions about one's street and neighbourhood: could something like that happen here too? In the summer of 2003, France was shocked by the number of people who had passed away alone during a heatwave that lasted several days. The informal network of family, friends, acquaintances and neighbours was apparently insufficient or entirely absent, and the professional system was incapable of reacting adequately. There are other harrowing examples of social isolation in our modern society. We regularly read about single men and women who neglect themselves and their dwelling. In recent decades, the street scene in large cities has witnessed the increase of homeless people: the man who looks for food leftovers in garbage containers, the woman who rambles the streets mumbling to herself. The sight of such people leads us to wonder how things got so far, and whether no one looks after these people anymore.

These dramatic examples of socially isolated people raise the question of whether we are dealing with a small group of dropouts from society or with the tip of an iceberg – for the rest a fairly invisible one. In other words, are there many more individuals in our society who for all kinds of reasons are cut off from the social and societal outside world? And are these specifiable categories – for example, older immigrants who never connected to the society to which they moved and live in total isolation, lone mothers who no longer see possibilities to participate in social or societal life – or can social isolation affect any member of society? Can it be specified as a personal risk of modern society?

The different manifestations of social isolation become more poignant when you consider the major importance our society attaches to personal relationships and a rich social life. An expression of this is 'emotion television', which can spotlight persons who want to enter into new relationships or restore broken ones. We have reality TV, which shows how people live with each other for several weeks or months and how relationships between them develop. Television viewers identify with the characters from the soap operas that 'come into their homes' every day and seem to form a surrogate for contacts with family and friends: the viewers are made part of the emotional highs and lows in the lives of these characters. The importance social relationships have acquired can also be seen in the blooming market of dating and matchmaking services and the increasing space that personal ads are taking in newspapers and dating websites. Also remarkable are the general appeals to people from organizations like the Salvation Army and non-commercial advertising on television to create civic awareness for lonely fellow human beings.

1.2 Social isolation: a phenomenon of our times?

Is there reason to assume that in our modern times it has become much more difficult to make and maintain social contacts, and has the risk of social isolation grown? Are the consequences of individualization in our society among these risks? The individual is unquestionably more self-dependent, and less able to fall back on traditional social bonds like church, neighbourhood, family, work, political party or labour union, since these have lost a great deal of meaning. Obviously not all social bonds have disappeared, but the individualistic lifestyle has changed the character of society. The effects can be noticed in personal life, in the dealings between people and in the general social environment. Whereas people used to have a limited number of relatively stable bonds (marriage, family, work, neighbourhood, club life), nowadays there are many relatively fleeting bonds. The fairly small communities in which people used to live have made way for a multiplicity of social bonds within which people have to function. Within each of these bonds, people have to deal with different expectations and role patterns.

In a certain sense parallel to the individualization of western societies, welfare states developed in the second half of the twentieth century, mainly in Western Europe. Differences may indeed exist between the Scandinavian countries, England and the Netherlands, and southern Europe, but everywhere a more or less extensive system of public social benefits has been established that has made people less dependent on members of the community than they used to be (Esping-Andersen, 1990). All kinds of societal institutions now fulfil a role in people's social lives, as a result of which informal contacts between individuals have been partially formalized (for example, in health care). In recent decades, many personal contacts have been replaced with institutional associations.

These developments offer more freedom and possibilities for self-determination, but also require new skills. The disappearance of widespread social patterns and structures not only presents possibilities for emancipation, development and self-government but also entails great insecurities. In this context, Beck (1986) speaks of risks of individualization, risks that are more person-bound than the class-bound inequalities of other times. Whereas traditions and its related rules guided actions, these days people have to find their own way and choose from the many possibilities available. Not everyone is equally equipped to do this (Knorr-Cetina, 2001; Orbach, 1998). While for some people the new situation produces more freedom and a wealth and variety of contacts, others feel lost in the midst of large-scale associations and the superficiality of contact patterns – hence individual freedom and vulnerability end up very close together. This is even more the case in recent decades, now that in Western European welfare states the social benefits system is undergoing a process of austerity, and cuts in professional care and welfare facilities are a necessity. On the basis of the above-mentioned theoretical assumptions we may assume that increasing numbers of people are unable to keep themselves going and build a network of meaningful contacts around them. At the same time government policy has made a greater appeal to people's ability to cope independently, thus increasing the importance of good informal social networks and informal social support.

1.3 Social isolation: how does it happen?

Although we assume that it has become more difficult to build and maintain meaningful social contacts, the importance of social contacts has in fact increased in terms of both personal and societal functioning. How come some people fail to build a stable and supportive network around them while others are successful? Is their social isolation caused by personal and societal factors, or is there a combination of both? People tend to imagine social isolation as a consequence of ageing, long-term unemployment or loss of a partner. Is it indeed mostly these life circumstances that can lead people into social isolation? Or do other factors play a role? Could personal characteristics be instrumental in the emergence of social isolation, like a lack of self-respect or self-confidence and poor social skills that makes entering into stable relationships with others more difficult (Hortulanus *et al.*, 1992)? Perhaps other youth experiences or other life events, such as prolonged illness, affect people in such a way that their personal contacts are severely affected.

For growing numbers of citizens the workplace has assumed an increasingly significant role when entering into (meaningful) social contacts. Increased participation in the labour market also ensures that building and maintaining a social network in the home situation and one's own living environment is under increasing (time) pressure: the contacts established at work are often at the expense of contacts in the private sphere. We see this especially in the female portion of the population. For a long time it was primarily women who maintained these social contacts with family, friends and neighbours. The demand to participate in the labour process implies that their daily contacts too must compete with social contacts from their professional environment. Does this make those people who do not (or cannot) participate in the labour process (like the long-term unemployed or the disabled) better-off or worse-off in terms of their social contacts?

The living environment can also play a role in the emergence of social isolation. For many people, neighbourhoods have acquired a different meaning than they used to have, not only due to increased labour participation but also because of greater geographic mobility. It is therefore interesting to find out to what degree social isolation is associated with local circumstances and the social environment. People nowadays assume that social isolation is a typical phenomenon of the big cities, as this is where one finds the greatest cultural and ethnic diversity. Due to a heterogeneity of lifestyles and etiquettes, people in urban neighbourhoods have less contact with each other than used to be the case. However, in recent decades small communities have also undergone developments that could foster social isolation: the populations of many small towns have dropped significantly, and many local facilities have disappeared. More and more residents have to leave their villages in order to participate in all kinds of societal activities (for example, work, recreation, entertainment) or use facilities (like libraries or social work services). It is the less mobile groups in particular – the elderly, housewives, households without a car – that experience the negative consequences of the spatial scale increase and the concentration of such activities and facilities. Such outcomes make them more dependent on personal networks and hence more vulnerable to social isolation.

In addition to personal characteristics, life events, degree of societal participation and the modern neighbourhood environment, the living situation of certain categories of people can also be identified as a factor in the emergence of social isolation. For example, a large-scale national study in the Netherlands showed that lone-parent families have great difficulty with social contacts. Of the lone parents with a low societal position, as many as 20 per cent are socially isolated (Hortulanus et al., 1992). Another factor is the precarious living situation of lone seniors who live on their own.

1.4 Social isolation: private matter or societal problem?

In addition to inquiring into the factors that play a role in the emergence of social isolation, there is another question – whether we should see social isolation as a private matter or a societal problem. Social contacts are important to people's personal and societal well-being (Hortulanus et al., 1992). They increase self-respect and fulfil a key role in dealing with problems: people in somebody's social network can more readily be there for someone with a problematic situation without giving problem accumulation a fighting chance. Moreover, social contacts have become more important for societal functioning: persons from the social network can provide access to assorted societal resources like work, an education, etc. To 'belong', societally speaking, it is also necessary to have the right contacts and to 'network'.

The impact on personal well-being and threat to societal functioning can be reason enough to view social isolation not exclusively as a private matter but also as a societal issue. Social networks, however, are also relevant when seen from the perspective of society as a whole. People who are part of social networks are more active in societal life: they participate more in club life, provide more informal care, do more volunteer work and are more involved in all kinds of societal organizations. This is important to society because this societal participation forms a feeding ground for social activity and involvement with the 'weaker' and 'dropouts' of society.

In a different way, social isolation can also constitute a threat to social cohesion and solidarity within society. The intrusive way in which the social isolation of drifters, the homeless and junkies in neighbourhoods and urban centres manifests itself can be experienced as a direct threat by other users of the public domain. Less visible forms of social isolation do not seem to be directly unfavourable to social cohesion, but if people are no longer part of regular society they can also lose contact with the norms and values prevailing in that society – values that are essential for social integration and societal stability.

What happens with people who cannot meet the demands our individualized and complex society makes of them? Those who do not participate in the labour process and are unable to build a supportive network in their private life end up outside of society, in a social as well as a societal sense. Furthermore, this category of people who cannot manage on their own is not assertive enough to present their interests and needs to professional agencies. They alienate their social and societal environment, and their bonds with it keep dwindling. Social isolation could therefore be designated as a new form of social inequality.

1.5 Social isolation: a theme for social policy?

If in addition to psychological factors, societal circumstances also play a role in the emergence of social isolation problems. As the consequences of social isolation do not only affect the individual but also cause societal disruption, one should expect social isolation to be an important theme of social policy. However, until now social isolation has received little policy-related attention. Most of the focus in social policy, at the local level, still lies on battling societal disadvantages and thus material issues. Important focal points are work, income, education and the neighbourhood environment. Governments tend to emphasize societal participation and the assumed active involvement of citizens. Next to these classic disadvantage indicators, more recent goals of social policy – under the denominators of ability to cope independently, personal responsibility and mature autonomy – have been defined mainly in the light of societal participation and active involvement.

Must the government also create conditions to strengthen the social competency of individuals so that people can have a properly functioning personal network, or can it make do with offering a safety net for those who do not make it on their own? Can practising professionals in the sphere of care and welfare provide adequate answers to these problems when confronted with social isolation? Primary physicians and social workers are under enormous pressure: they usually lack the means to give extra time and attention to these clients, if they come into contact with them at all. Mental health institutions are oriented specifically towards severe mental problems. Institutions such as the Social Services Department, neighbourhood police, housing corporations and municipal health services only intervene after the situation has taken extreme forms, for example, if public health or the public order is threatened. Still, attention to social competency and a properly functioning social network could sometimes prove to be a decisive condition or point of reference for the success of assistance in other areas of life. In terms of social policy, more knowledge about social isolation allows for better recognition of the value of preventive interventions, anticipation of risk factors, and relief or elimination of social isolation that is already there.

1.6 Research aim

Given the developments in society, it is possible that the problems of social isolation may worsen further. Changed relationship patterns, increasing numbers of inactive people, higher demands on social competences, greater cultural and ethnic diversity, crumbling social bonds, problems bringing up youth: all these issues influence people's social functioning. Despite all these signals, little is known at this point about the nature and scope of social isolation. There isn't even an unambiguous definition of social isolation. Although much research has been done in recent years into loneliness and social isolation, it has focused mainly on familiar high-risk groups like seniors, the long-term unemployed and people with poor health. A wide and systematic study into the nature, scope, causes and consequences of social isolation is missing. *Social Isolation in Modern Society* attempts to interpret these aspects of social isolation. We have deliberately chosen information on the average population. Hence the book does not report on social isolation among a specific group like the homeless, drug addicts or illegal aliens: it mainly provides a glimpse into the lives of normal, ordinary citizens. We have also limited ourselves to personal social networks; contacts of a functional or fleeting nature do not belong here. Feelings of loneliness or the urge to retreat into oneself for a while are part of human nature. In this study we do not deal with temporary but with structural forms of social isolation. The book not only examines social isolation but also provides insight into the lives of people who, socially speaking, *are* competent.

The aim of this study is to gain insight into the nature and scope of social isolation in a modern western society, into the background as well as the causes and consequences of this phenomenon. Individual and societal aspects of social isolation will be discussed extensively. To realize these aims, the following questions are formulated:

1 What are the scope and nature of social isolation?
2 What individual and societal causes are behind it?
3 What are the consequences of social isolation for the individual and the social well-being of individuals?
4 What can the insights of this study mean for theories on social isolation?
5 How can these insights have an effect on policy on social isolation?

The research questions are answered on the basis of data from a major survey project, *Sociaal isolement in Nederland* (Social Isolation in the Netherlands), which took place between 1995 and 1998 at the initiative of the Dutch Ministry of Health, Welfare and Sports (Hortulanus, Machielse and Meeuwesen, 2003). The project was executed in four Dutch municipalities, including two large cities (Amsterdam and Utrecht) and two rural areas (Binnenmaas and Het Oldambt) (Adriaanse and Hortulanus, 1997; Hortulanus *et al.*, 1996, 1997; Turkenburg and Hortulanus, 1997).

1.7 Method

The study was carried out in the form of an oral survey, gathering data in two phases. When compiling the extended questionnaire, use was made of various data sources. Prior to the composition of the questionnaire, key informants in all the research locations were consulted, such as public servants, professionals working in health care and welfare institutions, and volunteers who have knowledge of and experience with different facets of social isolation. Use was also made of policy documents, existing statistic data and specialized literature. Based on this different information resources the questionnaire was developed.

In the first phase of the study, 2,462 persons were interviewed in a face-to-face setting. The questionnaire used here consisted largely of items with pre-coded answer categories. Next to several general questions about the background and living situation of the respondents, questions were included about the social contacts maintained by the respondents, the evaluation of these social contacts (for example, in terms of loneliness), the mutual exchange of help and support, health, any hindrances in daily functioning and the use of facilities. There were also questions on societal and neighbourhood factors, like participation in society, social contacts in one's social environment, views on neighbours and attachment to one's neighbourhood. An important part of this first survey concerns a series of questions to map out the social networks of the respondents. This was done using the exchange approach of Fischer (1982), which attempts to find out the persons with whom respondents (regularly) undertake concrete activities and/or from whom they expect support. The quality of these social contacts was determined with a validated loneliness scale (De Jong-Gierveld and Van Tilburg, 1990). Appendix I offers an overview of the topics of the first questionnaire.

In the second phase of the study, an in-depth interview was taken of a smaller group of respondents (460 persons), selected from the first group. This second questionnaire focuses mainly at personal factors such as personal competencies, life attitude and socialization. The questionnaire also contains questions about important life events, the support people have found in such situations, and its consequences for the social network and social participation. It also asks about protective factors, uplifts and sources of comfort. A self-evaluation scale for depression has also been included (Zung, 1965; Dijkstra, 1974). Finally, questions are asked about respondents' satisfaction with all kinds of factors of their life, such as work, living situation, health, leisure activities, and having or lacking a partner, children and friends. Appendix II offers an overview of the subjects of the second questionnaire. Information about the specific items will be further explained in the corresponding chapters.

The study group was compared on several points with the total Dutch population aged eighteen and older: sex, age, marital status, living situation, ethnicity and education. (For an overview see Appendix III).

When comparing the respondents in the first phase of the study with the total Dutch population, the sample does not seem to show significant deviations from the total population in terms of the distribution of men and women. The sample is also representative of the total Dutch population for ethnicity. The sample shows no significant differences either with regard to the total population in terms of age distribution.

The sample does show significant deviations from the total Dutch population in civil status and living situation (in both cases $P<0.000$). Married people are under-represented in the sample, whereas divorced and widowed individuals are over-represented. The deviations in the living situation can be explained partially by the way this variable is composed. The data of the population only refer to persons who are part of a private household; what is known as the institutional population, i.e. people who have been staying for at least one year in nursing homes, homes for the elderly, convalescent homes and children's homes, boarding schools, rehabilitation centres and prisons are not included. This excludes about 2 per cent of the total Dutch population aged eighteen and older from this classification. The sample does include persons who are staying in institutions; they fall under the 'other' group, which is hence considerable larger (9 per cent) than in the total Dutch population (1 per cent). Of course, the disproportionately high number of older people in the sample also contributes to this large difference. The share of lone parent families is equal for the sample and the total population.

The main differences are found in the share of persons living in a single household and those living in a shared household. The sample has relatively more singles and less people from multiple-person households than the total Dutch population. The share of singles is closely connected with the degree of urbanization of the various research locations: in the urban areas (Amsterdam and Utrecht), the number of singles is considerably higher (respectively 33 per cent and 40 per cent) than in the rural areas (in Binnenmaas and Het Oldambt it is respectively 8 per cent and 17 per cent).

It is not possible to determine the representativeness of the sample on the basis of the educational levels of the respondents because the data in the sample cannot be properly compared with the data from the total population. The data on the educational level of the total population is available only for the working population, defined as persons between the ages of fifteen and sixty-four who work at least twelve hours per week or are available twelve hours per week for the labour market. The sample was drawn from all those individuals aged eighteen and older. The classification used is the same in both cases: lower, secondary and higher education (including university and higher vocational education). The relatively high number of persons with a lower and secondary education in the sample can be explained largely by the fact that 18 per cent of the sample is in the sixty-five-and-older age category, a group whose general educational level is lower than the other age categories.

To conclude, we can determine that the study group of the first research phase corresponds on several important points with the total Dutch population. The respondent group is in any event representative in terms of men—women ratio, age distribution and ethnicity of the respondents. The sample differs significantly from the total population in marital status and living situation, although the ratio between single households and common households is comparable with the ratio within the total Dutch population. The representativeness on the basis of educational data cannot be determined.

As expected, the small sample in the second research phase showed more significant deviations than the large sample. Only the distribution of men and women and the ethnicity correspond with the distribution in the total Dutch population. The frequency distribution of the background data shows significant deviations from the total population. The representativeness of the sample will be further discussed in Chapter 13. The findings in the following chapters relate to the data sets of the large and the small sample. In the analyses we have clearly indicated which data set the data was derived from.

1.8 Structure of the book

In addition to this chapter, Part I of this study consists of three further chapters. In Chapter 2 we start by presenting the main concepts and theories that are relevant for the study of social contacts in general and social isolation in particular. Views on social relationships and the meaning of personal networks are discussed, for both the personal lives of people and from a societal perspective. We also find out how social relationships are shaped in these times, and what it means when people become socially isolated. Chapter 3 presents a new typology of social contacts in which network size as well as quality of social contacts are taken into account in terms of feelings of loneliness. Based on these social contacts typology we describe four groups: one socially competent group, two groups risking social isolation and one group that is actually socially isolated.

In Chapters 4 to 9 of Part II we discuss different possible causes of social isolation. One subject is central per chapter, and its relation with the social contacts typology and social isolation is investigated. The personal factors that may play a role in the emergence of social isolation are: life events (Chapter 4), personal competencies (Chapter 5) and health (Chapter 6). We also look at the relation between social network and dependence on professional facilities (Chapter 7). We then examine several societal factors: societal participation (Chapter 8) and the neighbourhood (Chapter 9).

Part III consists of three chapters. Chapter 10 focuses on the comparison between urban and non-urban areas. We find out whether clear differences exist between the social world of citizens in more urban areas as against small communities in rural areas. Chapter 11 summarizes the main findings. We examine the relative importance of the different factors in terms of social isolation. The factors that were discussed in previous chapters are interrelated here and analysed in this context. In Chapter 12 we further distinguish the four basic types of our constructed social contacts typology into several interesting and unexpected subcategories, each with its own profile. Here we look at the relation between our social contacts typology, personal competencies and societal participation, and the individual and societal well-being of the respondents.

The study is concluded in Part IV with two chapters. Chapter 13 contains a method and theory review. We take a critical look at the research methods and questionnaires used and discuss the relevance of the results for modern western societies. We also show the points of reference that existing theories on subjective well-being and social networks offer for the study of social isolation, and how our research can make a contribution. Chapter 14 sketches the contours of a social policy aimed at preventing and reducing social isolation. In addition to a new policy vision, we make recommendations for intervention strategies.

2 Theories on social contacts and social isolation

Anja Machielse

2.1 Introduction

Social relationships are an essential part of human life. People are social beings who depend on each other for many things (see, for example, Myers, 1999). They are connected to each other and embedded in a network of relatives and non-relatives in all kinds of ways; they are also part of numerous communities they identify with. By having a variety of social contacts people give shape to their social life.

An effective way to study social contacts is through network analysis. In this tradition, a distinction is made between whole networks (a well-defined group of people, for example a department in a company) and *personal* (or ego-centred) networks of people (a system of relationships with a specific individual as the central figure) (Van der Poel, 1993a). This book is about personal networks; about the group of persons someone is involved directly with. This involvement can be regarded in three different ways. First, formally, meaning that the involvement relates socially recognized roles to mutual rights and obligations, for example parent–child, employer–employee. Second, it can be regarded sentimentally where people care for each other and have feelings of closeness. Finally, involvement can be regarded as an interaction or exchange where persons are involved with people with whom they undertake activities or exchange material and emotional services. Although the three forms of involvement largely overlap, most network research is focused on the third form, involving relationships in which interaction and an exchange of goods takes place (Fischer, 1982).

In this study we assume that diverse types of interactions should take place within relationships and that parties have a substantial influence on each other's life (cf Van der Poel, 1993b). The personal network may include individuals with very different social roles: family members, friends, acquaintances, neighbours, fellow students, colleagues, fellow members of an association or organization, etc. The scope of the personal network can vary strongly. Some people have a very extended network with many family members, friends and acquaintances, whereas others have networks that are limited to a select number of persons. The quality of relationships can also vary considerably: relationships between family members are often affective with a strong sense of mutual involvement, whereas relationships with colleagues or with persons who are members of certain associations or organizations are generally more practical or functional. The importance that people attribute to the different relationships in the personal network vary per individual and per culture (Billington *et al.*, 1998).

Social relationships have always been an important theme in social science disciplines. Social psychology focuses mainly on the importance of social relationships for personal functioning. Sociology regards social relationships primarily as a building stone for society. Before we delve into the actual theme of the book – social isolation (the lack of meaningful relations) – we will present the current leading concepts and theories about social relationships. We will successively discuss the importance of social relationships for people's personal lives and their relevance from a societal perspective (Section 2). We will then describe how the form and meaning of social relationships has changed in the course of time under the influence of social developments. The psychological, social and societal consequences of these change processes will also be discussed (Section 3). We will then proceed to indicate what it means when people become socially isolated and why social isolation should be seen as a social problem. Thereafter we will look at the main backgrounds and the main approaches of social isolation as described in the literature (Section 4). Although the importance of social relationships is recognized widely in the social sciences, until now there has been no systematic analysis of the phenomenon of social isolation. For this reason, we will discuss two theoretical approaches that are relevant for a study of social isolation: the network approaches oriented towards various aspects of someone's network, and the loneliness approaches that emphasize the subjective evaluation of the network. On the basis of these approaches, a definition of social isolation will be formulated in this study (Section 5). We will end with several conclusions (Section 6).

2.2 The importance of social relationships

2.2.1 Social relationships and personal well-being

The personal network is an important factor in people's daily lives. It is therefore not surprising that people give a high ranking to social contacts if asked to make an assessment of the issues that are important to their sense of well-being. This is especially the case for primary relationships (partner and family), but social relationships in a broader sense are also relevant (Hortulanus *et al.*, 1992). In recent years, many studies have confirmed that people who are embedded in a network of personal relationships generally experience a higher level of well-being than those who are socially isolated (see, for example, Heller and Rook, 2001). They also tend to be healthier (Tijhuis, 1994; Sarason *et al.*, 2001; Pescosolido and Levy, 2002; Jehoel-Gijsbers, 2004).

The positive relation between someone's personal network and health and well-being is explained in different ways. Some consider the concrete social support that members of a network share with one another decisive (see, for example, House and Kahn, 1985). Although the social support exchange greatly influences well-being and health, the meaning of social relationships seems to go beyond this specific function and lies more generally in the way relationships are regarded and valued (Sarason *et al.*, 1990). For this reason, we will discuss several functions of social relationships which may play a role with regard to well-being and health (Heller and Rook, 2001; Sarason *et al.*, 2001).

A first categorization of the more general functions of social relationships can be found in Weiss (1974). He posits that social relationships afford six basic 'social provisions': *attachment*, a sense of security, closeness and comfort provided by others; *social integration* into a network of like-minded individuals; *reassurance of worth* provided by the reactions of others that affirm one's role performance; opportunities to provide *nurturance* to others; the establishment of *reliable alliances* for the provision of mutual assistance; and the opportunity to obtain *guidance* for dealing with various stressful events (Weiss, 1974; Heller and Rook, 2001). Thoits describes a somewhat different list with functions that have derived from theoretical and empirical analyses of social relationships: social integration, the development and maintenance of identity and esteem, coping assistance, affect regulation and social control (Thoits, 1985: 124).

Here we will delve further into three functions that are quite relevant for the present study: the contribution to identity and self-respect, the importance of social integration, and the meaning of social support (most of the aspects that Weiss and Thoits mention can be categorized under these three concepts).

Social relationships are important to the development and maintenance of the *identity and self-resp*ect of people. This importance is described mainly in the social-psychological tradition of self-identity. In general, it is assumed that people develop their personal identity and self-respect by internalizing the appreciation of significant others (Cohen and Syme, 1985; Heller and Rook, 2001). This appreciation takes place permanently in daily life, given that people's behaviour in interactions with others is constantly judged and evaluated by themselves as well as by others. People develop within and through relationships with others: they need the appreciation and recognition of others to develop self-respect and self-confidence, and people from their personal network can provide this appreciation. Contact with others offers people a social identity and a frame of reference that greatly influences the values and norms they develop and the choices and plans they make (Myers, 1999). In this context, social scientists speak of 'network support', which gives someone the feeling of belonging to a network with mutual obligations, and of 'appreciation support', which has the form of appreciation and respect (Cobb, 1976).

A second explanation for the greater well-being of people with a good personal network is that social relationships contribute to the *social integration* of people. They meet the basic human need to 'belong', a need that is mentioned in all psychological literature. Social relationships offer people the possibility to feel part of a social group they can identify with and in which they experience personal involvement, intimacy and friendship. The social interaction with others, the comfortableness and the pleasure of 'being together with others' has positive effects on personal well-being. Being part of a group also means that people create and share a vision of reality with others, and thus are less bothered by feelings of insecurity (Dykstra, 1990). It is important that relationships be accompanied by role relationships that are embedded in the network and which give a feeling of personal and group identity (Heller and Rook, 2001). An aspect that relates closely to social integration is social control, meaning that the behaviour of network members can confirm socially desirable behaviour (see, for example, Hughes and Gove, 1981; Umberson, 1987).

A third explanation for the importance of social relationships is *social support*. People depend on each other to live and survive and to function optimally; this is what makes social support a basic condition of existence. This social support does not have to be constantly present: the expectation that in times of need one can count on help and support from others is crucial and this potential supportive function of personal relationships with others is positive for well-being and health (Berkman and Syme, 1979; Fischer, 1982; Hall and Wellman, 1985; Sarason *et al.*, 1994; Tijhuis, 1994; Pescosolido and Levy, 2002). A general distinction can be made of two important types of support: instrumental or practical support, and emotional or affective support (Van der Poel, 1993a). Instrumental support is when members of the network offer advice or concrete help to solve a problem. This is about material or practical help that meets the immediate need of the involved person, such as money, food, clothing, household help, advice or information. Emotional help gives those involved the feeling that others care about them, that attention is being paid to their experiences and feelings and that they can talk about personal problems. Next to these two forms of support, there is also support in the form of 'social companionship', that is the joint undertaking of social activities such as shopping, going to a see a movie, having a cup of coffee together or an evening playing cards (Fischer, 1982: Van der Poel, 1993a).

Social psychologists pay attention to social support, especially in relation to stress and regulation of emotions (Cobb, 1976). The idea is that, thanks to their supportive effect, social relationships form a protective factor when problems occur. People from one's personal network can help in different ways to control the stress, for example, by changing the stressful situation, by changing its meaning, or by alleviating the emotional reactions to it. This involves not only emotional support aimed at reducing stress, fear and insecurity, but also instrumental support (cf. Van der Poel, 1993a). Based on this idea, some posit that social relationships only influence personal well-being in a stress context, whereas there is no positive influence at times in which no dramatic events occur; this is known as the 'buffering hypothesis' (see Cohen and Wills, 1985). Others believe that social relationships contribute to well-being regardless of the stress level, but in different situations do have another function. In a stressful situation, significant others can offer immediate help, assistance, distraction or emotional regulation. In normal social interactions, persons from the network offer intimacy, company, the feeling of belonging, possibilities for social role determination and social comparison, and support for personal aspirations (see, for example, Vaux, 1988). In this last view, social relationships are not only important in order to solve problems or offer help in crisis situations, they also strengthen positive feelings (see, for example, Heller and Rook, 2001).

Beside the positive effects of social relationships, some theorists also focus on the negative consequences of social relationships (Schrameÿer, 1990; Badr et al., 2001; Dykstra, 2001; Heller and Rook, 2001), although these negative effects have been hardly investigated (Lincoln et al., 2000). While social relationships in general terms contribute to a person's emotional well-being and health, they can also be burdensome and limiting. Behaviour of members of the network can cause extra stress or form a basis for negative social comparisons (Myers, 1999; Heller and Rook, 2001). A person can belong to a social group whose members encourage socially deviating or unhealthy behaviour and discourage joining other social groups (Schrameÿer, 1990; Heller and Rook, 2001). When persons cannot meet the role expectations within the group they belong to, there is no appreciation from the members of the network and this has negative consequences for personal identity and self-respect (Heller and Rook, 2001). In addition, the social support offered does not always meet the need: the help could be inadequate, or be offered in a way that undermines the competence of the recipient, making him dependent. Network members can hinder someone in looking for adequate or professional help (Schrameÿer, 1990). These negative effects do not take away from the major importance of social relationships. We can conclude by stating that social relationships contribute substantially in different ways to the personal well-being of people.

2.2.2 The societal importance of social relationships

Social relationships presume a certain degree of social integration and thus fulfil an important role aimed at cohesiveness and stability in society. For this reason, sociologists regard social relationships as elementary building stones for more complex forms of contacts between people (see, for example, Tönnies, 1887; Durkheim, 1893; Simmel, 1908). In the previous section we saw that social integration gives an indication of the degree to which someone is involved with other persons or groups in society. Social relationships also provide a certain degree of regulation in the sense that the actions of people are to some degree controlled and guided by the embedment in a certain community or group (see, for example, Durkheim, 1893). This will contribute to social solidarity and cohesion.

Social integration is very important for the way in which people evaluate and assess social reality. From different (social-)psychological perspectives (e.g. the social identity theory and the social categorization theory) it has been shown that the social groups an individual identifies with are decisive for the thinking, feeling and social behaviour of that individual (Myers, 1999). Members of a community transfer their philosophies, values and norms to one another. At birth, children have an undifferentiated multifaceted behavioural pattern that develops through upbringing and socialization within a historically and socially determined symbolic-moral order. They assume social roles and values through relationships they have within the family, at school and in other socialization domains such as sports clubs or associations. This makes them internalize an image of behaviours that are morally acceptable or unacceptable. By being part of social groups and the identification with a specific community, people find out about the values and norms prevailing in their society (Fischer and Philips, 1982; Myers, 1999).

Thus, the socialization process provides *moral bonding*. It is accompanied with a system of positive and negative sanctions that serves to regulate the social behaviour of people in correspondence with prevailing values and norms. This social control is important to the continuity and stability of the social system. Within this formal system, people develop a social identity next to a personal identity. This social identity is based on collectively prescribed roles that people learn during the socialization process. In the socialization process people become social: they learn social roles and become social actors (Billington *et al.*, 1998; Myers, 1999). Against this background, the German philosopher and psychotherapist Erich Fromm introduced the concept of 'social character' that relates to the similarities in the character of people and groups within a specific society. He posits that a society can only function by forming its members in such a way that their behaviour corresponds with the objectives and needs of that society (Fromm, 1941). Cohesion within a social system thus implies that people within that system can appeal to each other morally. Moral bonding in society is always embedded in an infrastructure of formal rules and societal institutions within which people think and act and develop a social identity. This formal infrastructure also moulds the context within which people can strive towards their own ideals and goals. The actual bonding power of the formal infrastructure with its corresponding system of norms and values depends on the degree to which people believe in those norms and values. When the belief in the prevailing values of a community decreases and the will to live up to them wanes, a feeling of diminished bonding ensues (Schuyt, 1997). This is the case, for example, when the social institutions in which the moral bonding is embedded change character or disintegrate; as a result, there is no longer clarity on which social norms are still binding.

In addition to the positive effects of social relationships for society, negative effects can also be signalled. Social integration is per definition accompanied by separation, namely from all those who do not possess the feature that distinguishes the group. This can lead to an increasing 'in-group' mentality that only upholds the group's own norms and values at the expense of those who disagree and outsiders (Schuyt, 1997; Myers, 1999).

In conclusion social relationships fulfil an important intermediary role between the individual and society. They are important for the social integration of single individuals in society, and provide moral bonding and societal stability.

2.2.3 Social relationships as social capital

Social relationships are important resources that contribute to the capacity of individuals to lead a relatively independent life and thus to personal well-being. Social relationships also form an elementary aspect of society and provide in different ways for cohesion and bonding within society. The major relevance of social contacts at the personal and societal levels is known as *social capital*, a term used in various scientific disciplines (e.g. sociology, anthropology, political sciences, economics). The term points to the importance of social relationships between people for their personal functioning and for the functioning of the family, the organization, the community and the society they belong to (Schuller *et al.*, 2000; Stolle, 2000; Field, 2003; Flap and Völker, 2004). Social relationships are seen as a resource that is important to the realization of (social) goals.

Although the term social capital is used frequently, there is some confusion about the concept. What's more, several people are mentioned as having coined the term, for instance Becker, Loury, Homans, Coleman and Bourdieu. In the literature, the term is defined and applied in different ways. To begin with, the concept can involve different levels. Social relationships can be subsequently regarded as a resource to realize goals at the individual (micro) level, the group (meso) level and the societal (macro) level (Stolle, 2000; Scheepers and Janssen, 2001).

When social capital is seen as a characteristic of individual persons, it is part of the total human capital a person possesses (Becker, 1964). It points to the close social networks someone belongs to and within which rules of reciprocity apply. Social capital as a characteristic of a group refers to the durable network of reciprocal and as such recognized relationships between people (Bourdieu, 1984; Coleman, 1988). It refers to a set of informal values and norms that apply within the group and that enable cooperation between members of that group. Putnam (1993) uses the term in an even broader sense. He regards social capital as a characteristic of a culture or society, and defines the concept as the presence of reciprocity norms, a strong degree of generalized trust and the presence of networks of generalized trust. In this view, social capital says something about the presence of trust in fellow citizens and the willingness to work together. The generalized trust in fellow citizens is viewed by him as important to win over the 'powerlessness' of individual persons.

There are also different views on the definition of social capital. A common starting point is the idea that networks are important to enable the existence of collaborative connections and collective actions. There is also agreement on the three core elements of social capital: trust, reciprocity and networks that exist within a group or society (Stolle, 2000; Leeuw, 2001), however, these components are not seen as equally important by everyone. Most theorists emphasize the aspect of *mutual trust* that people in a durable network of relationships have in each other and which has a positive influence on the entire society (Dasgupta, 1988; Putnam, 1993; Cohen, 1999). Attitudes of generalized trust and the norm of reciprocity are central here, as without this mutual trust social interactions would not be smooth and it would be difficult to arrive at collaborative relationships. This mutual trust is of vital importance for a democratic society: it has a favourable influence on the economy and on the democratic content of society (Fukuyama, 1995). Others (e.g. Coleman and Bourdieu) emphasize not so much the mutual trust as the *institutionalized networks* in a community or society within which social interaction takes place. They emphasize mainly the (positive) consequences that social interaction in different types of networks has for individuals and groups that are part of that network. Within such a network there are obligations and expectations, channels of information (through which individual members of that network receive useful information), rules and effective sanctioning possibilities, social organizations and authority relationships. This social structure makes certain actions possible, and it is therefore advantageous to be part of such a durable institutionalized network (Bourdieu, 1984; Coleman, 1988). The amount of social capital for individuals within such a network depends on the size of the network of relationships that someone can mobilize effectively and of the amount of economic, cultural and symbolic capital that each member of the network has. According to this view, persons gain more social capital because the members of their networks have more expertise, influence or competence (Bourdieu, 1984; Lin, 1982, 2001).

According to some sociologists, a person's social capital is determined by what are known as the 'weak bonds' in the networks, i.e. the members that belong to the network only marginally and can form a bridge towards relevant contacts outside one's own networks (Granovetter, 1973; Burt, 1990). The idea is that these bonds add more to the social capital than overlapping, strong bonds in the network; what they provide is access to resources that a person cannot reach via members of his own network. Others are of the opinion that it is precisely a 'close' network (one in which the network members are closely interconnected) which offers more possibilities for indirect return favours than a less tightly-knit network (see, for example, Coleman, 1988). This difference in views has to do with the emphasis theorists put on either the personal or the societal usefulness of social relationships.

In the past, theories on social capital concentrated exclusively on the advantages of *formal* or *institutionalized* social relationships, such as membership in formal groups and organizations or participation in club life. In recent years greater attention has been paid to the fact that *informal* relationships are also a crucial part of the social capital (Portes, 1998; Komter et al., 2000). It is gradually being recognized that personal relationships that people maintain with their relatives, friends, acquaintances and neighbours can also constitute a resource in the realization of personal life plans, and the supportive factor of social relationships is frequently focused on. People who are in solid social networks can deploy resources in their environment at moments when this becomes necessary: members of the network can help each other with practical things, offer emotional support for important life events, undertake joint activities and keep each other company (Sarason et al., 1990; Schrameijer, 1990). Those in the personal network can also provide access to all kinds of societal resources, such as information, work or an education. In this sense, various sociologists point to the importance of personal networks for someone's career chances and employment possibilities (Granovetter, 1974; Boxman et al., 1992). Some theorists posit that people invest deliberately in certain relationships in order to optimize their amount of social capital (Bourdieu, 1984). This view presents the expectation that the potential of a certain relationship in the short or the long term is an important consideration when entering into new relationships or maintaining existing ones. In any event, the presence of others in one's immediate surroundings does not guarantee that someone can really count on help or support. The willingness to support depends not so much on the existence but mostly on the quality of the relationship. Among other factors, this is related to the investments that have been made earlier in the contact, and so mutual trust and reciprocity play a role here (Flap, 1987; Rusbult and Buunk, 1993; Buunk and Schaufeli, 1999).

It is remarkable that little attention has been paid until now to the more emotional and affective roles that social relationships play in the daily lives of people. The emphasis lies mainly on the usefulness and functionality of such relationships. They are primarily considered to be resources that contribute to the ability of people to realize their own goals, and from this perspective investments in social relationships are based chiefly on exchange considerations (in the longer or shorter term). This pragmatic view of social relationships is closely related to the way in which modern society has developed under the influence of the modernization process, namely in the direction of individualization and rationalization and it is these changes that are the focus of the following section.

2.3 Changes in the social environment

2.3.1 Modernization

Social relationships belong in all times and places. Still, social developments greatly influence the way interpersonal relationships take shape. The rise of modern industrial society in the nineteeth and twentieth centuries drastically changed the social structure of society and thus also the social environment in which people spent their lives. The most important dimensions of this change process will be described below.

A first development that had a major influence on the social structure of society is the process of *differentiation*, that is, the increasing specialization of people (task differentiation) and organizations and institutions (system differentiation), aiming at greater productivity and skills. Tasks which used to be fulfilled in a family context have been now largely taken over by specialists who have made it their profession. This is how bringing up and caring for children, caring for the sick and elderly family members, and the production of goods for personal use, which used to take place within the family, now take place largely in schools, hospitals and companies (see, for example, Durkheim, 1893).

A second development that had important consequences for social culture is the process of *rationalization*, whereby mythical and religious explanations of reality were replaced by rational and practical knowledge about society (Weber, 1920). A starting point in modern society is that everything can basically be managed by means of practical, empirical knowledge and by rational actions. At the level of collective actions, this means that thoughts and deeds are increasingly geared towards pre-set goals for which people use the most suitable means. Finally, rationalization has consequences for individual actions. It leads to a more planned lifestyle in which efficiency rules (Weber, 1920).

A third development that is strongly related to the differentiation and rationalization of society is the process of *individualization*. In modern society, people have released themselves from traditional ties of family, community and religion. Individualization implies an increase of individual freedom of choice: the collective identity that used to be expressed in a shared lifestyle is making place for a diversity of lifestyles (see, for example, Beck, 1986; Giddens, 1991; Beck and Beck-Gernsheim, 1994, 2002; Baumann, 2001).

A last development that has major consequences for the social environment is the process of *globalization*, which in the twentieth century has led to an enlargement of the scope of society. The term globalization points to 'the development of multiple social relations and interdependencies that rise above the level of the nation-state (society) and which together form the modern world system' (Van Steenbergen, 1996: 467). The world has become by now one large social system in which people communicate with each other and depend on each other (see, for example, Castells, 1996; De Swaan, 1996).

2.3.2 Psychological and social consequences

The decreasing importance of traditional institutions and the emerging individualism has changed the character of society and permeated all its aspects. This encroaches upon the identity of citizens as well as the interaction between individuals and groups of citizens.

In the first place, the process of individualization is expressed in the rise of the *reflexive* self (Giddens, 1990, 1991). The development of the self is no longer a fixed, socially allocated role but a project people permanently work on. Striving towards self-realization and self-development and the search for the proper means for their attainment has important consequences for the personal sphere. The construction of the self has become a reflexive process, in which individuals are continuously forced to make choices, also when it comes to relationships with others. Family ties between generations have become looser and views on marriage and family have drastically changed. This is why Giddens (1992) speaks of 'a transformation of intimacy'. This transformation means that people have to reflect on their emotional needs and must consider self-consciously what type of relationships they want.

Modernization processes have also led to a remarkable expansion of the *social space* in which people live. They now deal with a large number of relationships in a wide array of situations (De Swaan, 1996). People are part of very different circles, for example their family, their circle of friends, their job, the neighbourhood and club life. In all these social contexts people take social positions and they have to meet the corresponding role expectations. Functioning in all these changing situations requires social competencies: people have to adjust constantly to the surrounding social structures and comply with socially established norms and rules, they have to feel comfortable with others and be able to get along with them in socially acceptable ways (Billington *et al.*, 1998).

A third change relates to the bureaucratization of society (Weber, 1920). People are expected to adjust their general behaviour to the demands of modern '*organized society*'. As people increasingly live in more complicated dependencies and become part of a ramified network of institutions, rules and procedures, it becomes more necessary for them to mutually coordinate their behaviour. Their actions are primarily rational and thought-out. People are forced into a calculating attitude in relation to others in order to realize their own goals, while feelings and emotions are considered 'irrational' (see, for example, Habermas, 1981). Some theorists posit that instrumentality is characteristic mainly of certain life domains, seeing involvement and affection not as having disappeared but belonging mostly to the private domain. Here we see intimate, supportive relationships based on mutual involvement and appreciation (Lofland, 1989).

2.3.3 Societal consequences

The increasing individualization appears to bring the danger of social disintegration closer. Individualization and globalization provide an increasing heterogeneity that is expressed on various fronts: family, education, work, health care, living environment, etc. In modern society social and cultural groups with different backgrounds and lifestyles exist side by side. Finding a common basis for societal life and reaching a consensus over rules and norms that are acceptable for all social groups seems to be becoming increasingly difficult.

Some sociologists believe that individualization is disastrous for society's community life (Tönnies, 1887; Wirth, 1938; Hobsbawm, 1994; Putnam, 2000). Hobsbawm goes as far as to call the disintegration of old patterns of human relationships the most disturbing social change of the twentieth century. According to him, the falling away of traditional, meaningful integration frameworks has mostly negative consequences for the social bonds between people and for the development of solidarity and mutual loyalty. In modern society, collective awareness has disappeared as a basis for behaviour and solidarity.

Durkheim (1893) does not fear for disintegration but points to the emergence of new institutions (such as the division of work) which can contribute to modern forms of social and moral integration. He states that a new form of a more abstract and anonymous solidarity has come about that is accompanied by the new dependency patterns of society. In addition, many traditional institutions (despite the fact that their character has changed) still have a culturally binding function: family, club life, education, health care, the professional world, public administration and politics are still tightly anchored in modern societies (Bovens and Hemerijck, 1996).

Sociological theories list various motives that can lead to solidary behaviour in modern western societies. The rational choice approach of solidarity assumes that it is in everyone's interest to integrate into social networks; instrumental motivation (rational self-interest) leads to solidary behaviour (see, for example, Hechter, 1987; Raub, 1997). Others see norms, values and emotions as a basis for solidarity. Next to instrumental forms of solidarity they assume a socially-motivated solidarity that is based on involvement and feelings of commonality. Motives for solidary behaviour can be attraction, loyalty, identification and association (see, for example, Gouldner, 1960; Mayhew, 1971; Etzioni, 1988).

2.4 Social isolation as an issue for social sciences

2.4.1 Social isolation as a form of social exclusion

Although processes of social change have had an effect on the social experience of people, the need for relationships and communication with others has not waned. Individualization assumes precisely that people enter into relationships with others and are part of well-functioning social networks or groups so that they can integrate into modern society. This also means, however, that they have to build deliberate relationships and participate in networks that are relevant to the realization of their life plans.

At the same time, the terrain of social relationships in modern society has become more diffuse. Modernization processes have led to a remarkable expansion of the social space in which people live. They now deal with a large number of relationships in a wide array of situations (De Swaan, 1996). People are part of very different circles, like their family, their circle of friends, their job, the neighbourhood and club life. In all these social contexts people take social positions and they have to meet the corresponding role expectations. Functioning in all these changing situations requires social competencies: people have to constantly adjust to the surrounding social structures and comply with socially established norms and rules, they have to feel comfortable with others and be able to get along with them in socially acceptable ways (Billington *et al.*, 1998). This, however, makes high demands from the individual, as it assumes independent and autonomous persons who are capable of shaping their own lives beyond the ties of a specific community or group. They need all kinds of social and cognitive skills to function in very different situations. People who lack these skills and see no possibility of integrating through social ties become socially isolated.

Social isolation has negative effects for the functioning and well-being of individuals, and for solidarity and social cohesion within society. Personal quality of life is very much affected by being part of a social network. By rationalizing relationships in the public domain, the intimate nature of social relationships in the other domains has become increasingly important. Some believe that the need for social relationships has even grown now that people can no longer rely on self-evident, traditional cultural models (e.g. Beck and Beck-Gernsheim, 1990; Zoll, 1990; Kunneman, 1996). Individuals are basically free to make their own choices and choose their own lifestyles, but they can only develop their own identity in social contexts, in relationships with others, especially in relationships that are based on feelings of friendship, mutual intimacy and involvement (Beck and Beck-Gernsheim, 1990, 2002; Giddens, 1991). The lack of affective relationships constitutes a serious threat to individual well-being. People who do not maintain stable and meaningful relationships with each other and have no one to turn to in case of an emergency end up pretty much on their own. This often leads to serious personal problems such as depression, low self-esteem, social problems and physical symptoms (Peplau and Perlman, 1982).

Besides affecting one's personal life, social isolation also has negative consequences for the unity and stability of society. When a society has too many members who do not participate in societal life, cohesion and solidarity are adversely affected. This is the case if the inability to participate at a societal level is accompanied by a shortage of moral or social integration in the society. Social isolation can be accompanied by cultural exclusion, that is, people are cut off from the dominant patterns of behaviour, lifestyle orientations and values of society, or institutional exclusion, due to not having access to the facilities intended for them (Fischer and Philips, 1982; Hills *et al.*, 2002).

So, social isolation cannot be dismissed as a private problem for it is clearly a public issue. First of all its effects are not limited to people's personal lives but touch society as a whole. Second, social isolation is not grounded on just personal factors (competencies, characteristics and circumstances), as suprapersonal causes and social processes can also be signalled. Social isolation is a phenomenon that cannot be seen separately from the way in which modern western societies are designed. It is a result of structural developments and processes that have occurred – and still do – in society. A characteristic of social problems is that they say something about that society's social structure and opportunities for everybody (Mills, 1951).

Social relationships in modern society are indispensable for the social and personal functioning of people. Because of this, people who do not manage to participate in society and are unable to build and maintain meaningful relationships are at a great disadvantage. The lack of a personal network can result in a situation of marginalization or social exclusion, meaning that people no longer see a way to participate in society; they no longer have access to functional social networks where they voice their own interests, and socially speaking have no significant role to play (see, for example, Hirschman, 1975; Komter and Schuyt, 1993; Hills *et al.*, 2002; Jehoel-Gijsbers, 2004). As their relationship with society becomes disrupted, their chances to participate decrease (Wilson, 1987). The consequence is a process of accumulation and reproduction of social inequality in which those who have better access to social resources can create better life conditions for themselves by using these resources, whereas the disadvantages for people without these resources correspondingly increase (Flap and Tazelaar, 1988; Komter, 1996). Hence social isolation points to a new form of social inequality, namely in the distribution of immaterial resources. When people have fewer chances and possibilities to participate or be involved in society and do not have or have lost personal contacts they can count on in case of an emergency, they are worse off than people who do have a well-functioning network.

It is clear that social isolation is a complex issue that requires further analysis. Although there are numerous views and theories on the importance of social relationships, until now there has been no theory that focused exclusively on social isolation. Nonetheless, countless empirical studies have been carried out into the relationship between personal networks and various background factors.

2.4.2 Causes for social isolation

Studies in the social sciences relate very contrasting factors to social isolation. Here we will briefly sketch a number of important findings. To begin, many studies establish a relation between social isolation and *background factors* such as age, sex, income, education, living conditions, ethnicity and environment. This highlights several population groups that have greater chances of becoming socially isolated: the elderly, the sick and those with disabilities; people with lower incomes, lower educational levels or a low social status; the long-term unemployed; single people (especially men); lone parents; and (non-western) immigrants (see, for example, Hess and Waring, 1978; Fischer, 1982; Fischer and Philips, 1982; Marsden, 1988; Dykstra, 1990; De Jong-Gierveld and Van Tilburg, 1995).

Besides its relation with background factors, social isolation can also be related to personal and societal factors. First, social isolation is often related to people experiencing *major life events*, like the death of a partner, divorce, unemployment, disability or moving (see, for example, Fischer, 1982; Flap and Tazelaar, 1988; Broese van Groenou, 1990; Broese van Groenou and Van Busschbach, 1991; Dalgard *et al.*, 1995). Such events are often accompanied by a loss of relationships or a reassessment of the remaining relationships. The literature shows that establishing a family is one of the most important life events for women, whereas the most important changes for men are related to work (Fischer, 1982; Van Busschbach, 1992). In particular, life events that are not directly related to a specific life phase (like a divorce) lead to major changes in the personal network, whereas events that are related to the life phase (such as retirement) will have a rather stabilizing effect on the network (Broese van Groenou and Van Busschbach, 1991). In recent years, social isolation has also been related to traumatic youth experiences and victimization. Several studies confirm that people who have been the victim of incest, abuse or threats have considerably more chances of becoming socially isolated than people who have not come into contact with such events (see, for example, Draijer, 1990; Gersons, 1995).

Another explanation for social isolation is sought in physical and mental *health problems*. Handicaps or (chronic) disease can put people in a position that makes them more vulnerable to isolation. Physical or mental limitations often form a hindrance to participation in society (Mallinckrodt, 2001; Kal, 2001; Pescosolido and Levy, 2002; Jehoel-Gijsbers, 2004). The image people have of the disabled and (chronically) ill can also considerably hinder the establishment of contacts (Gorter and Winants, 1993). The personal network becomes especially fragmented for people with a severe 'social' disease, i.e. a disease that is frightening to others, is clearly visible and entails functional limitations that make considerable demands for help and support from others. From the medical science perspective, studies have been done particularly on the relationship between social networks and specific groups of patients: the chronically ill (e.g. De Boer, 1990; Janssen, 1992), people with severe cardiac problems (Brummett *et al.*, 2001) and cancer patients (e.g. Ros, 1990). Longitudinal studies have also been carried out into the relationships between social networks and death (e.g. Engel, 1971; Berkman and Syme, 1979; Taylor, 1986; House *et al.*, 1988; House, 2001).

Social isolation is also frequently related to certain *personality characteristics* that influence the way people interact with others. Certain factors increase the chances of someone becoming lonely or socially isolated. Examples of such factors are shyness, introversion, a lack of social skills and the willingness to take social risks (Peplau and Perlman, 1982; Asendorpf and Wilpers, 1998). Building and maintaining social relationships requires certain competencies like self-confidence, self-respect, sociability, dependency and a sense of personal control (De Ridder, 1988; Dykstra, 1990; Smith and Petty, 1995). Some authors emphasize that earlier life experiences within the family are determinant for the confidence level and the development of reciprocity that is necessary for interacting with others (see, for example, Wuthnow, 1997). Attitudes towards strangers, evaluation criteria and attitudes towards collaboration and a feeling of trust arise during the socialization process and are decisive for a person's attitude towards others in adult life (Stolle, 2000). Social psychologists also establish a frequent relation between social skills and attachment patterns, in the sense that a more successful attachment may influence interaction with others positively (see, for example, Bowlby, 1983; Smith *et al.*, 1999).

A concept we encounter often in theories on social relationships is that of *coping*, or people's *problem-solving ability* – all the strategies that can be used when there is a threat or if the consequences of that threat can become a reality (Lazarus, 1966; Lazarus and Folkman, 1984). Coping is seen here mainly as a stabilizing factor that allows individuals to face stressful situations they are confronted with in everyday life. Important forms of coping are the development of planned problem-solving behaviour, the mobilization of social support and the use of defence mechanisms such as avoidance, acceptance or tolerance of the situation (Pierce *et al.*, 1996). With regard to social relationships, theorists mention three 'social' coping styles, that is, three ways of dealing with an unsatisfactory social network (Van Tilburg, 1982). First, people can focus on the problem and adjust their network to their own wishes. They can increase the quality of their personal network by utilizing the existing contacts more, entering into new relationships or looking for surrogate relationships, for example with a pet. People can also opt for an emotion-oriented strategy. They can lower their social needs or desires in terms of relationships, for example doing more activities on their own. Another strategy is to repress feelings of loneliness by rationalizing ('others are worse off'), denying the problem, avoiding certain situations or through resignation (Linneman *et al.*, 1990).

Next to individual factors, social isolation is also often associated with societal factors. In many studies, social isolation is identified with low *societal participation*. This is not only about participating in the labour process, but also in other societal forms of participation such as club life, religious organizations, cultural or recreational activities and volunteer work. Societal participation is seen generally as an important source of social contacts (see, for example, Berkman and Syme, 1979; House, 1981; Fischer and Philips, 1982; House et al., 1982). At the same time, it is observed that societal participation is no guarantee for a satisfying personal network: people with paid jobs can still become socially isolated if they fail to maintain relationships with others in their personal life (Machielse, 2003, 2006).

Other studies relate social isolation with the person's *living environment*. The premise is that the spatial environment can support and stimulate or discourage social contacts. For example, a neighbourhood in which most people are at work during the day offer few possibilities for social contacts (Reijndorp, 1998). The composition of the population in the neighbourhood also plays a role: when people have little in common (age, household type, ethnicity, socio-economic status), the interaction potential is smaller and chances of remaining an outsider greater (Dignum, 1997). The same applies when neighbourhood residents have completely different lifestyles or when there are annoyances or neighbour's quarrels. Chances of social isolation are even greater when people no longer feel safe in their neighbourhood, for instance due to high criminality or if the composition of the neighbourhood population changes rapidly in a short period of time (Hortulanus et al., 1992).

Although many different factors that can increase chances of social isolation are described, no crucial factor has been identified that can explain it. Intensive research into socially isolated people shows that in most cases there is a complicated combination of different factors and circumstances, none of which separately have to necessarily lead to social isolation (Machielse, 2003, 2006). Such an accumulation of problems happens to people who in several ways are dealing with factors that affect their life chances negatively. The cause, then, lies in a specific constellation of events, circumstances and personal characteristics. In the end it is not about the amount of problems but about the balance between strength and burden, which can become disturbed (Bakker et al., 1999). To gain more insight into the emergence of social isolation, a more systematic analysis of the phenomenon is necessary. In the following section we will discuss two theoretical approaches that can provide leads for such an analysis.

2.5 Theoretical approaches to social isolation

2.5.1 Network approaches

A first approach that is relevant for a study on social isolation is network analysis. This tradition stemmed from cognitive and social psychology in the 1930s, and developed further into sociological and social-anthropological theory. In this approach, social relationships are seen mainly as building stones for social structures, with a focus on group relationships and the structural characteristics of social configurations. Next to sociological concepts, use is also made of sociometric techniques of network analysis. This is how social network analysis has become a specialized research field within sociology (Scott, 1991).

Within the tradition of network research there are three approaches, each oriented towards a different dimension of the social network: the social integration approach, the social network approach and the social support approach (House and Kahn, 1985; Dykstra, 1990; Snijders, 2001). None of these approaches pay explicit attention to social isolation, but they present derived definitions of social isolation as the lack of certain characteristics in the personal network. The *social integration approach* focuses on the scope of the personal network and the type of relationships and attempts to determine to what degree a person is integrated into society. Characteristics of the relationships in the network serve here as indicators of the degree of social integration. Important factors are the composition and size of the household, the share of family and friends, membership in associations and religious groups, having work or being unemployed, etc. All these types of relationships are seen as channels along which the integration of a person in society comes about. The degree of social integration is measured by the number and type of social relationships, membership in organizations and frequency of interactions with others. It is usually assumed that one is more socially integrated if one belongs to more different networks that are not fully interconnected (Berkman and Syme, 1979; House et al., 1982). From this approach, social isolation is defined in terms of the scope (even if limited) of a one-sided or multifaceted composition of the personal network.

In the *social network approach* the emphasis lies on the formal structure of the network, on the relationships between the relationships in the network (Fischer, 1982; Wellman and Hall, 1985). This type of research is oriented towards characteristics of the network someone participates in. The characteristics can be the closeness of the network (do the members of the network know each other), the heterogeneity of the network (e.g. family, sex, social status), the range of the network (the social layers the network has access to), and eventually the multifunctionality of relationships (Fischer, 1982). In this approach, social isolation is not related to a limited scope of the network but to specific characteristics of the structure of the network. The general premise is that the degree of closeness and homogeneity can say something about the social embedment of a person within that network and thus over the risk of social isolation. As more members of the network get to know each other, solidarity and mutual involvement grows, reducing the possibility of members becoming socially isolated. The same goes for a homogenous network in which the members are more or less equal in terms of several structural characteristics (such as their sex, age, social class, civil status, education, profession, religion, political conviction or ethnicity).

In the *social support approach* the focus lies on the quality of the relationships. The quality is detected from the function a relationship has for someone, especially the amount and type of support the relationship provides (Cohen and Syme, 1985; Sarason *et al.*, 1985). This involves two forms of functionality: instrumental and social or inter-relational functionality (Arts *et al.*, 1989). Instrumental functionality relates to activities that produce a practical result, like helping around the house or running errands (practical support). Social functionality relates to manners and joint activities between people who are not instrumental but can give someone a feeling of integration, involvement and acceptance (emotional support and companionship support). This approach does not map out the entire personal network, only relationships in which support is exchanged. It sees social isolation as the lack of supportive relationships in the personal network (Felling *et al.*, 1991; Van der Poel, 1993a).

Common to this network approach is that social isolation is measured by more or less factual data about the personal network of people: this is about the scope of the network, about structural characteristics or the presence of persons that can offer certain forms of social support. Social isolation is equalled to having a personal network of a reduced scope or a one-sided composition; as a personal network becomes smaller, closer or more homogeneous, or when supportive relationships are lacking, chances of social isolation increase. Empirical research shows that there is only a weak correlation between the network size and the subjective experiencing of the network. Data on the scope, composition and structure are not good indicators to determine whether relationships meet the expectations. Empirical research also shows that people with a large network can have considerable feelings of loneliness. The other way around, people with a small network can be very satisfied about the quality of their social network because the quality of the relationships meets the expectations (De Jong-Gierveld, 1984; Hortulanus *et al.*, 1992). Neither are structural characteristics conclusive about the subjective experience of the network. People who are embedded in a close and homogeneous network can nonetheless feel lonely. The homogeneity can hinder or curb functioning outside the close network, as a result of which someone can feel social isolation with regard to groups outside the network (Tijhuis *et al.*, 1992; Hortulanus, 1995a). The amount and types of support in the network guarantee even less of a positive appreciation: the support that members of the network have to offer not necessarily has to meet someone's needs (Schrameÿer, 1990; Lincoln, 2000; Dykstra, 2001; Heller and Rook, 2001). Hence the scope, composition and structure of the network and the availability of social support say little about the relative importance of the existing contacts. To gain insight into social isolation, the network approach must be supplemented with an approach in which this subjective dimension is central, as is the tradition of loneliness research.

2.5.2 Loneliness research

A second approach that is important for the study of social isolation is the tradition of loneliness research. It does not focus on the factual data of the social network but on the quality of the relationships in that network as people themselves experience. It is thus about the subjective experience of the personal network and emphasizes the lack of valuable and meaningful contacts with others (see, for example, Perlman and Peplau, 1981; De Jong-Gierveld, 1984; Van Tilburg, 1988; Sumbadze, 1999; House, 2001). Within this tradition we find various theoretical approaches and conceptualizations of loneliness.

In *psychodynamic* models, the cause of loneliness lies with the individual (see, for example, Zilboorg, 1938; Sullivan, 1953; Fromm-Reichmann, 1959). In this approach, loneliness is ascribed to influences and experiences from youth. Although these early experiences are essentially interpersonal, this tradition focuses exclusively on individual factors that lead to loneliness (Perlman and Peplau, 1982).

In *sociological* explanations, loneliness is seen as the product of social forces that lie per definition outside the individual; it is an inherent aspect of society and not something that lies with the individual (Perlman and Peplau, 1982). Bowman (1955) lists three social developments that lead to loneliness: the disintegration of primary group relationships, the increase of family mobility and a general increase in social mobility. Others see the changed social environment as causative of the increasing loneliness. Riesman, for example, posits that individuals in modern (American) society have become 'other-directed', that is, they constantly have to adjust their behaviour to their interpersonal environment. This cuts them off from their inner self, their feelings and their aspirations, and together they form the 'lonely crowd' (Riesman, 1961). Slater (1976) sees individualism as the big problem. He is convinced that every individual longs for community, involvement and dependency: people want to trust others and work together with them. These basic needs are not satisfied in the individualized society due to a commitment to individualism, the belief that everyone must strive for their own goals. This results in loneliness.

Given that in this study social isolation is seen as a social problem in which individual as well as societal factors play a role, these one-sided theories are not very usable for the purpose of this study. An approach that assumes that the causes of loneliness can lie in the individual as well as in the situation is the *interactionist approach*. This approach claims that loneliness is the result of personal and situational factors that influence one another mutually. Two interactionist approaches are the deficit approach and the cognitive approach. Both see loneliness as a *feeling* that people have and is not equalled to feeling 'alone'. Another common starting point of these approaches is that loneliness has to do with experienced shortages in personal relationships, and that this shortage can be experienced as unpleasant or stressful, and is accompanied by negative feelings. Explanations on the nature of this shortage vary (Perlman and Peplau, 1982).

According to the *deficit approach*, loneliness arises when certain relationships in the network are absent. The thought behind it is that different types of relationships fulfil more or less unique functions, and that the functions of one type can only be fulfilled by another type to a limited degree, if at all. An important representative of this approach is the American psychologist Robert Weiss, who theorizes that feelings of loneliness can be the result of the experienced shortage in one or more relational functions, namely social integration, nourishing, validation, a feeling of trust and help in stressful situations. In this theory of relational loneliness he distinguishes between two types of loneliness: loneliness due to emotional isolation and loneliness due to social isolation (Weiss, 1973). Both forms of loneliness are related to the lack of certain types of personal relationships. Emotional loneliness arises from the absence of an exclusive attachment relationship, for instance with a partner (see attachment theory of Bowlby, 1983). Other supportive relationships (like friendships) cannot compensate for this absence, which is why someone with many social relationships can still feel emotional loneliness. Emotional loneliness manifests itself in fear, restlessness and emptiness. The second form of loneliness is caused by a lack of social integration and embedment in a broader network of support providers. Social loneliness arises in people who have a relatively small personal network and therefore experience a shortage of meaningful friendships or of a feeling of communality with others. Social loneliness is manifest in weariness and feelings of social exclusion (Weiss, 1973; De Jong-Gierveld and Raadschelders, 1982; Van Baarsen *et al.*, 2001).

In the *cognitive approach*, loneliness is the result of a discrepancy between the desired and the present relationships (Dykstra and Fokkema, 2001). Feelings of loneliness are seen here as the product of the meaning persons themselves ascribe to their experiences with others. The most important aspect in this approach is the emphasis on cognition as a mediating factor between shortages in sociability and the experience of loneliness. The approach is based on the attribution theory, a psychological theory that deals mainly with the way in which people intuitively try to understand the causes of behaviour, for example in internal (dispositional) or external (situational) circumstances. This is specifically about a subjectively experienced difference between realized and desired relationships (see Peplau and Perlman, 1982). It clearly distinguishes 'subjectively experienced loneliness' from 'objective isolation'. This definition of loneliness contains two elements: the number of realized relationships with others is lower than a person would find pleasant or acceptable, or the relationships do not reach the desired level of intimacy (De Jong-Gierveld, 1984). Not only the realized network of personal relationships is involved, but also the preferences and desires regarding these relationships (Van Tilburg, 1988; Dykstra, 1990; Dykstra and De Jong-Gierveld, 1999).

This cognitive approach to loneliness emphasizes the experience of the individual, which is why it offers better points of departure than the deficit approach for a study into social isolation. In the deficit approach, the composition of the personal network (the type of existing relationships) is determinant to its subjective experience: there is an absence hypothesis that assumes unfulfilled needs due to the lack of specific types of relationships (Dykstra and Fokkema, 2001). By contrast, the cognitive approach explicitly distinguishes subjectively experienced loneliness from objective isolation. It focuses on psychological processes that are not so much related to an objectively observable lack of relationships, but mostly to the appreciation and adequateness of existing relationships (Van Tilburg, 1988; De Jong-Gierveld and Van Tilburg, 1990). This approach can therefore form an indispensable complement to the previously discussed network approaches.

2.6 Summary and conclusions

This book focuses on personal or ego-centred networks, that is, personal relationships between people who undertake things together and exchange goods and services (e.g. support), and in which the partners have a substantial influence on each other's lives. Countless social-psychological studies have evidenced that social relationships contribute in an essential way to the personal well-being and health of people. There are various explanations for these positive relationships. Besides the basic human need to belong and psychological functions of relationships with others for the identity and self-respect of people, it is mainly the potentially supportive function of personal relationships that is important.

Social relationships are not only meaningful for personal life, they also serve a societal interest. In sociology, social relationships have always been seen as elementary building stones for more complex forms of contact between people. They are instrumental in the conveyance of views, attitudes, values and norms that are common to society and thus in the socialization of individuals into citizens that fit into society. In this way, social relationships fulfil an intermediary role between the individual and society.

The vital importance of social relationships is expressed in the term 'social capital'. The term points to the importance of social relationships between people for their personal functioning and for the functioning of the community or society they belong to. The amount of social capital, seen as a resource at the individual level, depends on the size of the network of relationships that a person can mobilize effectively and the amount of economic, cultural and symbolic capital each of the members of that network has. At a societal level, it refers chiefly to the existence of trust in fellow citizens and the willingness to work together. Especially this last form of social capital has received much attention in recent years. This attention is coupled with the consequences that modernization processes have had on social bonds between people. Traditional, meaningful integration frameworks have dissolved and common forms of experience and expression have made way for an individualistic lifestyle in which people are increasingly focused on themselves. The central question in contemporary sociology is, then, what this means for the solidarity and cohesion of society. In addition, much empirical research has been done into social capital at a societal level ('civil society') – research into the willingness of people to do volunteer work, into changes in the forms of solidarity and into new types of ties.

Social capital theorists understand social relationships mainly instrumentally. They are regarded as resources that contribute to people being able to realize their own goals, and from this perspective investments in social relationships are based primarily on exchange considerations. The focus is mostly on formal relationships between people, whereas the more affective and emotional aspects of informal social relationships are hardly explained. In this study we want to show that these aspects of social relationships deserve theoretical attention too.

Social change processes that have taken place in recent centuries in modern western societies not only affect cohesion and solidarity but also people's personal lives. The types of relationships that are available for people in modern society and the conditions under which social interactions are possible have changed considerably. This affects the way in which people interact. Building and maintaining social relationships has become more complicated. People associate with different social contexts in which they have to constantly assume other social positions and meet the corresponding role expectations. They must be able to move in an impersonal sphere, speak up for their own interests and act efficiently and methodically.

Not everyone is capable of creating a relationship with people around them and to integrate into social contexts. When people do not succeed in building a network of supportive relationships and in participating in social life, they become socially isolated and end up in a situation of social exclusion. Given the fact that personal relationships are essential in an individualized society, their position is unfavourable. Social isolation should therefore be seen as a complex social problem that demands further analysis.

Although the issue of social isolation is recognized widely in the social sciences, until now there has been no systematic analysis of the phenomenon. In recent years we have seen an increase in the number of (social-)psychological and sociological studies into personal networks. Although different factors show a correlation with (objective) characteristics of the personal network, no single study has identified a crucial factor that can explain the emergence of social isolation. Neither has the weight of the various factors and how they inter-relate, strengthen or weaken one another been investigated. There is no clarity either on whether and to what degree a well-functioning social network can protect against certain negative situations or events, and what the lack of such a network means in terms of problem accumulation. The present study aims to fill this gap.

To this end, it is important to start by arriving at an adequate definition of social isolation in which not only objective aspects but also the quality and assessment of relationships in the personal network are weighed out. To arrive at such a definition, we use two theoretical approaches that are relevant for a study of social isolation: the network approaches that focus on factual aspects of the network, and loneliness approaches, which focus on the subjective experience of the network.

In the network approaches actual data on the personal network of people are mapped out. Although these network approaches have contributed significantly to knowledge about the personal network of people, they do not offer insight into the subjective experience of that network. Empirical research shows that emotional aspects play an important role in the assessment of social contacts, and that there is only a weak correlation between this subjective assessment and objective forms of isolation such as those described in the network approaches. The cognitive approach of loneliness sees loneliness as the product of the meaning that a person ascribes to their experiences with others. This approach focuses on the subjective experience of the existing relationships and thus constitutes a useful complement for the network approaches.

In this study we use a definition of social isolation in which next to the more factual element (the network approach) the subjectively experienced quality of the social contacts (in terms of loneliness) is also studied (see Chapter 3 for the operationalization). Using this definition we will study social isolation as an independent phenomenon. We will subsequently look at a number of important personal and societal factors that can play a role in the emergence of social isolation. We will also attempt to gain insight into the relative importance of those factors and how they are inter-related.

3 A typology of social contacts

Ludwien Meeuwesen

3.1 Introduction

In the past two decades we have witnessed growing psychological and sociological research into loneliness and social isolation (e.g. Hughes and Gove, 1981; Peplau and Perlman, 1982; De Jong-Gierveld and Van Tilburg, 1990; Brummett et al., 2001). As discussed in Chapter 1, for some time there have been indications that social isolation is more apparent throughout the population, and is not restricted to people who are in poor health, the unemployed or the aged (Hortulanus et al., 1992). This chapter explores a meaningful empirical approach to social isolation.

3.2 Definition of social isolation

Although there is no clear-cut definition of social isolation, a common characteristic is the lack of meaningful social networks (De Jong-Gierveld, 1984; Schrameijer, 1990; Sumbadze, 1999; Lincoln, 2000; House, 2001). The word 'meaningful' refers to the fulfilment of the individual's social needs. People can have extensive social contacts and still lack something, resulting in feelings of loneliness. On the other hand, people may have just a few social contacts that are quite sufficient and comforting for them. The lack of a meaningful social network can have serious consequences for the well-being of individuals. People without personal contacts do not receive social help and support, do not feel comfortable, and barely have access to social resources. In our western societies, when people lack meaningful social contacts their quality of life and personal functioning is negatively influenced. They stand alone and find themselves in a position of social isolation. Enduring loneliness often results in serious problems such as depression and poor self-esteem. Social isolation also has negative consequences for society as a whole, and detrimentally affects social cohesion (Komter et al., 2000).

As discussed in Chapter 2, a social network that functions well has positive effects on individuals as well as the society they live in. Social relations provide a sense of security, comfort and self-esteem. People derive their identity from their personal contacts in their immediate surroundings. They acquire self-esteem and self-confidence and, to a certain degree, a sense of competence and resistance to stress. Moreover, social networks provide access to social resources such as education, jobs and information. From a societal point of view, personal networks are relevant because they contribute to social integration and participation in society.

A common approach to the issue of social isolation is via the social network (Fischer, 1982; Tijhuis et al., 1992; Van der Poel, 1993a). This network approach makes it possible to describe the size of someone's personal network, its functions in terms of support, and some qualities of the contacts in terms of type of relationship, distance, intensity and frequency. Although only a specific part of a person's personal network is relevant to well-being, delineating personal networks provides ample relevant information about potential social support. Although it is still common in research to view social isolation as synonymous with a small network (e.g. Brummett et al., 2001), most authors agree that a fruitful approach to social isolation or the lack of meaningful social contacts should incorporate objective as well as subjective elements (De Jong-Gierveld, 1984; Schrameijer, 1990; Van Sonderen, 1995, Sumbadze, 1999). In an excellent overview, Lincoln (2000, p. 242) rightly cautions that the negative side of social interaction has been largely overlooked in research: 'Simply assessing the structure of a person's social network (e.g. size or number) provides little information about the quality, amount, and experience of positive and negative interactions.'

The degree to which personal networks are meaningful largely depends on the degree of support the contacts provide. People's subjective feelings about these contacts are essential for their well-being.

The two elements of social isolation are composed of a more objective criterion, network size or potential social support, and a more subjective criterion, namely the quality of a network in terms of subjective well-being. In line with De Jong-Gierveld (1984), who distinguished between objective and subjective isolation, the concept of loneliness is preferred. The presence or absence of feelings of loneliness lie at the core of subjective well-being. The term loneliness is often used as a synonym for social isolation, although it is not the same. Perlman and Peplau (1981, p. 31), hold that 'Loneliness is the unpleasant experience that occurs when a person's network of social relations is deficient in some important way, either quantitatively or qualitatively.'

Van Tilburg (1988) stresses the relevance of the subjective evaluation of social contacts as opposed to more objective facts about network size, by reporting rather low correlations ($r = 0.30$) between network size and feelings of loneliness. In an effort to understand this phenomenon, Van Sonderen (1995) distinguishes between potential support, i.e. a person's perception of the expected support in the event of problems, and the actual support that is needed and received – which is not quite the same. In other words, an important function of the social network is the social support it can provide for an individual (Sarason et al., 1990; Van Sonderen, 1995;

Sumbadze, 1999; Lincoln, 2000). The actual support that is needed and received is decisive for the functioning of the network as it is meant to be.

In addition to the concept of actual social support, there is the notion of reciprocity. The process of giving and receiving is usually characterized by reciprocity, an expectation that people will help those who have helped them (Gouldner, 1960). It seems relevant to devote attention to the interdependence or reciprocity of actual social support (Badr *et al.*, 2001). Reciprocity is essential to human relations and contributes to social cohesion (Komter *et al.*, 2000), and a lack of reciprocity coincides with negative feelings such as loneliness and depression (Buunk and Schaufeli, 2001). In the event of reciprocity an individual can be regarded as more socially balanced than when there is a lack of reciprocity. To achieve social balance, an individual needs to have competences in multifarious fields. Personal competences such as social skills or coping behaviour are instrumental in dealing with major and minor life events (Sarason *et al.*, 1990; Mallinckrodt, 2001).

Although the relevant dimensions (objective and subjective criteria) for a successful approach to the issue of social isolation may be clear, an approach explicitly incorporating these two elements is not common yet for the social isolation issue, even if there are studies in which both elements are studied. For example, Brummett *et al.* (2001) report that in a sample of medical patients 12 per cent are socially isolated, based exclusively on network size. Of the isolated group, 57 per cent are satisfied with their relationships as compared with 83 per cent of the non-isolated group. In our study we explicitly take these two elements as a starting point for defining social relationships in terms of a typology of social contacts.

3.3 Towards a typology of social contacts

The combination of an objective component in terms of network size and a subjective one about quality of social contact in terms of feelings of loneliness offers four possibilities (Table 3.1).

The combinations (A) and (D) are both unambiguous: individuals have extensive networks and they do not feel lonely (A), or they have small

Table 3.1 Combination of network size and feelings of loneliness

		Network size	
		Large	*Small*
Feelings of loneliness	Absent	large network and not lonely (A)	small network and not lonely (B)
	Present	large network and lonely (C)	small network and lonely (D)

networks and do feel lonely (D). The first group feels strong and is not at risk; the second group is quite vulnerable. The combinations (B) and (C) are more complex. In the case of (B) the network size is small, but the subjects do not feel lonely at all. The potential support is adequate and meaningful, but there is a risk: someone with a small network is definitely more vulnerable than someone from group (A). Individuals from the (C) group have large networks, but they feel lonely. In this situation, the potential network support does not seem to be adequate or meaningful enough. There is also a risk of social isolation.

This classification underlies the typology of social contacts, containing four groups: the 'socially competent', the 'socially inhibited', the 'lonely', and the 'socially isolated' (Hortulanus et al., 2003). They can be characterized as follows:

1 The socially competent have many social contacts, their social network functions adequately and they are satisfied with their social life. They do not run a risk of social isolation.
2 The socially inhibited have only a few contacts, but their network is adequate and meaningful for their social needs. They feel satisfied and in fact do not feel lonely. However, they are vulnerable in a specific way. If, for whatever reason, one or two people are removed from their social network, they would lose the greater part of their support system. In this sense, there is a risk of social isolation.
3 The lonely have numerous contacts but nonetheless feel lonely. For whatever reason, they have an inadequate support network. There is a discrepancy between the number and the quality of the contacts, which implies a clear risk of social isolation.
4 The socially isolated have few contacts and they do not feel happy about it. They meet the social isolation criteria formulated above: the network size is small and they feel lonely; there is a desire for changes in one or both of these aspects.

The main advantage of this social contact typology is that two essential aspects, size and quality, are systematically taken into account, and different forms regarding the risk of social isolation are included. By designing a social contact typology, we formulate the aim of this chapter, which is to explore relevant features of the four social types. We expect this type of approach to reveal more about social isolation than the sole use of either an objective or a subjective criterion. The questions to be answered in the present chapter are:

1 What can be said about the network size, its quality in terms of loneliness, and the classification of the typology of social contacts of the research sample?
2 How does the social contact typology differentiate actual social support?

3   How can the various groups be characterized in terms of demographic variables and other relevant personal characteristics?
4   What is the relevance of the typology for a successful approach to social isolation?

Additional questions that will be dealt with here refer to the functions and composition of the potential support network, changes in network size over time, protective factors against social isolation, features of a rich social life, and risk factors for social isolation. Based on relevant literature (Van Sonderen, 1995; Lincoln, 2000), we expect the typology to differentiate between actual social support and other relevant variables. We expect the typology to be more informative than an approach based exclusively on network size or loneliness.

3.4 Measures

The data was gathered in two phases. Most information was obtained in the first phase, with some 2,400 respondents having been personally interviewed (details are given in Section 1.7). This section offers a description of the operationalization of the main concepts. These are network size, different kinds of potential support, loneliness, actual support received and given, satisfaction with social contacts, changes in network size, protective factors and demographic variables.

Network size

As stated above, social contacts make a significant contribution to people's welfare, especially regarding emotional, social and instrumental support (Fischer, 1982). Personal networks are delineated by an adapted version of the exchange approach of Fischer. This method traces the number of people the respondent can count on for regular support or companionship. In terms of validity and objectivity, the exchange method is generally considered the most appropriate. The network relations delineated by this method refer to personal relationships, and the items can be interpreted in the same way by the respondents (Van der Poel, 1993a). In order to delineate the personal network, seven name-generating questions were asked concerning specific supportive interactions: emotional, instrumental and social companionship. An eighth question was added referring to possible significant persons not yet mentioned. Since the potentially supportive relationships could be traced, the questions were formulated hypothetically, apart from the two social support items. The items were formulated as follows:

Emotional support
1   Suppose you have serious personal problems and want to talk to someone about them, who would you talk to?

2 Suppose you need advice on a major change in your life, such as changing jobs or moving to a different area, who would you go to?

Instrumental support
3 Suppose you need help with chores in or around the house, running an errand, cleaning, repairing or painting, who would you ask?
4 Suppose you are going on holiday and the plants need to be watered or the mailbox needs to be emptied, who would you ask?
5 Suppose you need to borrow a large sum of money, who would you ask?

Social companionship
6 Who do you go out with once in a while, shopping or to a restaurant, movie or theatre?
7 Did you visit anyone last month, or did anyone visit you?

Other
8 Are there any significant persons you have not mentioned yet?

In response to each of these questions, the respondent can mention up to three persons, including the partner. With eight questions there are theoretically a maximum total of $8 \times 3 = 24$ different names that can be generated. Several methods could be used to assess whether the personal network size is small or large, depending on the aim of the study, e.g. a cut-off score 3/4 or 4/5, or the lowest decile of the sample recognized as 'extremely isolated' (Tijhuis *et al.*, 1992; Fischer and Phillips, 1982, Brummett *et al.*, 2001). For our study, the cut-off score was determined at 4/5. Respondents with a total score between 0 and 4 were viewed as having small networks, respondents with a total score between 5 and 24 as having large networks.

Loneliness

De Jong-Gierveld developed a cognitive model for loneliness (De Jong-Gierveld, 1984; De Jong-Gierveld and Kamphuis, 1985). In this model, the discrepancy between an individual's desire for affection and intimacy and what the individual has in reality is emphasized. The larger the discrepancy, the greater the feelings of loneliness. This model underlies a designed eleven-item scale of loneliness, which met the criteria of the Rasch model for dichotomous variables and has been validated for the Dutch population.

Items on the loneliness scale:

1 There is always someone I can talk to about my day-to-day problems.
2 I miss having a really close friend.
3 I experience a general sense of emptiness.
4 There are plenty of people I can lean on in the event of trouble.

5   I miss the pleasure of the company of others.
6   I feel my circle of friends and acquaintances is too limited.
7   There are numerous people I can count on completely.
8   There are enough people I feel close to.
9   I miss having people around.
10 I often feel rejected.
11 I can call on my friends whenever I need them.

The scores on the loneliness scale run from 0 (not lonely at all) to 11 (very lonely). Following the guidelines of De Jong-Gierveld (1984), the borderline for being lonely or not was determined by a cut-off score of 2/3. A score of 0, 1 or 2 means 'not or slightly lonely'. A score of 3 or higher means 'moderate or very strong feelings of loneliness'. The internal reliability in terms of Cronbach's alpha is 0.89 in our sample.

By combining these two dichotomized variables (small and large network size, feelings of loneliness absent and present) we arrive at a social contact typology, containing four values as described in Section 3.3.

Actual support received and given

Since the network questions were somewhat hypothetical and focused on the potential social support, a number of comparable explicit questions about the past month were also asked. These items focused on the actual support received. While recognizing the relevance of reciprocity in human relations, the same items supplied information regarding 'actual support given'. The questionnaire contained nine items on a three-point scale, mostly referring to practical support, and an overall measure was a summation of the nine items. This was done for 'support received' as well as 'support given'. Appendix IV contains more detailed information about the separate items.

Additional measures

The additional measures comprised a general measure regarding satisfaction with social contacts, a measure for changes in network size, a measure for factors which protect against isolation, and demographic variables.

Satisfaction: Regarding general satisfaction with social contacts, a report mark was given on a scale between 0 and 10.

Changes in network size: To get an indication about stability and change in network size, an item was included containing a comparison of the current network size with the situation of five years ago.

Protective factors: To get an idea of respondents' own ideas on what protects against social isolation, respondents were asked to indicate this on a list of seventeen items. They were also asked to formulate spontaneously which factors people with a rich social life were blessed with.

Demographic variables: The effects of the following risk factors on social isolation were assessed: age, gender, marital status, ethnicity, education, income, socio-economic status, and location.

3.5 Network size

The average personal network size, assessed with the instrument of eight name generators, was $X = 7.8$ (sd = 3.0). Figure 3.1 shows the frequency distribution of the personal network size, partner included.

While the network size ranged from one to twenty-two, about 38 per cent of the subjects had seven to nine people they could rely on for emotional, instrumental or social support. According to a cut-off score of 4/5, 14 per cent of the subjects were viewed as having small networks, meaning a potential risk of social isolation. Subjects with larger networks evaluated their social contacts more positively, but this correlation was rather small ($r = 0.14$, $P < 0.05$).

How many respondents could not appeal to anybody for specific support? Ten per cent didn't know anybody to ask for advice on a major change in their life, and 9 per cent lacked someone to go out with or go shopping once in a while. Seven per cent did not succeed in asking someone to water the plants or empty the mailbox when going on holiday. When it came to talking about personal problems, visiting someone or having visitors, or getting help with chores in or around the house, 6 per cent was lacking someone else. When someone's partner was not included in the network, the above-mentioned percentages tripled (e.g. 23 per cent had nobody to talk with about personal problems). The partner is the first person to appeal to in all areas, especially for emotional support.

Regarding the effect of the demographic variables on network size, stepwise regression analysis showed that educational level, ethnicity, age and degree of urbanization explained 13 per cent of the variance. To illustrate, the percentage of the older (>65) respondents having small networks (23

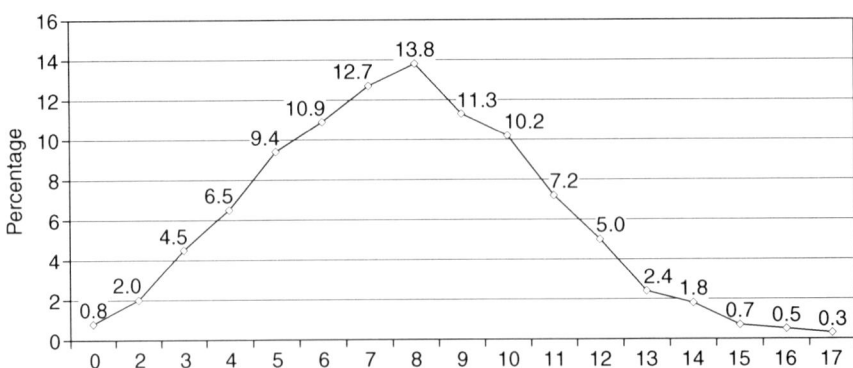

Figure 3.1 Network size (N = 2,443).

per cent) is somewhat higher compared with the total group (14 per cent), but the differences are small.

3.6 Loneliness

The mean score on the loneliness scale was $X = 1.9$ (sd = 2.5) (Figure 3.2); 28 per cent of all the participants indicated they had mild to strong feelings of loneliness, such as 'experiencing a sense of emptiness', 'not having enough people to count on', 'missing people around them' and 'having no friends to call on when in need'. Subjects with larger networks had a smaller chance of feeling lonely ($r = -0.23$, $P < 0.01$); again, this correlation was small, which is an indication that network size and loneliness are two different concepts. The correlation between loneliness and general satisfaction with social contacts was substantially stronger ($r = -0.40$, $P < 0.01$); both measures refer to a subjective experience.

The lonely lacked their parents more often, or the parents were not reckoned into their network. They had a child living on his/her own slightly more often, and lacked a best friend more often. Socio-economic status, degree of urbanization, ethnicity and marital status together explained 10 per cent of the variance in loneliness. The other variables were not significant, not even age. An increase in feelings of loneliness from 28 per cent for the whole group to 37 per cent for the older subjects (>65) is not very large. Nevertheless, more than one out of three of the older subjects indicated having feelings of loneliness. Probably this is mostly explained by socio-economic status.

3.7 Social contacts typology

When combining someone's network size (large versus small) with the presence or absence of feelings of loneliness, the following interesting partition emerged (see Figure 3.3).

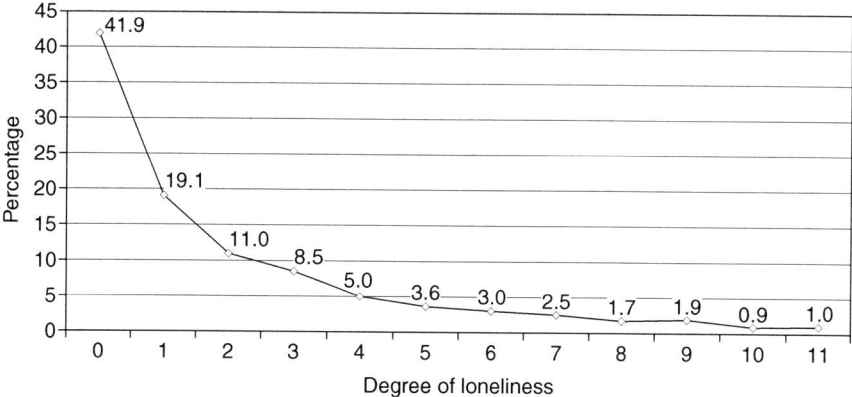

Figure 3.2 Loneliness (N = 2,443).

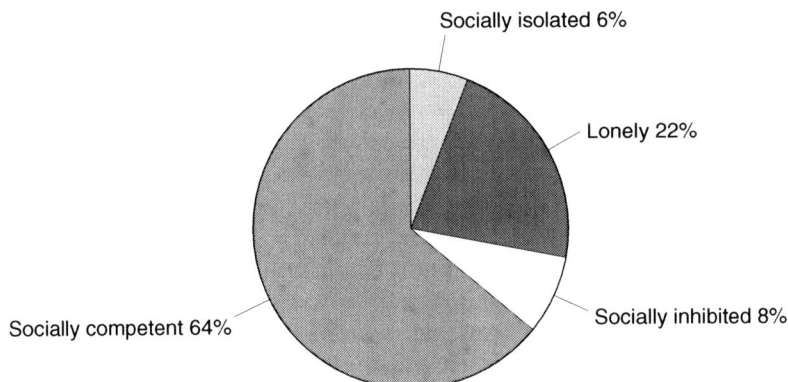

Figure 3.3 A typology of social contacts (N = 2,406).

Two out of three respondents (64 per cent) stated that they had large networks (of five persons or more) and did not feel lonely – they were the socially competent; 22 per cent seemed to have large networks but still felt lonely – they were the lonely; 8 per cent of the respondents indicated they had small networks, but no feelings of loneliness – they were the socially inhibited. Finally, 6 per cent of the subjects scored negatively on both network size and feelings of loneliness – they were socially isolated.

A sound question is whether there are any differences in the degree that respondents are in need for social contacts. It was striking that the four distinct social contact groups did not differ from each other in their need for social contacts, nor in the time they claimed to spend on social contacts. There were, however, significant differences in the degree of feeling at ease with others. While 79 per cent of the subjects of the total sample indicated feeling at ease with other persons, this percentage was significantly lower for subjects who were isolated (56 per cent). But even in the group of the lonely, 40 per cent did not feel at ease despite having extensive networks. Apart from the need for contacts and the time spent on them, it is evident that whereas one person draws support from social contacts, for someone else social contacts would seem to be a source of trouble.

Regarding a number of network features (type of relationship, distance), it was found that the group of the socially competent indicated three times more that their parents belonged to their network, compared with the socially isolated (51 per cent versus 17 per cent). The isolated also had to get on without a best friend twice as much, and if they had a best friend, he/she was less frequently available for giving support. When combining the results of the socially isolated, a picture shows up in which the parents are largely absent, any children are living relatively far away, and friends are poorly available when needed.

Attention has also been paid to the role of religion. Off all respondents, 73 per cent indicated having no religion, 8 per cent was religious but not active, and 19 per cent was more or less involved religiously. There was no relation with feelings of loneliness, and only a small relation with someone's network size ($r = -0.10$). Those who practiced a religion were a bit more highly represented among the socially competent and the lonely, and relatively less among the socially inhibited and the socially isolated (see also Sections 10.5.2 and 10.5.4 regarding participation in religious organizations).

3.8 Network support functions and typology

In Section 3.5 it was indicated that for the respondents as a group, practical support was the least difficult to realize, while emotional support seemed more difficult to realize. How many respondents indicate to have nobody to appeal to for support is shown in Table 3.2.

The four contact groups differed greatly on all items. This makes sense, as network size was one of the criteria to construct the typology. Therefore, the reasonable resemblance between the answers of the socially competent and the lonely fits expectations. The socially inhibited indicated considerably fewer other persons to appeal to, while the socially isolated were by far the worst across the board. The main differences were manifest on the level of social companionship. Thirty-nine per cent of the socially isolated and 19 per cent of the socially inhibited did not know anybody to ask to go shopping or go out together. While 6 per cent of the whole sample indicated that they had not visited anyone or been visited last month, this percentage was 15 per cent for the socially inhibited and 26 per cent for the isolated. More than 20 per cent of the socially isolated could not appeal to anybody to discuss personal problems, and 26 per cent for personal advice on a major change. For the socially inhibited, the percentages were 12 per cent and 17 per cent respectively. They have to cope without direct personal support. For everyone, instrumental support was easier to realize, although again the socially isolated and the inhibited were worse off.

Women and men did not differ on instrumental support, but on emotional support and social companionship women were a bit better off. The total network size of women was larger than men's. If corrected for overlapping (e.g. the same person mentioned for emotional as well as instrumental support), the gender differences disappeared. It seems that, compared to men, women make a more varied use of the same number of people. Additionally, both men and women appealed more to members of their own sex.

In conclusion: the socially isolated, and to a lesser extent the socially inhibited, miss all sorts of support (emotional, instrumental, companionship) more often compared to the other groups. The largest differences are manifest regarding social companionship. Women appeal to their social network members in a more varied way than men.

Table 3.2 Social typology and percentage of respondents who have nobody to ask for support (N = 2,443)

	Socially competent	Socially inhibited	Lonely	Socially isolated	Total
(E) talking about personal problems**	4	12	5	22	6
(E) advice on major changes**	8	17	10	26	10
(C) visits**	4	15	5	26	6
(C) shopping or going out together**	4	19	11	39	9
(I) help in or around the house**	4	12	7	19	6
(I) caring for plants or mail when going on holiday**	4	14	6	30	7
(I) borrowing a large sum of money**	42	53	46	68	45

Notes
**$P < 0.01$; Chi^2 test.
E = emotional support; C = social companionship; I = instrumental support.

3.9 Giving and receiving support

Is there any relation between potential support in terms of network size and actual received social support? This correlation was $r = 0.17$ ($P < 0.01$), which is rather small. Although they are related, network size is not the same as social support. The same can be said of loneliness and actual received social support ($r = 0.05$, $P < 0.05$). The subjects with large networks differed significantly from those with small networks on the actual support received ($X = 3.47$ versus $X = 2.75$, $t = 4.262$, $P < 0.001$). The 'lonely' and 'not lonely' groups did not differ that much ($X = 3.17$ versus $X = 3.43$, $t = 1.871$, $P < 0.1$). Regarding 'received support', the main differences were in terms of network size.

Analysis of the 'given support' presents the following picture: the 'large network' group gave more support than the 'small network' group ($X = 3.77$ versus $X = 2.24$, $t = 8.352$, $P < .001$), as did the 'not lonely' group compared to the 'lonely' group ($X = 3.82$ versus $X = 2.79$, $t = 6.965$, $P < 0.001$). Regarding 'given support', the main differences were in terms of network size as well as loneliness.

Paired t-tests show that the group with large networks gave more support than it received ($X = 3.81$ and $X = 3.43$, $t = 4.943$, $P < 0.000$), and the group with small networks received more support than it gave ($X = 2.59$ and $X = 2.17$, $t = -0.2,72$, $P < 0.01$). Lonely people also received more than they gave ($X = 3.10$ versus $X = 2.79$, $t = -2.410$, $P < 0.05$), and the 'not lonely' group gave more than it received ($X = 3.86$ versus $X = 3.40$, $t = 5.715$, $P < 0.001$).

Table 3.3 contains the mean scores of received support and given support for the total group, as well as the four separate types of social contacts (see also Appendix IV for more detailed information).

Table 3.3 Received support and given support in relation to the typology of social contacts (N = 1,758)

	Socially competent***	*Socially inhibited*	*Lonely*	*Socially isolated***	*Total****
Support received					
X	3.49	2.91	3.40	2.61	3.37
(std)	(2.67)	(2.48)	(2.55)	(2.36)	(2.69)
Support given					
X	3.95	2.76	3.18	1.64	3.56
(std)	(2.67)	(2.48)	(2.55)	(2.36)	(2.69)

Notes
**$P < 0.01$, ***$P < 0.001$ (paired t-tests between support received and support given on each column).

The four groups of social contacts differed significantly in 'support received' ($F = 6.205$, $df = 3$, $P < 0.001$). The socially competent received the most support, the socially isolated the least. The patterns of the socially competent and the lonely were similar. The patterns of the socially isolated and the socially inhibited were also similar, the latter being better off. The socially isolated were the worst off in almost all cases. Bonferroni tests show that the socially competent differed significantly from the socially isolated and the socially inhibited. The lonely also differed from the isolated.

The four groups of social contacts also differed significantly in 'support given' ($F = 33.907$, $df = 3$, $P < 0.001$). The socially competent differed from all three other groups; the same can be said of the socially isolated. Only the socially inhibited and the lonely did not differ significantly from each other. For receiving and giving support, the means of the socially inhibited and the lonely were in-between.

Across the board, the subjects indicated they gave help more often than they received it; paired t-tests show that the scale tipped in favour of giving support. A closer look at the four distinct types of social contacts presents quite a different picture though. The results show that this general image only held true for the socially competent (the largest group, 64 per cent). The observation for the socially isolated was quite the opposite: on all the issues, they claimed they received more support than they gave. The same can be said of the socially inhibited and the lonely, although the differences were less pronounced.

The typology of social contacts presents a more differentiated picture than just the network approach or just loneliness. Although network size does differentiate, we cannot conclude that having small networks is the same as social isolation.

3.10 Changes in network size

One can imagine that as a consequence of being lonely and isolated, a person's social network may change. But reasoning the other way round is as legitimate: what are the consequences of changes in network size for lonely and isolated people? The present study was not designed longitudinally, although respondents were asked to compare their current network size with their situation of some five years ago (Table 3.4).

About half of the respondents (46 per cent) indicated that no changes had taken place over the past five years. A decrease in contacts took place for 27 per cent of the respondents, and the same percentage indicated an increase in contacts. Again, a more or less linear relation showed up with the social contact typology: the lonely and the isolated indicated most frequently a decrease in contacts, and the socially competent the least. Across the board, the latter group showed an increase in contacts over the past five years. The socially inhibited seemed the least confronted with changes in network size. From the bare fact that more lonely and isolated respondents experienced a

Table 3.4 Changes in network size in the past five years, percentages (N = 2,366)

	Socially competent	Socially inhibited	Lonely	Socially isolated	Total
Decrease in contacts	24	23	37	41	27
Contacts not changed	47	55	41	42	46
Increase in contacts	30	22	23	18	27

Notes
$Chi^2 = 56.03; P = 0.000$.

decrease in contacts, it may be concluded that for a number of them the mere presence of feelings of loneliness may interfere with entering into new contacts and keeping them up. If a person's network is small already, it apparently becomes even more difficult. The socially competent show the reverse pattern.

The reasons for an increase in social contacts are numerous and are mostly related to positive life events; sometimes negative events offered new relational possibilities. The main reasons for a decrease in contacts were life events such as getting a new job, losing a job, moving to another house, loss of partner, or more prolonged processes like getting older or a deteriorating health condition. Chapter 4 will deal with life events in more detail.

When a person's network size increased, it involved mostly neighbours, people having children, or couples, and to a lesser extent family members and fellow sufferers. Large decreases in network size particularly referred to people living at great distances, (ex) colleagues or fellow students, relatives of the (ex) partner, and less to acquaintances. This pattern was most explicit in the socially competent, where the network increase was also complemented with people having a job. The network of the socially inhibited was often increased by their relatives, neighbours and contemporaries. Network decrease in this group particularly referred to relatives of (ex)partner, acquaintances, people living at distance, (ex)colleagues, and somewhat to the group of singles. Network decrease of the lonely was comparable to that of the socially inhibited, but the pattern was much more intensified (especially family of the (ex) partner and people living at a great distance), and an increase was due particularly to strengthening contacts with fellow sufferers. The socially isolated as a rule reported dramatic decreases over the past five years on all types of contacts, even regarding relatives, neighbours, people with children, and couples. The decrease intensified in the case of people living far away, acquaintances, relatives of the (ex) partner, people with jobs, (ex) colleagues, singles, contemporaries and fellow sufferers.

Particularly the contrast between the socially competent and the lonely, and especially the isolated, catches the eye. While the socially competent seem to be creative in orchestrating their social relations, in the isolated group an ongoing process of social shrinking takes place for all kinds of contacts. This is partly due to divorce or death of a partner, and increasing age: the networks of the older gradually shrink because one's partner or contemporaries have passed away.

It seems that changes in network size do not take place arbitrarily, however, they can be understood from the perspective of someone's life course. Every period in a life span is accompanied by a number of major events which may have implications for the ongoing social relations. The birth of a child or a new job offers new possibilities socially speaking. Deterioration of health, the process of getting older, and relatives passing away are events which may affect existing social networks. However, there are great individual differences in the way people will manage a situation and the individual risk of becoming isolated in the long run varies. Among other factors, a person's problem-solving capabilities and ability to cope are highly relevant (see Chapter 5).

As a rule, one may assume that an increase in social contacts is evaluated as desirable, as human beings are regarded as social beings. The evaluation of the shrinking of one's social contacts is usually more complex. Sometimes the loss of contacts will be a welcome relief from social burden, but more often it is experienced as a matter of loss and of thinking back wistfully. However, it is not easy to capture such experiences. People often accommodate change, especially when they have little control over what direction their social life takes. The mental incongruence between deep-seated desires and the actual situation will be relieved partly by adjustment to the situation, which will contribute to less dissatisfaction with the situation. In general though, analysis of the evaluation of changes in the social situation teaches us that a stable network or an increase in social contacts results usually in greater satisfaction than a decrease in contacts.

The differences between the socially competent on the one hand and the socially inhibited, the lonely and the isolated on the other are nonetheless striking. An increase in social contacts did not lead to greater satisfaction in the socially competent (they were already satisfied with their stable relationships), while the other three groups benefited greatly from the increase of their social network. The socially competent are the most balanced: their network is relatively large, and a decrease or increase does not affect their social satisfaction. The socially inhibited also look fairly balanced, although they seem to benefit from network increase. The lonely and especially the socially isolated are the least balanced: a decrease in contacts results in considerably greater dissatisfaction, while an increase will lead to significantly greater satisfaction. These patterns illustrate the vulnerability of the social situation of the isolated, and to a lesser extent, of the lonely too.

3.11 Sources of protection

3.11.1 Protection

As a prelude towards gaining more insight into the possible causes of social isolation (see further Chapter 12), it is necessary to learn more about the respondents' own ideas on this matter. To this end, a smaller group of respondents was interviewed for the second time (see Section 1.7). In this sample, the socially competent were relatively less represented (54 per cent), and the respondents at risk of social isolation were more represented. They were asked which factors (of a list of seventeen items) they thought protected them against loneliness and isolation.

Table 3.5 shows that in the top ten, personal factors (such as character, joy of life, good health) were named most frequently, followed by social relations and satisfaction with living, plus one societal factor of 'having a job'. Apparently, more value is attached to personal and relational factors than to societal factors. If a distinction is made between having had experience with the forenamed items as a protector against loneliness and isolation, and not by giving an assessment/estimate, the differences between the four groups become even greater. For example, of the 'experienced' group, respectively

Table 3.5 Sources of protection against isolation, in percentages (N = 428)

	Socially competent	Socially inhibited	Lonely	Socially isolated	Total
Joy of living****	93	90	86	61	88
Character***	93	82	85	77	88
Satisfactory living conditions **	83	73	70	73	78
Friendship**	82	80	70	61	77
Good memories**	77	74	75	55	74
Good health***	77	58	68	59	71
Partner relationship****	79	60	62	47	70
Relation with child*	72	55	64	63	67
No debts	59	55	54	46	56
Job*	56	54	54	27	53
Physical appearance*	52	56	39	55	50
Relationship with parents	48	52	48	28	47
Age	47	53	48	39	47
Clubs/voluntary activities**	47	29	47	31	43
Religion	38	28	42	33	38
Success in society*	39	51	33	27	38
Grandchildren	37	24	38	32	35
Other	19	14	30	21	21

Notes
*$P < 0.1$, **$P < 0.05$, ***$P < 0.01$, ****$P < 0.001$; Chi^2 test.

90 per cent, 72 per cent, 72 per cent and 59 per cent (for the four contact groups) indicated the relevance of satisfactory living conditions.

If a total score for protection is calculated (range between 1 and 17), the socially competent named an average of eleven factors which they had experienced as protective, the socially inhibited named ten factors, the lonely 9.5, and the socially isolated 7.5. Again, major differences between the four contact groups show up: the socially isolated feel the least protected. The socially inhibited and the lonely have a position in between.

3.11.2 A rich social life

Respondents were also asked to formulate spontaneously factors which blessed people with a rich social life (it was possible to give more than one answer, see Table 3.6). At the top of the list, the respondents gave answers which could be categorized as 'character' (57 per cent), followed at a great distance by 'having a job' (18 per cent), which was mentioned by the isolated and the socially inhibited twice as much. They also introduced 'being young' more frequently, while 'being successful and well-known' was named more often by the socially inhibited.

A factor analysis (varimax rotation) of all the items resulted in four main factors (see Table 3.7):

1 Character and coincidence.
2 Youth and health.

Table 3.6 Blessed with a rich social life, in percentages (N = 411)

Category	Socially competent	Socially inhibited	Lonely	Socially isolated	Total
Character	60	61	52	44	57
Having a job**	16	30	16	30	18
Many contacts via someone else	12	21	13	13	13
Having a lot to give	14	16	9	9	13
Being healthy	10	14	12	22	11
Having children	10	19	10	17	11
Neighbourhood**	7	21	9	13	9
Having a lot of time*	5	14	4	9	6
Being successful and well-known***	3	19	2	9	5
Young of age***	2	12	5	22	5
Attractive physical appearance**	3	9	2	13	4
Coincidence	1	7	4	4	3
Other**	56	35	55	39	53

Notes
$*P < 0.1$, $**P < 0.05$, $***P < 0.001$; Chi^2 test.

3 Neighbourhood and social contacts.
4 Being successful.

Of these four factors, the mean scores were calculated. It is noticed that the four contact groups did not differ regarding the factor 'character/coincidence'. However, the factors 'healthy and young' and 'successful' were absent in the socially competent. Especially the socially inhibited and the isolated stressed the importance of being young and healthy, and only the socially inhibited listed 'being successful'. The relevance of a good neighbourhood is absent in the answers of the competent group. Apparently, the younger, healthier and more successful one is (as is the case with the socially competent), the less important one's neighbourhood is. This is confirmed by other studies, which show that the less positive one's situation is regarding other factors, the more important one's neighbourhood becomes (Van Wel and Hortulanus, 2002). It seems as if the socially competent do not (yet) realize their blessings. They take it for granted, and the positive values are only realized if the casualness has disappeared or if it took much effort to realize.

Parallel to the protective factors, being blessed with a rich social life is particularly a matter of personal factors. Obviously, respondents attach more value to personal matters than to societal factors as far as a rich social life is concerned. Individuals who are joyous and vital have a better understanding of the art of controlling situations in various circumstances.

3.12 Risk factors

Other studies have shown that a number of demographic factors indicate a risk of social isolation (Dykstra and De Jong-Gierveld, 1999; Brummett *et al.*, 2001). Table 3.8 shows the demographic variables relevant to the different types of social contacts.

The percentage of socially isolated people was six times higher among the

Table 3.7 The four main aspects of a rich social life, mean scores (N = 411)

	Socially competent	Socially inhibited	Lonely	Socially isolated	Total (%)
Character/coincidence	0.31	0.34	0.28	0.24	57
Healthy/young/attractive/ having a job/children***	–	0.17	–	0.21	18
Neighbourhood/contacts via others*	–	0.21	0.11	0.13	13
Successful, a lot of time, a lot to give**	–	0.16	–	–	13

Notes
*P < 0.1, **P < 0.01, ***P < 0.001; Chi^2 test.

Table 3.8 Percentages within risk factors of the four categories of social contacts

	Socially competent (64%)	Socially inhibited (8%)	Lonely (22%)	Socially isolated (6%)
Age*				
18–29	66.7	7.6	22.0	3.7
30–44	68.3	7.0	19.8	4.9
45–64	64.9	7.0	22.2	5.9
≥65	53.4	10.1	24.6	11.9
Gender				
male	64.7	7.9	21.5	5.9
female	64.1	7.5	22.2	6.2
Marital status*				
unmarried	64.6	9.8	19.5	6.2
married	68.6	6.5	20.8	4.1
divorced	53.8	5.8	27.6	12.8
widowed	43.1	9.8	32.8	14.2
Ethnicity*				
Dutch	66.2	8.4	19.8	5.6
Surinamese/Antillean	54.9	15.7	13.7	15.7
Moroccan/Turkish	38.9	8.8	38.1	14.2
Other	52.9	11.0	25.1	11.0
Education*				
low	58.6	8.4	24.2	8.8
average	69.7	7.3	20.3	2.7
high	74.4	5.5	16.7	3.3
Income*				
low	53.1	7.9	29.6	9.4
average	66.6	8.8	21.6	3.0
high	73.8	4.8	18.4	3.0
SES*				
low	4.7	8.6	32.2	11.9
average	68.2	6.3	22.2	3.3
high	78.5	5.5	14.3	1.7
Location*				
urban	54.2	12.3	23.8	9.8
rural	74.0	3.4	20.0	2.6

Notes
*$P < 0.001$; Chi^2 tests.

subjects with a low socio-economic status than among those with a high socio-economic status (12 per cent versus 2 per cent). The percentage of lonely people was 32 per cent in the low socio-economic group and 14 per cent in the high socio-economic group. Social isolation increased with age: 12 per cent of the subjects above the age of sixty-five belonged to this group. Divorced or widowed subjects formed an at-risk group, and 16 per cent of the immigrants from Surinam or The Antilleans and 14 per cent of people from Turkey or Morocco were socially isolated. Subjects living on their own or without a regular job were also at risk. Although these factors do increase the risk of loneliness and isolation, it should be viewed in the proper perspective. For example, 50 per cent of the socially competent group are poorly educated, and 15 per cent are above sixty-five. The correlations lie between the minimum of $r = 0.01$ for sex and the maximum of $r = -0.25$ for socio-economic status. Stepwise discriminant analysis shows that only 14 per cent of the differences can be reduced to three factors, i.e. socio-economic status, location and age. The other factors were not significant. This means social isolation is a relatively autonomous phenomenon and cannot be reduced simply to structural variables.

3.13 Discussion

The findings of this analysis are grounds for a number of relevant conclusions and some critical comments. First, in this sample every type of social contact classification has been empirically assessed. About two-thirds of the subjects can be considered socially competent, they have many contacts and do not feel lonely. Although having an extensive personal network can improve a person's well-being, it is not necessarily always the case. Despite their extensive contacts, 22 per cent of the subjects feel lonely. On the other hand, 8 per cent of the subjects do not feel lonely despite their small networks. However, this last group is vulnerable in a way, because it is quite dependent on a small number of other people. A risk of isolation arises if one or two other people are removed for whatever reason. The socially isolated (6 per cent) were the worst off in both aspects.

The results of the core variables underlying the social contact typology, network size and feelings of loneliness are largely comparable with other findings. De Jong-Gierveld and Van Tilburg (1990) report the results of sixteen studies with mean loneliness scores between $X = 1.8$ and $X = 4.6$, which are somewhat higher than in our study. As far as network size is concerned, Van der Poel (1993a), reports a mean size of nearly ten, whereas Tijhuis *et al.* (1992) report a mean of almost four. These results differ from ours – nearly eight – due to differences in the method used; e.g. Van der Poel used ten items, in the present study eight items were used, and Tijhuis had a maximum of six persons who could be named. The percentages in our study are also comparable with Brummett *et al.*'s (2001). In comparing the effects of different approaches (network size, loneliness) on social support, the combined approach gives a more differentiated picture.

Elaborating on the typology, the contrast between the socially competent and the socially isolated is considerable according to the measures applied. The socially inhibited and the lonely group occupy an inbetween position. As a rule, they do worse than the socially competent but better than the socially isolated. However, there is a pattern of linearity between the typology and the measures applied, implying that the socially inhibited are generally better off than the lonely group, but not always. The results on giving and receiving support, and the opinions about protective factors confirm the concept underlying the typology of social contacts.

In addition to the linear increase in the risk of social isolation, another feature of the social typology is the degree of social balance. The socially competent are the most balanced group. The socially isolated are generally out of balance as is expressed, for example, in the results about receiving and giving support. In contrast with the socially competent, the socially inhibited, the lonely and the socially isolated run the risk of isolation in a specific way. The socially inhibited are generally content and appear stable, but have relatively small networks. They are dependent on a small number of people, and a possible disruption of this pattern renders them vulnerable. The lonely have extensive networks but are not quite satisfied, as there is an obvious discrepancy between their ideal and their reality. The socially isolated do poorly on both aspects, but seem to survive on a daily basis. Our study confirms Komter's notion (1996) that, in general, socially competent people say they give more than they receive, but this is not confirmed for the groups at risk of social isolation. On the contrary, the three risk groups say they receive more support than they give.

Regarding the issue of social isolation, subjective feelings of loneliness are more indicative than network size. Finally, it is the quality of the contacts that is decisive and not the quantity. The main virtue of this study, however, is that it shows empirically that applying a combination of two criteria offers a surplus value, which differs from exclusively applying a subjective criterion in terms of loneliness or an objective criterion in terms of network size (Schrameijer, 1990; Lincoln, 2000). The two criteria measure different aspects, but together they encompass the two most essential components of meaningful social contacts versus social isolation. Although reality is much more complex and diverse, this model based on dichotomization of objective and subjective criteria is a good starting point for investigating social isolation. Further analysis is needed to differentiate within the four groups. The two dimensions of the loneliness scale, social and emotional loneliness, could probably offer a fruitful approach (Van Baarsen et al., 2001).

This study evokes several methodological comments. As is noted in the method section, different cut-off scores are applied regarding network size depending on the purpose of the study (Fischer, 1982; Tijhuis et al., 1992; Brummett et al., 2001). For example, when applying a cut-off of 3/4, the percentage of isolated people dropped to 4 per cent in our study. Criteria about cut-off scores are always somewhat arbitrary, but the results do resemble those of other studies. Regarding the operationalization of social support, which is rather complex (Van Sonderen, 1995; Lincoln, 2000), we preferred actual support given and received. This approach has some limitations, as the items were mostly instrumental. Our measure was mainly restricted to instrumental support, and information about emotional support was limited. A more extended measure would have been preferable. For example, the measure for network size, which was based on hypothetical support situations, contains three kinds of support (emotional, instrumental and social companionship).

This chapter aimed at pursuing a meaningful approach towards a typology of social contacts based on objective and subjective criteria. The next step will be to investigate further the causes and effects of social isolation. Topics such as life events, personal competences, health issues, dependence on professional care, neighbourhood, and societal participation seem to be relevant to the issue of social isolation. These issues will be addressed in the following chapters.

Part II
Personal and social factors

4 Life events and social isolation

Ludwien Meeuwesen

4.1 Introduction

Certain life events may cause a decrease or an increase in a person's network size. This chapter will focus on the nature of important events that may occur in someone's life span, and the way these events are related to the typology of social contacts. Which events do occur in most people's life span? In what way and to what extent is social isolation related to specific life events? Do certain life events trigger the onset of a process of social isolation? Or are they the consequence of social isolation? It is these types of questions that will be discussed in this chapter. To start with, it is necessary to pay attention to the concept of life events and how it is defined. What is the relative importance of the concept for processes of well-being?

4.2 Definitions of life events

The concept of major life events or important life events was introduced more than twenty-five years ago, particularly in psychological literature (e.g. DeLongis *et al.*, 1982). While seeking for causes of illness and well-being in human beings, it was hypothesized that unwell people could have experienced more burdensome events or crises in their lives. Because these events might be very stressful, they could have a negative impact on people's course of life and health condition. If there was ample knowledge about which type of events captured a potential risk for these individuals, it would be possible to formulate preventive steps, such as strengthening a person's social network, enhancing their problem-solving capabilities, or social measures to prevent unemployment and discrimination. On the other hand, events do happen which are experienced as rather positive and may buffer impending non-well-being or poor health. Positive events are mostly manageable, joyful and stimulating, such as marriage, having children or one's first job. Except for humanist psychologists like Rogers and Maslow, attention has been paid predominantly to the negative events like death of a partner or family member, divorce, serious illness, loss of a job, problems at work, or lacking a school certificate.

While researching causes for illness, the dominant thinking was that negative events triggered substantial stress, which resulted in cognitive, emotional, behavioural and physiological changes (Taylor, 1986). In turn, these changes would lead to minor or major illness. There are even known examples in which very critical events have resulted in death. Engel (1971) describes a story of thirty-nine-year-old twins who were never separated from each other; the sudden death of one resulted in the death of the other within a week. In this case, a biomedical cause could not be diagnosed.

Although a great deal of research has been done on the effects of negative life events and the onset of illness, the predictive value is low (9 per cent) (Taylor, 1986). Gradually as insight grew, it became clear that it was not the occurrence of an event per se, but the way the situation was perceived by an individual in terms of stress, which counted. In other words, an event is not inherently stressful, it depends on the way an individual perceives and interprets the event and its consequences. This does not preclude negative, unmanageable, unpredictable and/or ambiguous events from being generally experienced as stressful. In this context it is also helpful to discern between more or less normal life events (death of parents, moving, relationships, having children, changing jobs) and abnormal or traumatic events (sexual abuse, extreme aggression, criminality) (Gersons, 1995). It is much less clear how a person will deal with traumatic events. Repeatedly going through such experiences or denial of these events will lead a person to seek professional help (Mol et al., 1999). The distinctions between life events may elucidate their potential to provoke a broad range of stressful experiences and greater chances for an individual to cope.

In addition to the 'major life events' approach to illness, the relevance of minor events was emphasized later on. Compared with major stressful events, people experience on a daily basis all kinds of small inconveniences and recurrent stress which may be irritating – what we know as 'daily hassles' (for example, standing in a long line to buy a train ticket, noisy neighbours, social obligations). These hassles have proven to be an even better predictor of physical health than major life events (DeLongis et al., 1982). The opposite of hassles are 'uplifts', daily-recurring smaller delights and windfalls (receiving compliments, finding something that was lost, tax refunds) that can buffer daily stress. Another infrequently used, but nonetheless important concept, is non-events. This concept refers to obvious events that one would normally expect to occur, but which do not happen and turn into a source of frustration. Examples are not finding a suitable romantic partner, performing under level for years, being involuntarily childless. Non-events can relate to realistic as well as unrealistic expectations in life.

Confronted with all these different situations, an individual is challenged to cope. In the course of life a person develops many coping strategies (see Chapter 5), one of which is social support of close family members, friends and acquaintances. This brings us to the importance of a person's social network. To what degree can someone in need of support turn to others?

Life events and social isolation 65

And will this result in the expected effect, namely a decrease of discomfort and an increase in subjective well-being?

There are indications that effects of a negative event will be mediated by personal (e.g. character, coping and social skills) and societal (e.g. participation in society) factors. A person who is quite active in the community (having a job, working as a volunteer, member of clubs or unions), will have larger personal networks and will have better access to finding support (see Chapter 8 for the relation between the social contacts typology and participation in society). It is supposed that if individuals have larger networks, the possible effects of negative events will be less dramatic, for example, in the case of losing a job. Many positive events protect people from loneliness and isolation.

Studies show that social support functions as a buffer and will protect against developing mental disorders in case of negative life events (Dalgard *et al.*, 1995), especially if individuals feel relatively powerless and have little control of their own lives. It is expected that if socially isolated people receive any support, they will benefit much from it. In Section 3.10 we showed that if the number of social contacts increased within a certain time span, the socially isolated benefited the most. However, if meaningful support is absent, chances of accumulation of problems are great. This shows the importance of paying attention to the role of life events in relation to processes of loneliness and isolation. What unpleasant and nasty events are individuals confronted with, and are these still bothering them? How are life events related to the typology of social contacts? What is the importance of social support when dealing with the consequences of important events? What are the social consequences of important events? What will offer consolation? What will protect against the negative consequences? Which are important risk factors for the negative consequences of life events? These questions will be answered in the next sections of this chapter; the analyses are based on the smaller dataset (N = 460; see Section 1.7).

4.3 Life events and the social contacts typology

4.3.1 *Positive and negative events*

The respondents filled out a list of eighty-eight important life events (pleasant and unpleasant) by answering the question 'which events still play an important role in your life at the time of the interview?', based on an adapted version of Van de Willige *et al.* (1985). The event itself could have taken place in the recent or distant past, but the question referred to the impact of the event. Respondents were also asked to indicate how they experienced a specific event (mainly positive/ mainly negative/ both positive and negative).

The respondents mentioned a mean number of seven events ($X = 7.1$, std = 6.92, N = 451) (Figure 4.1).The four contact groups differed from each other: the socially competent mentioned a mean of six, the lonely and

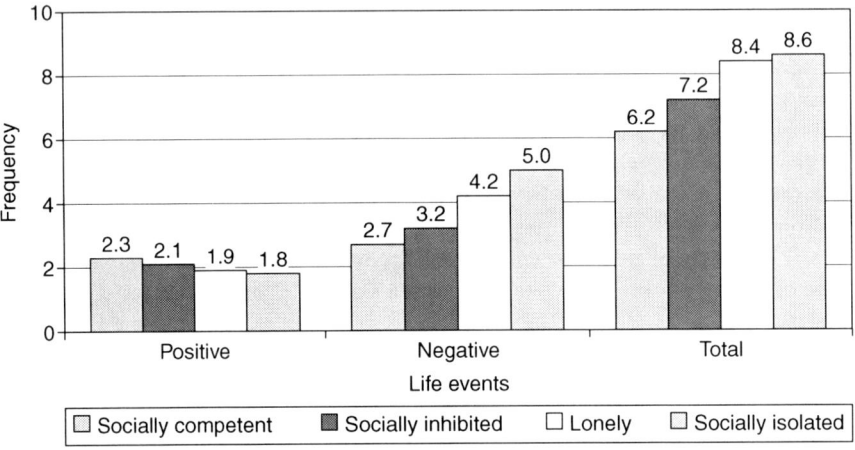

Figure 4.1 Number of life events related to the typology of social contacts (N = 451).

the socially isolated had a score between eight and nine (F = 3.18, df = 3, $P<0.05$). Respondents did not differ in the number of positive events (X = 2.2). They did mention more negative (X = 3.3) than positive events, but the differences between the four contact groups especially catches the eye (F = 7.25, df = 3, $P<0.000$). There was a linear connection with the social typology: the socially competent recalled the least negative experiences, the socially isolated reported twice as many (respectively 2.7 and 5). While the number of positive and negative events among the socially competent was fairly balanced, the lonely mentioned twice as many negative events, and the socially isolated three times more. The groups did not differ on the events experienced as ambivalent (X = 1.4, std = 4.4). What kinds of events still bother the respondents, in a negative or a positive way? Table 4.1 contains the most frequently mentioned positive events.

The eight most frequently mentioned positive events belonged mostly to personal domains like relationships and children, and the childhood period. Two items referred to moving, and one had to do with realizing a major achievement. Nearly 75 per cent of the respondents emphasized having had a happy childhood. Regardless of age, this event was quite decisive towards someone's course of life in a positive way. Half of the group mentioned marriage/living together, one in four brought up the occurrence of having children, and 20 per cent mentioned becoming involved in a new relationship. There were mostly no differences between the four contact groups. The socially inhibited and isolated recalled the event of moving more frequently. Although not significant, it is noticeable that the socially inhibited mentioned achieving something major in life.

Table 4.1 Percentage (≥10 per cent) of positive life events (N = 402)

Positive event	Socially competent	Socially inhibited	Lonely	Socially isolated	Total
A happy childhood	72	83	68	75	73
Marriage or living together	49	56	47	54	50
Addition to the family (a child)	28	24	28	21	27
A new relationship, being in love	22	34	18	26	22
Pregnancy	16	19	15	10	16
Moving to another house*	11	24	12	32	14
Moving to another city or town	11	17	10	15	11
Big achievement	8	20	10	5	10

Notes
*$P < 0.05$; Chi^2 test.

Regarding the recalling of negative events, Table 4.2. shows quite another picture. First, a number of negative events – twenty-two – exceeded the positive ones substantially. For the most part, the events were personal (such as death, illness, relational problems), and four of them referred to societal aspects (education, work disability, retirement, problems at work). The loss of a parent, another significant person or a pet were mentioned most frequently (51 per cent, 36 per cent and 22 per cent), followed by events relating to personal illness or illness of a significant other (between 10 per cent and 30 per cent). Themes like childhood and relations were also fairly represented. A shortage of positive attention and love in childhood was mentioned (20 per cent), whereas 24 per cent indicated having a problematic relationship or did not succeed in finding the right romantic partner. Themes like schooling and work were also represented. 20 per cent indicated having problems at work, and 18 per cent did not succeed in finishing their education. Last, 11 per cent indicated keeping a secret, and another 11 per cent were heavily disappointed somehow.

Which negative events do the socially inhibited, the lonely and/or the socially isolated report more frequently than the socially competent? Nearly half of the events showed substantial differentiation according to the typology. Illness and shortage of love in youth was mentioned less frequently by the socially competent compared with the three other social groups. Illness was mentioned much more by the socially isolated. Further, the lonely and the isolated reported two to three times more cases of being disabled compared with the socially competent. Even events such as retirement and relational problems were more frequently raised by the socially inhibited and the isolated. The impact of having small networks is visible here. All three risk groups, especially the inhibited and the isolated (up to 30 per cent), reported more non-events such as being heavily disappointed while not succeeding in realizing targets in life compared with the socially competent. About the same could be said with regard to keeping a secret. In addition to

Table 4.2 Percentage (≥10 per cent) of negative life events (N = 451)

Negative event	SC	SIN	L	SI	T
Death of parent	50	50	48	69	51
Death of significant other	36	43	35	29	36
Serious or chronic physical and/or mental problems (self)****	21	41	35	68	30
Loss of a pet*	19	36	22	30	22
Great shortcoming of love and attention in childhood***	13	26	30	32	20
Intensive care of sick spouse, parent, child or significant other**	16	30	18	35	20
Serious/chronic physical and/or mental problems (partner, parent, child)	17	18	17	29	18
No school certificate or finished education****	11	34	21	38	18
Becoming disabled for work (self)***	12	18	29	30	18
Death of spouse or own child**	12	28	20	32	17
Great uncertainty about appearance or achievements	14	22	15	19	15
Retiring (self)*	13	23	10	27	14
Having a problematic relationship*	10	24	14	24	13
Prolonged hospitalization (partner, parent or child)	10	12	12	25	12
Being the black sheep or maverick of the family	11	15	12	22	12
Dismissal/jobless	9	15	13	14	11
Not succeeding in finding the right spouse*	8	21	11	19	11
Major problems with/at work	9	9	16	15	11
Serious or chronic physical and/or mental problems (significant other)	9	17	9	14	10
Keeping a big secret**	7	17	15	20	11
Big disappointment while not having realized ideals****	5	24	16	30	11
Major financial problems**	10	3	9	29	10

Notes
*$P<0.1$, **$P<0.05$, ***$P<0.01$, ****$P<0.001$; Chi^2 test.
SC = socially competent; SIN = socially inhibited; L = lonely; SI = socially isolated; T = total.

the above-mentioned data (>10 per cent), Table 4.3 draws attention to the significant negative events mentioned by less than 10 per cent of the respondents. A substantial part of these events are considered traumatic (see Section 4.2).

The socially competent mentioned nearly all the events the least frequently. Most of the events tended to be recalled by the socially isolated, such as mistreatment, difficult social integration, hospitalization, and relational, sexual and/or psychiatric problems. The socially inhibited and the lonely groups mostly took a position in between (difficult integration, hospitalization, relational problems). Sometimes the pattern of the lonely

Table 4.3 Percentage (<10 per cent) negative life events, significant (N = 451)

Negative event	SC	SIN	L	SI	T
Victim of criminal act (sexual or otherwise)***	5	23	12	16	9
Mental or physical assault**	5	3	10	24	8
No or difficult social integration****	4	12	11	30	8
Prolonged hospitalization (self)****	4	12	9	32	8
Prolonged work above achievement level**	4	13	14	15	8
Parents disabled*	5	15	11	5	7
Moving of significant other***	5	21	9	5	7
Prolonged hospitalization of significant other**	7	18	4	–	7
Raised in negative neighbourhood*	3	12	10	10	6
Major relational problems****	2	9	8	24	6
Hopeless love affair**	6	9	4	20	6
Psychiatric hospitalization (self)***	3	7	6	20	5
Prolonged work under achievement level***	2	13	4	15	4
Alcoholism/drug abuse**	2	9	4	10	4
Dismissal/no job (partner)**	1	6	8	5	4
Sexual problems****	2	6	3	14	3
Leaving a religion/sect*	3	–	1	11	3
Childlessness	1	9	5	5	3
Discrimination by environment**	1	3	3	10	2
Loss of volunteer work**	1	–	–	10	1
Having been imprisoned***	1	–	–	10	1

Notes
*$P<0.1$, **$P<0.05$, ***$P<0.01$, ****$P<0.001$; Chi^2 test.
SC = socially competent; SIN = socially inhibited; L = lonely; SI = socially isolated; T = total.

group resembled that of the socially competent (addiction, hopeless love affair), and sometimes that of the socially isolated (achieving above one's own capacities, raised in a bad neighbourhood). The socially inhibited resembled the isolated in having chronically worked under achievement level. Some events were most frequently recalled by the socially inhibited, such as victimage, moving away of significant other, prolonged hospitalization of significant other, and involuntary childlessness.

4.3.2 Personal and societal events

In describing the results of the relation between events and social typology, sometimes one refers to the distinction between more personally-tinted events and more societal events. Table 4.4 contains a summary of such a classification of the events, grouped by themes. Also included is the dominant perception (mostly positive, mostly negative or ambivalent) of them by the respondents.

70 *Ludwien Meeuwesen*

Table 4.4 The mentioning of personal and societal events, and respondents' evaluation (in percentages) (N = 451)

	Mentioned[a]	Positive	Negative	Positive and negative
Personal	94**	74	74***	47
Childhood	66*	55	18	15
Relationships and children	65	51t	18***	15t
Loss	64	6	48	14
Victimage	16	–	14	2
Acceptance	27	8	15t	8
Justice	6	1	3	2
Illness (other)	38	6	28	12
Illness (self)	32***	3*	25***	7
Other	39**	14	23	12*
Societal	53***	19	34***	14
Education	18**	1	9t	5
Employment and income	43t	13	25***	10
Other	4t	6	6t	3

Notes
a A minimum of 1 item being part of the specific section has been mentioned by the respondent. The number of items being part of a specific section varies from minimally 2 (e.g. education) to maximally 14 (e.g. acceptance).
t $P = 0.1$; *$P < 0.05$, **$P < 0.01$, ***$P < 0.001$; Chi^2 test; per cell, the percentages of the four contact groups are tested.

Personal events include the subjects of childhood, relationships and children, loss, victimage, acceptance (problems in accepting oneself and being accepted by others), justice, personal or significant other's illness, and a section of 'other events'. Societal events refer to school, employment and income of oneself and the significant other. Almost everyone mentioned personal events, and well over half of the respondents mentioned societal events.

The differences between the four social contacts groups were especially manifest along the personal theme of personal illness and along the societal theme of education. Although the groups did not differ in positive perception (see also Figure 4.1), there is one exception: only socially isolated respondents indicated their own illness as being mainly positive. They possibly value the effects of secondary illness gains (e.g. getting attention).

In regard to the negative personal events, most differences related to personal illness and problems with relationships and children; for the societal events the differences concerned employment and income. The socially competent reported the least problems, the socially isolated the most. The subject of loss was presented most frequently (48 per cent), regardless of the contact group – after all, every person is sooner or later confronted with the demise of a family member, close friends and acquaintances. Feelings on personal subjects like childhood, relationships, children and loss, regardless of the contact group, were for the most part ambivalent.

In reviewing the results, it is concluded that:

- the four social contact groups differ substantially from one another in the number of major life events they experience;
- there are no differences in the number of positive events;
- there are substantial differences when reporting negative events between the contact groups, quantitatively as well as qualitatively.

Major differences are expressed towards events related to relationships and children, illness, employment and income, as well as some traumatic events. Again, we see a linear relation in the typology: the socially competent are the best off, the socially isolated the worst, and the socially inhibited and the lonely are in between. With regard to the reporting of burdensome life events, we conclude that subjective feelings of loneliness are more indicative compared with network size.

4.4 Hassles and uplifts

What about daily hassles and uplifts? Respondents were presented with fourteen situations that could annoy them. The items referred to nuisance, dog-do, litter, vandalism, street gangs, tinkering in the street, scolding/discrimination, drugs, traffic, feeling threatened, poor lighting, burglary, nasty smells, and others (see also Chapter 9). Based on these items, an irritation index was composed with scores ranging between 1 and 14. The contrast between the mean of the socially competent and the three other groups was great (respectively $X = 5.3$ (the competent group); $X = 7.1$ (the inhibited); $X = 6.6$ (lonely); $X = 7.7$ (isolated)). For example, 36 per cent of the socially competent were (sometimes too often) irritated by noise, compared with 53 per cent of the socially isolated. The isolated felt four times more threatened (27 per cent versus 7 per cent), complaining three times more about drug nuisance (35 per cent versus 13 per cent) and a lot more about tinkering in the street (28 per cent versus 12 per cent).

In interpreting these results, it is necessary to realize that the index used here is focused mainly on inconvenient situations in one's neighbourhood, and not on situations in other contexts. It is probably not so much of a general irritation index, but is more informative about the kind of neighbourhoods people live in and the degree to which this may give reason for becoming annoyed (see also Chapter 9).

To learn more about uplifts, respondents were asked to what degree they were able to enjoy life, and to what extent they received compliments. Again, the same pattern showed: the greater the risk of isolation, the less enjoyment and the less compliments. While the socially competent and the socially inhibited did not differ from each other, the situation looked grimmer for the lonely, especially for the isolated. Eighty-five per cent of the socially competent received enough compliments versus 46 per cent of the socially isolated. Just as with life events, hassles and uplifts show about the same linear pattern in relation to social typology.

4.5 Important events and social support

Which of all life events was bothering interviewees the most? For all four groups, the subjects of loss, illness, relationships and children took the highest toll, followed far below by childhood, employment and income, victimage and issues regarding acceptance (see also Section 4.3.2.). And what was respondents' reaction on the most bothersome event mentioned? Two-thirds indicated having accepted the situation, 17 per cent changed the situation, and another 17 per cent had suppressed it. Although the four contact groups did not differ substantially in their reaction, personal competences do play a role: the less competent someone was in terms of self-confidence, problem-solving and social skills, the greater the chances of suppression ($r = -0.13$; see Section 5.7).

One of the most effective strategies to cope with a painful event is asking for and getting support from others. How many respondents received this kind of support? And what type of support was it? Seventy-eight per cent of all respondents indicated having received help or support from others, but only 55 per cent of the socially isolated ($P < 0.01$). The reasons for not having received any support vary: 59 per cent indicated not feeling in need, 17 per cent experienced it as inconvenient, 18 per cent said there was nobody available, and 6 per cent asked for help without succeeding (Figure 4.2).

The reactions of the socially isolated are in glaring contrast with the other three contact groups. Nearly half of the isolated indicated not having received any support (45 per cent). The fact that 80 per cent of this group is in need of support but has nobody to appeal to reflects the poignant situation of the isolated respondents.

Regarding the whole group who did receive support, the nature of the support was mostly emotional (86 per cent), as is understandable. Of the received support, 68 per cent was mainly informal (partner, friends, family and neighbours), 7 per cent was formal (organizations, agencies, telephone help services), and 25 per cent was both formal and informal. There were no great differences between the four contact groups, although the lonely and the isolated received a little more formal support. The socially competent and the lonely could appeal to a large variety of persons (colleagues, neighbours, parents and children included), whereas this was more limited for the socially inhibited and the isolated. This is understandable, considering that having a relatively small network partly defines these two contact groups (see Section 3.3), in contrast with the socially competent and the lonely.

Life events and social isolation 73

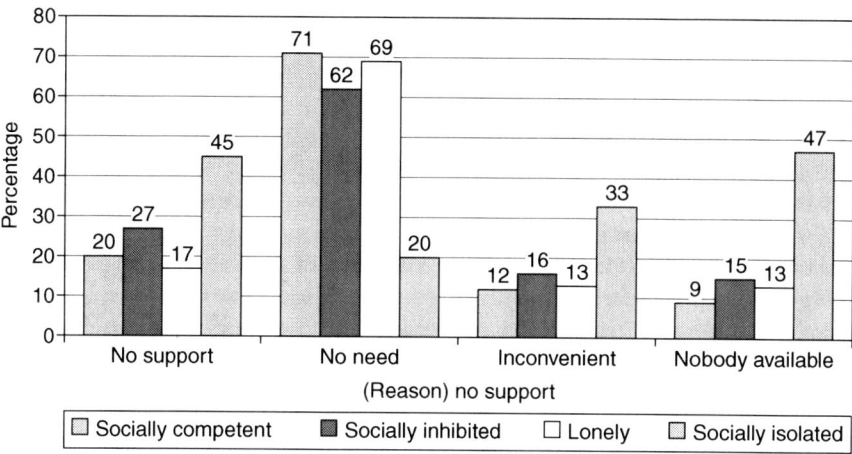

Figure 4.2 Percentage of 'no support after important event' and reason for it (N = 407).

The formal support respondents received (N = 78) came mainly from psychiatrists and social workers and was of an emotional nature; they also received practical support in the form of information or education (Chapter 7 elaborates further on formal and informal support).

Those respondents who indicated not appealing to an organization gave the following reasons:

- it did not fit with their character (57 per cent);
- they preferred asking for help from close relatives (19 per cent);
- they were unfamiliar with the existence of these agencies and organizations (13 per cent);
- they did not expect that much from such organizations (11 per cent).

The socially isolated did not indicate a preference towards asking close relatives for help, compared with the three other groups. One out of three isolated respondents (36 per cent) turned out to be unfamiliar with the organizations concerned. It is observed that precisely the target group these organizations aim towards is hardly reached, if at all (see also Chapter 7).

To summarize, the results emphasize that after the occurrence of a major event there is an obvious lack of adequate help and support for a substantial group, especially for the socially isolated. It is conspicuous that those who are in the greatest distress have to go without this urgent support. Professional organizations fail notably in reaching one of their most important target groups – the most distressed. These findings are in line with the situation that persons entitled to welfare and the elderly are often unfamiliar with their rights and possibilities, and are not reached well by the proper organizations (Van Oorschot, 2000; Jehoel-Gijsbers, 2004).

4.6 The effects of important life events

What are the effects of the occurrence of a major life event on the social contacts and activities of the person in question? The social life of some will shrink, for others it will remain the same or even expand (see also Section 3.10). Thirty-six per cent of the respondents answered that after the major event there was a shift in contacts in the form of diminishing or even stopping contacts with family members, friends, colleagues or fellow students in particular. Diminishing or stopping with activities referred to paid/unpaid work, sports, visiting cafes/restaurants and/or going to the theatre/movies, neighbourhood activities, church attendance, watching television. There were no appreciable differences between the four groups, except for a remarkably higher drop of neighbourhood activities among the isolated.

On the other hand, about an equally big group (42 per cent) indicated that their social life had intensified, although this was much less the case for the isolated (21 per cent) and the socially inhibited (26 per cent). The positive change related especially to friends, family, neighbours, sport activities, voluntary work and television-watching. Apparently, a major event will intensify or diminish one's social life. How is such a change related to feelings of loneliness? What are the effects of major life events on loneliness? (see Table 4.5).

If a person is already wrestling with loneliness, a negative major event will not change the situation that much. Most respondents were not lonely and they did not become lonely (59 per cent). However, 24 per cent of the respondents who did not generally feel lonely had become lonely after a major event. There exists an obvious linear relation between the increase in feelings of loneliness and the typology of social contacts: the socially competent were the least vulnerable, and the socially isolated the most. At the same time it is observed that 16 per cent of the socially competent could

Table 4.5 Effects of a major life event on feelings of loneliness, percentages (N = 387)

	Socially competent	Socially inhibited	Lonely	Socially isolated	Total
Lonely, same as before	6	6	6	21	7
More lonely	5	6	6	9	6
Less lonely	4	4	6	3	5
Not lonely, same as before	69	55	50	30	59
Not lonely, but have become lonely	16	29	32	36	24

Notes
$Ch^2 = 32.13; P < 0.01$.

also become lonely as an effect of an event, against as many as 29 per cent of the socially inhibited.

4.7 Consolation and protection

In Section 4.3 we discussed that some specific events are related to social isolation, yet there are individuals who have gone through the same distress without becoming lonely or isolated. Are they better protected against becoming isolated? If this is the case, how come? Or do they have specific sources of consolation at their disposal which others lack? Who or what offers comfort, who or what protects an individual? Answering the question of whether a significant other person is available for giving comfort in case of grief or major distress, most respondents were affirmative (92 per cent). They had one or more significant others they could turn to. However, 17 per cent of the lonely group and 20 per cent of the isolated group could not mention one single other person to turn to. Half of them said they had someone at their disposal in former days, but this important pillar had been largely lost through death or divorce.

The most important persons available for offering comfort were spouses, friends, children, other family members and parents (Table 4.6). Professionals like a health care provider, social worker, vicar, imam or pastor, or even a colleague were mentioned occasionally. While both the socially inhibited and the isolated lacked a consoling partner more often, the first group had more access to appealing to friends or parents. Except for turning to children and other family members, in general both the lonely and the isolated had less comforting persons at their disposal compared with the socially competent and the socially inhibited. Having large networks (such as in the case of the lonely group) is not a guarantee for having the right persons to offer the right comfort. When it comes to human consolation, quality is much more important than quantity (as with the socially inhibited). Besides appealing to significant others of a person's network, there are other means to find consolation. Figure 4.3 contains the other sources of comfort ('What offers comfort?').

Table 4.6 Persons who offer comfort (>5 per cent) (N = 422)

	Socially competent	Socially inhibited	Lonely	Socially isolated	Total
Partner**	76	49	64	44	69
Child	29	36	32	33	30
Parent*	24	41	18	11	24
Other family member	28	31	27	28	28
Friend*	44	56	37	33	43

Notes
*$P<0.05$, **$P<0.01$.

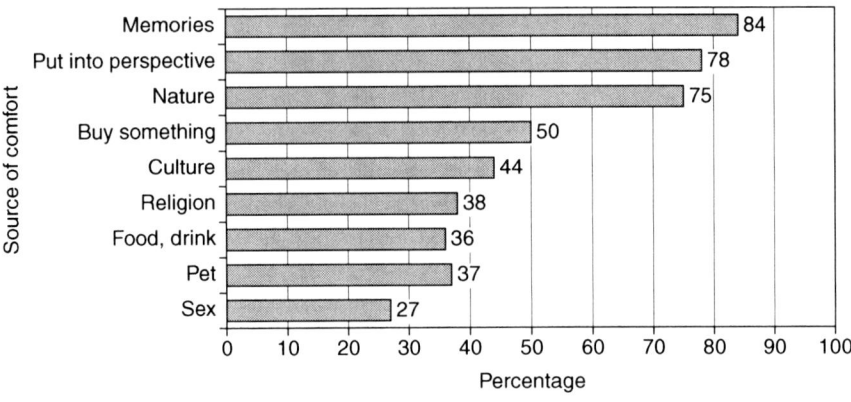

Figure 4.3 Sources of comfort, percentages (N = 422).

Good memories played an important role for almost everyone, regardless of network size or degree of loneliness. This is comparable with the data on positive events (Section 5.3.1). Being able to put things into perspective was also very important; the socially inhibited seemed to be best at it (95 per cent versus 72 per cent of the other groups). In general, there were few differences between the contact groups. On average, sex was less often a source of comfort for the lonely and the isolated (18 per cent and 12 per cent) compared with the other groups (32–33 per cent).

Apart from having these types of sources of comfort at one's disposal, there are many other possibilities that can offer protection to persons in difficult times. In Section 3.11 we already ascertained that the socially isolated lacked remarkably more resources, e.g. health, joy of living, relationships, living conditions, employment, compared with the other three groups. The more sources of comfort and protection people have at their disposal, the better they are able to cope with the situation under a variety of circumstances, the more positive impulses they receive, and the more adept they become at steering clear of negative influences.

4.8 Risk factors

Before discussing results, this section will provide a review of some additional statistics (correlations and regression) of important risk factors for life events. The following topics will be dealt with successively: the relation between loneliness and network size, some report marks, demographic variables, childhood, personal competences and participation in society.

Loneliness and network size: The more negative events respondents introduced, the more lonely they were ($r = 0.24$). There was no relation with network size ($r = 0.02$). The relation between social typology and negative events was r = 0.21. These correlations reveal that subjective feelings of loneliness are more indicative compared with network size.

Report marks: Negative events correlated negatively with report marks for work (r = −0.28), finances (r = −0.21), and health (r = −0.23). The report mark for 'relationship' was positively correlated with positive events. The more satisfied people were with their partner, the more positive events they introduced. In contrast, single persons introduced on average more negative events than persons with a partner and/or family.

Demographic variables: People living in urban areas introduced more negative events and positive events (r = −0.13) compared with people in rural areas. Urban life seems to be more dynamic, leading to experiencing more peaks as well as more setbacks. A relation also showed up between income and positive events (r = 0.13). The more people had to spend, the more pleasant events they could experience and remember. Regression analysis with the demographic variable shows that only the age variable gives an effect on total number of events (2 per cent of explained variance). It is remarkable that no effect at all was observed regarding negative events. Regarding positive events, there was an effect of socio-economic status and gender (4 per cent of explained variance). The higher someone's socio-economic status, the more positive events were reported, and women mention more pleasant events than men.

Childhood: Respondents were asked if they had a happy childhood, and whether they felt their parents loved them unconditionally. The correlations with negative events were substantial (respectively r = −0.34 and r = −0.36). This means that a happy childhood and loving parents buffer against negative events in later life. We saw in Table 4.1 that nearly three-quarters of the respondents introduced a happy childhood as a positive event.

Personal competences: Individuals may have personal qualities that enable them to resist setbacks. Among these competences are a certain degree of emotional independence and a fighting spirit, which enables people to function well as self-relying human beings in relation to themselves and others. These competences can be relatively fixed features or personal traits, or they can be shaped as a result of life experiences. The measure for personal competences applied here is composed of three subscales: self-confidence, coping and social skills (see Chapter 5). There was a negative relation between personal competences and negative life events (r = −0.31), and no relation with the positive events. The more people were personally competent, the less they came across negative events, or they were better equipped to cope with them. Self-confidence, coping abilities and social skills buffer the effects of negative events.

Participation in society: It is observed that there was no relation between the number of events and the degree of respondent's participation in society. (See Chapter 8 for further discussion.)

In sum, it is observed that most demographic variables show a small or non-existent relation with the negative events. Network size is of no importance. Having a partner and/or money will lead to a somewhat higher number of pleasant events. However, more decisive are having had a happy childhood, affectionate parents and personal competences at one's disposal. These may buffer the negative impact of important life events.

4.9 Discussion

The analysis of life events gives rise to a number of remarkable findings and some comments. Respondents mentioned more negative than positive events which still bothered them. The negative events have a substantial effect on the typology of social contacts. There is a pattern of linearity between the typology and the negative events: the greater the risk for isolation, the greater the number of negative events mentioned, regardless of the personal or societal emphasis of the events, and of normal or traumatic events. The same pattern is observed with regard to hassles and uplifts. The contrast between the socially competent and the socially isolated is considerable according to the measures applied. The socially inhibited and the lonely group take a position in between.

Another important finding is that the impact of negative events is more decisive when it comes to feelings of loneliness compared with network size. Subjective feelings and thus the perception and experience of events are important factors in determining the length and intensity of carrying the burden of a negative event. Network size seems less relevant, but the way people appeal to their support system and significant others does count. However, network size does play a role in daily hassles and uplifts. These daily occurrences are considered as important mediating factors with regard to perception and experience of major events.

While demographic variables have little importance, we observe that a happy and loving childhood seems quite decisive in overcoming setbacks. The same holds true for personal competences. It is not educational level, sex or age which are decisive to burdensome events, but the availability of self-confidence, coping abilities and social skills. It appears that a positive childhood is a good foundation for future life, enabling a person to establish personal capital such as personal competences and strength. This in turn increases the likelihood of a rewarding social life.

An intriguing question is whether people become socially isolated because they encounter many negative events, or whether they are already somehow programmed early in life to be or become isolated. Put another way, were they already isolated or did they become isolated by an accumulation of specific events? This is a complicated issue which we will try to shed some light on. Reasons for social isolation are manifold, and there is a clear link between isolation and life events. As observed in Section 5.6, a substantial part of the two groups at risk (the socially inhibited and the lonely) and the socially isolated indicate having become (more) lonely as a consequence of an important event. The occurrence of a major negative event may have triggered feelings of loneliness. In particular, the isolated appear to be most in need of support, which unfortunately is not available. Either they had nobody else to turn to, or they did not know how to mobilize others in their circle of acquaintances. This may have to do with their isolated position and/or personal competences. When focusing exclusively on the isolated group, the relation between events and personal competences was considerably stronger compared with the whole group ($r = -0.50$). The isolated group with low self-confidence and less competences mentioned twice more (namely 9) negative events compared with the isolated group that had enough self-confidence and competences. This provides yet another cue that personal competences matter. As we saw, the same holds true for having grown up in happy and affectionate surroundings. We can conclude that regarding the incidence of social isolation, several conditions seem to be essential but do not explain the phenomenon sufficiently. People of course are ignorant of what will cross their path, yet it is observed that the socially competent are the best protected in many ways and have the best personal and social baggage, while the isolated are the least protected.

Regarding the kind of help people are in need of after a major event, it is striking to observe that both private and professional support fails for a substantial number of respondents, especially for the socially isolated. They are in most urgent need, but have to refrain most often. The kind of support they need most, in the first instance, is emotional. Direct personal contact is essential and spouses, family, friends, neighbours and acquaintances are the first to offer it. In the case of traumatic events, professional help such as medical and psychosocial care is more appropriate. This is not an easy job though. For example, general practitioners – gatekeepers of the health care system in most European countries – are not always able to accurately diagnose certain problems (Verhaak, 1995). There is also a gap between patients' experiences triggered by traumatic events and doctors' specialized knowledge of such events. Mol et al. (1999) observed a big difference between the lay person's reports and the GP's 'diagnosis'; based on data from physical assault and sexual abuse, the GP has little indepth knowledge of these events. The psychic and psychosomatic impact of experiencing such major events is considerable and requires prompt and adequate primary health care (Van der Ploeg et al., 1985). Offering this kind of support not only reduces the suffering caused, but also prevents it from worsening. The problematic nature of isolation is indeed expressed by an accumulation of problems which can be halted in time professionally and can potentially be turned in a positive direction.

From the viewpoint of social welfare policy, a number of recommendations can be formulated based on the results of life events (see further Chapter 14). For example, attention needs to be paid to the observation that 11 per cent of respondents mention carrying a secret (20 per cent for the isolated group), or another 11 per cent mention being heavily disappointed (30 per cent for the isolated) (Table 5.2). Carrying a secret could be interpreted as a form of denial – at any rate, it is a denial for one's social network. Studies show that there is a relation between the coping strategy of denial and high blood pressure (Taylor, 1986). A specific form of coping by avoidance may have direct physiological consequences for an individual. The aspects of personal competences and health will be further elaborated in Chapters 5 and 6. Here suffice it to conclude that many people will not, cannot, might not talk about what is bothering them, even when it is obvious that it is experienced as a burden. Could it be that they are disappointed having not realized their life's ambitions. Professional care needs to be available, through health care as well as in the form of persons one can trust, for example, social workers or therapists. This type of support needs to be initiated in a broader context.

5 Personal competences and social isolation

Ludwien Meeuwesen

5.1 Introduction

In the previous chapter we saw how people at a high risk of social isolation have encountered more major negative events throughout their lives that still worry them. Such negative events make everyone – whether or not at risk of social isolation – commit to the task of adequately coping with the effects, which include negative feelings. Not everyone manages equally well though. We already saw that one in four respondents became lonely due to such an event, while indicating not having felt lonely before the event (Section 4.6). How come that some individuals worry or separate themselves from others, while others go looking support from people in their surroundings, seek distraction, or tackle the problem? How do individuals deal with the many negative feelings? Do they get over these feelings, do they know how to face the threatening event head-on, or does the event fixate into a person's life, contributing to a worsening of the situation in terms of loneliness and isolation? The way in which people cope depends strongly on certain personality traits, on socialization and on a number of societal factors.

This chapter focuses on the role of several *personality traits* and *socialization factors*. The proposition involved here is that social isolation is chiefly a question of personal incompetence, which is related to someone's personality or character. In Section 3.11 we observed that respondents consider that someone's character and joy of living offer by far the most protection against loneliness and isolation, and are considered most important for a rich social life. Just like a happy youth and loving parents, personal competences form a solid buffer against the effects of negative events (Section 4.8) (Sarason *et al.*, 1990; Mallinckrodt, 2001). They also seem to be more decisive than demographic variables (such as age or education) or network size. When there hasn't been a happy youth, the personal competences become even more important. How important these personality traits can be have also been described by Rubin (1996) in several penetrating portraits of people who underwent very traumatic youth experiences but carried themselves through them and turned their lives around successfully. As reasons why some do manage, Rubin indicates that they realized very early on that their primary contacts, mostly relatives from whom they depended, were not good for them. They succeeded to detach themselves emotionally from these relatives at an early age already and attract people who were good for them. They adopted, as it were, new adults around them, who could heal the deprivation and damage from their past. A strong feeling of self-esteem plays a decisive role here. Another example is the street children of Latin American countries. Those who are known to have been saved, despite harrowing circumstances, can attribute this largely to their array of problem-solving skills (Hoynck van Papendrecht and 't Sas, 1997).

With regard to personal competences, concepts such as self-confidence and self-respect, social and communicative skills, and problem-solving capacities are essential (Hortulanus et al., 1992; Shadid, 1998). How do these personal competences relate to social isolation? Theories on stress and problem-solving describe two important mechanisms (Lazarus, 1966; Sarason et al., 1990). What are the effects of personal competences on people's personal well-being, such as type of contacts, social support system and feelings of loneliness? Which personal competences work against loneliness and social isolation? The second mechanism involves the search into the effects of social isolation or social competency on personal competences. In other words, what is the meaning of social contacts for someone's personal competences? To answer these questions, it is necessary to delve a bit further into the concepts of personality, socialization and personal competences.

5.2 Personality, socialization and personal competences

5.2.1 Personality

What do we mean by someone's character, temperament or personality? These concepts are closely related. Temperament points to a typifying quality of an individual that contributes to shape reactions and process all kinds of occurrences. Personality traits refer to characteristics and noticeable behavioural patterns of a person, which occur in a broad spectrum of situations and which are relatively stable in time (Luteijn et al., 1985). We speak of someone with a 'strong personality' or 'character' when the person in question has a generally good attitude, is trusted by many people and knows how to act adequately in different situations. Such a person will be relatively balanced, relaxed and healthy, will radiate high spirits, will be sure of themselves and able to take setbacks, and will be open, easy and sociable. In short, we are talking here about a type of personality that is a desirable goal for most people yet attainable to few, but which can serve as a personal example on how to act. The absolute opposite to this can be identified in gloomy, unstable people who face the world and their fellow human beings with distrust and fear. Such people can also have smug and dependent traits, have pessimistic dispositions and not be devoid of some rigidity.

In reality, all of these traits rarely come together in one and the same person. We have deliberately sketched here a black-and-white picture, to sharpen the contrasts. The ideal picture is seldom encountered, but we do have an image of it. Those among us with developed self-reflection capacities know more or less of themselves and of others how to stand in life and what their strengths and weaknesses are. This notion of personal identity or self-image is the answer to someone's question, 'Who am I?'. Our personal schemes – the perception of ourselves in terms of a number of traits (athletic, thin, fat, etc.) – determine to an important degree how we process social information. They influence how we perceive, remember and assess other people and ourselves (Myers, 1999). Our self-image involves not only our notions about who we are, but also who or how we would eventually like to be. These potential self-images contain visions about the self that we dream about, as well as aspects of the self that we fear (e.g. being jobless or sick).

A skilful person will understand how to bring forward their personal capital and create circumstances to present this capital in the best light possible. In this sense, good social contacts are of the utmost importance for everyone. People will try to shape their lives together with others in the most pleasant manner possible, taking into consideration one's own strengths and limitations as well as those of others. A person's strengths and limitations are subject to change, and circumstances only add to this. There are early bloomers and late bloomers, and per life period each individual will use their personal capital to various degrees of success.

A person with self-confidence and self-esteem will be able to accept more easily who they are, who they look like, what they can do, etc. A basic feeling of being satisfied with oneself tends to put a rosy tint on one's skills and experiences, and contributes to maintaining positive emotions and well-being (Smith and Petty, 1995). It forms, as it were, a buffer against negative influences. People with a positive feeling of self-esteem are usually happier, they get sick less easily, and failure upsets them less (Brown, 1991). In a study into well-being among the population of the Dutch city of Dordrecht, it was confirmed that greater self-respect was related to general well-being (Hortulanus *et al.*, 1992). Hortulanus *et al.* speak in this context about self-respect that consists of self-determination, self-assurance and self-esteem. The degree to which people have their social contacts and societal position basically under their own control contributes to a greater feeling of self-determination. Self-assurance is rooted mainly in one's societal position, where societal appreciation can be found, and in one's social contacts, which provide social support and appreciation. Self-esteem is much more related to personal characteristics than to one's societal and social environment.

Our self-concept thus involves not just our personal identity (notion of personal characteristics) but also our social identity. The social definition of who we are is related to group memberships such as race, religion, gender, education, etc. We compare ourselves with those around us and become aware of our social identity and how we differ from others or are similar to them. Our self-image is also formed by our daily experiences in terms of success and failure, recognition and underestimation. Success leads to an increase of self-respect and self-esteem, whereas failure can lead to a low self-esteem. Positive evaluations of other people can also help us think positively of ourselves. What's more, the renowned social-psychological experiments of Rosenthal (1966) have shown that positive expectations elicit positive behaviour and vice versa. The process of formation of someone's personal and social identity begins at birth and continues throughout life. This process is mostly described as the result of a complicated interaction of individual and environmental factors and of innate and acquired qualities. In any event, a solid basis for someone's personality and self-image is laid during youth. This process is known as socialization.

5.2.2 Socialization

Socialization involves the process in which the individual acquires certain desirable values, norms, expectations, skills and behavioural traits. It is a process in which an individual is formed by the social and cultural environment, and that process actually goes on throughout one's entire lifetime. Socialization theories tend to presume that roles and behaviours are acquired. One of the most important mechanisms of this learning process is that of modelling: a child sees all kinds of images, examples and habits, and imitates the behaviour of his carers. The social environment in which children grow up is very influential to what they imitate and learn. In our society, the family is seen as an important 'socialization body'. Socialization is essentially about how people learn to manage basic emotions such as love, aggression, joy, grief, anxiety and satisfaction, and how they relate to authority and intimacy from their personal tendencies and biographies. Families are characterized by a unique combination of informality, affectivity and inequality, where intimacy is expressed in a very specific manner (Blum-Kulka, 1990). This unique combination of authority and intimacy within the family has repercussions on the social, moral, emotional and cognitive development of individuals. In the family or among the primary carers, a solid basis is – or should be – established for self-confidence and trust in others, for a basic attitude towards life, and for a feeling of safety and personal identity. One of the prerequisites for this is the unconditional love and care of parents or guardians, who make it possible for the child to grow in a safe and accepting environment. In this context we often speak of a safe attachment (Bowlby, 1983), which constitutes the basis for healthy social contacts later in life. Socialization also takes place outside the family: at school, among one's circle of friends, and later on at work. Each of these socialization bodies contributes in its own way to the formation of personality. Experts differ in their opinion about the relative importance of family, school and peer groups for the socialization of youth (Feldman and Elliott, 1990; Harris, 1998). The family is usually ascribed the greatest formative power. The way in which this formative process elapses has changed significantly in recent decades though. A characteristic of our western society is that norms and values are not as fixed as they were about fifty years ago. A far-reaching democratization and individualization of human relationships has occurred (see Chapter 2). This has led to the theory that human relationships, in the private sphere as well as in countless societal terrains, have become more egalitarian (De Swaan, 1979). Such a cultural shift entails that relationships between people, be it in the private sphere or societal life, have become more dynamic. This also means, however, that our society demands a lot from individuals in terms of social competences and problem-solving skills. In a strongly individualized society, like most western societies, individuals are left more to their own devices. Possibilities of developing one's talents have greatly expanded, but so has individual responsibility.

5.2.3 Personal competences

The concept of personal competences refers to the personal traits of people which can facilitate competent actions in a normative sense. The normative refers to that which is generally considered desirable in our society. This is not fixed and is subject to change, and tends to be determined by the specific culture people belong to or want to belong to. These competences can be classified into cognitive, social, moral and emotional aspects, and are interwoven in a complex fashion. They are acquired and used when things go well, or when people want them to go well. They become more important as an individual faces a difficult situation, such as the major negative events mentioned or daily recurring annoyances. Such events have stressful effects which will appeal more intensely to a person's social skills and problem-solving capacities – the professional term for it is coping. Coping involves a collection of strategies that can be used when there is a threat or when the effects of that threat can become a reality (Lazarus, 1966; Lazarus and Folkman, 1984). The relation between stress and coping will be discussed in more detail in Chapter 6, with a perspective on well-being and health. We will now delve further into coping. A frequently used classification of personal coping strategies encompasses two axes: one involves change and avoidance, the other cognitive and behavioural strategies (Moos, 1990). Figure 5.1 offers an overview of these coping strategies.

Such a classification offers four general possibilities: cognitive or behavioural change and cognitive or behavioural avoidance. The positive reassessment strategy is an example of a cognitive strategy that is aimed at change, its behavioural counterpart being the problem-solving action strategy. Avoidance or denial of a problem can happen at a cognitive and/or emotional level, for example, not wanting to think about something or emotional denial. Seeking guidance and support is placed in this diagram under 'behavioural change'. The strategies aimed at change fit mainly a tendency towards an internal locus of control, those aimed at avoidance fit more an

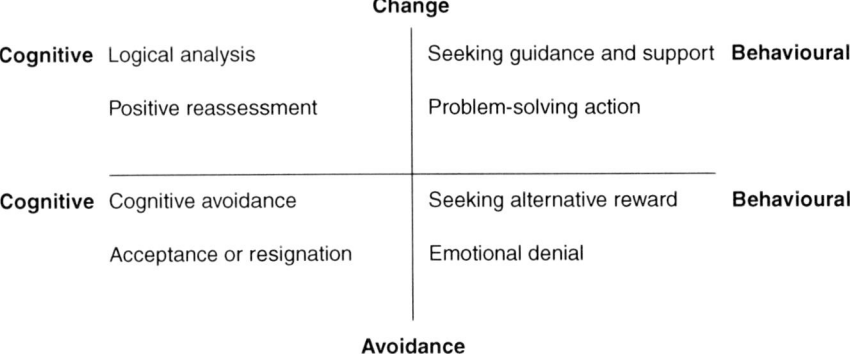

Figure 5.1 Personal coping strategies.

external locus of control. The first situation occurs when an individual has a feeling of being more or less in control of a situation, in the latter case the opposite happens. When an individual has developed over a long period of time the feeling of having no control over his situation, we speak of an acquired helplessness. A disposition of acquired helplessness does not foster a person's well-being and shows a relation with depression (Seligman, 1975) (see Chapter 6).

Adequate coping always involves a combination of cognitive and behavioural factors. Further, insight in one's own emotions and those of others also plays an important role (Fischer and Manstead, 1998). The basic premise is that people who understand their emotions and can also express and regulate them adequately are more satisfied with and happier in their lives. When, following a negative event, people start worrying about the ensuing negative feelings, they may encourage depression (Nolen-Hoeksema, 1991). When people otherwise seek distraction or tackle the problem, depressive feelings are reduced. People who understand emotions better tend to worry less about them. People who are aware of their feelings and those of others, are open to the negative and positive sides of emotional life, and are capable of recognizing and if necessary communicating them. They will be able to regulate their own emotions and those of others more effectively. Such people also receive more social support and know how to make better use of it, because they are skilful in communicating, recognizing and understanding emotions. Those who have these skills are more easily recognized as warm, human and friendly, which contributes to their social attractiveness (Fischer and Manstead, 1998). In addition, people who have received a lot of social support from a young age have been able to develop the corresponding competences more easily. They are also more skilful in offering help to others, and will have the feeling they can offer something to others. They do not shy away from it and can usually indicate their limits.

In other words, they are able to estimate what their own competences are and what is needed in a specific situation.

As we mentioned, communicative competency is an important element of social competency (Hymes, 1972). An essential aspect of it is openness and self-disclosure, a process in which people tell their conversation partner factual and emotional information about themselves (Shadid, 1998). Disclosure forms an essential component of a good social relationship, among other things because it indicates the degree of mutual involvement and trust of the communication partners. Mutual involvement (friendship, intimacy) becomes stronger as the partners' mutual trust increases. A satisfying relationship is only possible when both partners reveal something about themselves. Socially competent people have developed an antenna for their own and their partner's changing need for intimacy and privacy. They are also sensitive to the tension between honesty and vulnerability. How does one talk about emotionally-loaded issues like severe illness, violence or a family secret?

Another aspect of social competency is the importance of shared knowledge in relationships. A person is socially skilful when he develops and uses mutual knowledge in social contacts. Proper use of it can make a person an interesting conversation partner, and different roles of networking (social, emotional and functional) can be realized. Improper use of it can lead to misunderstanding or insults, and/or ultimately to social estrangement. Ended friendships, death of loved ones or divorce always mean the loss of common knowledge. Such a loss may encourage the onset of loneliness. The essence of loneliness could be formulated as a lack of shared understanding and knowledge (Planalp and Garvin-Doxas, 1994).

To summarize, personal competences are the result of a complex interaction of many factors. When dealing with personal competences we will limit ourselves to the most relevant ones – self-confidence, problem-solving and social skills. We will also discuss briefly topics such as primary socialization, attitudes towards problem-solving and experiences with offering help. At the end of this chapter we will look at personal competences from the perspective of several risk factors.

5.3 Measures

Personal competences

Because the present study focuses on the way people manage their interpersonal relationships, social skills are of relevance here. To what degree are people capable of fulfilling each other's need for autonomy and intimacy? Another relevant skill is problem-solving or coping. A third relevant aspect is self-confidence. The concept of personal competency will therefore be conceived as a combination of three measures: self-confidence, social skills and coping behaviour. A questionnaire of seventeen items was used to get an indication of the subjects' personal competences, based on the work of

Luteijn et al. (1985) and Bandura (1997). The items require yes/no answers (Cronbach's alpha = 0.68).

Self-confidence
1 I am satisfied with myself.
2 I find myself being self-reliant enough.
3 I can keep myself good company.

Social skills
4 I like to make conversation just like that.
5 I make new friends easily.
6 I like to have a lot of people around me.
7 A day regularly goes by in which I speak to no one.
8 I don't feel shy in the company of unfamiliar people.
9 I like going to parties.
10 I am not embarrassed when talking to strangers.
11 I feel at ease, not just with familiar people.
12 I get along easily with other people.

Coping behaviour
13 I do not find it difficult to trust other people.
14 I don't have the feeling I have to do it all alone.
15 I don't have bitter feelings because of negative experiences.
16 If I wish to achieve something, I usually persevere.
17 I can handle my own problems.

The items appeal to someone's self perception, which is not always concordant with actual behaviour. However, the item list gives an indication of someone's personal competences. Regarding coping behaviour, the term self-efficacy is probably more convenient, as it refers to someone's feeling of being competent (Bandura, 1997). The internal reliability of the questionnaire was satisfactory (Cronbach's alpha = 0.68). The analysis of the personal competences is based on the smaller dataset (N = 460) (see Section 1.7).

Additional measures

Questions were also asked about a person's socialization process, memories of youth, parents, life events, attitude towards life, attitude towards problem-solving, attitude towards giving help, experiences with giving help and a number of risk factors (see Sections 5.6–5.9).

5.4 Personal competences and social isolation

The cut-off score between being personally competent or not was assessed at 10–11 (scores between 0 and 17; 0 = not competent at all, 17 = highly com-

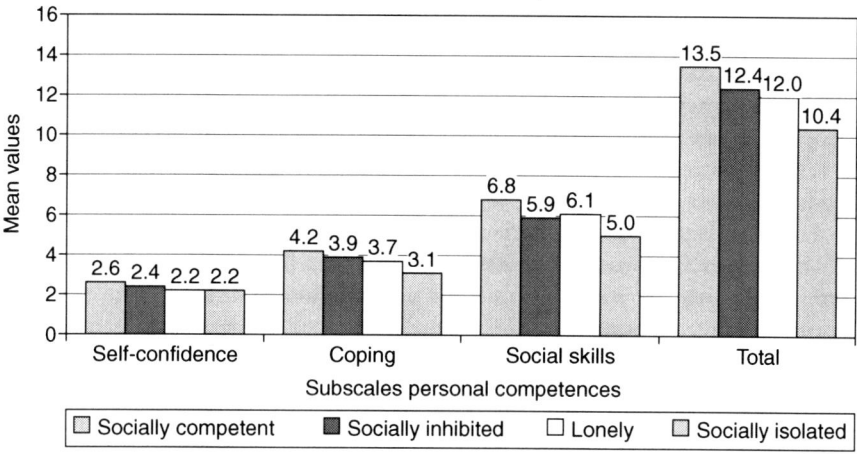

Figure 5.2 Social typology and personal competences (N = 394).

petent)). The majority of the respondents (82 per cent) indicated feeling fairly competent on a personal level, while 18 per cent felt less competent. The four social groups differed substantially from each other (Figure 5.2).

The results were as follows: the socially inhibited, the lonely and the socially isolated felt less competent than the socially competent. They had less self-confidence, less effective coping behaviour and fewer social skills ($F = 16.423$, $df = 3$, $P = 0.000$). Results for the socially inhibited and the lonely were similar and occupied an in-between position: these groups had more competences than the isolated but fewer than the socially competent. The differences between the socially inhibited and the lonely were that the lonely were more socially skilled than the socially inhibited, who in turn were more self-confident and better at coping.

5.5 Personal competences at the item level

Table 5.1 offers an overview at the item level. What do most people do relatively well in? Nearly everyone (97 per cent) believes they get along with people well. The number of respondents who claim being satisfied with themselves or having sufficient self-confidence is relatively high (86 per cent and 79 per cent). These percentages correspond fairly well with what is mentioned most frequently under the protection theme, namely character and joy of living (88 per cent) (Section 3.11). When it comes to tackling problems, most people seem to make no bones about it (85 per cent), and if people want to achieve something they will usually persevere (88 per cent). So far, the picture looks relatively favourable. This applies to a much lesser degree to the social aspects. It is remarkable that one in three people find it difficult to trust others (36 per cent). About the same number (41 per cent) indicates feeling at ease only around people they know well. One in four people indicate having become bitter because of negative experiences. This corresponds fairly well with the percentage of respondents who indicate having become lonely due to the main life event (see Table 4.5). One in five people (21 per cent) says that a day in which they speak to no one occurs on a regular basis. And of all respondents, 13 per cent have the feeling of having to do it all alone.

For most questions we observed that the picture the socially isolated give of themselves is considerably less rosy than that for the other three contact groups. Again, the socially inhibited and the lonely usually take an inbetween position. Among the lonely we also see that shyness often plays a role, and/or that people are not happy with themselves. For about one in two of the isolated group there is a feeling of having to do it all alone, more negative experiences have caused bitterness, and trusting other people is difficult. The socially isolated find considerably more often that they get along less well with others, feel less at ease with others and do not enjoy parties that much. They make new friends less easily, and for one in three of them a day regularly goes by without talking to anyone.

In fact, they have fewer social contacts, whereas there is not less of a need

Table 5.1 Personal competences at an item level, in percentages (N = 425/435)

	SC	SIN	L	SI	Total
1. I am satisfied with myself***	91	90	75	80	86
2. I find myself being self-reliant enough	83	78	73	71	79
3. I am happy with my own company	83	77	75	71	79
4. I like to make conversation	79	68	73	69	75
5. I make new friends easily**	67	52	53	46	60
6. I like to have a lot of people around me	55	54	49	42	52
7. A day regularly goes by in which I speak to no one**	14	31	25	37	21
8. I am shy in the company of unfamiliar people	25	25	33	29	27
9. I like going to parties*	61	58	48	35	55
10. I don't like talking to strangers*	12	22	13	26	14
11. I only feel at ease around familiar people***	34	48	42	71	41
12. I get along easily with other people***	98	97	97	83	97
13. I find it difficult to trust other people**	30	36	43	53	36
14. I have the feeling I have to do it all alone***	5	12	20	43	13
15. Negative experiences have made me bitter***	18	37	35	54	28
16. If I wish to achieve something, I usually persevere	90	92	86	80	88
17. I can handle my own problems	87	86	80	83	85

Notes
*$P < 0.05$, **$P < 0.01$, ***$P < 0.001$; Chi^2 test.
SC = socially competent; SIN = socially inhibited; L = lonely; SI = socially isolated.

Personal competences and social isolation 91

for such contacts than among the other contact groups, as we saw in Chapter 3. Apparently there are some aspects in the areas of less self-confidence, fewer problem-solving capacities and more limited social skills that are mutually enhancing and foster isolation.

Finally, it is very revealing to observe that the competent do better than the socially isolated in having a good time by themselves, while it is more likely that, objectively seen, the socially isolated will miss company more often. This also shows that the need for autonomy (being alone) and the need for connection (togetherness) are usually more balanced among the competent.

5.6 Socialization and contact typology

To the question of how respondents experienced their youth, 80 per cent answered they generally had a happy one. This means that 20 per cent of the respondents considered their youth unhappy. For the lonely and the socially isolated, this percentage is slightly higher (29 per cent). These data correspond with the finding that 73 per cent of the respondents indicate having had a happy youth as a positive event that still has meaning for them (Table 4.1).

Eighty-seven per cent of the respondents say that their parents or guardians gave them the feeling that they loved them unconditionally. There seem to be no differences between the contact groups. There is a fairly strong correlation ($r = 0.48$) between unconditional parental love and a happy youth. Still, this does not apply to everyone; it could also be that the presence of unconditional parental love did not result in a happy youth. All kinds of factors could be causing this.

It is also interesting to observe that as the memory is more positive, the youth period is seen as more determinant to a person's current life ($r = 0.28$), just like with the unconditional love of the parents ($r = 0.24$). Hence those who have no happy youth memories and/or had no parents/guardians who loved them unconditionally tend to consider this as less relevant to the satisfaction with the further course of their lives. In other words, as individuals are more satisfied with their lives, they will be more prone to ascribe it to a happy youth and loving parents than when satisfaction over one's life is lower. In this sense it is interesting to observe that the four contact groups differ from each other strongly in the degree to which they ascribe the importance of their youth to their satisfaction with their current life. Almost three-quarters (72 per cent) indicate that their youth was very determinant to the further course of their life; the socially isolated agree considerably less (51 per cent), as they are usually less satisfied with their lives. The socially isolated may attach more importance to environmental or societal factors as (one of the) causes for their current situation. This is understandable from the perspective of social-psychological insights into attribution processes, which among other things posit that when people are doing well they tend to attribute it to internal factors (in this case 'a good nest'), and when they are not doing (so) well they tend to blame external factors (Heider, 1958).

Given the relevance of the quality of upbringing for personal competences later in life, it is interesting to ascertain that we keep seeing a positive relation between personal competences and the ability to look back at a happy youth. The correlation between the total measures amounts to $r = 0.24$, and for the respective subscales of self-confidence $r = 0.17$, social skills $r = 0.14$ and coping $r = 0.22$. Seen this way, the obvious conclusion is that a happy youth establishes a certain basis for the acquisition of a number of personal competences.

5.7 Personal competences and life events

How important are personal competences and socialization for coping with life events? Memories of a happy youth and affectionate parents buffer against negative events later in life (the correlations were $r = -0.34$ and $r = -0.36$ respectively, see Section 4.8). Personal competences also are related to negative events ($r = -0.31$), and not to positive events. This means that as people become more competent they encounter fewer burdensome events (see also Section 4.8). We can conclude that self-confidence, problem-solving capacities and social skills form a buffer against negative events. This is underscored by the finding that there is a strong relation between personal competences and the degree to which people feel protected against social isolation ($r = 0.32$). In this way they also form a buffer against loneliness. This has been examined explicitly by linking personal competences to the social consequences of life events. In Section 4.6 we saw that 24 per cent of those who are not lonely have become lonely after the most important event. It now seems that, as people have less competences, they will become lonely more often after an important event, while they were not lonely before that ($r = -0.28$). We also see that whether or not one gets help makes no difference. There is thus help or there isn't, but in neither case can the situation prevent people from becoming lonely.

In Section 4.5 we also discussed what the reaction of an individual is to the most important life events in terms of general coping strategies, i.e. acceptance, change or repression. When we examine these reactions, we observe a connection with parental love, in the sense that more unconditional love keeps a person from repressing events to some degree. Personal competences also play a role here ($r = -0.13$). As people have fewer personal competences, chances are greater of them repressing problems caused by life events. This seems to be related mainly to self-confidence ($r = -0.21$), to some extent to social skills ($r = -0.13$), but not to coping ($r = -0.02$). If this is indeed the case, it is an interesting data to keep in mind when planning policy. Adequate processing of life events seems to have more chances of success in people with sufficient self-confidence and social skills, while problem-solving skills hardly play a role. This is understandable too, if we realize that when processing negative events it essentially comes down to mobilizing the right people for emotional support. Good support for an individual depends on having the right people around, who know how to be sensitive to a particular situation. Those who need this support will be asked mainly to express themselves as well as possible. This becomes easier the more self-respect people have, whether they can put aside feelings of fear and eventually shame or guilt, and can be as open as necessary.

There is another remarkable finding. In Section 4.6, on the social consequences of life events, next to loneliness there was also an increase and decrease of social contacts. We now see that, as people are more competent, negative life events will lead less quickly to a decrease in contacts and activities ($r = -0.13$). It is striking that social skills are not relevant here, but self-confidence and coping are. This is understandable if we realize that social skills have already led to a certain social network. Both phenomena are interesting, especially when seen in combination. Whereas self-confidence is important in both, we see that shortly after a negative event an appeal is also made to a person's social skills, although to stabilize the situation in the longer term it is coping that comes to the fore.

So far we have paid attention to rather major life events. In terms of daily recurring annoyances and uplifts, we can ascertain that the first shows no relation to personal competences, contrary to what happens with uplifts. The degree to which an individual can enjoy daily life and the degree to which compliments are given is strongly related to personal competences (respectively $r = 0.35$ and $r = 0.31$). Having personal competences contributes to people's increased enjoyment of life and their ability to 'make the most of it', gets them more compliments, and makes them better at understanding how to fish for them.

5.8 Social responsibility

In relation to personal competency, it seems relevant to learn more about respondents' attitude towards problem solving and giving support to others.

5.8.1 Attitude towards life

According to western values, the competency of having control over one's life is evaluated positively. Individuals differ a great deal in the degree to which they are successful in orchestrating their own life. About half of all respondents indicate having success in arranging their life course according to their own wishes, while the other half take life as it comes (49 per cent versus 51 per cent). The socially isolated and especially the socially inhibited indicate more frequently taking life as it comes (respectively 59 per cent and 68 per cent). People's life attitudes differ according to network size and not according to degree of loneliness. The larger a person's network, the greater chances are of arranging one's life course according one's own wishes. It is remarkable that there is no relation between general attitude towards life and personal competences, or feeling protected. This lack of a relation with personal competences is puzzling at first glance, but if we recognize that personally competent individuals assess correctly if something is important enough to worry about (or not) and at the same time are capable of assessing if taking action is necessary at that time (or not), it does make more sense.

5.8.2 Attitude towards problem solving

Individuals may feel lonely or isolated during different lifetime periods for a variety of reasons. In modern western society, some citizens believe that lonely and isolated individuals need to solve their problems by themselves. Others consider it is the responsibility of society to support these people. What are the respondents' opinions on problem solving? About one in three find that the person in trouble needs to find a solution by herself. Half of the respondents indicate that it would be better to solve problems with the help of others, and 21 per cent think that in that case professional help should be deployed. The contact groups do not differ substantially; the socially inhibited and the socially isolated have a bit less confidence in appealing to others (36 per cent and 37 per cent), but the differences are not significant. There is no relation with personal competences either.

These attitudes towards problem solving seem fairly consistent in people's lives, and are not influenced by network size of feelings of loneliness. There probably is a dominant idea in our society about how to share matters of responsibility.

5.8.3 Attitude towards giving help

What is the general attitude towards giving help? Respondents were asked: *'Imagine that one of your acquaintances or friends seems lonely or isolated. At what stage do you, as an acquaintance or friend, think you need to take action?'*

Over two-thirds of the respondents would intervene if they suspected something, 15 per cent would intervene if the person in question clearly had problems, 14 per cent believed that the person in question would first need to indicate having these problems, and only very few people would do nothing at all (Figure 5.3). While the socially competent, the socially inhibited and the lonely reacted very similarly, the socially isolated were considerably more reluctant in offering help. A comparable pattern of answers was observed regarding the balance between giving and receiving help (Section 3.9). The socially isolated are much less prone to take help initiatives in case of suspicion – the person in trouble would need to ask for help more often. How can this be explained? Will it be a matter of reacting more slowly, or do the socially isolated think they do not have that much to offer? Or perhaps they have a lot to offer but dare not, or they interpret the situation inappropriately.

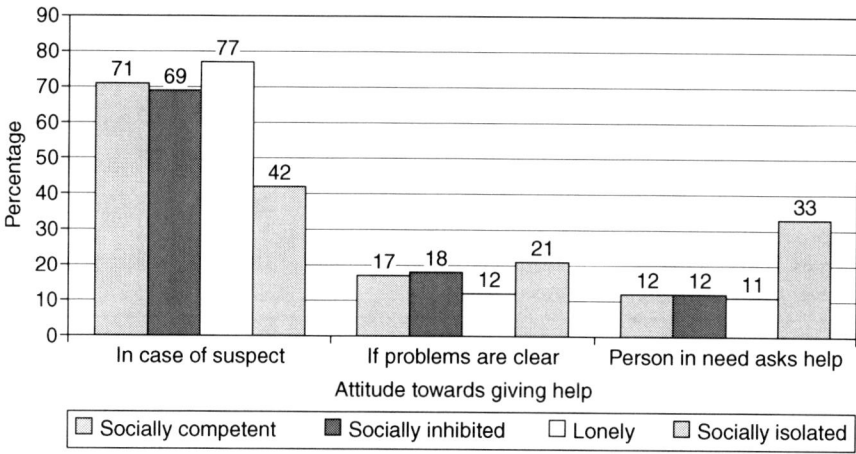

Figure 5.3 Motivations to offer support to friends or acquaintances, related to the social typology, percentages (N = 446).

In addition, with regard to neighbours or colleagues in trouble, all the respondents are considerably more passive. The percentage for taking action when they suspect something is only 29 per cent and 38 per cent respectively, with no differences between the contact groups. The question as to whether a respondent ever gave help to someone else in case of loneliness or isolation was answered affirmatively by two-thirds of the respondents, with no differences between the groups of the social contact typology. The type of support given was mainly emotional (64 per cent) and instrumental (25 per cent). There is no relation with personal competences. How often someone really has given support remains unclear.

5.8.4 Evaluation of giving support

In the light of the above-mentioned results on proneness to offer support actively, it seems relevant to learn more about the respondents' evaluation of the actual giving of support. For some people it is very satisfying to give support in cases of loneliness, for others it seems rather frustrating; socially isolated people do not accept support easily, or it is very consuming to them. In general, one would expect there to be more or less of a balance between asking/getting support and offering help ('what goes around comes around'). What are the respondents' assessments of offering help? In Chapter 3 we already showed that giving and receiving support was reasonably balanced among the socially competent, while the other social contact groups, especially the isolated, experienced more often being the receiving or dependent party. To take a closer look at the experience of offering support,

Table 5.2 Assessment of offering support, percentages of positive answers (N = 287/304)

	SC	SIN	L	SI	T
I did it wholeheartedly	98	92	95	92	96
I would love to do it again	92	87	92	79	90
I received very much in return*	65	49	57	33	59
It took a lot out of me	24	24	37	17	26
Upon reconsidering, it was a job for a professional	22	29	31	17	25
It was fighting against windmills	18	24	28	25	22
It was a one-time thing, but never again	7	11	13	16	10

Notes
*$P < 0.05$; Chi^2 test.
SC = socially competent; SIN = socially inhibited; L = lonely; SI = socially isolated.

respondents were asked to answer a set of seven statements (Table 5.2) with a yes/no answer.

Almost everyone evaluated the offering of support positively – they did it wholeheartedly (96 per cent) or 'would love to do it again' (90 per cent). Fifty-nine per cent indicated that they received a lot in return. One in four respondents found that it cost them a lot, and upon reconsidering it should have been a professional's job. The more demanding the support, the more they thought a professional was needed. There were no large differences between the four social contact groups, except that just one in three of the socially isolated indicated receiving a lot in return. The results reconfirm the conclusion that the socially competent are more balanced than the socially isolated (Section 3.9).

When computing a total score of the evaluation of giving support (range between 1–7), the results show a linear negative relation with the typology analogue to personal competences (Section 5.4): the socially competent are the most positive ($X = 5.8$), the lonely and the isolated the least ($X = 5.3$) in evaluating the offering of support. Only the socially inhibited take a position inbetween ($X = 5.5$). There was no relation with life attitude, and only a small relation with having had a happy youth ($r = 0.11$). Personal competences contribute to a positive evaluation ($r = 0.22$) along all three subscales. It is also interesting that the more positive the evaluation, the less prone a respondent is to indicate the need for professional support. Those who are the most positive are the most active regarding fellow citizens who are in need of support (friends, acquaintances, neighbours, colleagues), and have actually given support.

In summary, people love to give support in general, and they would do it again immediately if necessary. Their success increases the more self-confidence, social skills and problem-solving capacities they have. The personal competences are not just for their own benefit but also for that of others. In this regard the socially competent constitute the most balanced group, as they are more successful in taking care of themselves as well as in supporting others. They are more active in supporting others and it seems very satisfying to do so.

5.9 Risk factors and personal competences

What are the risk factors regarding personal competences? A review will now be presented of the correlations with loneliness, network size, a number of evaluative reports, demographic variables and societal competences.

Loneliness and network size: There was a negative relation of personal competences – on all three subscales – with loneliness ($r = -0.26$), and a positive relation with network size ($r = 0.21$). The more competent people feel personally, the less lonely they are and the larger their network size.

Life events: There was a negative relation between personal competences and negative life events ($r = -0.31$), and no relation with the positive events. The more people were personally competent, the less they came across negative events, or they were better equipped to cope with them. Self-confidence, coping and social skills buffer the effects of negative events.

Evaluative reports: The more competent people are, the more satisfied they are about their work ($r = 0.15$), health condition ($r = 0.25$), financial situation ($r = 0.14$), relationship with their children ($r = 0.14$), living condition ($r = 0.11$), and not being single ($r = 0.17$). Those who are not single are generally more competent in coping and socially skilled, but they do not have more self-confidence.

Demographics: The correlations varied from $r = -0.03$ (location) to $r = 0.27$ (socio-economic status). Stepwise regression showed someone's socio-economic status explained 12 per cent of the variance, and the other factors did not add to this. What was remarkable was that self-confidence did not show any relation at all to the demographic factors; for coping skills, a person's income and educational levels explained 15 per cent of the variance, and for social skills the factors of age and socio-economic status explained 10 per cent of the variance.

Participation in society: The more personally competent someone is, the more active in society ($r = 0.12$). This relation holds especially true for social skills ($r = 0.14$) but not for self-confidence or problem-solving capacities (see Chapter 8).

Upon review, there are some correlations but most of them are not very strong. The concept of personal competences seems to be a relatively autonomous concept, relevant to people's lives. To the degree that there are relations, they especially apply to health condition. Additionally, a person's socio-economic status offers some explanation of variance in personal competences. The higher someone's status, the more socially skilled they are and the better they can cope. What's more, younger people are slightly more socially skilled compared with the elderly. Remarkably, there is no relation at all between demographics and self-confidence. The concept of self-confidence cannot be understood by sociological categorization.

5.10 Discussion

Individuals who experience a major life event will be challenged to cope with the negative effects. Not everyone is as skilled in coping: one in four persons will be affected by more permanent feelings of loneliness. The degree to which people are successful in coping with the negative effects of life events will depend greatly on specific personal features, on the socialization process and on societal factors. The thesis of this chapter was that social isolation is principally a matter of personal competences. Personal competences may form a strong buffer against the negative consequences of life events, just as a happy youth does. Based on a number of theoretical notions, a measure for personal competences was composed containing three main factors, i.e. self-confidence, coping behaviour and social skills. How are these competences related to the social contact typology?

The majority of the respondents feels personally competent. A consistent pattern emerges which shows that the socially isolated feel less competent compared with the socially competent. The lonely and the socially inhibited take a position inbetween; they indicate feeling more competent than the socially isolated, but not as competent as the socially competent group. Upon comparing the lonely and the inhibited, it turned out that the lonely felt a bit more socially skilled, and the socially inhibited a bit more self-confident and skilled in problem-solving. Most remarkable was that the lion's share of the respondents felt self-confident and that they had sufficient problem-solving capacities, while only 60 per cent felt socially skilled. It is the social capital that most people indicate not possessing enough of. If they are confronted with major negative events throughout their life, they fail socially to a considerable degree. This will result in feelings of bitterness and loneliness for 25 per cent of the respondents. Such a result will have important consequences for social policy.

Most respondents indicated having had a happy youth, with parental love having indeed played an important role in it. Most are also convinced that the quality of their youth was quite influential towards their ongoing life course, however, the socially isolated share this opinion less frequently. The quality of the youth period forms a strong basis for mastering personal competences; this has an ongoing influence on processes later in life. The less competent someone is, the greater chances are of becoming lonely after major life events. As we saw, the socially isolated are at a greater risk of being confronted with negative events; it is important that social support is mobilized immediately after such an event.

The more personally competent one is, the easier it will be to mobilize social support. The other way around is also true: the more an individual is embedded in a social support network, the better the personal competences will be developed. At the same time, these people are also less reserved in offering help to others in need. Generally, people like to offer support to others. The more self-confident, socially skilled and capable in problem-solving they are, the more successful. The personal competences are not just for one's own benefit, but also to support others in need. The aforementioned observation that the socially competent are the most balanced group in this respect (see Chapter 3) is confirmed here again. These people know how to take good care of themselves, and at the same time are able to care for others more adequately. They are less reserved in their support for others, and helping others is satisfying in itself.

Socio-economic status explains the variance in personal competences only to a limited degree. This holds true for problem-solving and social skills, but not at all for self-confidence. Self-confidence is a trait that does not allow itself to be categorized sociologically. It is a basic feeling of someone's fundamental attitude towards life, and is shaped mostly in early childhood.

In considering the effects of personal competences on a person's well-being, the various analyses confirm the thesis that personal competences – which contain the dimensions of self-confidence, problem-solving capacities and social skills – contribute positively to someone's well-being and firmly buffer against negative influences of life events. The latter dimension, social skills, seems difficult to realize at this point. The other way around, we see that processes of becoming lonely and socially isolated entail a deterioration of the quality of personal competences, so that self-confidence, social skills and coping will diminish. When individuals do not succeed in mobilizing adequate support at critical moments in life, the risk of becoming lonely increases, thus making it more difficult to find support. As far as the group of the socially isolated is concerned, an accumulation of problems has been taking place in the course of time. Many aspects of the life of the socially isolated will turn out negatively. In that process, their (lack of) personal competences play a crucial role.

The different types of analyses show that the concept of personal competences is a relatively autonomous one, and an autonomous aspect of human life. As far as the concept has been studied by itself, the thesis that social isolation is a matter of personal competences is confirmed. In many aspects, the effect of personal competences on social contacts and social isolation is larger than the classic demographic variables. Accordingly, personal competences are independent from other variables relevant to processes of social isolation. However, in Chapter 2 we saw that social isolation can be explained by many factors in terms of personal and societal causes, which are more temporal or more structural in character. In Chapter 12 a more comprehensive analysis will be discussed that elaborates on the relative effects of personal competences on the social scale, which accounts for as many other relevant factors as possible.

6 Health and social isolation

Ludwien Meeuwesen

6.1 Introduction

After life events and personal competences, this chapter focuses on the theme of health and its relation to social isolation. Common sense explains isolation with health-related factors next to causes such as character, age, unemployment and being single. Scientifically too, health is identified as one of the causes of isolation (see Section 2.4.2). In section 4.3.1 we saw that 30 per cent of the respondents (up to 68 per cent of the socially isolated) are bothered by serious chronic illness. As people feel more lonely and/or isolated, they indicate experiencing their health as less good. It has been known for longer that there is also a relation between health and social inequality (Mackenbach, 1994). Recent research has shown that health status is the main predictor for exclusion from society (Jehoel-Gijsbers, 2004). The degree to which people have personal competences at their disposal is also indicative of their health situation – the more reason to pay special attention to the role of health in the social well-being of people and vice versa. We will use a broad definition of health from the World Health Organization (WHO), which also emphasizes social health in its policy. The social functioning of people is seen in itself as either health-promoting or health-inhibiting.

In western cultures, health-threatening events such as war and poverty play less of a role, but issues related to social cohesion, mutual involvement and social-emotional functioning are more at the forefront when it comes to well-being. They determine much more the quality of life nowadays, and a well-functioning social life can be seen as a modern type of lifebuoy in terms of someone's well-being (Hortulanus *et al.*, 1992; Tijhuis, 1994; Sarason *et al.*, 2001). In her dissertation, Tijhuis (1994) underlines the relation between health and a well-functioning personal network. She observes, among other things, a shrinkage of the network of people with a 'socially' severe illness, an illness that invokes fear in others, is clearly visible and entails limitations in daily functioning. In contrast, a meaningful social network has a positive effect on physical and mental health (see also Section 2.2.1). This positive influence is related to the social support that a personal network can provide and the contribution it makes to social integration (Tijhuis, 1994). Next to physical health, the relation between mental problems and personal networks is increasingly identified; this relation is even stronger than that with physical health (Hooley and Hiller, 2000).

There has been a focus for quite some time on the importance of stressful events for health, although the connection is somewhat complex (Lazarus, 1966; Linas and Bieliauskas, 1982). People who are sick indicate having had more negative experiences than others (De Boer, 1990). The way in which someone copes with such events is decisive (Lazarus and Folkman, 1984). One way of coping is to seek support from others (Moos, 1990, see also Section 6.2.3).

This chapter will focus on the health situation of the respondents and the connection to social isolation. The effect of several explanatory and relevant factors of a societal as well as personal nature on people's health will be examined.

6.2 Explanatory models for health

Some important factors in relation to health have already been mentioned. The causes of poor health are less clear and are often complicated. Two explanatory models are relevant in this context. One emphasizes lifestyle and living conditions, the other selection by health (Ten Dam, 1997). The first model – lifestyle and living conditions – is about factors such as the social environment, lifestyles and care which influence health (the causation explanation). In this study we will emphasize the physical environment to the degree that it involves the living environment, and especially the social environment in the sense of social bonds in which people live and the support they get from them. There are indications that the causes of poor health can probably be found in an accumulation of poor living habits and unfavourable living conditions (Commissie-Albeda, 2001). Not only do aspects of socio-economic status influence health, but also social isolation and the experience of major negative life events (Brown and Harris, 1989).

The other model, selection by health (known as the selection explanation), holds the view that health influences societal classification processes. Health is seen as a factor that can influence one's chances for an education, a profession, personal competencies, societal participation and social networks. Disability is an example of downward mobility. The selection mechanism does exist and has an effect, but not as strong as the first model. Among non-western immigrants and single-parent families, lifestyles and living conditions seem to be especially influential. Both hypotheses seem to apply to the long-term unemployed and the homeless. For the homeless, for instance, the reasoning is as follows: people can end up in a certain social position, and/or due to predisposition and upbringing can find themselves in a downward spiral that can lead them to a position of social isolation through unemployment and (mental) diseases, thus further reducing their chances of work and societal participation (RMO, 2001). At the moment, the philosophy that integrates both models seems to offer the most perspectives (Ten Dam, 1997).

Both for the lifestyles and living conditions model and for the selection by health model it is relevant in finding out a number of mediating factors. Again, one important mediating factor in relation to health is someone's personal competences, underlining problem-solving capacities or coping as well as the person's potential support network and how one takes advantage of it. Let us take a closer look at these factors.

6.3 Coping and health

Stress is adversely related to health. In other words, stress increases chances of becoming sick (e.g. Linas and Bieliauskas, 1982). An important cause or reason for stress are major life events or daily recurring hassles. Such events have a stressful effect and make considerable demands on one's social skills and problem-solving capacities – what is known in technical terms as coping. Coping includes a combination of strategies that can be used when there is a threat or when the consequences of a threat can become a reality (Lazarus, 1966; Lazarus and Folkman, 1984). Lazarus emphasizes that this is about the subjective experience of an event and not so much about the event itself. A hospital stay can thus cause a lot of stress for someone who has never stayed in a hospital, whereas it will not be as burdensome for someone who has been through it more often. This means that someone's perception of the situation may be more important than the stressful situation itself. Accordingly, Lazarus defines stress as being present in a relationship between a person and the environment which the person experiences as dangerous to their well-being. Various estimates are made when assessing a situation. First we estimate the severity of the situation ('should I do something?') and then the possibilities are weighed out ('can I do something?') (Te Vaarwerk and De Ridder, 1994). This second estimate involves the arsenal of social support and problem-solving skills that an individual has at their disposal. In Section 5.2.3 the following relevant coping strategies were mentioned: actively tackling a problem, seeking distraction, avoidance, social support, passive reaction, expressing emotions and using comforting thoughts (relativizing) (Schreurs *et al.*, 1993). Someone's orientation towards being in command (internally and externally) also plays a role. When an individual develops a feeling for a prolonged period of time that he has no control over his situation, we speak of an 'acquired helplessness', a disposition that does not foster a person's well-being and shows a link to depression (Seligman, 1975). Which strategy is best depends on the nature of the events and circumstances. For instance, when a situation cannot be changed, actively tackling a problem is not the most effective strategy. The experienced stress will not decrease in that case. A form of cognitive restructuring would probably be more effective. Certain strategies that are effective in one situation need not be effective in another. The factor of time does not play an unimportant role in the question of which coping strategy is the most effective. Coping strategies that initially have a positive effect can be disadvantageous in the long term. Avoidance and waiting, even distraction can be good at first but detrimental in the end. The strategy that works best thus depends on the situation. However, when the situation *can* be changed, actively tackling it is the most effective way to go.

If we assume that coping has an indirect influence on health and behaviour, this influence can be positive as well as negative. Going to the doctor when one is ill can prevent a worsening of the health problems. Denial or seeking distraction (through the use of alcohol, drugs and cigarettes) may well lead to a reduction of the experienced stress but will influence health negatively (Rice, 1987).

There may also be a direct influence on health through physiological changes. Blood pressure research has shown that denial of the death of someone close causes increased blood pressure (Taylor, 1986). People with a positive outlook tend to have fewer problems with high blood pressure. It is known that older people have a poorer health condition when they are in denial or passive (Lazarus and Folkman, 1984). The relation can be the other way around too, as health can influence the choice of a coping strategy. In this case there may be less of an active approach and more of a passive reaction.

6.4 Social support and health

We would like to explain the relation between social support, one of the coping strategies mentioned, and health, expanding this connection into personal networks. We have already distinguished three types of approaches for the study of personal networks (see Section 2.5.1): the social integration approach, the social support approach and the social network approach. The first involves the presence or lack of certain relationships and focuses on four different characteristics of social integration (composition and size of household, frequency of church attendance, club membership and number of 'real' friends). The second, the social support approach, involves the various functions of social contacts, i.e. emotional and practical support and companionship support. The social network approach focuses on the structure of someone's network in terms of type of relationship, closeness, contact frequency and number of family members.

Several links have been observed between social networks and health. Social integration leads to better health. Social support seems to combat the negative effects of stress on health, which implies that people with a large social network are healthier than people with a small network (Dalgard *et al.*, 1995; Tijhuis, 1996). Social support can be seen as a social resource, and whoever can 'summon' more resources has a greater chance of reaching their goal – in this case, good health (see also Section 2.2.3). Still, it is not self-evident that people who have many social resources can always effectively deploy them for health problems. Social resources are often goal-specific and hence not always equally deployable (Tijhuis, 1994). For example, if someone lives far away, you can ask that person for emotional support but not for practical (physical) support.

The positive effect of social integration on health can be explained by the social regulation of health-related behaviour, which entails that people within a group behave according to the values and norms of that group, which among other things have to do with health-related behaviour. Members of a group will comply with these behavioural rules and may thus live longer and stay healthier for a longer period of time (Tijhuis, 1994).

There are also the buffer effects: social support leads to better health or prevents illness, because negative consequences of stress are buffered (see also Section 2.2.1). If a person's well-being is threatened by stressful events, the consequences of such events can be limited by appealing to the social resources (Tijhuis, 1996). Major life events can cause psychological and physiological changes that can be conducive to a depressive mood. By using social resources adequately, such a mood has less chances of developing (Cohen and Wills, 1985). Buffer effects occur only when a stressful event has taken place, direct effects take place earlier. These effects occur without an appeal being made to another person: it is just the knowledge that one can appeal to others in case of need.

Finally, there is some correlation between coping strategies and social support. There are indications that people with few social contacts do not use the most effective coping strategy to reduce stress. They will rather tend to avoid or deny the situation, or distort reality (De Ridder, 1994). People who have many social resources usually have more coping strategies, and these are more effective. We saw this already in the previous chapter: there is a positive link between personal competences and network scope, and as people's competences increase they are better at mobilizing social support.

In summary, life events and daily hassles can merge as sources that invoke tension and appeal to a person's adaptive and creative capacity to face a situation. The degree to which this is successful affects health. A person's coping strategies and the availability of social resources weigh particularly high on this scale.

This section focuses on the physical and mental well-being of people, aiming to establish relations with various relevant factors as they have been elaborated upon above. We will first analyse how health can be measured.

6.5 Operationalization of health indicators

Health can be defined in different ways, and this is highly related to cultural values and norms that can vary considerably by social group, time and place (Helman, 1994). Professionals also use different definitions than lay people. A professional will tend to define health in terms of medical-biological abnormalities, whereas a lay person will point to having symptoms or the fact that they feel sick. This introduces the distinction between subjective experiences and verifiable conditions with regard to physical symptoms. In the present study, we will limit ourselves to someone's subjective health experience. We are interested in how people themselves experience their health.

Various measures have been developed to this end: a general assessment of health expressed in a report mark, a measure for physical vulnerability and for mental vulnerability, and a list that assesses the degree of depression. The measures can be described more specifically as follows:

1. A rough measure is the *report mark* that people give for their health.
2. A measure for *physical vulnerability* is based on a combination of three indicators. When people indicate that they have been bothered for more than a month by physical symptoms that limits their freedom of movement, when they cannot leave the house because of their physical health, and when the report mark of their own health situation is unsatisfactory, we speak of physical vulnerability. The scores lie between 0 (physically competent) and 3 (physically very vulnerable); people with scores of 1 and 2 are considered physically vulnerable (see also Section 7.2).
3. A measure for *mental vulnerability* is also composed of a number of variables. There is mental vulnerability when people indicate that they have had psychological problems for more than a month, and have a high score on the loneliness scale (between 6–11) and a low score on the personal competences scale (0–5). Here too the scores lie between 0 and 3: 0 means mentally competent, 1 mentally vulnerable, 2 and 3 mentally very vulnerable (again, see Section 7.2).
4. The degree of *depressiveness* was examined in this study on the basis of a self-assessment scale of W. Zung (Zung, 1965; Dijkstra, 1974). Respondents indicate on a four-point scale (1 = never/seldom, 2 = sometimes, 3 = often, 4 = always) to what degree 20 statements apply to them recently. The items relate to affect (2) and to physiological (8) and psychological (10) equivalents of depression. Examples of statements are 'I feel gloomy and despondent' (affect), 'I have palpitations' (physiological), and 'I have the feeling that things are more difficult than they used to be' (psychological).

Table 6.1 contains an overview of the separate items. The Zung depression list is not a diagnostic instrument but a screening one. It highlights the experience of people themselves and indicates the degree of being at risk for a disorder, but does not specify whether there is a clinical depression.

The analyses over the first three measures are based on the large data set (Section 1.7). The analyses over the degree of depression are based on a separate dataset of 733 respondents who live mainly in rural areas and are on average older and less educated than the respondents from the large data set. The reliability of the depression scale among these respondents is high (Cronbach's alpha = 0.85).

We will now report the results of the various indicators separately. The emphasis lies on a description of relevant relations in terms of social typology and social support potential, life events, socialization, protective sources and comfort, personal competences and relevant background variables. An overview of the statistical correlations of the four health measures with the mentioned variables has been included in Appendix VI.

6.6 Report mark on health

The respondents give an average report mark of $X = 7$ (std. $= 1.4$) (N = 1,814) for their health, in other words a generous satisfactory mark. The mark of the socially isolated lies almost one entire point lower than for the socially competent (the averages are respectively 7.6, 7.5, 6.9 and 6.7 for the socially competent, the socially inhibited, the lonely and the socially isolated). Five per cent of the socially competent gave themselves an unsatisfactory mark, compared with 21 per cent of the socially isolated, 10 per cent of the socially inhibited and 18 per cent of the lonely. There is a linear relation with the social typology: the more isolated, the unhealthier ($r = -0.23$) (Appendix VI). There is a correlation especially with loneliness, the subjective dimension of the social contacts typology, at $r = -0.28$. There is also a correlation, albeit less substantial ($r = 0.084$), with network size, and this is mainly because of the potential of companionship support. This also evidences that as people are unhealthier, they also feel more lonely (and vice versa). For example, people who see themselves as unhealthy tend to be more disappointed in others and see themselves more as a burden to others.

The change of contacts over the last five years shows a slim relation with health assessment, so health benefits from an increase in contacts. This corresponds with the relation with social support, and seems to apply particularly to the lonely and not to the socially competent or the socially inhibited. Especially for the lonely, an increase in meaningful contacts leads to better health or, looking at it the other way, better health leads to more contacts.

With regard to major events, there is a substantial relation with negative life events: as the respondents have undergone more negative events, they feel less healthy ($r = -0.31$). Positive events, by contrast, contribute somewhat to better health ($r = 0.11$). The correlation with the negative events is stronger though. Moreover, people who feel less healthy feel more at risk of becoming lonely after an important event. As people are healthier, fewer things cause annoyances. They receive more compliments too, and most of all are more capable of enjoying daily things. They have more protective sources and get more comfort from putting things into perspective.

From the angle of socialization, it is worth mentioning the following. Unconditional love of the parents and the ability to look back at a happy youth contribute to positively experienced health. There is also a substantial correlation with personal competences. This applies most to problem-

Health and social isolation 107

solving skills (r = 0.27). It is followed to a lesser degree by self-confidence (r = 0.16) and social skills (r = 0.15). As people's problem-solving skills improve – or at least their ability to believe in them – so does their health.

The correlations with the background variables we used vary from r = 0.03 for gender to r = 0.28 for socio-economic status. Three variables, namely socio-economic status, location and age, explain together 9 per cent of the variance; the other variables are not significant. This means that, as people's socio-economic status is higher, do not live in a big city and are younger, they ascribe themselves a better health condition.

6.7 Physical vulnerability

Of the group examined, 72 per cent indicates being physically healthy, 25 per cent is physically vulnerable and 3 per cent is very vulnerable. Figure 6.1 shows the percentages of physical vulnerability in relation to the typology.

Here too there is a linear relation with the social contacts typology: as people are more lonely or isolated, they are also physically more vulnerable. Among the group of the lonely, 37 per cent are physically (very) vulnerable, compared with 46 per cent among the isolated. The lonely and the isolated correspond highly in this sense, which confirms that quality of contacts weighs more than quantity.

The relations studied between the different variables and the degree of physical vulnerability show a pattern that very much resembles that for the 'report mark' measure, although they tend to lie lower. Hence the relation with the loneliness scale is greater than with network scope. The potential for companionship support is the most important here too. In addition, an

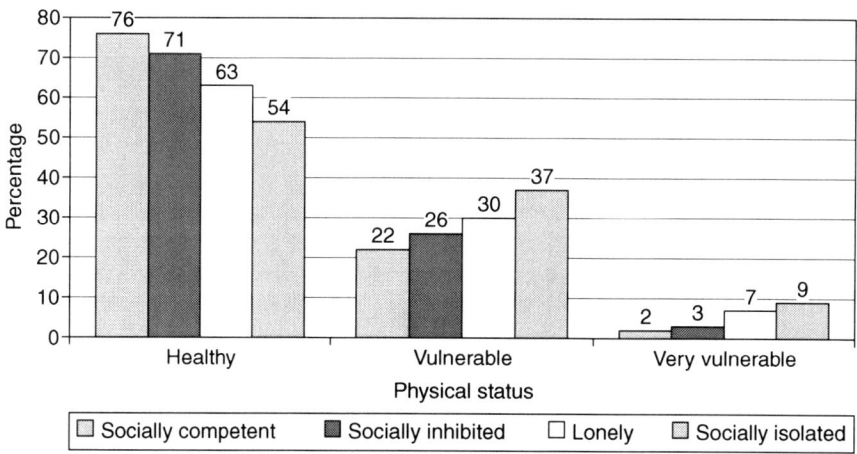

Figure 6.1 Social typology and physical status (N = 2,459).

increase of substantial important contacts in the last five years leads to greater physical competency. This applies mainly to the lonely and the isolated (r = −0.13 and r = −0.18). The moral of the story is the same: more social contacts make you less physically vulnerable. Negative events make people physically vulnerable, and those who are already vulnerable are at a greater risk of becoming lonely after such an event. Problem-solving capacities, next to self-confidence and social skills, are what weighs more in the scale here too.

The correlations with the different background variables vary from r = 0.02 for ethnicity to r = −0.31 for socio-economic status. Regression analysis shows that socio-economic status, age, city and gender together explain 11 per cent of the variance. People with a lower status and the elderly are more vulnerable. City dwellers and women are slightly more vulnerable than non-urbanites and men.

Our conclusion so far is that we have identified an important factor, but this on its own it does not explain the social typology: 54 per cent of the isolated are healthy.

6.8 Mental vulnerability

Of the group examined, 79 per cent indicated being mentally healthy, 17 per cent mentally vulnerable and 4 per cent very vulnerable. Figure 6.2 shows in percentages mental vulnerability in relation to the typology.

Here too we see a linear relation with the social contacts typology: as people are more lonely or isolated, they are also more mentally vulnerable. Among the lonely, 48 per cent are mentally (very) vulnerable, compared with 63 per cent of the isolated. We keep seeing a large difference between

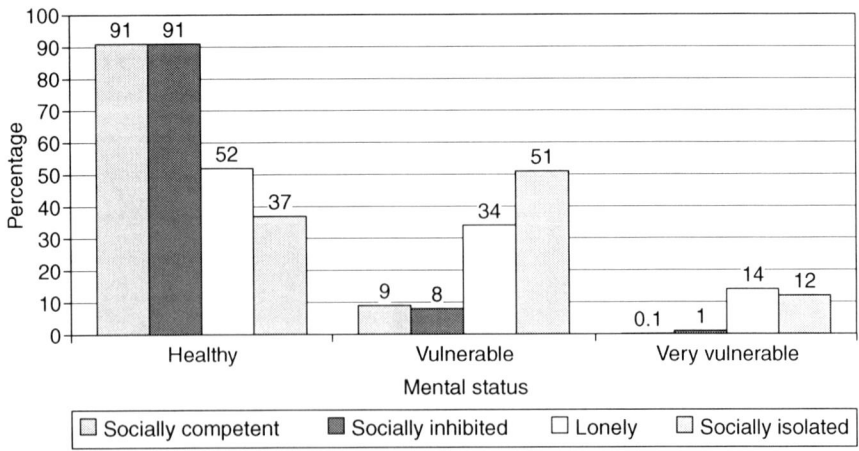

Figure 6.2 Social typology and mental status (N = 2,459).

the competent and the socially inhibited on the one hand and between the lonely and the isolated on the other. This has to do with the fact that one of the criteria for mental vulnerability is derived from the score of the loneliness scale. The connection sketched here is therefore partially tautological. For that reason, the correlation with the loneliness scale is very high ($r = 0.66$).

The potential for companionship support weighs again the most in the scale ($r = -0.12$). Negative events take their toll on mental competency. Youth plays an important role, and once again there is a substantial correlation with personal competences ($r = -0.24$), i.e. problem-solving skills ($r = -0.29$), self-confidence ($r = -0.27$) and social skills ($r = -0.09$).

The correlations between mental status and the different background variables vary from $r = 0.02$ for gender to $r = -0.22$ for socio-economic status, and do not deviate from the previously observed pattern. Regression analysis with eight variables shows that socio-economic status, city and age together explain 9 per cent of the variance. Urbanites with a lower status and the elderly are more mentally vulnerable.

6.9 Depression

6.9.1 Scale averages

We will be discussing the Zung depression scale in detail. The average score on this depression self-evaluation scale amounted to $X = 35.3$ (std. $= 8.2$). The minimum score was 20 and the maximum score 66. A breaking point of 40–41 was used as criterion for mildly depressed, 50–51 for considerably depressed. On this basis, 76 per cent of the respondents appeared not to be depressed, 19 per cent mildly depressed and 5 per cent considerably depressed. These percentages correspond very well with the measure for mental vulnerability described above.

Figure 6.3 shows the distribution once more. In theory, the scores are between 20 and 80; in this data set they lie between 20 and 66. To compare, Mook *et al.* (1989) report a slightly lower average of $X = 34.5$ among a group of about 300 students. The difference may be related to differences in age and education.

As expected, there was a strong correlation between the depression list and the loneliness scale of De Jong-Gierveld ($r = 0.42$). The relation with the network scope is much smaller ($r = -0.14$). This is also reflected in the averages of the depression score per contact group. The averages of the socially competent and socially inhibited are close ($X = 33.3$ and $X = 34.3$), similar to those of the lonely and the socially isolated ($X = 40.6$ and $X = 40.8$). The question of whether the distinguished contact types differ in degree of presence of depressive feelings can be confirmed. Figure 6.4 also depicts these findings.

The number of considerably depressed individuals goes from 1 per cent

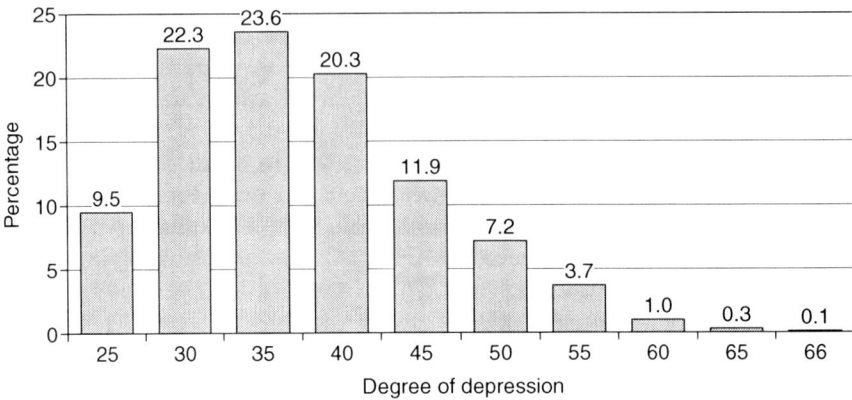

Figure 6.3 Scores on the Zung depression scale, percentages (N = 733).

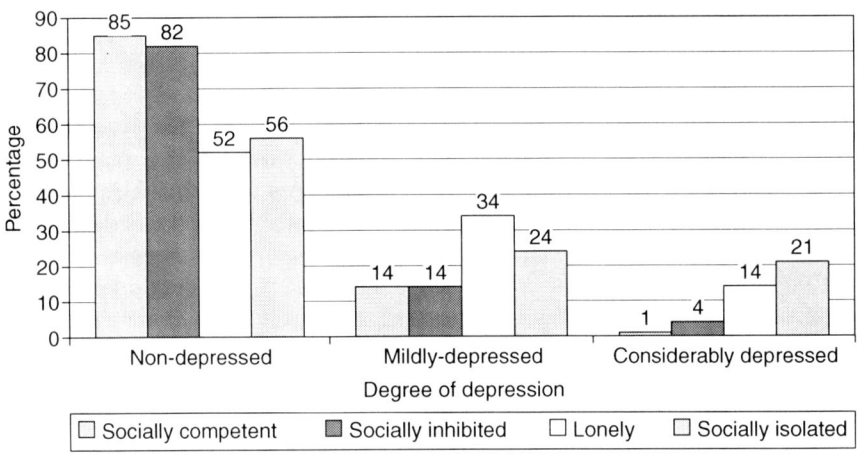

Figure 6.4 Social typology and degree of depression (N = 664).

among the socially competent to 21 per cent among the socially isolated. These differences between the socially competent on the one hand and the lonely and the isolated on the other are dramatically contrasting. The percentage of mildly depressed people is highest among the group of the lonely (34 per cent). It is also striking that the percentage of non-depressed people among the socially competent (85 per cent) almost corresponds with that from the sample of Mook *et al.* (1989) among students (84 per cent).

6.9.2 Results on item level

It is interesting to examine the answer patterns of the separate items, especially in relation to the contact typology. What are the common complaints or symptoms, and who mentions them? Table 6.1 contains the overview.

The most mentioned physical symptoms are agitation, poor sleep, fatigue and irritability, and to a lesser degree palpitations, slow bowel motion and crying bouts. Two-thirds to three-quarters of the respondents indicate that they are as clear-headed as before, look forward to the future full of confidence, have as much pleasure in things as they used to, and have the feeling of being useful and needed. A not inconsiderable number, however, denies this in their answers. In combination with the contact typology, many questions show respectively a linear increase or decrease of the percentages, depending on the direction of the questions. Poor sleeping, for example, is three times more common among the socially isolated than among the socially competent; the same applies to irritability. Relatively speaking, twice as many socially competent individuals indicate having the feeling of being useful and needed, compared with the socially isolated (78 per cent

Table 6.1 Zung depression items, percentage of respondents with confirmative answers (N = 686)

	SC	SIN	L	SI	T
I feel broody and despondent**	2	2	11	22	5
I feel best in the mornings	49	48	39	52	47
I have crying bouts or want to cry***	2	4	10	17	5
I sleep poorly***	11	10	27	34	16
I eat as much as I used to*	55	58	49	54	54
I have as much pleasure having sex as I used to***	61	57	42	36	55
I have the feeling that I am losing weight	5	10	9	6	6
My bowel movements are slow*	5	6	8	14	6
I have palpitations***	4	4	10	11	6
I am tired from nothing***	6	14	21	23	11
My mind is as lucid as ever***	75	65	59	40	69
I have the feeling that things are as easy as ever***	54	65	35	44	50
I feel agitated and cannot stand still	21	29	27	24	23
I face the future with confidence***	76	59	54	56	68
I am more irritable than I used to be***	8	10	20	25	12
I find it easy to take decisions***	61	49	42	56	56
I have the feeling that I am useful and needed***	78	74	51	40	70
My life is quite full***	93	69	66	49	83
I feel that people would be better off if I was dead***	1	6	4	11	3
I enjoy things as much as I used to***	86	63	58	44	76

Notes
*$P < 0.1$, **$P < 0.01$, ***$P < 0.001$; Chi^2 test.
SC = socially competent; SIN = socially inhibited; L = lonely; SI = socially isolated.

versus 40 per cent). The socially isolated fall prey to feelings of gloominess eleven times as much compared with the socially competent and the socially inhibited, and twice as much compared with the lonely. Especially noticeable in the group of the lonely is that, compared with the other groups, including the socially isolated, they seem to have the most difficulty with taking decisions (58 per cent) and that things are more difficult for them than they used to be (65 per cent).

6.9.3 Depression related to other variables

The relations between depression and general assessment of health, physical and mental status, and the loneliness scale are large (varying from $r = 0.42$ to $r = 0.49$). The correlation with network scope is $r = -0.14$. Here too the focus is on companionship support ($r = -0.16$) as well as practical support ($r = -0.15$). Fewer contacts tend to be related to depressive feelings, mostly for the socially inhibited (for the contact types, respectively $r = -0.04$, $r = -0.22$, $r = -0.10$ and $r = 0.04$). Negative events take their toll in the sense of depression ($r = 0.17$), but positive events offer a good counterbalance to this ($r = -0.16$). As people are more capable of running their own lives, they have less chances of becoming depressive, compared with people who have a life attitude of taking things as they come.

With regard to socialization variables, a happy youth is important. Non-depressed people tend to have (more) protective sources, and find comfort more often in religion and sex. People who understand the art of putting things into perspective are at a lower risk of falling prey to depressive feelings. Here too a substantial correlation with personal competences has been observed ($r = -0.38$), in order of strength of the relation: social skills, coping and self-confidence.

The correlations with the background variables fluctuate from $r = 0.09$ (gender) to $r = -0.35$ (socio-economic status). Socio-economic status and age explain 15 per cent of the variance.

In summary, the depression list greatly overlaps with the loneliness scale, as well as with the three other health indicators. The nature of the observed correlations corresponds largely with that of the three other health indicators.

6.10 Inter-relatedness

The health measures used here assess different things, yet also show a significant overlap. Thanks to this, the results patterns are comprehensible, like the strong relation with feelings of loneliness (especially with depression). The 'general health assessment' measure is quite strong. Based on this general measure we can delve further into the meaning of several network characteristics for health, as well as examine the relevant factors together (see also Appendix V).

As we observed, there is a strong correlation with loneliness as well as with network scope. This last relation, however, is much more limited and is present mainly with regard to companionship support. On this basis we determined a linear relation with the social contacts typology. There is also a substantial correlation with personal competences, especially with problem-solving skills (coping). Negative events weigh heavily in the scale, and age and socio-economic status are influential. These are the most important findings so far.

We have also investigated whether different network characteristics play a role with regard to the assessment of health. Degree of closeness, strong/weak bonds and number of family members of someone's network do not appear to play a decisive role. There is, however, some relation with contact frequency, which is lower with poor health ($r = -0.12$). We also see that, as people consider themselves as less healthy, they are more dependent on all sorts of formal support facilities ($r = -0.20$) (see Chapter 7).

Upon looking at the joint effect of the most important factors – age, socio-economic status, negative life events and personal competences – we observe that the three factors of age, negative events and personal competences together explain 21 per cent of the variance. Socio-economic status plays of course an important role, but is shoved aside by age (there is naturally a strong link between the two). Hence as people age they have undergone more negative events, and chances are greater of them experiencing their health as poorer; this also increases as respondents have fewer problem-solving capacities.

Let us look at some figures in more detail. The percentage of respondents giving a 5 or less to health amounts on average to 9 per cent, for young adults it is 4 per cent and for seniors (>65) 18 per cent, more than four times as much. Of the group with an 8 or higher (53 per cent), the percentage is 63 per cent among young adults and 36 per cent among seniors.

A comparable pattern can also be seen with regard to the typology: an unsatisfactory assessment for health is 5 per cent among the socially competent and 21 per cent among the socially isolated. Among the competent, 58 per cent considers their health as (very) good, compared with 38 per cent of the isolated.

Despite the clear relations of age and typology with the assessment of health, we also observe a considerable diversity among the different groups.

We would finally like to point to the fact that a person seeing themselves as unhealthy can be considered as a life event in itself, especially when an illness is involved. We have observed that the more people list illness as a life event, the more negatively they assess their own health ($r = -0.35$). Also striking is the finding that illness of a respondent is often accompanied by illness of a significant other person ($r = 0.38$). For the lonely and the socially isolated, this can even rise to respectively $r = 0.58$ and $r = 0.48$.

6.11 Conclusions

The analysis of the four health indicators we used produced several relevant results. There is a substantial linear relation with the typology of social contacts. The relation between health and coping mentioned in the introduction, in terms of problem-solving capacities and social support, comes forth from the analyses in different ways. Having effective problem-solving skills contributes to better health and, the other way around, good health leads to more effective problem solving. Social support also weighs in the scale, but mainly when it comes to companionship support. Here we find an indication of the existence of buffer effects. When a person's well-being is threatened by stressful events, the damage can be contained by appealing to social resources (Tijhuis, 1996). Life events and daily annoyances do cause stress, appealing to a person's adaptive and creative capacity to face the situation. The degree to which this is successful also affects health. A person's coping strategies and the potential for companionship support are very important here. At the same time, positive events offer a good counterbalance, as they have a protective effect on health. Enjoying daily things and being surprised by compliments are also fostered by this.

If we examine several relevant factors together, a persons' age, negative life events experienced and problem-solving capacities weigh importantly in the scale with regard to the assessment of health.

Although the health measures assess different things, they do show a large overlap – with the loneliness scale too. The overlap with the loneliness scale applies the most for the depression scale. As we keep finding the same trend in types of relation, even when there are smaller differences, we can conclude that the results can be ascribed their due importance. This applies in any event to the subjective experience of health; the results say much less about insight into the 'objective' health situation of those involved.

7 Social isolation: formal and informal support

Anja Machielse

7.1 Introduction

Social isolation is often associated with a strong dependency on professional facilities. The idea behind this is that people who have little informal support in their immediate surroundings tend to rely on formal help or appeal more often to professional facilities than people with enough sources of support.

This chapter focuses on the relation between the availability of informal support and the use of formal facilities. Are people with a small network or a network that cannot provide the desired support more dependent on formal facilities than others? And how do they experience this dependency?

To answer these questions, we will examine the relations between the informal support people can expect from their personal network and the use of professional facilities (Section 7.3). Because not everyone has the same need for support or help, we will discuss several forms of vulnerability that can lead to a higher use of facilities (Section 7.4). We will also compare the personal network of people with a specific care or help need with the network of persons who are not vulnerable (Section 7.5). We will proceed to analyse the relationships between vulnerability, the personal network and the use of professional facilities (Section 7.6). Finally, we will discuss views on the dependency on professional facilities (Section 7.7). We end with the main conclusions (Section 7.8). The chapter starts with discussing relevant concepts and definitions (Section 7.2)

7.2 Relevant concepts and definitions

Informal support is defined in different ways. The term usually relates to the wide concept of 'social support', a collective term for different types of support from the social network (see also Section 2.2.1). This involves different types of help and support that people can give each other: practical support (help with chores or errands, information), material support (money, goods), emotional support (guidance, consolation, intimacy) and companionship support (sociability, doing things together) (see, for example, Fischer,

1982; Van der Poel, 1993a; Sarason *et al.*, 2001). Sometimes a smaller definition is used, designating informal support as 'informal care' or 'informal help'. This involves care for persons who as a result of chronic illness and/or old age get into a problematic situation and are dependent on the help of others in their immediate surroundings (De Boer, 1994). The care entails practical help with household tasks, daily life activities and personal care, and is usually provided by members of the household, the family, the neighbourhood or the ethnic community someone belongs to. In this sense it distinguishes itself from regular professional (formal) care by employees or volunteers from certain institutions that are not part of the social network of the person asking for help.

Research shows that informal support towards others involves a certain selectivity in the sense that people would rather provide informal help to family and friends than to people outside their personal network. This 'philanthropic particularism' (Komter *et al.*, 2000) implies that people can expect informal help only if they belong to a personal network with family and friends. This selectivity is enhanced by the fact that people who deal with certain forms of vulnerability tend to have less of an adequately functioning network than others. Several studies have shown that the personal network of people with (chronic) health problems disintegrates slowly (e.g. Tijhuis, 1994) and that prolonged poverty also leads to the withdrawal of informal support (Engbersen *et al.*, 1998). Whereas it is precisely these people who have a greater need for (informal) help or support, their vulnerability has unfavourable consequences for the social network and they are more prone to appeal for help from the professional circuit. In the present chapter we will further examine this relation between vulnerability, informal support and the demand on professional facilities.

We will define informal support as *the practical, emotional and material support that people can expect from their own personal network*. This definition is based on the expectation that these three types of support can be important for the daily functioning of people who are vulnerable due to poor physical or mental health or a critical financial position. To map out the *informal support*, we have used a selection of items from Fischer (see Section 3.4 on the exchange method). All respondents were presented with the following three hypothetic questions about practical, emotional and financial support:

1 Suppose you need help with chores in or around the house, running an errand, cleaning, repairing or painting, who would you ask?
2 Suppose you have serious personal problems and want to talk to someone about them, who would you talk to?
3 Suppose you need to borrow a large sum of money, who would you ask?

We also asked what the relationship was between the respondents with the person(s) mentioned: partners, relatives, friends/girlfriends, colleagues/fellow students, immediate or residential neighbours, fellow members of an organization/club, volunteers, professionals or employees of agencies. Because this section discusses informal support, this last category of support is excluded from the analyses. This makes the figures deviate slightly from the data on social support from Section 3.8.

To get a picture not only of the support potential but also of the *actual support received*, respondents were asked whether they received certain types of informal help from persons outside their own household in the last year. We will limit ourselves to a number of very common support situations such as being picked up or brought home, borrowing things, being cared for during illness and getting help to take care of children and/or pets (see also Section 3.9).

To get a general impression of the *quality of social contacts*, respondents were asked to give a report mark. The scope and experience of the personal network are expressed in the *typology for social contacts* as presented in Chapter 3. Let us briefly review the four contact groups. According to the typology, about two-thirds of the respondents (64 per cent) can be seen as socially competent, meaning that they have a wide social network that functions adequately and do not suffer from feelings of loneliness. The rest of the respondents belong to one of the two groups at high risk for social isolation or is already socially isolated. Of these two groups, the lonely are at 22 per cent the largest; they may well have many contacts, but feel nonetheless lonely because the support in the network is insufficient or not effective. The socially inhibited (at 8 per cent) only have a few contacts but experience them as sufficient because they meet their social need, so they do not feel lonely. The socially isolated (6 per cent) have a small network with few contacts; in contrast to the socially inhibited, they deal with strong feelings of loneliness.

To examine the relation between informal support and vulnerability, we constructed three separate measures for vulnerability: (i) physical vulnerability, (ii) mental vulnerability, and (iii) financial vulnerability. The first two measures of vulnerability are also discussed in Section 6.5.

The measure for *physical vulnerability* is based on a combination of three indicators: the presence of physical symptoms that persist for longer than a month, the experience of hindrances to leave the house for health reasons, and an insufficient report mark for the personal health situation. The scores lie between 0 and 3: people scoring 0 are physically competent, people scoring 1 or 2 are considered physically vulnerable, and a score of 3 indicates that someone is physically very vulnerable. Based on this scale, 25 per cent of the respondents can be considered *physically vulnerable* and 3 per cent *physically very vulnerable* (see also Section 6.7).

The *mental vulnerability* is based on the following three indicators: the presence of mental symptoms that last longer than a month, a high score (6–11) on the loneliness scale, and a low score (0–5) on the self-confidence scale (for the loneliness scale, see Section 3.4; for the self-confidence scale see Section 5.3). Here too the scores lie between 0 and 3: people with a score of

0 points are considered mentally competent, a score of 1 means being mentally vulnerable, and people with a score of 2 or 3 are mentally very vulnerable. Based on this scale, 17 per cent of the respondents are among the *mentally vulnerable* and 4 per cent among the *mentally very vulnerable* (see also Section 6.8).

A third form of vulnerability goes together with the financial situation someone is in. *Financial vulnerability* is based on the following three indicators: a low household income,[1] the need to incur in debt or use one's savings to make ends meet each month, and experiencing financial hindrances to leave the house. We consider someone to be financially competent if the income is moderate or high, or if the income is low but no debt is incurred or no savings used. A person is financially vulnerable when the income is low and there is debt or use of savings. Financially very vulnerable are people with a low income who are in debt or use their savings, and that lack of money is the reason they do not leave the house (see also Hortulanus *et al.*, 1997). Based on this scale, 7 per cent of the respondents can be considered to be among the *financially vulnerable* and 2 per cent among the *financially very vulnerable*. This picture is somewhat distorted because many respondents did not answer the questions about their financial position; as a result, the financial data of a large number of them is missing (N = 1,329). Because we know from research practice that particularly people with extreme low or high incomes are less willing to answer questions about their financial situation, it can be assumed that the number of people with financial vulnerability will be higher in reality

The formal *facilities* that are involved in the study offer support to people with physical, mental and financial problems. Home care and meal services are intended primarily to support people with physical health problems. General Social Work and hotlines are oriented primarily towards people with mental problems, and the Social Services Department and the (Municipal) Credit Bank (a money-lending institution) were created for people who need financial support. Most of these facilities are optional, that is, people may decide themselves whether they want to use them or not. This is the case, for example, with the meal services or hotlines. In some cases, like the Social Services Department, there are no alternatives people can turn to. Because people with health problems will tend to first go to their primary physician, we will also report on such visits.

The results on the use of facilities and the relation with the social contacts typology and vulnerability are based largely on data from the nearly 2,500 respondents surveyed in the first research phase (see Section 1.7). We indicate when the results refer to the second research phase.

7.3 Use of facilities and informal support

7.3.1 *The use of facilities: a first impression*

To get a general impression of the actual use of facilities, we presented respondents with a list on which they could indicate which facilities they or their family members had used one or several times in the last twelve months. Table 7.1 gives an overview of the percentage of people that use these facilities

As expected, the primary physician is mentioned the most; four out of five respondents go regularly to a GP. Though most respondents simply do not need these forms of support, they may be essential for people who are vulnerable on the physical, mental or financial field.

Which people rely – temporarily or permanently – on professional forms of help and support? Although we have not yet taken into account the support that people have from their immediate surroundings or the degree to which they need help, we see clearly that certain groups are more dependent on formal facilities than others. People with poor health use all the listed facilities more often than healthier individuals. Lone parents also make frequent use of facilities. More than a quarter of them are dependent on the Social Services Department (29 per cent), whereas the average use is 4 per cent. They also make more use of social work (12 per cent versus 5 per cent) and go more often to a primary physician (86 per cent versus 81 per cent). A similar pattern can be seen in people with a low socio-economic status. They not only make more frequent use of financial aid agencies, but also of other formal facilities, such as home care (17 per cent versus 9 per cent), social work (8 per cent versus 5 per cent) and meal services (5 per cent versus 2 per cent). A last group with a relatively high use of facilities is formed by non-western migrants. This is related partly to the fact that they often belong to the lower social strata. They tend to appeal extensively to financial institutions and social work (13 per cent).

Table 7.1 Use of professional facilities (in the last year), in percentages (N = 1,825/2,459)*

Facility	Use
Primary physician	81
Home care	9
General social work	5
Social Services Department	4
Municipal Credit Bank	2
Meal services	2
Hotlines	1

Note
*The type of question asked could differ a bit per site.

Seniors, people with poor health, lone parents, people with a low socio-economic position and migrants are thus more dependent on facilities than others. Upon examining the total use of facilities, we observe that the relation is not very strong; the correlations vary from $r = 0.08$ (age) to a maximum of $r = 0.25$ (socio-economic status). The expectation is that the availability of a personal (support) network will produce greater differentiation in the use of facilities.

7.3.2 Informal support

We will now explore how the support that people have from their personal network relates to the use of professional facilities. In Chapter 3 we already saw that most people do have individuals in their surroundings who can offer practical, emotional and financial help. The majority (86 per cent) have two or three types of support. About 10 per cent have only one of these sources of support, whereas 4 per cent have none of these three forms of support in their immediate surroundings. If we look at the separate forms of support, we see that about 10 per cent of the respondents have no one for practical help, and that the same number cannot mention anyone for emotional support. Financial support seems even more difficult to get than practical or emotional support, because as many as 52 per cent of the respondents indicate having no one for it.[2] Apparently, people do not appeal that quickly to family or friends for monetary support. This high percentage could, however, also be related to the question posed, which offers little insight into the actual financial support that people have in their immediate surroundings because it only asks about lending large amounts. The most common possibility has not been taken into account, namely that people have someone in their surroundings that gives them small amounts regularly or supports them financially in another way, for example, as a guarantor.

Given that this is about potential support, we also looked at whether the expectation of people regarding informal support that they can expect from their network corresponds with the actual support they have received in the last year. This involves several practical forms of help and support: borrowing things, being picked up or brought home, being cared for during illness or getting help caring for children or pets. Among those who indicated they do not expect any form of informal support, nearly two-thirds (62 per cent) indeed received none of the listed types of help, as against 36 per cent of those who expect two or three types of help. This means that more than one-third of the people with a potential support network receive no actual support from others. The relation between potential support and support actually received is therefore minimal ($r = 0.17$, see also Section 3.8). This is probably related to the fact that many people simply have no need for support.

What does the presence or absence of (potential) informal support mean for the appeal to professional facilities? We see that the use of most facilities increases as fewer types of support are available in the immediate surroundings. Use of meal services and home care rises particularly when someone has little or no informal support, although the correlation is weak (respectively $r = -0.08$, $P < 0.01$ and $r = -0.05$, $P < 0.05$). Not all forms of support have a lot of influence on the use of facilities. Having or lacking practical support seems to have consequences in particular, whereas the presence of emotional support has hardly any influence on the use of facilities – not even the use of social work, even though that is a facility oriented par excellence towards providing emotional support. The same goes for financial support: its presence hardly makes a difference for the appeal to financial aid institutions. Consequently, although there is a relation between the presence of informal support and the appeal to facilities, the correlation is not strong ($r = 0.07$).

All of this raises the question of whether there is a relation between the *experience* of the personal network and the appeal to facilities. In Chapter 3 we saw that the quality of the network is related, among other things, to the support that a relationship produces (see Section 3.8). Is it so that people who experience their own network as insufficient appeal more to professional facilities? If we look at how respondents assess the quality of their social contacts, we see that the average assessment is satisfactory ($X = 7.3$, std $= 1.2$). Nearly half of the respondents (48 per cent) give a 6 or a 7, a slightly smaller portion (46 per cent) gives a generous satisfactory mark (8 or more), and 6 per cent give an unsatisfactory mark. The assessment of one's own network does show a connection with the support actually received. Respondents who assess their network as unsatisfactory received no help twice as often (22 per cent) as those who give a generous satisfactory mark for their network (11 per cent). Persons with a 6 and a 7 are inbetween, at 18 per cent. All of this has little influence on the use of formal facilities. Although people make more frequent use of facilities as their assessment of their social contacts drops, the correlation is not very strong ($r = -0.05$).

7.3.3 The social contacts typology

The presence or absence of certain forms of informal support and the subjective assessment of the network show a (limited) relation with the appeal to formal facilities. It is interesting to examine whether the use of professional facilities shows a relation with the social contacts typology in which both the scope of the total network and its experience (the score on the loneliness scale) are calculated (see also Section 3.7). Table 7.2 shows the relation between the social contacts typology and the use of formal facilities.

The socially isolated and the groups at high risk for social isolation (the socially inhibited and the lonely) make more use of most facilities than the socially competent; only the hotlines and the Social Services Department show a different pattern. The socially isolated make much less use of the

122 Anja Machielse

Table 7.2 Use of professional facilities by the four groups of the typology, in percentages (N = 1,804/2,406)

	Socially competent	Socially inhibited	Lonely	Socially isolated	Total
Home care**	8	10	11	15	9
Meal services**	1	2	5	5	2
Social work**	4	5	9	10	5
Hotlines	1	2	1	–	1
Social Services Department**	3	5	5	4	4
Municipal Credit Bank**	1	1	3	4	2
Total (six facilities)**	13	18	26	29	18

Notes
**$P < 0.01$ (home care $r = 0.74$, meal services $r = 0.11$, social work $r = 0.10$, Social Services Department $r = 0.06$, Municipal Credit Bank $r = 0.06$).

Social Services Department than the other two high-risk groups, and just like the lonely call hotlines less often. The socially inhibited call hotlines more often.

Upon looking at the entire use of facilities, we see that there is a relation between the social contacts typology and the use of professional facilities. As the assessment of the network and the support potential wanes, people appeal more to facilities. The relation between the total use of facilities and the social typology is $r = 0.16$. The assumption that people with a poorly functioning network are more dependent on formal facilities than people with an adequately functioning network is probably confirmed here, but the differences are not large. The connection with the scope of the network and loneliness is respectively $r = 0.08$ and $r = 0.17$.

7.4 Use of facilities and vulnerability

7.4.1 *Physical, mental and financial vulnerability*

Professional facilities are oriented towards reducing or neutralizing the vulnerability of people. The facilities discussed in the previous section are intended to support people with poor health or a precarious financial position. In this section we investigate to what degree these professional facilities are used by the people for whom they are intended.

To begin with, there is a positive relation between physical vulnerability and the use of two important facilities that are pre-eminently intended to meet this specific form of vulnerability, namely home care and meal services (respectively $r = 0.12$ and $r = 0.16$). Nonetheless, most people who are physically vulnerable or very vulnerable do not avail themselves of these services. Apparently, despite their illness or physical discomfort many people are able to manage otherwise; this corresponds with the assumption that help comes primarily from one's personal circle. Only primary physicians are visited by most of them, but this should not be surprising, given that 81 per cent of respondents go to a GP at some point (r = 0.17).

A second category of vulnerable people is formed by persons dealing with mental problems. Most general facilities for this group are social work and hotlines. Research results show that the appeal to social work presents a relation with mental vulnerability (r = 0.10). We can say less about the use of hotlines because the figures are small. It is clear, however, that people call such hotlines more often when they are mentally vulnerable; the most vulnerable are not able to find such services, or ignore that this is an option. Most people with mental problems do not appeal to the facilities intended for them either.

The last form of vulnerability we discuss here is financial vulnerability. The main facilities for financial help are the Social Services Department and the (Municipal) Credit Banks. Both facilities are used more as people's financial vulnerability increases (respectively r = 0.16 and r = 0.14).

When we look at the relation between the various forms of vulnerability and the total use of professional facilities (the six facilities mentioned), we see about the same relations with physical vulnerability (r = 0.18), mental vulnerability (r = 0.17) and financial vulnerability (r = 0.16).

7.4.2 Problem accumulation

The various problems are often intertwined, and people end up having to deal with an accumulation of vulnerabilities. Prolonged physical or mental problems can lead, for example, to a worsening income position, due to which financial problems will occur in the long term and people will be increasingly dependent on all kinds of government facilities, certainly when an adequately functioning network is missing. Thirty-five per cent of the physically vulnerable also have mental problems, and 14 per cent of them also have financial problems. Prolonged financial problems may also result in mental and physical problems.

When looking at the degree to which various vulnerabilities are simultaneously present in one person, we see that most respondents (59 per cent) are not vulnerable on the mentioned fields. About one-quarter (27 per cent) are vulnerable on one field, and 7 per cent are vulnerable on two or more fields. In addition, about 7 per cent are *very* vulnerable on one or more fields. It is to be expected that people's use of professional facilities will increase strongly as the problems become simultaneously manifest on several fields.

In Table 7.3 we see that the appeal to all the mentioned facilities increases as the problems accumulate (r = 0.23). Still, it appears that most vulnerable people make no use of these professional facilities, even when there is an accumulation of problems. Various reasons can be identified for

Table 7.3 Individual problem accumulation and use of professional facilities, in percentages (N = 1,825/2,426)

	Not vulnerable	Vulnerable on 1 field	Vulnerable on 2–3 fields	Very vulnerable on 1 field	Very vulnerable on 2–3 fields	Total
Primary physician**	76	87	89	87	100	81
Home care**	6	12	16	16	–	9
Meal services**	1	3	7	9	8	2
Social work**	4	6	10	10	23	5
Hotlines**	–	2	2	2	–	1
Social Services Department**	2	5	7	8	8	4
Municipal Credit Bank**	1	3	6	3	23	2

Notes
**$P<0.01$ (correlation of individual problem accumulation with GP $r = 0.14$, home care $r = 0.12$, social work $r = 0.09$, hotlines $r = 0.08$, meal services $r = 0.16$, Social Services Department $r = 0.10$, Municipal Credit Bank $r = 0.12$).

the vulnerable's *non-use* of facilities, for example, the fact that potential users ignore what certain facilities can mean for them, or the presence of enough people in their immediate surroundings who can take over the function of facilities or institutions, cancelling out the need to deploy formal facilities. On the other hand, the facilities are also used by people who are not vulnerable, which is the case with temporary inconveniences or problems (such as after having surgery).

7.5 Vulnerability and the personal network

7.5.1 *Vulnerability and informal support*

We have seen that the scope and experience of the support network can be influential to the use of professional facilities. We also know that certain groups of people have a specific need for support and help because they are in a more vulnerable position than others. For them, social contacts are much more important because they can derive various types of support from these contacts. The question is, then, to what degree do the vulnerable have informal support. Which forms of support can they expect from their personal network, and how do they assess that support and that network?

When we look at the availability of different types of informal support, we see that the vulnerable are clearly at a disadvantage compared with people who are physically, mentally and financially competent. The *physically vulnerable* have most often no single form of support; for the very vulnerable this is almost three times as much as the average (11 per cent as against 4 per cent). Although this group benefits the most from practical support, it is often lacking; 14 per cent of the physically vulnerable has no one for support, compared with 16 per cent of the very vulnerable (the average is 8 per cent). In addition, 18 per cent of the physically very vulnerable have no emotional support. The *mentally vulnerable* also have less informal support than average; 16 per cent of them have no one to talk with about personal problems (against 9 per cent of the competent), whereas this form of support is especially important to them. Things do not look much better for the *financially vulnerable*: 14 per cent have no single form of support, 20 per cent have no one for practical support, and the same share has to manage without emotional support.

We can thus conclude that the vulnerable have less practical, emotional and financial support in their immediate surroundings than people who are not vulnerable (the relation between the availability of informal support and the degree of vulnerability is $r = 0.12$ for the vulnerable and $r = 0.07$ for the very vulnerable). The same applies for those who have to deal with an *accumulation of vulnerabilities*. The most vulnerable even seem to be the worst-off: whereas only 3 per cent of the vulnerable have nobody for informal support, this applies to 6 per cent of those who are vulnerable on two or three fields and even for 23 per cent of the very vulnerable on two fields.

Against this background, it should not be surprising that the vulnerable assess their network less positively than the competent: research data show that people give their personal network a lower assessment as they become more vulnerable. While an average 6 per cent give an unsatisfactory mark for the social contacts, the share of unsatisfactory marks increases with the degree of vulnerability. This is the case especially for persons who are mentally vulnerable; among them, the share of people giving unsatisfactory marks reaches 17 per cent for the vulnerable and 37 per cent for the very vulnerable. The relation between the assessment of the social contacts (report mark) with the different type of vulnerabilities is $r = -0.08$ for financial vulnerability, $r = -0.11$ for physical vulnerability and $r = -0.21$ for mental vulnerability.

The research data show that the vulnerable not only often have a more negative assessment about their personal network than the competent, but that they also receive less *actual help* than people who are not vulnerable ($r = -0.12$). The very vulnerable are in particularly bad shape here. The vulnerable only received help more often when sick. That makes sense, given that in such cases they would indeed need such help more often. The same applies, of course, to the very vulnerable, but with respect to this type of help they are also in an unfavourable position.

Examination of the type of vulnerability shows that the mentally vulnerable receive the least informal help; 51 per cent of them indicate not having received any of the types of help mentioned, and among the mentally very vulnerable figures reach as high as 60 per cent. Among the physically vulnerable, 44 per cent indicate not having received any form of support, whereas at 20 per cent this is less common among the very vulnerable.

If we look only at the care received during illness, we see that the vulnerable receive this type of support more often than people who are not vulnerable. This is especially the case with people with a physical vulnerability; here the care received rises from 25 per cent among the non-vulnerable to 38 per cent among the vulnerable and 49 per cent among the very vulnerable.

7.5.2 *Vulnerability and the social contacts typology*

The strong relation between vulnerability on the one hand and the minimal support potential and quality of the informal network on the other confirms that vulnerability implies a greater risk on the social level – in other words, the vulnerable expect less informal support from their immediate surroundings. How does vulnerability relate to the groups of the social contacts typology? Do vulnerable people belong more often to the groups at high risk for social isolation than the non-vulnerable? Table 7.4 shows to which groups the respondents with a varying degree of physical, mental and financial vulnerability are allocated.

Among those with a physical, mental or financial vulnerability there are proportionately many lonely and socially isolated individuals and few

Table 7.4 Social contacts typology of persons with a varying degree of physical, mental and financial vulnerability, in percentages (N = 2,406)

	Socially competent	Socially inhibited	Lonely	Social isolated
Total	64	8	22	6
Physically competent**	69	8	19	5
Physically vulnerable	56	8	26	9
Physically very vulnerable	30	6	48	16
Mentally competent**	74	9	14	3
Mentally vulnerable	33	4	45	19
Mentally very vulnerable	2	1	78	19
Financially competent**	69	7	20	5
Financially vulnerable	42	5	35	17
Financially very vulnerable	43	5	38	14
Non-vulnerable**	76	9	13	2
Vulnerable on 1 field	59	8	25	9
Vulnerable on 2 or 3 fields	36	6	39	19
Very vulnerable on 1 field	20	4	61	15
Very vulnerable on 2 fields	–	–	77	23

Notes
**$P < 0.01$ (correlation of social typology with physically vulnerability $r = 0.19$, with mental vulnerability $r = 0.48$, with financial vulnerability $r = 0.17$, with total vulnerability degree $r = 0.37$).

socially competent individuals. We also observed that there are fewer socially inhibited individuals among the vulnerable than among the non-vulnerable. The mentally very vulnerable are the worst-off; they have to deal almost always with loneliness or social isolation, whereas social competence is hardly ever the case with them. It should be noted though that this picture is somewhat distorted because this form of vulnerability presumes a high score on the loneliness scale – a factor that is allowed for in the social contacts typology. In Section 6.8 we saw that the relation between the loneliness scale and mental vulnerability is very high ($r = 0.66$). This is partially related to the fact that one of the criteria for mental vulnerability is derived from the score on the loneliness scale. However, since the report mark that people give to their social contacts shows the same pattern, we can assume that mental vulnerability has nonetheless the strongest relation with the typology

When there is an accumulation of vulnerabilities, the situation becomes even more unfavourable. As people deal with several forms of vulnerability, chances decrease of them being socially inhibited, whereas chances of loneliness and social isolation in fact increase; of those people with two or more forms of vulnerability, as many as 39 per cent are lonely and 19 per cent socially isolated. Among those who are very vulnerable on two fields none are socially competent, whereas the number of lonely individuals climbs to 77 per cent and the number of socially isolated individuals to 23 per cent. It is clear that the functioning of the informal network worsens as problems accumulate. In particular, the number of people that have to deal with strong feelings of loneliness rises dramatically when the problems are more severe.

We can conclude by stating that there is a strong relation between personal networks and certain forms of vulnerability, in the sense that people who are physically, mentally or financially vulnerable have less of a well-functioning network than people who are not vulnerable on these fields. Not only does their network contain fewer sources of support, its assessment is considerably more negative. Although the vulnerable generally have a greater need for support than the competent, they can expect much less support from their immediate surroundings than others. A large portion of the vulnerable thus belong to the group of the lonely or socially isolated. The relation between vulnerability and the scope of the network and loneliness is respectively $r = -0.13$ and $r = 0.39$ (both significant at a 0.01 level). The subjective factor is particularly decisive.

7.6 Use of facilities by the vulnerable in relation to the social contacts typology

7.6.1 *The vulnerable per contact group*

We have seen that people who are lonely or socially isolated appeal more to professional facilities than the socially competent and the socially inhibited. We have also seen that people who are physically, mentally or financially vulnerable are lonely or socially isolated more often than people who are not in a vulnerable position. Their greater dependency on facilities thus seems enhanced by the poor quality of their personal network. We will now find out what the use of facilities by the vulnerable in the four groups of the social contacts typology looks like.

People who are physically, mentally or financially vulnerable and at the same time are *socially competent* generally appeal less to the facilities than those who are not socially competent. They probably find most of the necessary support in their own surroundings. They do visit GPs and call hotlines more often (4 per cent in an average of 1 per cent). This is probably related to the problem-solving capacity of the socially competent; when necessary, they do manage to find their way (see also Section 5.3).

Although the *socially inhibited* generally make less use of professional facilities than people from the other risk groups, this does not apply to the vulnerable among them. For this group, the necessary support has to come chiefly from professionals. The socially inhibited who are vulnerable on one or several fields appeal more to meal services, social work and the Social Services Department.

The vulnerable who are *lonely* appeal more to the facilities that are oriented towards their specific vulnerability. The physically vulnerable who are lonely make more frequent use of home care and primary physicians, the mentally vulnerable go more often to social workers and call more hotlines, and the financially vulnerable appeal more often to financial aid institutions.

The vulnerable who are *socially isolated* appeal to formal facilities a great deal, just like the lonely. It is remarkable though that this use of facilities shows much less of a relation with the specific forms of vulnerability this group deals with than is the case with the lonely. The socially isolated with mental problems not only appeal to social work and hotlines, but also to home care and meal services. Socially isolated people with financial problems are relatively less dependent on the Social Services Department, but they do appeal extensively to social work and the Municipal Credit Bank.

We can conclude by positing that the lonely and the socially isolated in particular appeal a great deal to professional facilities. Vulnerable people who are lonely make more use of the facilities intended for them than those who have a well-functioning network. Vulnerable people who are socially isolated appeal more to all facilities. They also tend to make use of several facilities simultaneously (6 per cent against 3 per cent). Socially-inhibited vulnerable individuals seek mainly practical and financial support in the professional circuit.

7.6.2 *Informal support and use of facilities*

A next question is what the relation between informal support and the use of professional facilities by the vulnerable look like. The combination of vulnerability on the physical, mental or financial fields with loneliness or social isolation results in many cases in a high use of facilities that offer a very basic form of help, like home care, social work and the Social Services Department. At the same time we see that most vulnerable people do not appeal to these facilities, not even when they are lonely or socially isolated. The lonely and the socially isolated do not have sufficient support from their own network, and therefore tend to turn to the mentioned facilities (home care, meal services, social work, hotlines, the Social Services Department, Municipal Credit Bank) more than persons from the other contact groups. Still, more than half of them make no use of any of these facilities.

Table 7.5 shows how many people are in fact dependent on these professional facilities; 18 per cent of the respondents have used one or several facilities in the last year. The figures are of course much higher for the vulnerable. Among those who are vulnerable on one field, 22 per cent have appealed to one or several facilities, compared with 35 per cent among those who have to deal with an accumulation of problems. This figure reaches as high as 54 per cent among persons who are very vulnerable and deal with several problems. If we look at the relation with the social contacts typology, we see that especially the lonely and the socially isolated appeal to professional facilities

Table 7.5 Use of professional facilities^a by the vulnerable per group, in percentages (N = 2,406)

	Socially competent	Socially inhibited	Lonely	Socially isolated	Total
Average	13	18	26	29	18
Not vulnerable	10	15	12	18	11
Vulnerable on 1 field	19	25	27	27	22
Vulnerable on 2 or 3 fields	25	30	44	39	35
Very vulnerable on 1 field	27	14	39	32	34
Very vulnerable on 2 fields	–	–	50	67	54

Note
a Home care, meal services, general social work, hotlines, Social Services Department, Municipal Credit Bank.

(respectively 26 per cent and 29 per cent). Among the socially competent and the socially inhibited this is respectively 13 per cent and 18 per cent.

The relation between the total use of facilities (not including GPs) with vulnerability and the social contacts typology is respectively $r = 0.23$ and $r = 0.16$. From this we can derive that the vulnerability is more relevant than the adequate or poor functioning of the personal network. Given that vulnerability does show a strong correlation with the typology, in the sense that the vulnerable tend to have more of a poorly-functioning network than others, this effect is only enhanced.

Finally, it is interesting to note the relation between informal and formal support and the degree of vulnerability (see Table 7.6). Are there also vulnerable people who have no single form of support? And to which groups of the social contacts typology do they belong?

Most people have informal support at their disposal and do not appeal to professional facilities, whereas 17 per cent have formal and informal help. The group that has no informal support but does appeal to professional facilities is the smallest (1 per cent). Most people in this group are lonely or socially isolated. The group that has to manage without support is slightly bigger, at 3 per cent. In this group we find mainly socially inhibited and socially isolated individuals.

The existence of informal resources does not have to automatically lead to a more limited appeal to professional facilities. People in one's immediate surroundings can in fact urge a person to seek formal help or support. For example, people who are mentally or financially vulnerable and who have sufficient emotional support in their personal network make much more frequent use of mental health and financial support facilities than people who do not have such informal support. Apparently, they need to be urged by people in their immediate surroundings to actually go knocking on the door of professional help institutions. Network scope is not always an indication

Table 7.6 Professional facilities and informal support among the vulnerable, in percentages (N = 2,461)

	Not vulnerable	Vulnerable on 1 field	Vulnerable on 2–3 fields	Very vulnerable on 1 field	Very vulnerable on 2–3 fields	Total
Informal support, professional facilities	11	21	33	30	31	17
Informal support, no professional facilities	86	74	61	62	46	79
No informal support, professional facilities	–	1	2	4	23	1
No informal support, no professional facilities	3	4	4	4	–	3

of the appeal to formal institutions either. Although a small network is usually accompanied by an above-average use of facilities, in some cases one sees the opposite. This is clearest with the financially vulnerable who have a small network: these people make less use of financial aid institutions than those with a large network. Here too a stimulant is lacking from the immediate surroundings to seek the necessary help.

7.7 Views on the dependency on facilities

7.7.1 Dependency on facilities

Given that modern societies place an increasing emphasis on the ability to do things independently and citizens' own responsibility, it is interesting to find out how important professional facilities are for the daily life of the users, and how they experience their limited coping ability and their dependency on these facilities. To get a general impression of the degree to which people are dependent on facilities, we asked users of several chief facilities to what degree they consider such facilities important or even critical to their daily functioning. In Table 7.7 we see the importance that users attach to home care, meal services, the Social Services Department and social work.

More than one-third of the users of home care, social work and the Social Services Department do not find these facilities important for their daily functioning. Almost three-quarters of the users of the meal services feel this way. Others find these services critical to their daily lives though. Many socially isolated users experience home care as being of critical importance to their functioning (38 per cent); this varies between 26 per cent and 29 per cent among the other contact groups. Social work is considered critical by the lonely and the socially isolated – respectively 20 per cent and 21 per cent against 7 per cent among the socially inhibited and 6 per cent among the socially competent. Meal services are critical mainly for the socially inhibited (29 per cent) and the lonely (21 per cent), and the Social Services Department largely for the lonely and the socially competent. As people deal with several problems simultaneously, they consider these facilities more

Table 7.7 Importance of professional facilities for users, in percentages (N = 125)[a]

	Not important	Important	Critical
Meal services	72	7	21
Social work	46	39	15
Social Services Department	44	26	30
Home care	38	29	33

Note
a This question was only asked to users of professional facilities in Amsterdam.

important. This applies especially to home care and the Social Services Department; more than half of people with multiple vulnerabilities consider the help they receive from these services as critical to their functioning. It is mostly the socially isolated and the lonely who are greatly dependent on these facilities. From this we can conclude that people with severe problems not only appeal the most to professional facilities, but that they need this professional help the most in order to function or keep functioning.

7.7.2 Experiencing dependency

Another question is how people think about the fact that they are dependent on professional facilities. To this end they were presented with the following statement: *'You are better-off not depending on institutions, because in the end it will not work out for you.'* People could indicate on a five-point scale to what degree they agreed with this statement. If we look at the total respondents group, it appears that 50 per cent disagree with this statement, 23 per cent agree more or less with it, and 27 per cent find that dependency on institutions is indeed not good for people.

Persons who are physically, mentally or financially vulnerable think more negatively about dependency on institutions than competent persons; the relation between vulnerability and the assessment on dependency is $r = -0.11$. Whereas 19 per cent of the competent consider that dependency on institutions is not good, 31 per cent of the vulnerable and even 37 per cent of people dealing with an accumulation of problems feel this way. Vulnerable individuals who are lonely or socially isolated think the most negatively about institutions; the socially inhibited also have problems with dependency. The relation between the social contact typology and the assessment on dependency is $r = -0.15$. Only the most vulnerable socially inhibited people think positively about this. They are probably those who need these institutions the hardest to keep functioning in daily life because their network is simply too small (Table 7.8).

Table 7.8 Share of people that give negative assessments on dependency on institutions per contact group, in percentages (N = 2,324)

	Socially competent	Socially inhibited	Lonely	Socially isolated	Total
Not vulnerable	20	31	30	41	23
Vulnerable on 1 field	26	36	38	36	30
Vulnerable on 2 or 3 fields	25	20	34	31	29
Very vulnerable on 1 field	44	29	44	50	44
Very vulnerable on 2 fields	–	–	50	33	46
Average	22	31	36	39	27

Finally, it is interesting to find out whether the negative assessment on dependency on institutions of the lonely and the socially isolated can be explained by the fact that they are the actual users of these professional facilities. The research data show that those who have to rely the most on facilities indeed assess this dependency the most negatively; a negative assessment on dependency on institutions is much more common among persons who appeal to facilities than among vulnerable non-users. Thirty per cent of the most vulnerable non-users assess dependency on facilities negatively, as against 43 per cent of those who do use facilities. It seems that they end up in such problematic situations that despite this feeling they are forced to appeal to formal help.

7.8 Summary and conclusions

The analysis of the use of facilities produces a number of interesting results, which we will now expound. Most people do not use professional facilities. This is mainly because they have no need for the services offered and are able to shape their daily lives without needing professional support. Still, some groups make relatively more use of facilities than others, even if we do not take into account a specific need for care that accompanies health problems or a precarious financial situation. These are people who have a specific need for support due to their age (the elderly), poor health or a disadvantageous social position (e.g. lone parents and migrants).

The use of professional facilities is influenced by the help and support that people can expect from their personal network. As people have fewer types of support in their own circle, they have to turn to professional help. The availability of practical support – or the lack thereof – is relevant here, whereas a lack of emotional or financial support has less of an influence on the use of facilities. The existence of informal sources of support does not mean, however, that the help from formal facilities is redundant, because it is not always self-evident that people appeal to members of their personal network. Whether they enlist the help from people from their personal network depends mainly on the experiencing of that network. Someone can have enough informal relationships yet still recur to professional facilities because the quality of the network is not such that help can be expected from it. Other considerations can of course play a role in the decision to appeal to the available sources of support; for example, it is possible that people do not want to bother members of their personal network. The study gives no definite answer on this though.

It does seem clear, however, that the emotional dimension with regard to the personal network is stronger than the presence or lack of certain types of support. People who find the quality of their own network unsatisfactory appeal more to facilities than those who assess their network positively. From the study we cannot derive how the assessment of the network and the appeal to persons in that network are related exactly. What does become clear is that especially those with a specific need for care experience their network negatively. It would be interesting to know whether those persons were already unsatisfied about their network before they needed support, or whether their assessment of the network worsened as the problems lasted longer. Is the experienced support unsatisfactory when the chips are down, and is that the reason why the vulnerable are spontaneously more critical of their own network? Or does the network of the vulnerable disintegrate slowly as the problems become more severe and last longer? Personal interviews could give more information on this question.

The research results confirm the assumption that the lack of an adequately functioning informal network lead to a greater appeal on professional facilities, especially among the vulnerable. They depend more on facilities for their daily functioning than people with a network that can offer the desired and needed support. At the same time, we see that people who are physically, mentally or financially vulnerable have to manage more frequently without a supportive network. They have less support in their immediate surroundings and experience their network much more negatively than the non-vulnerable. This means that they have a greater need for support, whereas they actually can expect less from their personal network. This picture is confirmed by the actual support received. People who are vulnerable tend to have received less help than the non-vulnerable. Especially the very vulnerable end up in an unfavourable position.

The vulnerable are more often lonely or socially isolated, and less often socially inhibited than the non-vulnerable. The lonely and the socially isolated among them appeal a lot to facilities, although each group does it its own way. The vulnerable who are lonely make more use of facilities that are intended for their specific form of vulnerability than the vulnerable who are not lonely. The socially isolated resort largely to professional help for their daily functioning, regardless of their vulnerability.

The socially inhibited also turn more frequently to facilities than the socially competent, but this is because they simply have fewer people around them to whom they can appeal. If necessary, they turn to formal facilities, but they do not experience this as a shortcoming in their own network. They apparently make a deliberate choice to set up their life in that way. The same applies to the socially competent who appeal to facilities. Among the lonely and the socially isolated this is different, as they experience a greater discrepancy between the desired and the actual support they receive from their personal network. In contrast to the socially inhibited, they are not pleased with having to seek help in the professional circuit. The fact that they would prefer things to be different is evident from their more negative assessments on the use of institutions. This mean that those who have to rely the most on professional institutions assess this dependency the most negatively.

Notes

1 The classification into income groups is based partly on household composition; a low income for single people means a net monthly income up to €770, for lone parents it is a net income up to €861 and for shared households a net income up to €1,068.
2 In Section 3.9 this number is lower (45 per cent) because in that section the support of professional agencies is also calculated.

8 Societal participation and social isolation

Roelof Hortulanus

8.1 Introduction

In academic and policy circles, much attention has been paid in recent years to the social participation of citizens. Each adult citizen providing his own livelihood and being involved in society is highly valued. Participation in the labour market is seen as a crucial factor. In many European countries, policy focuses on the fight against unemployment, the promotion of labour participation of women and the reintegration of people with labour disabilities (Serrano Pascual, 2004)

There are also great expectations on welfare policy, focusing on education and paid labour as fighters against societal disadvantage. Several authors point at the complexity of this disadvantage, calling it 'modern poverty'. This involves not only a precarious financial situation but also exclusion from society: in other words, a permanent dependence on all kinds of government arrangements, habitation of stigmatized neighbourhoods and the use of particular cultural adaptation mechanisms (Jordan, 1996; Pearson, 1998; Van Berkel and Horneman-Moller, 2002).

Modern poverty is thus characterized by *societal isolation* – the inability to participate in society in all aspects. This societal isolation is also defined as a form of *social exclusion* (Room, 1997). In spite of the complex interwoven character of the issues of societal participation and social exclusion, government policy has changed very little. It sees a good education as an important condition for paid labour, paid labour as a guarantee for an autonomous existence, and an autonomous existence as accompanied by societal involvement. Paid labour and societal involvement are presumed to benefit individuals' personal networks, and not only because they know more people: they benefit in many other respects. Hence the absence of paid labour, an autonomous existence and societal involvement are always bracketed together with social isolation and social exclusion. Social life is thus seen as a result of the way in which people function in society. The further conceptual specification of social life, however, gets little attention, whereas societal functioning gets a specific connotation: it is identified with the availability of paid labour, participation in corporate and cultural life, and political and community involvement (Hortulanus *et al.*, 1992).

Therefore, in this chapter we will focus on the presumed reciprocity between societal participation and proper functioning of personal networks. The key issue is what influence people's societal participation has on the proper functioning of their personal network and social life. Under discussion are several questions. First we discuss a few operationalizations of the concept of societal participation (Section 8.2). We develop our own measure for societal participation based on seven more or less objectively formulated indicators. This measure is then compared with respondents' own (subjective) notions of societal participation. Next we examine the question of whether societally passive people have less informal support at their disposal and are more socially isolated than societally active people (Section 8.3). We will also look at the different meaning that societal participation has in the eyes of certain categories of respondents in terms of proper functioning of their personal network. We focus on the difference between the elderly and youth, the healthy and the sick, women and men, singles and cohabitants (Section 8.4). Finally we draw our conclusions, arguing that societal isolation may not be identified with social isolation (Section 8.5).

8.2 A measure for societal participation

8.2.1 *Indicators for societal participation*

Before we develop our own measure for societal participation we discuss several other operationalizations. If we simply measure respondents' societal participation in terms of their labour situation or income, we are implying insufficient societal participation of all persons aged sixteen to sixty-five who do not have paid labour, do volunteer work or are unemployed or disabled, and all persons with a low household income (respectively 25 per cent and 37 per cent of our respondents). Paid labour and income are important yet insufficient indicators for societal participation. We can also emphasize participation in all kinds of societal activities – for example, the degree to which people are members of or participate in activities of associations, sports clubs and cultural organizations, volunteer organizations and informal support, are part of informal groups, go out shopping in their free time, to the theatre, the movies, sporting events, etc. If we look at participation in clubs and organizations, 28 per cent of the respondents are members of sports clubs and cultural organizations, and only 7 per cent are members of common-interest organizations. Of all respondents, 33 per cent do volunteer work and 29 per cent give informal support on a regular basis; 49 per cent are part of informal groups (family and friends not included). No fewer than 82 per cent participate in recreational outdoor activities such as going to the market, the theatre, sporting events, the movies, and so on. There is thus a great variety in the scale of participation, depending on the chosen criterion.

The specified indicators for societal participation apparently do not make clear to which extent a person who builds up a respected position in society

Table 8.1 Relation between income and societal activities, in percentages (N = 839/1,607)

Societal activities	Income			
	Low	Average	High	Total
Common-interest associations	6	6	9	7
Sports clubs/cultural organizations	14	33	38	28
Informal groups	58	55	48	52
Informal care	20	31	33	28
Volunteer work	26	36	42	35
Recreational outings	89	98	99	95

does not experience societal isolation. The indicators refer to societal participation in which either a minority or most of the citizens are interested. People who are very active in clubs and organizations or as volunteer workers are not the ones who are better-off in terms of income or labour situation (Table 8.1). Low-income groups participate slightly less often in activities of sports clubs and cultural organizations, give less informal support and participate less as volunteer workers. And then there is a percentage – albeit small (11 per cent) – of people with low income who say they never go out to visit a market, the theatre, the movies or sporting events.

Upon looking at respondents' positions in the labour market, the differences become apparent (Table 8.2). With regard to participation in common-interest organizations, informal support or volunteer work, the differences are negligible. There are, however, differences in activities of sports clubs and cultural organizations. Employed people are members of such organizations more often, the disabled and retired less often. The least memberships are found among the unemployed, students and the 'other' category (which includes many housewives). People who say they never participate in recreational facilities are almost always disabled or retired (respectively 12 per cent and 17 per cent never go out). Health problems are probably an important factor here. Participation in informal groups (family and friends not included) shows few differences for several income groups and for people with and without paid labour.

In spite of the observed differences, we have to conclude that income and participation in the labour market do not coincide with the several forms of societal participation. Even the majority of people with high incomes and paid jobs are not members of organizations or participate in informal support or volunteer work. At the same time, a substantial proportion of members of organizations, informal carers and volunteer workers belong to the low-income category. We can therefore say that income, participation in the labour market and all other kinds of societal participation are not closely connected.

Table 8.2 Relation of the labour situation with societal activities, in percentages (N = 1,209/2,277)

Societal activities	Labour situation						
	Works	Labour Disabled	Retired	Seeks work	Studies	Other	Total
Common-interest associations	6	7	7	5	3	9	7
Sports clubs/cultural organizations	34	24	22	9	6	14	26
Informal groups	46	62	62	41	36	57	50
Informal care	30	24	20	35	32	31	28
Volunteer work	35	28	27	29	52	35	34
Recreational outings	99	88	83	98	100	96	95

Societal participation can be seen as an achievement, but also as a potential capacity to attain a good position in society. Almost 22 per cent of our respondents have only attained elementary school level and few finished elementary school. Education is an important factor for income and participation in the labour market. Of all respondents with a higher educational level, 70 per cent have a high income and only 13 per cent a low income. Among respondents with a lower educational level, 47 per cent have a low income and 31 per cent a high income. The labour market position is also linked closely to educational level. The number of employed people (71 per cent) is very high within the category of the highly educated. The educational background of disabled workers is especially remarkable. Chances of becoming disabled are four times higher for respondents with lower educational levels than for those with higher educational levels (respectively 14 per cent and 3 per cent).

A higher education level has few consequences for someone's broader societal participation (Table 8.3). Chances of someone being more active in a common-interest group or a sports club or cultural organization hardly increase for people with a secondary or higher education. Only participation in volunteer work and recreational outings are somewhat higher for this group.

Clearly it is not so easy to measure societal participation. Paid labour and income are not univocally connected with participation in club life, informal care, volunteer work and leisure-time activities. Not even educational level plays a decisive role. Because in this study it is essential that we have a measure for societal participation at our disposal, we combined several of the indicators mentioned above, especially those referring to people's actual activities. We made use of the following indicators:

1   having paid work or studying;

Table 8.3 Relation between education and societal activities, in percentages (N = 1,284/2,427)

Societal activities	Educational level			
	Lower	Secondary	Higher	Total
Common-interest associations	8	6	8	7
Sports clubs/cultural organizations	24	26	29	26
Informal groups	51	49	43	49
Informal care	27	31	31	29
Volunteer work	29	39	39	34
Recreational outings	91	99	99	95

2 being a member of a common-interest group or being a member of or participating in a sports club or a cultural organization;
3 doing volunteer work;
4 giving informal support to other people, not including family members;
5 giving informal support to family members;
6 participating in informal groups (not including family and friends);
7 going out in one's free time.

With the help of these criteria we typify people to the extent of their societal activity or passivity. We presume active societal participation can have the following forms: having paid labour or studying, doing volunteer work or giving informal support to others (family members not included), or participating to some extent in activities of clubs and organizations. The remaining indicators – giving informal support to family members, participating in informal groups, and visiting sporting events and going out – are used to make a difference in the extent of societal activity or passivity.

We differentiate four categories of increasing societal participation: very passive, passive, active and very active people (Figure 8.1).

1 *Societally very passive people* do not have paid labour, are not studying, do not participate in clubs or organizations, do not work as volunteers, do not give any informal support to others, are not active in informal groups (family and friends not included) and do not go out or visit recreational facilities.
2 *Societally passive people* neither have paid labour nor are studying, are not members of clubs or organizations, do not work as volunteers and do not give any informal support to others (except for their own family circle). Contrary to very passive people, we regard societally passive respondents as people who indeed give informal support to their own family *or* participate in informal groups *or* visit recreational facilities.
3 *Societally active people* have paid work *or*, study, *or* work as volunteers, *or*

give informal support to others (family members not included) or participate to some extent in activities of clubs and organizations.

4   *Societally very active* people *combine* paid work or a study with volunteer work, give informal support to others and participate to some extent in activities of clubs and organizations.

Based on this classification, 5 per cent of our respondents can be seen as societally very passive, 26 per cent as passive, 39 per cent as active and 30 per cent as very active (Figure 8.1).

Now that we have a broad measure for societal participation we can see to what extent it coincides with respondents' educational level and socio-economic status. There is a substantial correlation: $r = 0.33$, $P < 0.000$ (Table 8.4).

We find there are hardly any very passive people in the secondary and higher educations category. Among those with a lower education, more than twice as many passive people are found compared with those with a secondary education. For the category of active people, education doesn't really matter. Twice as many very active people are found among the respondents with secondary and higher educations. Instead of our own participation measure, we could have used a well-known indicator for someone's position in society: socio-economic status (a combination of labour market position, income and educational level). The two measures are expected to strongly coincide, if only because the labour market position is a criterion in both measures. The correlation is indeed unmistakable: $r = 0.47$, $P < 0.000$ (Table 8.5).

The majority of very passive people have a low socio-economic position. Active and very active people mostly have an average or high socio-economic

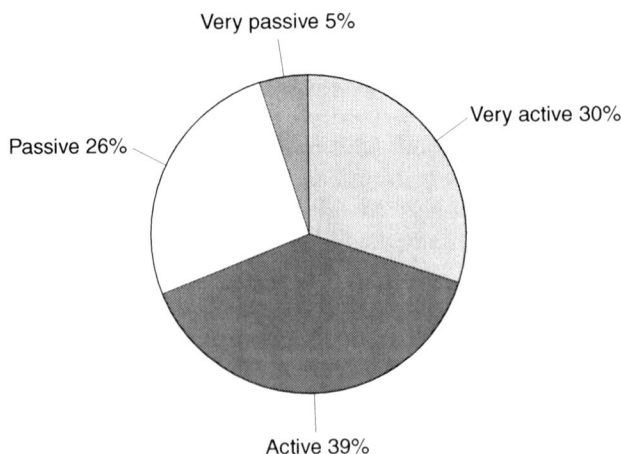

Figure 8.1 Societal participation (N = 2,265).

Table 8.4 Relation between educational level and societal participation, in percentages (N = 2,250)

Societal participation	Educational level			
	Lower	Secondary	Higher	Total
Very passive	8	1	0	5
Passive	36	16	10	26
Active	36	41	45	39
Very active	20	43	45	30

Notes
Chi² = 280.52; P < 0.000.

Table 8.5 Relation of socio-economic status and societal participation, in percentages (N = 1,390)

Societal participation	Socio-economic status			
	Lower	Middle	High	Total
Very passive	14	3	–	5
Passive	52	21	7	26
Active	25	46	43	40
Very active	9	31	50	29

Notes
Chi² = 364.32; P < 0.000.

status. However, the two measures do not measure the same thing: there are very passive people with an average socio-economic position, just as there are very active people with a low socio-economic position. It is this that precisely justifies using our broadly formulated measure for societal participation. This measure shows that very passive people are not active at all, but that doesn't mean they have nothing to do. Therefore we asked our respondents the following question: '*What are your main daily activities besides or instead of your paid work?*' Of the very passive people, 46 per cent mention household work and 14 per cent a hobby (Table 8.6).

Of all the very passive people, 20 per cent say they do nothing, a percentage that is lower for passive people and even lower for active and very active people. The extent of passivity of very passive people is highlighted, because almost 70 per cent have a partner who also lacks paid work. This is the result of an over-representation of older people: two-thirds of the very passive group are sixty-five or older (in fact, among the older people only 15

Table 8.6 Other occupations according to societal participation, in percentages (N = 2,265)

Other occupations	Societal participation				
	Very passive	Passive	Active	Very active	Total
Household	46	48	35	20	34
Hobby/sport	14	16	14	12	14
Study	–	–	5	31	11
Nothing	20	12	6	3	7
Chores/moonlighting	4	4	8	7	6
Meetings	1	5	7	3	5
Volunteer work	–	–	6	8	5
Art	1	2	5	4	4
Other	14	13	14	12	14

Notes
$Chi^2 = 617.92$; $P < 0.000$.

per cent are very passive in society). Among passive, active and very active people, about 40 per cent have a non-working partner. Apart from that, the category of very passive people does not consist predominantly of housewives, as men and women take an equal share. We will return to potentially relevant subcategories within our typology of societal participation in Section 8.4.

8.2.2 Feelings of societal exclusion and well-being

Our broad typology of societal participation is not necessarily meaningful for the respondents themselves. In our second interview round we asked for their satisfaction with their education, labour market position, income, living conditions and recreational activities. We put these five questions together and considered them as indicators for respondents' own judgment about their societal well-being. In Table 8.7 we see hardly any differences between the four categories. Our more or less objective measure does not mesh with the subjective perception of our respondents: apparently they use other criteria to evaluate their well-being.

This is confirmed by asking respondents about possible feelings of exclusion. (*'Do you have a feeling of not belonging or not being taken seriously, and is this so because you: are ill, are of a certain age, are single, do not have paid labour, are unqualified, do not have good looks, cannot afford luxury, are gay or lesbian, cannot make yourself useful in society, know few people, cannot solve your own problems, are not from around here, cannot manage?'*)

Aspects of societal well-being (being unemployed, enjoying no luxuries, being unqualified) are mentioned less (average 7 per cent) than aspects such

Table 8.7 Satisfaction with societal well-being according to societal participation, in percentages (N = 434)

Societal well-being	Societal participation				
	Very passive	Passive	Active	Very active	Total
Lower	39	34	35	33	35
Average	42	26	24	29	27
High	19	39	41	38	38

Table 8.8 Societal exclusion according to societal participation, in percentages (N = 384)

Societal exclusion	Societal participation				
	Very passive	Passive	Active	Very active	Total
Not excluded	61	69	76	70	71
Excluded	39	31	24	31	29

as age, being single, sickness (average 11 per cent). Among respondents, 10 per cent feel excluded because they cannot make themselves useful in society. But it is precisely on that matter that very passive and passive people do not feel more excluded than active or very active people (Table 8.8).

The dissatisfaction of very passive people concerns other matters, such as having no qualifications (17 per cent against 5 per cent average), not being able to manage (10 per cent against 4 per cent average), not being able to solve one's own problems (16 per cent against 4 per cent average), knowing no people (10 per cent against 5 per cent average), being ill (18 per cent against 10 per cent average), feeling excluded because of age (23 per cent against 12 per cent) and particularly being single (36 per cent against 11 per cent). Given the over-representation of older people in the category of the very passive, this last item constitutes an important explanation for the feelings of exclusion mentioned. The differences between passive, active and very active people are altogether not so large.

8.2.3 *Conclusion*

In this section we formulated a broad measure for societal participation in which attention is given not only to paid labour or studying but also to participation in clubs and organizations, informal support, volunteer work, attending sporting and cultural events, and participation in all kinds of

146 *Roelof Hortulanus*

informal groups. We believe one can speak of societal isolation when people hardly get in touch with these aspects of society – or even not at all. Such isolation is underlined by looking at other indications for disengaging behaviour from public life. Half of the very passive people do not read a newspaper (compared with 30 per cent in the other categories), and 60 per cent of the very passive respondents believe that the makers of rules in a country only benefit themselves (compared with 42 per cent of the passive, 30 per cent of the active and 23 per cent of the very active).

Still, we have to conclude that such a broad but 'externally' formulated measure does not coincide with the feelings of our respondents about their societal participation. The well-being of passive and active people is almost as substantial. The same goes for feelings of exclusion. Besides, people mention more individual and less societal issues as a reason for exclusion. Does this mean that societal participation and societal isolation have less of an influence on the social functioning of people than we expect? The next section provides more insight into this matter.

8.3 Societal participation: a breeding ground for significant personal networks?

Active participation in society is generally presumed to help personal networks, as a person gets acquainted with more people and benefits from it (Berkman and Syme, 1979; Fisher and Philips, 1982). Unemployment and other forms of non-participation in society are considered as an important cause of social isolation. In that respect, societal isolation and social isolation are bracketed together (see Section 2.4.4). Therefore we look at the relation between our measure for societal participation and the typology for social contacts and social isolation presented in Chapter 3 (see Section 3.3). According to this typology, about two-thirds of the respondents are considered to be socially competent. They have a vast social network that functions adequately and they are not bothered by feelings of loneliness. The socially inhibited (8 per cent of the respondents) only have a few contacts, but they experience them as sufficient because they meet their social needs, and they do not feel lonely. The lonely (22 per cent of the respondents) may have many contacts but feel nonetheless lonely because the support in their network is insufficient of not effective. The socially isolated (6 per cent of the respondents) have a small network with few contacts, and have also to deal with strong feelings of loneliness.

8.3.1 *Societal participation and social competence*

We will start by looking at the connection between our social contact typology and our measure for societal participation (Table 8.9).

The category of very passive people contains many more socially isolated individuals than the category of the very active. At the same time, 39 per

Table 8.9 Degree of societal participation and social contact typology, in percentages (N = 2,224)

Social contact typology	Societal participation				
	Very passive	Passive	Active	Very active	Total
Socially competent	39	55	68	71	64
Socially inhibited	13	10	7	6	8
Lonely	29	26	20	21	22
Socially isolated	19	10	6	3	6

Notes
$Chi^2 = 97.55; P < 0.000$.

Table 8.10 Social contact typology acording to feelings of exclusion due to inability to be societally useful, in percentages (N = 394)

Social typology	Societal exclusion		
	No exclusion	Exclusion	Total
Socially competent	60	19	53
Socially inhibited	13	16	14
Lonely	21	45	25
Socially isolated	7	19	9

Notes
$Chi^2 = 26.41; P < 0.01$.

cent of the very passive are socially competent, whereas 30 per cent of the very active are socially inhibited, lonely or socially isolated. The picture becomes clearer when we look at the people who feel excluded because they don't feel useful in society (Table 8.10). Of all the people who feel excluded, only 19 per cent are socially competent, whereas among people who do not have that feeling 60 per cent are socially competent. Twice as many lonely and socially isolated people can be found among those who feel excluded from society.

The measure for societal participation also says something about the extent to which people receive or give informal support (see also Section 3.9). Very passive people receive the least informal support. The degree of giving informal support make the differences more pronounced (Table 8.11).

Can we assume that passive and active people differ in the composition of their personal networks? To this end, we focused on the differences between family-bound and mixed networks. A personal network that consists for

Table 8.11 Support received and given according to societal participation, in percentages (N = 1,548/1,660)

Societal support[a]	Societal participation				
	Very passive	Passive	Active	Very active	Total
Support received[b]	11	22	32	40	31
Support given[c]	8	22	35	52	35

Notes
a These two measures for support received and support given are based on a combination of three societal support items: 1) help looking for a job, 2) tips for doctors, household help, 3) introduction to a club or association.
b $Chi^2 = 47.33$; $P < 0.000$; $r = 0.18$.
c $Chi^2 = 122.99$; $P < 0.000$; $r = 0.27$.

Table 8.12 Network composition according to societal participation, in percentages (N = 2,238)

Type of network	Societal participation				
	Very passive	Passive	Active	Very active	Total
Predominantly non-family-bound	9	9	12	14	11
Mixed	63	66	66	72	68
Predominantly family-bound	28	26	20	15	21

Notes
$Chi^2 = 32.08$; $P < 0.000$.

more than 75 per cent of family members is considered to be family-bound, compared with a network with less than 25 per cent family members. Respondents who have a personal network with less than 75 per cent and with more than 25 per cent family members is called a mixed network. There is a little difference between passive and active people. In most cases, both categories have mixed personal networks made up of family, friends, acquaintances, neighbours and colleagues (Table 8.12).

Personal networks that are strongly family-bound have an advantage in terms of the extent to which people receive informal support (for example, with job-seeking, introduction to a club or help during illness). The degree of giving informal support to others is the same for family-bound, mixed and non-family-bound personal networks.

In Chapter 3 we revealed that our respondents see personal qualities and not so much aspects of societal participation as protective factors against

Table 8.13 Protective factors according to societal participation, in percentages (N = 310)

Protective factors[a]	Societal participation				
	Very passive	Passive	Active	Very active	Total
A little	35	36	31	26	32
A lot	65	64	69	74	68

Note
a The total degree of protection goes from 0 to 17. The criterion for classification into a little or a lot was established at 8 and 9.

loneliness and social isolation (see also Section 3.11.1). Are there differences in this respect between passive and active people? In any event, passive people do not feel less protected against loneliness and social isolation than active people (Table 8.13).

There are indeed differences in the type of protective factors mentioned. Very passive and passive people refer far less to paid work as a protective factor (33 per cent and 24 per cent), compared with active and very active people (60 per cent and 75 per cent). The same applies to club life and volunteer work: only 9 per cent of the very passive and 28 per cent of the passive see participation in club life as a protective factor for social isolation. Among the active and very active, respectively 48 per cent and 55 per cent see participation in club life and volunteer work as a protective factor. There are clear differences with respect to success in society too: 23 per cent of the very passive and 27 per cent of the passive name this factor, compared with 44 per cent of the active and very active. Passive and active people think the same with respect to all other protective factors such as character, health, partnership, living conditions and age. The only exception is friendship. Active people name this factor far more often: 87 per cent of the very active, 80 per cent of the active, 68 per cent of the passive and 54 per cent of the very passive.

Participation in society is not permanently fixed. A person can become unemployed or find paid work. One would suspect this change has consequences for the personal network. Twenty-eight per cent of respondents report fewer social contacts compared with five years ago, and almost the same percentage (26 per cent) report more. For 46 per cent the number of social contacts remains unchanged (see also Table 3.3 in Chapter 3). There are differences between very passive, passive, active and very active people (Table 8.14). The very passive state more often that their contacts decrease, the very active state just the opposite.

We also asked about the decrease or increase in social contacts, and can distinguish four reasons: socio-economic, personal effort, private circumstances (such as children and health) and moving. Changes in socio-economic

150 Roelof Hortulanus

Table 8.14 Changes in contacts and degree of societal participation, in percentages (N = 2,236)

Changes in contacts	Societal participation				
	Very passive	Passive	Active	Very active	Total
Fewer contacts	32	31	28	24	28
Contacts remain the same	56	48	46	43	46
More contacts	12	21	26	34	26

Notes
Chi^2 = 40.98; $P<0.000$.

Table 8.15 Reasons for fewer contacts and societal participation, in percentages (N = 445)

Reasons for fewer contacts	Societal participation				
	Very passive	Passive	Active	Very active	Total
Socio-economic	18	18	37	51	34
Personal effort	–	5	8	10	7
Private circumstances	77	71	41	32	49
Moving	6	7	14	7	9

Notes
Chi^2 = 57.71; $P<0.000$.

circumstances can cause an increase or decrease in social contacts to the same extent. The same applies to moving. Personal effort is named more often as a cause for an increase in social contacts. Private circumstances, on the other hand, are more often a reason for a decrease in social contacts.

Very passive and passive people have to deal with private circumstances more often; this is why they experience more decreases in social contacts. Active and very active people mention socio-economic reasons more often as cause for a decrease in their social contacts (Table 8.15).

When it comes to an increase in social contacts, passive, active and very active people give identical answers (Table 8.16).

Socio-economic factors and therefore societal circumstances are not the main reasons for changes in the number of social contacts. They play an important role only for very active people. Private circumstances are closer to being the main reason for changes in social contacts. To a considerable extent this applies to very passive and passive people. This picture is confirmed when we ask respondents about their major life events. Life events that can be seen as important negative changes in someone's societal circum-

Table 8.16 Reasons for more contacts and societal participation, in percentages (N = 320)

Reasons for more contacts	Societal participation				
	Very passive[a]	Passive	Active	Very active	Total
Socio-economic	50	33	30	42	37
Personal effort	–	34	37	37	36
Private circumstances	–	22	23	13	18
Moving	50	10	9	9	9

Note
a Percentages based on extremely few respondents.

stances (like poor living conditions, unemployed parents, being unqualified, problems at school, financial problems, being fired, loss of volunteer work, retirement, problems at work, overachieving, underachieving) are mentioned much less (see also Section 4.3). Moreover, very passive and passive people do not experience such societally negative life events more often compared with very active respondents.

8.3.2 Conclusions

Societal participation is a breeding ground for significant personal networks. The risk of social isolation increases unmistakably if we rely on someone's societal functioning in terms of passivity and activity. Looking at factual experiences with forms of social support, very passive people are worse off. For a specific portion of the very passive population, societal inactivity (especially as regards small-scale participation in informal groups and recreational facilities) coincides with an inadequate personal network. However, the significance of personal networks does not depend chiefly on societal participation. This becomes obvious when looking at respondents' reasons for their feeling of not being useful to society. These reasons apply more to a personal network that is not working properly or to inadequate personal competencies than to insufficient participation in society. We have to judge the functioning of a personal network on its own merits and not as a consequence of societal participation.

8.4 Societal participation and significant personal networks: not the same meaning for everyone

In the previous sections we made statements about the reciprocity between societal participation and the significance of people's personal network. It is possible that speaking in terms of very passive and very active people or socially competent and socially isolated people does not do justice to other important differences in people's social situation. Perhaps the relation between societal activity and social competence has to be defined otherwise for older people, because they no longer work. Singles have to go public to maintain social contacts and may therefore be more dependent on societal activities than couples. There are still differences between men and women with regard to their societal orientation and their own social environment. City dwellers are presumed to live in a more anonymous environment, unlike people living in the countryside (see also Chapter 10). Individuals with serious health problems are perhaps more hindered in their societal activity and have to appeal to their existing personal network.

Using the typology for social contacts formulated in Section 3.3 of Chapter 3 and the measure for societal participation presented in this chapter, we therefore examine if the interaction between societal participation and social functioning differs for the respondent categories mentioned.

8.4.1 Age

It is often older people who are at a higher risk ($r = 0.47$) of being socially isolated. The social contacts from their functioning days in society decrease and their personal network shrinks, among other things because people from that network die. The number of very passive and passive people increases as the years pass (Table 8.17).

As people become older, their social competence also decreases gradually and social isolation grows, but these differences are less significant (Table 8.18).

The fact that of all the *very passive* people older than sixty-five only 24 per cent are socially isolated is quite revealing. Likewise, the share of socially isolated people is not much larger for passive, active and very active older people compared with social isolation in all age categories. The same applies to loneliness and social inhibition.

The nature of the personal network – family-bound or not – does not

Table 8.17 Age and degree of societal participation, in percentages (N = 2,261)

Societal participation	Age				
	<29	30–44	45–65	>65	Total
Very passive	2	2	5	13	5
Passive	13	15	29	55	26
Active	40	44	42	25	39
Very active	45	39	24	6	30

Notes
$Chi^2 = 459.82$; $P < 0.000$; $r = -0.47$.

Table 8.18 Age and social contact typology, in percentages (N = 2,398)

Social contact typology	Age				
	<29	30–44	45–65	>65	Total
Socially competent	67	68	65	54	64
Socially inhibited	8	7	7	10	8
Lonely	22	20	22	25	22
Socially isolated	4	5	6	12	6

Notes
$Chi^2 = 47.62$; $P < 0.000$; $r = 0.13$.

change with increasing age: about 10 per cent of each age category has no family-bound network and is also very passive. Receiving actual support for practical and emotional problems is also the same for very passive older and younger people. The picture of very passive and socially isolated older people is only true for a very small group.

8.4.2 Marital status

Social isolation is often associated with living as a single. This does not seem to have much to do with societal participation, because singles are no more or less active than couples and cohabitants (Table 8.19). However, singles who live alone are socially isolated more often (Table 8.20).

When it comes to very passive, passive and active singles, they all have a greater chance of becoming socially isolated compared with couples from the same categories (only the very active singles are not more socially isolated). Things do not look good for very passive singles in this respect. Only 2 per cent of all singles are both very passive and socially isolated.

8.4.3 Other factors

We also looked at possible differences between men and women. Our typology of social contacts does not distinguish between men and women, but differences do appear when we include societal participation. Women belong to the (very) passive respondents more often, whereas (very) passive men are more socially isolated. In particular, socially isolated and (very) passive men lack emotional support (13 per cent of these men cannot mention any person for emotional support, compared with only 3 per cent of women).

In Chapter 7 we discussed the influence of a person's health situation on the availability of a significant personal network. People with health problems are less socially competent and more socially isolated. This applies to very passive and passive respondents to an even larger extent.

Table 8.19 Marital status and degree of societal participation, in percentages (N = 2,245)

Societal participation	Marital status		
	Single	Couples/cohabitants	Total
Very passive	6	5	5
Passive	30	25	26
Active	36	40	39
Very active	28	31	30

Notes
$Chi^2 = 7.97; P < 0.05$.

Table 8.20 Marital status and social contact typology, in percentages (N = 2,382)

Social contact typology	Marital status		
	Single	Couples/cohabitants	Total
Socially competent	55	68	64
Socially inhibited	11	7	8
Lonely	25	21	22
Socially isolated	12	5	6

Notes
$Chi^2 = 61.45; P < 0.000$.

The presumption that the urban environment brings more social isolation is confirmed by the results of our research. If we include societal participation, it appears that many more socially isolated and socially inhibited people can be found among all four categories of active and passive city dwellers than among rural residents (see also Chapter 10).

8.5 Conclusions

In the introductory section of this chapter we mentioned the academic and policy opinions about the significance of societal participation for social functioning. We presumed that people who are isolated from society also experience a certain form of social exclusion. In fact, isolation from society and social exclusion are considered so interwoven as to be interchangeable. In our opinion this is regrettable, our research results make that clear.

Judging isolation from society on the basis of paid labour, income or educational level points particularly at a greater risk and not at something obvious. Our formulated measure for societal participation fits the picture better, because it combines several characteristics for societal participation which are employed frequently. In that respect, the subcategory of very passive people we distinguished can be seen as isolated from society. Because this measure for societal participation does not coincide entirely with disability or poverty (our financially vulnerable respondents have proven not to be very passive or passive with more frequency), it acquires greater significance. However, our measure does not speak much to respondents' own perception of societal isolation.

In Section 3 we established that very passive, passive, active and very active people express the same degree of (dis-)satisfaction with their societal well-being, namely in terms of paid labour, education, leisure time and living conditions. If we ascertain to what extent the very passive feel excluded, there is hardly any difference. Is it possible that very passive people can live with their position in society and that some portion of the very active group is so pretentious that they still feel dissatisfied or excluded? Or is our measure for societal participation simply not a good predictor for societal isolation, and are other factors more important in the eyes of the respondents? Let us leave it at that.

To conclude, we can say that bracketing together social exclusion and poor societal participation is not very wise. First, citizens seem to employ other arguments for social exclusion than frequently-used policy criteria. Second, it is preferable to take social exclusion literally and regard it as an expression of poor functioning of someone's personal network. It is true social exclusion and societal participation are correlated, but social exclusion is more likely a cause or breeding ground for societal isolation than the other way around. People can feel isolated from society, but that is not so strongly linked with the factors we used in the composition of our broadly formulated measure for participation. A person's own health and the way in which their personal network is functioning are more decisive in this matter.

9 Social environment and social isolation

Roelof Hortulanus

9.1 Introduction

Social contacts and social isolation are frequently related to people's living conditions. The social environment plays a key role in people's social lives, but it can vary from person to person. This may have to do with demographic factors such as age or marital status, or with societal factors such as work, income or education. Still, it appears that the significance of social life depends more on one's lifestyle and opinions about the social environment. It involves the extent to which residents identify with their neighbourhood, the significance they attach to neighbourly contacts, and the extent to which they believe it is a matter of homogeneous beliefs that affect the essence of living together agreeably (Rigers and Lavrakas, 1981; Hortulanus *et al.*, 1997, 2001a). One resident may see the neighbourhood as a temporary residence or a situation one has to accept, another may prefer to stay in the neighbourhood for as long as possible. Some people like to interact with neighbours, others do not. Many prefer to live amid like-minded people while others do not mind if people of all sorts live in the neighbourhood. It is evident that the social environment can have a different significance for people. The literature identifies four important meanings of neighbourhoods, all of which may contribute to the resident's involvement with their neighbourhood (Hortulanus *et al.*, 1997).

First, the social environment is a breeding ground for social contacts, providing people with all sorts of possibilities to maintain these contacts (Wellman and Leighton, 1979). Second, neighbourly relations are preeminently exchange relations involving certain kinds of support and help. Especially practical support – borrowing things, having someone water the plants or running one's errands, babysitting – is very convenient. No profound social contacts are necessary here, just good relationships with and trust in neighbours (Unger and Wandersman, 1985; Lofland,1989). Third, neighbourhood facilities like local shops, playing grounds, social and cultural centres, parks, etc. can give residents the opportunity to meet and contribute to identification with the neighbourhood (Michelson, 1977). Finally, the neighbourhood can be a platform for joint activities and interests. When residents organize joint activities or try to prevent or promote certain developments, positive effects on neighbourhood ties can be expected (Warren,1978).

Many authors believe these traditional functions of neighbourhoods have lost their significance. Some even claim that the industrialization and urbanization of society have led to 'non-place communities', while concepts of spatial proximity and territorial bonds are outdated (Kasarda and Janowitz, 1974; Webber, 1968). Recent transformation to a post-industrial society with its world economy and information technology is supposed to have made the temporariness of people's residence more prominent (Boomkens *et al.*, 1997; Duyvendak and Hortulanus, 1999). It is true that community patterns experience unmistakably important changes, but this must not be exaggerated. Although the activity pattern of most people has become more all-round in spatial and social respects and has exceeded the boundaries of the neighbourhood, this does not mean that the immediate vicinity no longer has any social meaning (Wellman and Leighton, 1979; Lofland, 1989; Hortulanus, 1995a). In fact, there has been a recent emphasis on the growing need of people to provide themselves with a stronger local identity as a reaction to current globalization and unifying processes. The sense of community – the extent to which residents identify with their neighbourhood – and the social significance of the social environment are not so much diminished in the course of time, they have acquired a different meaning (Hortulanus, 1995b). The 'we' feeling of older times based on factual relations and activities is replaced by a comparable feeling of which shared values, manners and visible living patterns constitute the essence. People want to identify with their fellow neighbourhood residents in a way that is characterized by a certain standoffishness combined with compliant contacts. This is possible when residents cherish similar beliefs and rules of etiquette with respect to important residential issues. Even without factual contacts with neighbours, residents can promote attractive living conditions or just irritate each other. When neighbours have the same opinions about certain essential aspects of living, then residential satisfaction can be stimulated, whereas neighbours who cause trouble can undo the strong aspects of the neighbourhood. The same applies to the social environment as a whole. Residents who cause inconveniences or other forms of undesirable behaviour produce a negative identification with the neighbourhood. If, on the other hand, people's residential behaviour is mostly compatible and supports residents' status in society and in terms of lifestyle, then the neighbourhood evokes positive images.

In this chapter we will go more deeply into the question of how and to what extent residents identify with their neighbourhood, and what are the consequences if the needs and preferences of people do not coincide with the characteristics of the neighbourhood. The central question is whether people in a similar situation can feel isolated in a environmental sense, and what typifies the relationship between environmental and social isolation.

In this chapter we first examine which function people attribute to their social environment nowadays (Section 9.2). We then look into the three forms of environmental isolation and examine the role a relatively homogeneous social environment plays in preventing environmental isolation (Section 9.3). We then turn to the leading question of this chapter, that is, the relation between environmental isolation and social isolation (Section 9.4). Is it correct to bracket environmental isolation with social isolation? By themselves, the three forms of environmental isolation distinguished do not implicate damage to the personal network as a whole. We have to look closely to determine which residents experience social isolation as a result of environmental isolation. We also ask whether the social environment has a specific significance for people who are socially isolated. We finish with some conclusions (Section 9.5).

9.2 Functions of the social environment

For many residents, neighbourhoods can have several functions.

To judge to what extent respondents see their neighbourhood as a source for social contacts, we presented them with the following four propositions: *'I have many contacts with people in my social environment'; 'I don't search for friends in my neighbourhood'; 'I think good contacts with people in my social environment are very important'; 'A pleasant neighbourhood is very important for me'.* The respondents could indicate on a five-point scale to what extent they agree with the propositions. A small majority of the residents (56 per cent) has extensive contact with their fellow residents. Thirty-five per cent said they maintain few or no relations at all in their neighbourhood. This does not mean the latter category find smooth neighbourly contacts of no importance. One-third do not care, but two-thirds want – albeit to a limited extent – smooth relations with fellow residents. Apart from that, almost everyone thinks a pleasant social environment is important, but people have different ideas about what that entails. One would be inclined to pin down such differences to age, sex or marital status. Still, men do not show different patterns than women, single people do not have substantially different opinions than families, and the elderly have mostly the same views as young people. If anything, we can only say that elderly residents value social contacts and friends in their social environment more often.

A second function of neighbourhood contacts we looked at are exchange relations. They involve the factual practical support that fellow neighbourhood residents give each other, such as lending/borrowing things, giving someone a ride, taking care of a child or pet, offering care in case of illness, helping fill out forms, tipping someone about a suitable cleaning lady or babysitter, help finding a job, mediating in problems with authorities (see also Section 3.8). Such exchange relations between neighbourhood residents are not common. Only a small minority of the residents (16 per cent) has such an exchange pattern with their neighbours. The fact that residents do not have exchange relationships with their neighbourhood residents is not a problem in itself: after all, 91 per cent have a network within walking distance for practical and emotional support. Still, one should not underestimate that 9 per cent of residents do not maintain any neighbourly relationships in the sense of reciprocal support, and must also do without such relationships of family and friends within walking distance, even though they indicate having a need for it.

A third function of the neighbourhood relates to the degree to which residents make use of all kinds of neighbourhood facilities. We see that many respondents make no use of facilities in their own vicinity, even if we use a very broad definition of facilities and include shops, playing grounds, a community centre, childcare, a primary physician and a school. Even then, 37 per cent of the respondents make no use whatsoever of such neighbourhood facilities. Against that, 31 per cent make use of three or more of these facilities. This shows that nowadays it is quite possible to just live in a neighbourhood without making use of any neighbourhood facilities. Furthermore, whether people use the neighbourhood facilities is totally unrelated to their satisfaction with the neighbourhood as expressed in a report mark.

A fourth function a neighbourhood can have relates to the common activities that residents undertake. To get a picture of this, we asked respondents whether they participate in neighbourhood associations, resident committees, maintenance activities in the context of neighbourhood management, volunteer work in the neighbourhood, public inquiry procedures and the like. Almost a quarter of the respondents (22 per cent) has participated occasionally on these neighbourhood activities, but an equally large group (26 per cent) is not even aware of such activities. Although most residents are aware of it, they say they have no time for it or do not feel like participating, they don't see the point of it or say that the neighbourhood doesn't mean much to them.

To summarize, we can state that for many residents, neighbourhoods still fulfil all kinds of functions. It is also clear that not all respondents give the same meaning to their social environment. Residents can relate to their neighbourhood in all kinds of ways, and the social meaning of the environment can vary per person. There are many people who indeed live in a house in a specific neighbourhood but for the rest do not attach much importance to social contacts with neighbourhood residents, have no exchange relationships with their neighbours, do not use neighbourhood facilities and do not participate in neighbourhood activities or stand up for their neighbourhood. May we conclude from this that for these people the neighbourhood as a whole and their social environment in particular have no meaning? Or should we look at the other aspects that contribute to a neighbourhood forming an attractive social climate, such as agreements about residents' views on living conditions and lifestyles?

9.3 The many faces of environmental isolation

We have seen that there are all kinds of discrepancies between the living preferences of residents and the actual characteristics of their living environment. This justifies looking further at what the consequences are of such a mismatch between the needs and preferences of individual residents and the social characteristics of the neighbourhood they live in. In this section we will look at the three different forms of environmental isolation: two forms refer to factual isolation (objective) and one form refers to a feeling of isolation (subjective).

1. We speak of factual environmental isolation if people's need for social contacts in the neighbourhood does not coincide with the contacts they really have there. On the basis of two propositions ('*I don't have any contacts in my neighbourhood*' and '*I don't have any need whatsoever for any contact in my neighbourhood*') a classification has been made into four categories of residents. First we have residents who indicate having a need for neighbourly contacts and actually have them; this is not a environmentally isolated category. Second, there are residents who indicate having a need for neighbourly contacts but do not actually have them; we consider this a environmentally isolated category. Then there are residents who have no need for contacts and have no contacts, and residents who have no need for contacts although they do have contacts; these last two groups cannot be classified a priori as environmentally isolated or not.
2. A second form of factual environmental isolation refers to people's supportive relationships in the neighbourhood. In this sense we see people as environmentally isolated if they (*do not have a network of support within walking distance – less than 500 meters*) of their house. The support network can consist of family members, friends, neighbours, colleagues, and so on, who the respondent indicates offer practical or emotional support, or companionship if necessary.
3. The third form of environmental isolation refers to the situation in which people do not feel at home in a neighbourhood for one reason or another, or identify with their neighbourhood in a negative way because they experience nuisances, feel unsafe or have negative ties with their neighbours. To get a picture of environmental isolation in this subjective perspective, we asked the respondents for report marks on *their social environment's appreciation*. Respondents who gave their neighbourhood a report mark 5 or lower are seen as environmentally isolated, because that report mark indicates that their social environment evokes negative associations.

9.3.1 A mismatch between desired and actual social contacts in the neighbourhood

Let us first look at the eventual discrepancy between the need (desire) for social contacts in the neighbourhood and the degree to which residents actually have these contacts (Figure 9.1). There are respondents (15 per cent) who say they have no contacts at all in their vicinity. In addition, about 30 per cent have little contact and 55 per cent a lot of contact with fellow residents. A deliberate choice may be behind these differences in social contacts. To find out, we asked respondents to indicate whether they have a need for social contacts in their neighbourhood. About 20 per cent indicated having no need for it at all, for 10 per cent it did not make much of a difference, and 70 per cent had a real need for it. If we compare the data on the actual contacts and the need for them a clear picture emerges.

For 75 per cent of the respondents, the social contact pattern in their neighbourhood is going the way they like it. For 4 per cent of the respondents we can clearly identify environmental isolation: they indicate having a need for contact with neighbourhood residents, but do not actually have these contacts. The other two categories raise all kinds of questions from the perspective of environmental isolation. Seven per cent of the respondents claim having no need for social neighbourly contacts, although they do have them. This need not be a problem per se, but it can also involve a feeling of restriction. At first glance, the 14 per cent of respondents who claim to have no need for contacts and also have no contacts have it made. Their social contact pattern is going just the way they want it to. But from a neighbourhood perspective, these residents can be identified as environmentally isolated, for example, if relinquishing or rejecting neighbourly contacts is not so much related to personal preferences but is a reaction to the specific character of the neighbourhood they live in. By the way, the two categories of respondents who indicate having no need for neighbourly contacts do not

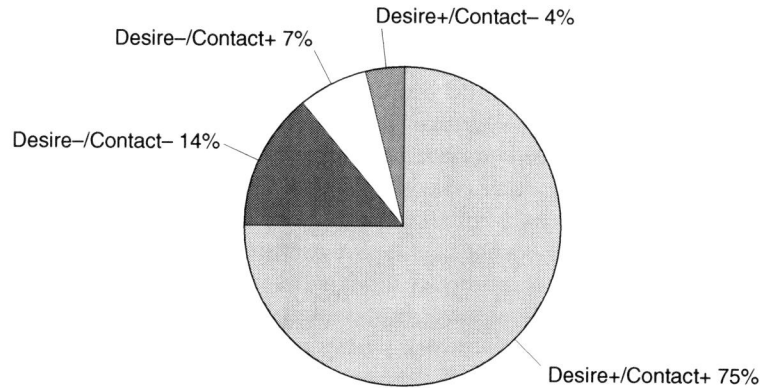

Figure 9.1 Desired and actual contacts in the neighbourhood (N = 2,119).

162 *Roelof Hortulanus*

say it because they find having social contacts unimportant. They have as much need for it as other respondents, they just don't really need the contacts to be in their vicinity.

The varying need for neighbourhood contacts cannot be explained either by obvious factors like marital status, age, sex or educational levels of the respondents. There are slightly more single people among those who have no neighbourly contacts though. This in itself is an important fact, because single people claim to have as much of a need for neighbourly contacts as people in other types of households. Families with children have neighbourly contacts more often and have more of a need for them. Older people tend to attach more importance to neighbourly contacts, and they have more of these contacts. Men and women do not differ with respect to their need for neighbourly contacts or actual contacts and this also applies to people with lower or higher educational levels. There are, however, differences between urban and rural locations. In rural areas, 85 per cent of the respondents had a need for contacts and had actual neighbourly contacts. In urban areas this percentage is lower, at 66 per cent, indicating that environmental isolation is more common in urban areas.

9.3.2 *The absence of a support network in the neighbourhood*

Environmental isolation can also be involved in – potentially – having a network for practical and/or emotional support. It is already remarkable that even in our times about 91 per cent of all residents claim to have a network within walking distance of their house. Only 9 per cent is unable to appeal for support from the direct social environment (Figure 9.2). Therefore, the importance of the neighbourhood in that sense can still be designated as significant. This is not just about support from parents, children or friends, because only 37 per cent of all respondents have them within walking distance. Besides, not all parents, children and friends fulfil a supportive function for our respondents. We see the same for the nearly 10 per cent of respondents who miss a support network within walking distance. About 22 per cent of these respondents does have parents, children or friends within walking distance, but they fulfil no function as a source of support, and 13 per cent has no parents, children or friends. This means that one-third (35 per cent) of these respondents has no support network outside the neighbourhood either. The other two-thirds can fall back on support from parents, children or friends, but these people live farther away. Hence the 10 per cent of respondents without a support network within walking distance is not a more vulnerable category of residents per definition. What is noticeable is that single people are over-represented here too: as many as 22 per cent do not have a support network within walking distance. It is not as if respondents who lack a support network in their own social environment generally have less of a need for social contacts. This is one more reason to be alert for environmental isolation in this category.

Social environment and social isolation 163

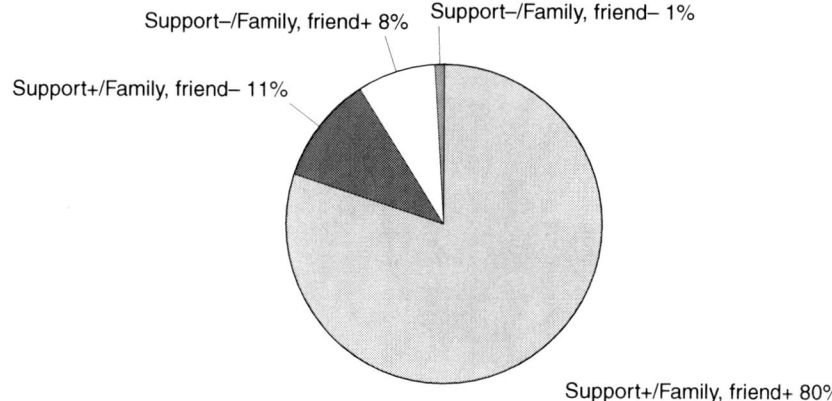

Figure 9.2 Availability of support from family/friends within walking distance (N = 2,438).

9.3.3 Negative identification with the neighbourhood

The social environment is not only important from the perspective of social contacts or practical support. It also has a certain emotional value in terms of security, pride, suitability, unsafety, shame and discomfort. Residents can identify, as it were, with their neighbourhood in a positive or negative way. There is environmental isolation in this subjective meaning if residents identify negatively with their neighbourhood, and reject the neighbourhood in certain ways. The general assessment over the neighbourhood is expressed in the report mark that respondents themselves give their neighbourhood (Figure 9.3). Of all respondents, 11 per cent give an unsatisfactory mark (5 or lower) to their neighbourhood, and 16 per cent a barely satisfactory mark (a 6). The vast majority (66 per cent) give a 7 or an 8. Another 7 per cent are very satisfied, and give a 9 or a 10.

If the report mark for the neighbourhood is a good indicator for a negative identification with it, this means that respondents are annoyed about certain things.

To gain more insight into the factors that play a role in negative neighbourhood identification, we constructed a few subscales for nuisance, unsafety and negative ties with neighbours:

- *Nuisance* is estimated in terms of ten items: noise from neighbours; dog dirt; rubbish lying around; destruction/vandalism/graffiti; loitering youngsters; fiddling with cars and motorbikes on the street; abuse/discrimination; nuisance from drug addicts/dealing; feeling threatened; odour nuisance.

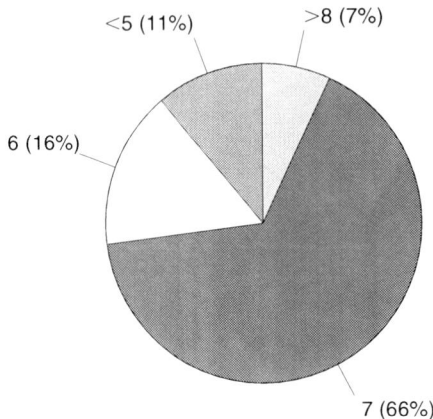

Figure 9.3 Report mark of the neighbourhood (N = 2,406).

- *Unsafety* is estimated in terms of six items: loitering youngsters; abuse/discrimination; nuisance from drug addicts/dealing; feeling threatened; badly illuminated streets; burglary.
- *Negative ties* are estimated in terms of three items: respondent's conviction that too many different types of people are settling in the neighbourhood; dislike of some people in the neighbourhood; having quarrels with some people in the neighbourhood.

We found out whether the report mark is related to issues like nuisance, unsafety or negative social ties (such as conflicts with fellow residents or the feeling that the differences between residents are just too great). Before doing this, we first looked at how these factors are interconnected.

Nuisance can refer to many things: from noise from neighbours to garbage lying around, discrimination and drug-related problems. When confronted with about ten examples of nuisance, 11 per cent of our respondents said they are never bothered by it, and 31 per cent are only bothered by some things. This against 25 per cent who are bothered by more than eight items and another 33 per cent who are bothered by four to seven items. Nuisance is not the same as unsafety in the eyes of the respondents, but apparently they are strongly linked ($r = 0.66$). A large portion of the respondents who said they experience no annoyances live in neighbourhoods where they feel very safe (this is the case for as many as 75 per cent). Respondents who said they experience a lot of nuisance have a correspondingly high feeling of unsafety (it is considerable for 33 per cent of them and even higher for 48 per cent). The main connection is caused by the fact that some nuisance items are also part of the unsafety score; this was done because some nuisance issues also cause feelings of unsafety.

Nuisance is also connected with the degree to which residents indicate having a negative social bond with the neighbourhood (r = 0.27). Such a negative bond becomes visible when residents say that too many types of people are coming to live in the neighbourhood, or if they hate some people in their vicinity or even have fights with them. When there are very negative ties, the chances of respondents indicating they experience nuisance too on many points are very high, at 63 per cent. The opposite does not hold true, though. It is possible for people to experience a lot of nuisance and still not have a negative bond with the neighbourhood (16 per cent). The same applies for the relation between feelings of unsafety and negative bonds with fellow neighbours (r = 0.25). Now that we have ascertained that the three scores on nuisance, unsafety and negative social bonds are importantly inter-related, we can establish a relation between these three scores and the above-mentioned report mark for the neighbourhood.

The report mark indeed shows a clear relation with all three scores. Of the respondents who gave an unsatisfactory mark to their neighbourhood, 56 per cent experience a lot of nuisance, while only 18 per cent of those giving a mark of 7 or 8 and 10 per cent of those giving a 9 or 10, experience this (r = −0.31). Feelings of unsafety are also higher in neighbourhoods with low assessments. Of those who give a 5 or lower to their neighbourhood, 37 per cent indicate strong feelings of unsafety; only 9 per cent of those giving their neighbourhood a 7 or an 8 and 5 per cent of those giving a 9 or a 10 feel that way (r = −0.26). Negative bindings with fellow neighbours are also mentioned more often by respondents who give an unsatisfactory mark to their neighbourhood (63 per cent); For those who give a mark 7 or 8 this goes for 37 per cent and those giving a 9 or 10 only for 29 per cent. (r = 0.23).

We can conclude that the report mark not only gives a good overall impression of residents' assessment of their neighbourhood, it also says a lot about the degree to which they identify with their neighbourhood. This is why we believe respondents who assess their neighbourhood with a 5 or lower are environmentally isolated, because with this mark they indicate that their immediate living environment invokes negative associations.

9.3.4 *The relation between the three forms of environmental isolation*

Until now we have distinguished three forms of environmental isolation. One form is that in which residents experience a discrepancy between their need for neighbourly contacts and the social contacts they actually maintain with neighbourhood residents. A second form is embodied by the situation in which residents cannot have a support network within walking distance. A third is environmental isolation seen as a situation in which a resident identifies negatively with the neighbourhood. These three forms of environmental isolation we have distinguished also seem to be inter-related. A positive assessment of the neighbourhood, the availability of a support network within walking distance and the situation in which the need for neighbourly contacts is actually fulfilled often go together. The opposite situation is also true, as the three forms of environmental isolation are equally inter-related in neighbourhoods that received lower marks: in neighbourhoods with low assessments one can find more residents that do have a need for neighbourly contacts but do not actually have them, and more residents lack a support network within walking distance. However, the relation is not that large that we can limit ourselves to one of the three indicators of environmental isolation. The relation between the three forms of environmental isolation does not have that much of a link with certain resident characteristics either, like socio-economic status, ethnicity or health status. The mental health of residents (see also Sections 7.8 and 7.9) relates most closely to environmental isolation. People with mental health problems often do not have a support network within walking distance, and are less likely to belong to the category of residents who have been able to actually realize their need for neighbourly contacts. They also tend to give their neighbourhood a lower report mark. It would be in the interest of mentally vulnerable individuals to live in a neighbourhood in which their need for neighbourly contacts is reflected in actual such contacts. When they are in that situation, only 16 per cent of them give a 5 or lower to the neighbourhood. If they do not succeed in meeting their need for neighbourly contacts, as many as 40 per cent give a low assessment to their neighbourhood.

Still, the predominant picture is that the three forms of environmental isolation stand pretty much on their own, and are influenced only to a very limited degree by many background characteristics, such as sex, age, marital status, socio-economic position, ethnicity and health. This still does not tell us whether our three forms of environmental isolation are related primarily to specific living preferences or to a characteristic of the social climate that brings about environmental isolation in residents.

9.3.5 Environmental isolation and the homogeneity of the neighbourhood

A factor that could be related to all three forms of environmental isolation is the *homogeneity of the neighbourhood*. To get an impression of the homogeneity of the neighbourhood, we measured the homogeneity of opinions on life and behaviour. We presented our respondents with the following six propositions:

1 People in my neighbourhood are living just like me.
2 People have the same opinions about raising kids as me.
3 All residents of this neighbourhood believe everyone has to keep their garden and doorway clean.

4   All residents of this neighbourhood are of the opinion that you cannot cause inconveniences to people in the neighbourhood.
5   Too many different types of people are settling in this neighbourhood.
6   Some times I feel threatened in my neighbourhood.

The question is whether shared values, manners and visible behaviour are more important to the enjoyment of one's living conditions than actual relationships and activities with other residents. Of all the respondents, 54 per cent say there is little homogeneity in their neighbourhood, while 46 per cent say they live among like-minded people. The research data show that the influence of such a homogeneous social environment on the three distinguished forms of environmental isolation is considerable. Nearly all respondents (93 per cent) in neighbourhoods where views on life are very homogeneous say that they have a need for neighbourly contacts and actually have them. In the very heterogeneous neighbourhoods this drops to 57 per cent (see Table 9.1).

Very heterogeneous neighbourhoods have four times as many residents (16 per cent against 4 per cent) without a support network within walking distance compared with homogeneous neighbourhoods (see Table 9.2).

The report mark for the assessment of the neighbourhood – understood as an indicator of the degree to which residents identify positively or negatively with their neighbourhood – is influenced by the degree of homogeneity in views on life and neighbourly behaviour (Table 9.3). There are very few respondents in homogeneous neighbourhoods that assess their neighbourhood with an unsatisfactory mark or a 6 (respectively 3 per cent and 9 per cent). In very heterogeneous neighbourhoods, by contrast, almost half of the respondents give a low assessment mark (respectively 26 per cent and 22

Table 9.1 Neighbourhood homogeneity according to desire for contacts and actual contacts, in percentages (N = 2,119)

Desire for contacts/ actual contacts	Neighbourhood homogeneity					
	Very heterogeneous	Heterogeneous	Neutral	Homogeneous	Very homogeneous	Total
Contact+ desire−	18	8	6	2	2	7
Contact− desire−	20	20	14	8	4	14
Contact+ desire+	57	69	77	85	93	75
Contact− desire+	5	3	4	5	–	4

Notes
$Chi^2 = 190.23$; $P < 0.000$; $r = 0.23$.

Table 9.2 Existence/lack of neighbourhood-bound support network (practical and/or emotional) according to neighbourhood homogeneity, in percentages (N = 2,438)

Neighbourhood-bound network	Neighbourhood homogeneity					
	Very heterogeneous	Heterogeneous	Neutral	Homogeneous	Very homogeneous	Total
Existing support network within walking distance	16	11	9	6	4	9
No support network within walking distance	84	89	92	94	96	91

Notes
Chi^2 = 45.03; $P < 0.000$; r = 0.13.

Table 9.3 Neighbourhood appreciation according to neighbourhood homogeneity, in percentages (N = 2,406)

Appreciation of neighbourhood	Neighbourhood homogeneity					
	Very heterogeneous	Heterogeneous	Neutral	Homogeneous	Very homogeneous	Total
(Very) unsatisfactory <5	26	11	7	5	3	11
Satisfactory 6	22	19	18	9	9	16
Very satisfactory/good 7	49	66	68	75	74	66
Very good 8>	3	4	8	11	14	7

Notes
Chi^2 = 255.03; $P < 0.000$; r = 0.30.

per cent). When a neighbourhood is seen by people as homogeneous, they seem to experience less nuisance and feel less unsafe.

We come to the conclusion that the three forms of environmental isolation we distinguished can be partially derived into different living preferences of individual residents, but that they can also be the result of a socially heterogeneous living environment. Not everybody has a need for neighbourly contacts, and we cannot claim that every resident who lacks a support network within walking distance misses that support as such. The third form of environmental isolation — a negative identification with the neighbourhood — can be related to physical as well as social neighbourhood characteristics. The degree of homogeneity of views on life also plays a role in the degree to which environmental isolation exists. Respondents who indicate they do not want contacts in the neighbourhood are reacting mostly to the heterogeneous environment they live in, and less because of a real preference issue. A support network within walking distance is very useful in many cases, even for people who have all kinds of support. Homogeneous neighbourhoods almost always procure such support networks within walking distance. And as attractive as heterogeneous neighbourhoods may be in terms of other characteristics – e.g. physically or spatially – chances of a low assessment of such neighbourhoods seem to be much greater than for a neighbourhood that is homogeneous in terms of views on life and neighbourly behaviour.

9.4 Environmental and social isolation

In the eyes of our respondents, satisfactory living conditions are not only an important aspect of a satisfactory life: almost three-quarters believe that it constitutes a protection against loneliness and social isolation. Still, in our analysis of environmental isolation up to now we have made a point of not mentioning social isolation. At first glance there was no reason for it, because in Section 9.2.1 we saw that residents who indicate having no need for neighbourly contacts attach as much value to social contacts in general. They have preferences in which neighbourly contacts do not take an important place. However, in Section 9.3 we also observed that the lack of a need for neighbourly contacts can also be a reaction to a living environment that is more heterogeneous in its views on life. For this reason, it would be good to explore more deeply the question of whether such a situation may lead to more social isolation in the lives of residents, in the meaning we gave it in Chapter 3. But first we will look at an eventual direct relation between environmental and social isolation.

9.4.1 *The relation between environmental and social isolation*

Before looking at the connection between environmental and social isolation, let us review the social contacts typology presented in Section 4.3.

According to this typology, about two-thirds of the respondents (64 per cent) can be considered to be socially competent, meaning that they have wide social networks that function adequately and have no feelings of loneliness. The rest of the respondents belong to one of the two high-risk groups for social isolation or is already socially isolated. Among them, the lonely form the largest group, at 22 per cent; they may have many contacts, but feel lonely nonetheless because the support in the network is insufficient or ineffective. The socially inhibited and the socially isolated comprise respectively 8 per cent and 6 per cent of the total respondents group. The socially inhibited experience their limited contacts as sufficient because these meet their social needs; they do not feel lonely. The socially isolated have a small network with few contacts, and in contrast to the socially inhibited must deal with strong feelings of loneliness.

A first indication of a relation between environmental isolation and social isolation in a more general sense can be detected in the answers our respondents give to the question of whether they feel they can count on their own social environment if they need help. For respondents who meet the indicators for our distinguished forms of environmental isolation, that feeling is less common. Of the large group of respondents whose need for neighbourly contacts corresponds with actually having such contacts, nearly everyone had the feeling that they could count on their environment if they needed help (70 per cent knew that for sure and only 9 per cent responded negatively). For the respondents who do have a need for neighbourly contacts but who do without them, the situation is completely different: only 39 per cent know it for sure and 30 per cent do not think so. Residents who have a neighbourhood-bound support network obviously also have more of a feeling that they can count on their social contacts. The same goes for residents with a positive neighbourhood identification. The tendency of residents themselves to provide support, for example, when suspecting social isolation of a fellow resident (see Section 5.8.3), is also greater in situations in which there is less environmental isolation. This suggests that neighbourhoods in which people indicate being environmentally isolated more frequently, not only is the mutual support of residents not as substantial but the chances of there being socially isolated residents is greater too. Environmental and social isolation (in the sense of the social contacts typology presented in Section 3.3) do not really go together, but a certain relation can surely be observed. Hence the lonely and the socially isolated are over-represented, and the socially inhibited and the socially competent are under-represented among those who do need neighbourly contacts but have not been able to realize this (Table 9.4).

Among residents who say they do not have a neighbourhood-bound support network we find more socially inhibited people and, again, more socially isolated individuals (Table 9.5).

In this form of environmental isolation too – a negative identification with the neighbourhood – there is a relationship with social isolation (Table 9.6). The socially isolated, the lonely and the socially inhibited tend to live in

172 Roelof Hortulanus

Table 9.4 Social contact typology according to environmental isolation (combination of desire for contacts/actual contacts), in percentages (N = 2,075)

Social contact typology	Environmental isolation				
	Contact + Desire −	Contact − Desire −	Contact + Desire +	Contact − Desire +	Total
Socially competent	60	49	68	41	64
Socially inhibited	9	11	7	7	8
Lonely	19	28	20	37	22
Socially isolated	13	12	5	16	7

Notes
$Chi^2 = 82.31; P < 0.000; r = -0.07$.

Table 9.5 Social contact typology according to environmental isolation (neighbourhood-bound support network), in percentages (N = 2,401)

Social contact typology	Environmental isolation		
	No existing support network within walking distance	Existing support network within walking distance	Total
Socially competent	45	66	64
Socially inhibited	17	7	8
Lonely	24	22	22
Socially isolated	14	5	6

Notes
$Chi^2 = 67.63; P < 0.000; r = -12$

Table 9.6 Social contact typology according to environmental isolation (neighbourhood report mark), in percentages (N = 2,361)

Social contact typology	Environmental isolation				
	(Very) unsatisfactory <5	Satisfactory 6	Very satisfactory/ good 7	Very good 8>	Total
Socially competent	50	58	68	71	65
Socially inhibited	10	8	7	8	8
Lonely	31	25	20	19	22
Socially isolated	8	9	5	2	6

Notes
$Chi^2 = 42.92; P < 0.000; r = -0.13$.

Social environment and social isolation 173

neighbourhoods with lower report marks. In neighbourhoods assessed as 'very good' we do not find many socially isolated individuals.

Despite the clear relation between the three forms of environmental isolation and social isolation, this link is not so significant that one should consider identifying them with one another. Whether there are homogeneous or heterogeneous neighbourhoods in the eyes of the respondents may, however, make some difference for the observed connection.

9.4.2 *The role of homogeneity*

In Section 9.3.5 we observed that the degree of neighbourhood homogeneity is one of the few factors that are relevant to all three forms of environmental isolation. The question now is whether this observed connection between environmental and social isolation in homogeneous neighbourhoods means the same as in heterogeneous neighbourhoods. If we start by concentrating on the residents who indicate having a need for neighbourly contacts but do not actually have them, then living in a homogeneous or a heterogeneous environment makes a huge difference (Tables 9.7 and 9.8).

Table 9.7 Social contact typology according to environmental isolation (combination of desire for contacts/actual contacts) in *very heterogeneous* neighbourhoods, in percentages (N = 400)

Social contact typology	Environmental isolation				
	Contact + Desire −	Contact − Desire −	Contact + Desire +	Contact − Desire +	Total
Socially competent	52	48	60	41	55
Socially inhibited	15	11	11	9	11
Lonely	21	26	21	23	22
Socially isolated	13	15	8	27	11

Table 9.8 Social contact typology according to environmental isolation (combination of desire for contacts/actual contacts) in *very homogeneous* neighbourhoods, in percentages (N = 697)

Social contact typology	Environmental isolation				
	Contact + Desire −	Contact − Desire −	Contact + Desire +	Contact − Desire +	Total
Socially competent	67	53	72	59	70
Socially inhibited	7	11	6	0	6
Lonely	13	30	19	36	20
Socially isolated	13	6	3	5	3

Respondents who suffer from environmental isolation (in the sense that people do have a need for social contacts but do not actually have them) and social isolation can be found much more often in heterogeneous neighbourhoods (as many as 27 per cent of the environmentally isolated are also socially isolated in such neighbourhoods). In homogeneous neighbourhoods this is only 5 per cent. The socially inhibited are better off in homogeneous neighbourhoods, because among the environmentally isolated no socially inhibited people can be found in such neighbourhoods. Just like the socially isolated, they have difficulty establishing contacts, but apparently this is somewhat easier in homogeneous neighbourhoods than in heterogeneous neighbourhoods. The opposite applies to the lonely. Lonely people among the environmentally isolated can be found more often precisely in homogeneous neighbourhoods; they do not lack social contacts, but feel very lonely anyway, and that feeling is more pervasive in a social environment in which the feeling of mutual solidarity is greater. The socially competent do justice to their name. To them it doesn't make a difference whether they live in homogeneous or heterogeneous neighbourhoods. They are under-represented in both types of neighbourhoods among the environmentally isolated.

If we assume that our social contact typology particularly influences the relationship patterns people have in their neighbourhood, the differences become smaller when we compare homogeneous and heterogeneous neighbourhoods. It doesn't seem to make so much of a difference whether we are dealing with socially isolated people, lonely people, the socially inhibited or the socially competent. Living in homogeneous neighbourhoods produces less environmental isolation for all four categories. In homogeneous neighbourhoods, for instance, as many as 75 per cent of the socially isolated are in a situation in which their need for neighbourly contacts corresponds with actually having these contacts. In heterogeneous neighbourhoods only 40 per cent of the socially isolated is in such a situation.

With respect to having a support network within walking distance and the degree of neighbourhood identification (two other criteria of environmental isolation), the socially competent, the socially inhibited, the lonely and the socially isolated benefit equally from a homogeneous neighbourhood. This confirms that the degree of homogeneity of neighbourhoods does not influence the existence or absence of social isolation directly. It is, however, relevant to preference patterns relating to neighbourly contacts and an eventually ensuing environmental isolation. Along these lines, the degree of homogeneity does influence social isolation, because all the forms of environmental isolation we distinguished are accompanied more often by social isolation in heterogeneous neighbourhoods.

9.5 Conclusions

In this chapter we distinguished three forms of environmental isolation: a mismatch between the need for neighbourly contacts and the actual existence of such contacts, the lack of a support network within walking distance of one's home, and a negative identification with the neighbourhood (indicated by the report mark for the living environment). A common factor that seems to be connected to these three forms of environmental isolation concerns the degree of homogeneity in terms of views on neighbourhood life and neighbourhood social behaviour. All three forms of environmental isolation are more common in heterogeneous neighbourhoods.

Environmental isolation is not the same as social isolation. Most people who are environmentally isolated are not necessarily socially isolated. There is nonetheless a specific connection between environmental and social isolation, and the degree of homogeneity plays a role in it. It is mostly in heterogeneous neighbourhoods that a higher-than-average number of socially isolated people can be found among the environmentally isolated. This is not the case in homogeneous neighbourhoods. In such neighbourhoods the environmental isolation is lower among the socially isolated as well as among the lonely, the socially inhibited and the socially competent.

Part III

Comparisons and differentiation

10 Social isolation in city and countryside

Anja Machielse

10.1 Introduction

Social isolation is often associated with city life. The assumption is that residents of rural areas are less likely to be lonely or socially isolated than city dwellers. Allegedly, villages have a strong sense of community, family ties are stronger, and societal participation and involvement are more self-evident than in the cities. For this reason, in this chapter we focus on the comparison between city and countryside. We look first at the composition of the population in urban and non-urban areas as this can have consequences for interaction patterns and social neighbourhoods. The presumption is that the possibilities for enduring social contacts are greater as people in the immediate vicinity have more common characteristics and as they share more values, norms and manners (Section 10.3). The place where people live forms the spatial context for an important part of their social and societal activities. The question we raise here is whether an urban environment offers fewer possibilities for social and societal participation than more small-scale rural environments. We will then compare the social neighbourhoods of residents of urban and non-urban areas (Section 10.4), various forms of societal participation (Section 10.5) and the orientation towards the social environment (Section 10.6). We will finish with the main conclusions (Section 10.7).

10.2 Relevant concepts and definitions

Differences between city and countryside have been the subject of social science studies since the nineteenth century. In particular, much has been written about the differences in *social environment*. These differences are supposed to accompany the modernization process in the western world. Ferdinand Tönnies (1855–1936) describes the development of traditional society into modern urban society as the transition into a new type of social alliance. He sees traditional society as a *Gemeinschaft* with emotional social bonds in which traditions, feelings of solidarity and unity play an important role. By contrast, he typifies modern society as a *Gesellschaft* in which relationships between people are entered into mainly in order to achieve a certain goal. It is not tradition and feelings but efficiency and functionality which are central here (Tönnies, 1887). This dichotomy between *Gemeinschaft* and *Gesellschaft* has long served as a model for the differences between city and countryside, in which the harmony and sense of community of small, surveyable village society is compared with the more individualistic lifestyle of the city (Van der Loo, 1996).

In the first half of the twentieth century, several social scientists elaborated further on this contrast. Louis Wirth (1897–1952) describes urban culture and its effect on social relationship patterns. He sees the stable, close community in cities as having been replaced by a heterogeneity of immigrants and newcomers, whereas the countryside is still characterized by communities with a more traditional character and tight-knit social structure. Because of the size of cities, it is impossible to know all residents personally, for which reason urbanites generally deal with each other only in functional capacities (Wirth, 1938).

In recent decades, it has mainly been sociologists and anthropologists who in the context of 'community studies' have determined that the changes in the social environment of city and countryside have not been equal, as a result of which cities represent a more modern part of society than the countryside. The assumption is that modernization and individualization in urban areas have made further progress than in non-urban areas, and that the mutual involvement that was characteristic of traditional society can only be found in the countryside nowadays.

The differences between city and countryside are becoming increasingly blurred. All kinds of developments in western countries have resulted in characteristics of urban culture and lifestyle having spread to the entire society. Individualization, expansion, technological developments and greater geographical mobility have caused rural areas to become increasingly urbanized and social contacts of villagers to be less bound to the neighbourhood or local community than they used to be. The question is, then, to what degree does the social climate in urban areas differ from that in non-urban areas in modern western society.

The profiling of the research locations into urban and rural areas is based on the *urbanization measure* used by Statistics Netherlands (CBS, 1992). This measure is defined as the average number of addresses in the surroundings of a location (the average address density within a circle within a 1 km radius). In this way the concentration of human activities in a specific geographical area is shown. For the classification into urbanization, the numeric values of the surrounding's address density for the separate Dutch municipalities were categorized into five classes, with class 1 as the highest degree of urbanization and class 5 applying to the non-urban municipalities. According to this measure, two of the four research locations (Amsterdam and Utrecht) are very strongly urban municipalities with a surroundings' address density of 2,500 addresses or more per square kilometre (class 1). The other two research locations (Binnenmaas and the separate municipalities of Het Oldambt) belong to the category with the lowest degree of urbanization, being non-urban municipalities with a surroundings' address density of less than 500 addresses per square kilometre (class 5) (see Section 1.6). On the basis of the CBS measure, in this chapter we designate Amsterdam and Utrecht as urban areas, and Binnenmaas and Het Oldambt as non-urban areas.

Most of the measures and scales used for the analyses in this chapter have been described in previous chapters. Here we will briefly review some important measures. The social networks of village and city dwellers are described on the basis of the *typology for social contacts* as presented in Chapter 3. According to this typology, about two-thirds of the respondents (64 per cent) are considered to be socially competent, meaning that they have a vast social network that functions adequately and are not bothered by feelings of loneliness. The rest of the respondents belong to one of the two groups at high risk of social isolation or is already socially isolated. The lonely, at 22 per cent, form the largest high-risk group; they may have many contacts but feel nonetheless lonely because the support in the network is insufficient or ineffective. The socially inhibited and the socially isolated make up respectively 8 per cent and 6 per cent of the total respondents group. The socially inhibited only have a few contacts, but they experience them as sufficient because they meet their social needs, and so they do not feel lonely. The socially isolated have a small network with few contacts, and in contrast to the socially inhibited have to deal with strong feelings of loneliness.

Another measure that is important when comparing city and village dwellers is the *measure of environmental isolation* as described in Section 9.4.1, characterized in terms of a mismatch between the need for contacts and de factual social contacts in the neighbourhood. Here four groups are distinguished: residents who have no need for social contacts in their neighbourhood and do not have them (14 per cent), residents who do have these contacts but do not really feel a need for them (7 per cent), people who do need contacts in their neighbourhood and also have them (75 per cent), and residents who indicate they find contacts in their neighbourhood very important but have not realized them (4 per cent). We designate this last group of residents as environmentally isolated.

To get a complete impression of attitudes towards the living environment, we have developed a scale for *local social orientation*. This scale is based on the following six factors that indicate a positive attitude towards the social environment in a person's current neighbourhood or town.

1   They have many contacts in the direct vicinity.
2   They attach great importance to these neighbourly contacts.
3   They do common activities regularly with their fellow residents.
4   They are not planning to move within the next two years.
5   They chose their current living environment because they grew up

182 *Anja Machielse*

there, because their family and friends live there, or because they have good contacts with other neighbourhood residents.

6   They stay in their current town out of their own choice, because they do not want to be away from family, friends and neighbours, or because they like the neighbourhood residents.

Each factor applies to all locations and is worth one point. There is a strong local orientation when residents meet at least four of the six conditions (score 4, 5 or 6). Persons with a score of 0 to 1 have a weak local social orientation. Persons scoring 2 or 3 have an average local social orientation.

The results presented in this chapter are based largely on data from about 2,400 respondents who were surveyed in the first research phase (see Section 1.7). When the results relate to a smaller group, it is mentioned expressly. We worked with two *weighing factors* in the analyses of this chapter. In one research location (Het Oldambt) a weighing was adjusted for age, given that the number of seniors in the sample was clearly over-represented. In another research location (Utrecht) a weighing was adjusted for sex because women were under-represented (for representativeness of the study group, see Section 1.7). The remaining deviations between respondent groups and population of the respective research locations gave no reason for weighing. Due to the weighing of these two aspects, the N number deviates from the actual number of respondents (N = 2,493 instead of N = 2,410). This can make the percentages in this chapter vary slightly from the data in the previous chapters.

10.3 Population composition of urban and rural areas

10.3.1 Demographic factors

Given that the population composition in an area influences the interaction patterns and social networks of people, we will start by looking at some important demographic differences between urban and non-urban areas. These differences go together with three social developments: ageing, individualization and increasing migration.

Ageing is visible mainly in rural areas. When we look at the *age distribution* of respondents, we see that the average age of the respondents in the non-urban locations is significantly higher than in the urban research locations; the average age in cities and villages is respectively 42.1 years [std. 17.1] and 46.9 years [std. 17.5]. Still, the number of people sixty-five and older in the villages is not that much higher (18 per cent) than in the cities (15 per cent). The higher average age in the villages is explained chiefly by the small share of young people that live there.

Shifts that have taken place in recent decades under the influence of individualization are especially perceptible in cities. If we look at the *living situ-*

ation and *marital status* of respondents, we see that the share of single people in the cities is more than three times higher than in the villages (37 per cent versus 11 per cent). Furthermore, the ratio of single and divorced people is about twice as large as in non-urban areas (respectively 47 per cent and 10 per cent against 18 per cent and 4 per cent). These last figures also explain the high number of lone-parent families in the cities (5 per cent versus 2 per cent).

Changes in population composition due to the arrival of *migrants* are also seen particularly in the urban areas. Nearly one-fifth of the urbanites were not born in the Netherlands (19 per cent), whereas it is mainly the native Dutch who live in the non-urban areas, where the share of migrants is only 3 per cent.

10.3.2 Socio-economic factors

Besides the demographic factors we also compared several socio-economic factors of the inhabitants of the urban and non-urban locations, namely work situation, educational level and income. If we look at the work situation of inhabitants of the city and rural areas, we see that the share of employed people in the cities is higher than that in the villages, but that the differences are minimal. The cities, however, do have higher numbers of labour disabled and unemployed individuals (respectively 10 per cent and 9 per cent versus 6 per cent and 3 per cent in the villages).

Income position and educational level show a clear relation with urbanization, although cities and villages each differentiate in another direction. The number of people with a high educational level is about twice as high in the cities as in the non-urban areas (24 per cent versus 11 per cent). The differences in educational level are especially large among youth. Of the urbanites under the age of thirty, 27 per cent have a higher educational level as against only 6 per cent of their peers in the villages. Among urbanites between ages thirty and forty-five, the number of highly educated individuals is twice as high (36 per cent) as in the villages (17 per cent). Among residents of forty-five and older there are hardly any differences in educational level between city and village dwellers. The differences are largely related to the fact that cities have many institutions of higher education.

The cities showed considerably more people with low incomes than the villages; this applies to all age categories. Although the average income in the villages is somewhat higher than in the cities, we also observed that the differences among village dwellers are much larger than among city dwellers.

To conclude, we can state that there are a number of significant differences in the population composition of cities and rural areas. Cities host proportionately more youth, singles and divorced people than villages, and the number of lone-parent families is also larger in the cities. Cities also have a higher percentage of labour disabled and unemployed individuals, but more

184 *Anja Machielse*

highly-educated young people. Finally, migrants rarely live in the rural areas – they make up a substantial portion of the population in the cities.

10.4 Personal networks

10.4.1 Scope, composition and experience

In Chapter 3 we saw that the network of the respondents, including their partner, consists on average of almost eight persons [X 7.78, std. 2.98, min. 1, max. 22]. The number of persons people can appeal to for concrete forms of support is generally slightly smaller. The average number of people that is mentioned to give practical, emotional and companionship support is slightly more than six [X 6.16, std. 2.29, min. 0, max. 16] (see also Section 3.4). The average scope of the total personal network and the average scope of the support network do not show any strong relations with the urbanization degree of the residential location. Still, there are significant differences between the networks of village and city dwellers. In the cities we find considerably more residents with a small network than in the villages: while 6 per cent of the village dwellers have a small network of no more than four persons, the same applies to 22 per cent of the city dwellers. City dwellers also have a greater tendency to have a small support network (32 per cent) than villagers (16 per cent) (respectively $r = -0.17$ and $r = -0.18$). For this reason, in the cities we find more people who have no form of support whatsoever in their vicinity. Table 10.1 shows how many people have no one in their network for practical, emotional and companionship support (see also Section 3.8).

Table 10.1 Number of respondents who cannot count on anyone for specific forms of support in city and countryside, in percentages (N = 2,478)

	City	Countryside	Total
Practical support			
Help in or around the house**	8	4	6
Water plants and get mail during vacations	8	5	6
Emotional support			
Talking about personal problems	7	5	6
Advice on major changes**	12	9	10
Companionship support			
Visiting someone or receiving visitors**	8	5	6
Shopping or going out together*	11	6	9

Notes
*$P < 0.05$ (correlation of urbanization degree with shopping/going out together $r = -0.05$), **$P < 0.01$ (correlation of urbanization degree with talking about changes $r = 0.10$, visiting someone $r = -0.07$, help around the house $r = -0.07$).

Urbanites have to live more often without any form of support than village dwellers: 6 per cent of them have no practical, emotional or social support, and that percentage is three times as high as that of villagers (2 per cent). They lack someone for practical support (2 per cent versus 1 per cent), social support (2 per cent versus 1 per cent) and emotional support (3 per cent versus 2 per cent) more often.

Given that this only says something about the *potential* support that people expect from their personal network, we also examined how things stand with the *actual* support that people receive from others in their daily life. To get an impression of this, respondents were asked whether and how often they received help from someone in one or more fields in the last year (see also Section 3.9). This involves help from people *outside* one's household; help from live-in partners, children or parents is therefore not counted. If we look at the total respondents group, we see that most village dwellers (85 per cent) occasionally receive concrete help from people in their direct surroundings, compared with only one-third of the urbanites (39 per cent). Urbanites who receive help from their direct surroundings can count on several sorts of help though, whereas this is much less the case for villagers. It is noteworthy that urbanites indicate more often (41 per cent) than village dwellers (24 per cent) that someone outside the household has cared for them during illness. In most cases this involves *incidental* help; a smaller percentage of the urbanites (9 per cent) has received such help often, but that percentage too is significantly higher than for the villagers (6 per cent). And if we take into consideration the presence or absence of a partner, the differences remain. Given that care during illness is a form of support that presumes a closer contact than the other types of help, this is a remarkable finding.

Besides the support that people can get from their network, the composition of the network is also interesting. Keeping an eye out for differences between city and countryside, the question into the share of family members is especially interesting (Table 10.2).

The research data shows that villagers indeed have more family-bound contacts than urbanites; for one-fifth of urbanites, more than three-quarters of the social network consists of non-family-bound contacts, and that is considerably more than in the villages. Because more individuals without a partner live in cities and the presence or absence of a partner can influence the number of family members in the personal network, we compared persons with and without a partner. We observed that persons without a partner indeed have less family-bound contacts than persons with a partner, but the number of urbanites with a non-familial network is still higher. When we only look at the number of close relatives (partner, parents, children, siblings), the differences are even slightly higher. In the cities, the number of people who have a network with few close family members is almost twice as large (30 per cent) as in the villages (17 per cent). Here too this appears to be the case for persons with and without a partner.

Table 10.2 Share of family members in city and countryside, in percentages (N = 2,459)

	City	Countryside	Total
*Share of family members***			
Predominantly not family-bound	17	6	12
Mixed	65	72	68
Predominantly family-bound	18	22	20
*Share of close relatives***			
Predominantly not family-bound	30	17	24
Mixed	58	69	63
Predominantly family-bound	12	14	13

Notes
**$P < 0.01$ (correlation of urbanization degree with family members $r = -0.13$, close family $r = -0.14$).

To get a global impression of the satisfaction with their network, we asked people to give a general assessment of their contacts with others in the form of a report mark. In Chapter 3 we saw that the average assessment that people give for the quality of their social network is well over seven [X 7.3; std. 1.2] (see also Section 3.5). The average assessment of city and village dwellers does not deviate from this. Villagers, however, are more unanimous in their assessment [std. 1.02] than urbanites [std. 1.5]. Almost half of the villagers give a seven, whereas there are more high and low peaks among the urbanites (52 per cent give an 8 or higher, 9 per cent less than a 6). Urbanites give unsatisfactory marks almost twice as often (9 per cent) as villagers (5 per cent). Hence the city hosts relatively more people who experience their network as very negative. It is therefore not surprising that there is a strong relation between urbanization and feelings of loneliness. At 34 per cent, the number of residents who feel lonely is considerably higher in the cities than in the rural areas (22 per cent). When we look at the average score on the loneliness scale (X 1.9; std. 2.54) (see Section 3.6), we see that the villagers with their average score of 1.5 [std. 2.1] remain far below, whereas the average score of the urbanites stands far above this at 2.3 [std. 2.8]. City dwellers indicate twice as often as village dwellers that they miss having a good friend or girlfriend (14 per cent versus 7 per cent), that they miss people around them (12 per cent versus 6 per cent), or that they find their circle of acquaintances too limited (15 per cent versus 9 per cent). And thus in the assessment of the networks we see again the differences between their scope and composition.

10.4.2 The social contacts typology

The social network of urbanites is generally less large than that of villagers. In addition, urbanites tend to experience their social network more nega-

Table 10.3 Social typology for city and countryside, in percentages (N = 2,359)

	City	Countryside	Total
Socially competent**	54	75	64
Socially inhibited	12	3	8
Lonely	24	20	22
Socially isolated	10	2	6

Notes
**$P < 0.01$; $r = 0.21$.

tively and have to deal with more feelings of loneliness than villagers. There is also a significant connection between degree of urbanization and risk of social isolation (Table 10.3).

The number of socially competent people is considerably higher in the villages than in the cities. The other three contact groups are more common in the cities. Upon closer examination of the group of the lonely and the socially isolated, we see that the composition of these high-risk groups in the urban and non-urban areas differs slightly. Urban singles are more often among the socially competent than rural singles. This could be an indication that being alone is more accepted in cities or that it is a more conscious choice than in the villages. It is also remarkable that the cities have more families belonging to the high-risk groups. Age and sex do not make a difference; in both city and village we find relatively as many socially inhibited, lonely and socially isolated people among men and women and in the different age categories.

We can summarize by stating that the social network of city dwellers is generally less favourable than that of village dwellers. Although the average scope of the network does not differ that much, we find more extremes in the cities, in a negative as well as a positive sense. This means that cities have relatively more people who are worse-off because they have a small network and lack potential sources of support. The large variation within the cities is also evident from the fact that only a small group of city dwellers get practical help from others, whereas most of them have to do without such help. In the villages, most people do get one form or other of help from others. Urbanites also experience their social network more negatively and deal with more feelings of loneliness than villagers.

10.5 Societal participation

10.5.1 Labour participation

In Section 10.3.2 we saw that there is no clear relation between labour participation and degree of urbanization. There are, however, significant differences between cities and villages in terms of specification of the jobless:

188 *Anja Machielse*

cities have more labour disabled and jobless individuals than villages (respectively 10 per cent and 9 per cent versus 6 per cent and 3 per cent). Against the expectation, the number of retired people in the villages is not much higher than in the cities (33 per cent versus 28 per cent).

When we consider how people spend their free time *next to or instead of paid work*, we see major differences between city and village dwellers. In the villages, 40 per cent of residents mention the household as the most important way to spend their time, as against only 27 per cent of urbanites. Of course, the fact that more families live in the villages plays a role here, but this can only explain the difference partially. Among the villagers without children, 31 per cent also mention the household as their main way of spending time, compared with 23 per cent of urbanites without children. The number of students, as expected, is much higher in the cities (15 per cent) than in the villages (8 per cent). It is remarkable that 24 per cent of the villagers mentioned a hobby or a sport as their most important occupation, compared with only 3 per cent of the urbanites.

10.5.2 Volunteer work

We found no strong correlation between urbanization degree and volunteer work (r = −0.06). The differences are related mainly to age and sex. In the villages, it is mainly people in the 30–65 age category who do volunteer work. We also see that in the villages there are more men who do volunteer work (41 per cent) than in the city (31 per cent). Villagers indicate more frequently that volunteer work is their main activity *next to* or *instead of* a paid job (respectively 8 per cent and 6 per cent), but this relation is not that strong either.

There are, however, differences in the *types of volunteer work* urbanites and villagers do. Villagers are more involved in the organization of social activities in the neighbourhood, like planning events, doing bar shifts in a community centre, or helping in the neighbourhood with chores and errand services. Villagers are also slightly more active in volunteer work for organizations and associations: one-third of the villagers does volunteer work for one or more organizations (33 per cent), as against 27 per cent of urbanites (r = −0.06). Volunteer work for a religious organization is also more common in the countryside; 14 per cent of villagers are active within a religious organization, as against 4 per cent of urbanites. Church activities take place in the villages among all age categories: for youth under thirty it is 7 per cent versus less than 2 per cent in the city. In the context of this study we are unable to say anything further about the time such forms of volunteer work consume.

10.5.3 Informal care

When defining informal care as *support that people give regularly to others outside their own household* (see Section 7.2), we see that providing informal care is more common among villagers than among urbanites. Most villagers provide informal care occasionally: they help people outside their own household with chores and running errands, offer help with problems, babysit, perform care tasks, etc. While 85 per cent of the villagers provide such forms of informal care once in a while for relatives or acquaintances, this figure is 38 per cent for the urbanites. The percentage of people who provide such informal care often is nearly twice as high in the villages (39 per cent) than in the cities (18 per cent).

If we examine who this informal help is given to, we see that villagers provide more help for family members, while urbanites tend to support mainly friends. Helping neighbours is about the same in cities and villages. Villagers and urbanites also differ in the *type* of help they provide. Villagers run errands for others more often, help more with chores and watch children and pets with more frequency. By contrast, urbanites take care more often of a sick person, and tend to offer more frequent help filling out forms, with personal problems, and with problems with an official agency or a third party. Those urbanites who do provide informal care tend to offer more types of help to others. Both men and women offer these types of help, although women are in the majority. In the villages there are more people of sixty-five and older who provide help to others than in the cities; 60 per cent of this age category provides one type or other of informal care, whereas this applies to only 26 per cent of seniors in the city.

10.5.4 *Club life and informal groups*

Another aspect of social participation is membership in clubs and being part of informal groups in which people undertake activities jointly (see also Section 8.2.1). The research data show that nearly all villagers are members of one or several clubs or organizations; only 0.1 per cent of the villagers is not a member of any association. In the cities that is about 3 per cent. When we look at the different types of organizations that people can be members of, we see that in all cases villagers score higher than urbanites. In the rural areas, about twice as many people are members of a religious organization (37 per cent) than in the cities (16 per cent). These data correspond with a high number of villagers that are active within a religious organization. More villagers are members of a political party than urbanites (9 per cent versus 4 per cent). The number of members of welfare agencies, help services or organizations like the Red Cross is twice as high in the villages (22 per cent) as in the cities (11 per cent). The fact that villagers are more involved in social activities in their own vicinity (13 per cent versus 7 per cent in the city) probably indicates a greater involvement and sense of community. Urbanites who do not participate much in club life often indicate as a reason that they cannot connect to the people in those organizations (17 per cent), that they are not familiar with the organizations (10 per cent), or that they find participation in such organizations too expensive (11 per cent). These reasons are almost never mentioned by villagers (respectively 3 per cent, 2 per cent and 2 per cent).

People do not always have to be members of a club to meet a specific group of people and do things together (see also Section 8.2.1). Upon looking at participation in informal groups, we see that village and city dwellers have such social meetings with others as often. What is interesting though is that the emphasis goes to different groups. Both villagers and urbanites focus mainly on relatives and friends. Next to that, villagers have more contact with people from the same religion, whereas urbanites socialize more with colleagues, fellow students and people with the same hobby. Urbanites and villagers do things as often with their neighbours or fellow neighbourhood residents. Most meetings take place at people's homes; more than half of the people visit each other (51 per cent); this applies to both city and village. In addition, urbanites meet each other more often in cafes and community centres, whereas villagers see each other more often at the sports club or the church they belong to. Participation in club life and informal groups has remained the same for most people in the last five years.

10.5.5 *Entertainment and the use of social and cultural facilities*

When we look at attendance for various places of entertainment, we see than villagers frequent museums, concerts, the theatre, movies, cafes and dance locales less often than urbanites. These findings should not be surprising, given that residents of rural areas have to leave their village for most of these facilities. The number of villagers and urbanites who never go to a place of entertainment is the same though (11 per cent). Most urbanites attend several of these places of entertainment regularly: 13 per cent even go to all, whereas only 1 per cent of villagers do. The differences in the entertainment behaviour of city and village dwellers are the largest among youth below the age of thirty. In the cities, 22 per cent of this group go to all the facilities, in the villages only 4 per cent (Table 10.4).

Villagers spend more time on sports. They attend more sporting events than urbanites and make more use of sports accommodations such as swimming pools and athletic fields. About a third of the villagers (34 per cent) visit a church, whereas only 19 per cent of urbanites do. Villagers are also visited more by someone from a church or ideological organization. The fact that the church plays a more important role in villages than in the cities is manifest in the large number of villagers active in a religious community.

10.5.6 *The measure of societal participation*

The differences in societal participation between villagers and urbanites is not expressed in *the measure of societal participation,* that differentiates four categories of increasing societal participation (very passive, passive, active and

Table 10.4 Use of facilities in city and countryside, in percentages (N = 2,395)

	City	Countryside	Total
Entertainment			
Museum**	49	39	44
Concert**	47	35	41
Theatre*	43	29	36
Movies*	58	34	46
Cafe**	63	40	52
Restaurant**	80	81	81
Dancing**	28	13	23
Religion			
Church/mosque**	19	34	24
Visits of other church members**	4	21	16
Sports			
Attending a sporting event**	31	47	38
Gym, athletic field, swimming pool**	48	61	52

Notes
*$P < 0.05$ (correlation with theatre $r = 0.15$); **$P < 0.01$ (correlation with museum $r = 0.10$, concert $r = 0.12$, theatre $r = 0.15$, movies $r = 0.26$, cafe $r = 0.27$, restaurant $r = 0.12$, dancing $r = 0.13$, church $r = -0.17$, home visits $r = -0.20$, sporting event $r = -0.16$, gym/swimming pool $r = -0.12$).

very active people, see also Section 8.2.1). This should not be surprising, given that the different types of social activities show a varied pattern: different elements score in the cities than in the villages. City dwellers make much more use of cultural facilities and places of entertainment, while village dwellers are more active in club life, and do volunteer work and provide informal care slightly more often. The degree of activity is almost the same for urban and non-urban areas, but in each case involves different social activities. The number of very active people in cities and villages is about the same. No general observations can be made about the other categories. There are, however, some differences that coincide for age. In the cities we see slightly more (very) active persons under age twenty-nine (88 per cent) than in the villages (82 per cent), while the number of (very) passive youth in the villages is a bit higher. Among urbanites in the thirty to forty-four age category, the number of very passive individuals is higher (3 per cent) than among villagers of the same category (1 per cent). The same applies for urbanites between ages forty-five and sixty-four: the number of very passive individuals in that group is more than twice as high (7 per cent) than in their peer villagers group (3 per cent). The share of very passive individuals is the highest among urbanites aged sixty-five and older (18 per cent against 10 per cent in the villages). The strong rise of the

192 Anja Machielse

number of very passive urbanites above age thirty has to do with the fact that the use of entertainment facilities – the most important form of social participation for urbanites – decreases strongly as people age. Whereas 95 per cent of the urbanites under thirty visit one or several places of entertainment regularly, only 61 per cent of those aged sixty-five or older do. The forms of social activity that villagers mostly engage in are much less related to age.

10.6 The social environment

10.6.1 Residential history and moving plans

The neighbourhood people live in forms the environmental context for an important part of their social and societal activities. In this section we will find out whether residents of villages are more involved in the social life of their own vicinity than urban residents.

A close bond with the social environment can only exist if people live somewhere for a longer period of time. Against this background, urban and rural areas are often typified on the basis of the *average residential history* of the residents of those areas. It is generally assumed that the social structure in villages is tighter because people live and stay there relatively longer than in cities. They are often born and raised in their village and thus have known each other their whole lives. The research data show that this line of reasoning falls short. Indeed, city and village dwellers have different reasons for living in their current town. About one-quarter of the villagers live in their current town because they grew up there, whereas this applies to only 8 per cent of the urbanites. Many villagers indicate they moved to their current town for work (19 per cent); only 2 per cent of urbanites gives this reason. Urbanites have ended up in their current vicinity mainly by coincidence or due to the allocation of a dwelling. They also seem less attached to their living environment, given that they have serious moving plans twice as often as villagers (respectively 21 per cent and 9 per cent). The moving plans are related chiefly to the suitability of the current dwelling; this applies to urbanites as well as to villagers. In addition, urbanites' plans are mainly motivated by dissatisfaction with the neighbourhood (4 per cent versus less than 1 per cent for villagers) and feelings of unsafety (4 per cent versus 1 per cent). Villagers indicate more often than urbanites that they are dissatisfied with the facilities in their vicinity (7 per cent against 1 per cent), that they want to live closer to their work (7 per cent versus 2 per cent), and that they want to move due to their age or health problems. More than 4 per cent of the villagers with moving plans mention as main reason that they want to live closer to family and friends (in the city this is 1 per cent).

Both urbanites and villagers who do not want to move indicate as main reason that they are satisfied with their dwelling (31 per cent in the city, 28 per cent in the villages). Villagers also indicate more often that they stay because they like the people in their vicinity (14 per cent against 8 per cent). The fact that they do not want to move away from their family or friends is an important argument for staying for 8 per cent of the villagers (against 5 per cent of the urbanites). For villagers, the quiet and greenery is another important reason to stay (9 per cent against 4 per cent of urbanites).

10.6.2 Neighbourly contacts and environmental isolation

To gain insight into the existence of contacts with neighbourhood residents and the importance that village and city dwellers attach to it, we presented respondents with several statements over the contacts in their own neighbourhood (Table 10.5) (see also Sections 10.2 and 10.3).

A pleasant living environment is important to most people, but there are major differences between urbanites and villagers. The latter have considerably more contacts with neighbourhood residents than urbanites. Whereas only 9 per cent of the villagers have no contact at all with neighbourhood residents, 22 per cent of urbanites do. Villagers not only have more actual contacts in their neighbourhood, they attach more value to it; only 14 per cent has no need whatsoever for neighbourly contacts, compared with more than a quarter of urbanites. The fact that villagers attach more value to contacts with neighbourhood residents is also evident from the fact that they do more things together. Most villagers know their fellow residents and talk regularly, many visit each other or do things together. This is less common among urbanites: they speak with each other less often, visit each other less and do not do as many things together. Borrowing things and taking care of each other's plants and animals is also more common in the villages than in

Table 10.5 Statements about contacts in the neighbourhood in city and countryside, in percentages (N = 2,374)

	City	Countryside	Total
I have many contacts with people in my neighbourhood**	42	69	56
I don't have any contacts in my neighbourhood**	22	9	15
I think good contacts with people in my neighbourhood are very important	72	88	80
I don't have any need whatsoever for any contact in my neighbourhood**	27	14	21
I don't search for friends in my neighbourhood**	50	31	43
A pleasant neighbourhood is very important to me	85	91	88

Notes
**$P<0.01$ (correlation with a lot of contact $r=-0.23$, no contact $r=0.20$, no need $r=0.16$, does not look for friends in neighbourhood $r=0.09$).

the city. Residents of villages also have more of a tendency to look for their friends in their own vicinity.

Not only seniors find neighbourly contacts important. Young villagers also have many contacts in the neighbourhood; among residents under thirty, 63 per cent have such contacts (against 27 per cent in the city). Urban youth find good contacts in the neighbourhood important, but do not look for friends in the neighbourhood per se. This is the case for nearly half of the villagers under thirty.

When we look at environmental isolation, defined as the discrepancy between the need for contacts in the neighbourhood and the actual existing contacts (see Section 9.4.1), we see a strong correlation between urbanization and environmental isolation ($r = -0.17$). In the city, the number of environmentally isolated individuals is significantly higher (32 per cent) than in the villages (20 per cent), that is, urbanites have more of a need for neighbourly contacts without actually realizing those contacts. In addition, the groups of environmentally isolated individuals are composed differently in the cities than in the villages. In the cities we find in this group twice as many young people under thirty (35 per cent) than in the villages (16 per cent). The environmentally isolated in the villages are generally older, most of them belonging to the 45–64 age category. Nearly half of the city dwellers is single (55 per cent), whereas two-thirds of the environmentally isolated in the villages have a partner (67 per cent).

10.6.3 Homogeneity and the social climate

It appears that in the city it is more difficult to realize contacts with neighbourhood residents than in the villages. This may be related to the greater heterogeneity in cities. In general, it is assumed that the city hosts more varied views on living together in a neighbourhood, and more competing lifestyles can be found next to one another (Van der Loo, 1996). To get a general idea of the homogeneity in the living environment of villages and cities, we presented respondents with several statements on living together with their own neighbourhood residents (Table 10.6). On a scale for the homogeneity of views on living and manners (see section 9.2), homogeneity in the villages is at 2.4 [std. 1.1] amply above the average of 1.9 [std. 1.2], while the average for the cities is 1.5 [std. 1.2]. The correlation between urbanization and homogeneity is a substantial ($r = -0.36$).

More than half of the villagers find that people in their vicinity live the same way they do; in the city, only one-third have this opinion. In the villages, more people tend to share the same views on raising children and on the fact that parents have to ensure that their children do not become a nuisance. Most villagers (87 per cent) also agree that you should not cause nuisances in the neighbourhood (57 per cent of the urbanites think this way too), and keeping one's doorstep or porch clean is more self-evident for villagers (85 per cent) than for urbanites (55 per cent). In the cities, 19 per

Table 10.6 Views on neighbourhood residents in city and countryside, in percentages (N = 2,374)

	City	Countryside	Total
People in my neighbourhood are living just like me**	33	53	43
People have the same opinions about raising kids as me**	25	34	30
All residents of this neighbourhood believe everyone has to keep their garden and doorway clean**	55	84	70
All residents of this neighbourhood are of the opinion that you cannot cause inconveniences to people in the neighbourhood**	57	87	73
Too many different types of people are settling in this neighbourhood**	27	20	24
Sometimes I feel threatened in my neighbourhood**	19	3	12

Notes
**$P < 0.01$ (correlation of urbanization with living like me $r = -0.13$, upbringing $r = -0.18$, porch/doorstep $r = -0.23$, nuisance $r = -0.17$, too many differences $r = -0.08$, threatened $r = 0.25$).

cent feel occasionally threatened in their own living environment; in the villages this is only 3 per cent. More than a quarter of the urbanites believe that too many types of different people have come to live in their vicinity, and 20 per cent of villagers share these feelings. Hence villagers indeed have more similar views and lifestyles, and are bothered less by each other than in the city. It should not be surprising, then, that almost three-quarters of the villagers (74 per cent) indicate wanting to spend their old age in their current town, whereas this applies to less than half of the urbanites (46 per cent). This can be seen in the report mark that village and city residents give to living in their neighbourhood. The average mark of villagers is a generous seven [X 7.5, std. 1.0] and that is precisely one point higher than the average six of the urbanites [X 6.5, std. 1.5]. More than half of the villagers give an eight, only 3 per cent give an unsatisfactory mark. Urbanites give an eight less often, and give more unsatisfactory marks and a six.

To conclude, we can state that the social aspects of the living environment are more important for villagers than for urbanites. Villagers have more contacts with residents and find these contacts very important. The contacts in the vicinity tend to be more intensive than the neighbourly contacts of urbanites; villagers visit each other more often and go out together more. Another important difference between city and village is that villagers

196 Anja Machielse

coincide much more on how they view life in the neighbourhood and are less bothered by nuisance from neighbours than urbanites.

10.6.4 Local social orientation

To what degree does living in a certain neighbourhood or town and the local social contacts constitute part of people's reference framework these days? Is it so that the social orientation of villagers goes mainly towards the local community they belong to, whereas urbanites emphasize more the social life outside their own local community? An important indicator of the degree to which residents are oriented towards the local society is an active attitude towards local social life, meaning that people are active in local associations and use local facilities. We have observed that most villagers participate actively in club life in their town, and that they do more volunteer work than urbanites. However, social orientation cannot be derived only from participation in local club life or the degree of volunteer work done. Aspects related to the living environment and local social contacts also play a role here. Table 10.7 gives an indication of the separate indicators that point to a positive attitude towards the social environment.

For all items it applies that villagers tend to be more positive than urbanites. Upon examining the score for local social orientation, we can observe

Table 10.7 Indicators for a positive attitude towards the social environment, in city and countryside, in percentages (N = 2,493)

	City	Countryside	Total
Has many contacts in the neighbourhood**	42	69	56
Finds good contacts in the neighbourhood very important**	72	88	80
Does things regularly with fellow neighbourhood residents**	32	52	42
Has no plans to move in the next two years**	57	78	67
Lives in the current neighbourhood/town because one grew up there, because family or friends live there, or because of the good contacts in the vicinity**	21	39	33
Wants to stay in current place due to conscious choice for this location, because one doesn't want to leave family, friends or neighbours, or because one likes the neighbourhood residents**	17	24	22

Notes
**$P < 0.01$ (correlation with many contacts $r = -0.23$, contacts important $r = -0.20$, active $r = -0.19$, moving plans $r = -0.23$, reasons for living there $r = -0.19$, reasons to stay there $r = -0.08$).

that the score of villagers is significantly higher than that of urbanites (Table 10.8). On a scale of 1 to 6, villagers score an average of 3.5 [std. 1.3], against an average score for urbanites of 2.5 [std. 1.5].

There is a significant relation between urbanization and the local social orientation of people. More than half of the villagers are strongly oriented towards the local environment, and this is more than twice as in the city. The share of urbanites with a low local social orientation is three times as high (28 per cent) as villagers (9 per cent). These data confirm the previously mentioned assumption that villagers – despite the social developments and the advancing urbanization of the countryside – are still more strongly oriented towards the local society than urbanites. Social aspects of the immediate living environment seem to play a larger role for villagers than for urbanites. In the context of this research it is interesting to know whether a strong orientation towards the local community protects people against loneliness and social isolation. The relation between the social contacts typology and the degree of social orientation can resolve this (Table 10.9).

It is clear that people with a strong local social orientation tend to be more socially competent than persons with a moderate or weak orientation towards the local community. As people's orientation towards the local community wanes, they tend to be part of the high-risk groups or the

Table 10.8 Local social orientation in city and countryside, in percentages (N = 1,834)

	City	Countryside	Total
Weak local social orientation**	28	9	15
Average local social orientation	47	38	41
Strong local social orientation	24	53	44

Notes
**$P < 0.01$; $r = -0.32$.

Table 10.9 The social contact typology and local social orientation, in percentages (N = 1,810)

	Weak local social orientation	Average local social orientation	Strong local social orientation	Average
Socially competent**	55	61	74	66
Socially inhibited	11	9	6	8
Lonely	22	21	17	19
Socially isolated	13	10	3	7

Notes
**$P < 0.01$; $r = -0.16$.

socially isolated. The number of socially isolated individuals is much higher among persons with a weak or moderate local social orientation. We also see more lonely and socially inhibited individuals as people are less oriented towards the local community. Hence the involvement with the social environment seems to be a good predictor of social isolation.

10.7 Summary and conclusions

In the preceding sections we made a comparison between the social networks, the societal participation and the social orientation of urban and non-urban respondents in this research project. Although the research locations are not completely representative of urban and non-urban communities in general, the research results offer sufficient options to make sound comparisons on several points. We arrived at the following conclusions.

First, we have observed that there are a number of significant differences in the population composition of cities and rural areas. Cities hold relatively more youth, singles and divorcees than the villages; the number of lone-parent families is also much larger in the cities. In addition, rural areas hardly deal with migrants, who make a substantial percentage of the urban population.

The social networks of urbanites are generally less favourable than those of villagers. The networks of villagers tend to be somewhat larger and more tight-knit that those of urbanites, and they are assessed more positively. Although the average network scope between city and countryside does not really differ, in the cities we find more residents with a small network and little or no support. The networks are also composed slightly differently. Villagers have more family-bound contacts in their network than urbanites. At the same time, we can observe that most urbanites do have a mixed or family-bound network. The networks of urbanites are, however, less stable and for them a drop in the number of contacts is at the expense of family members and fellow neighbourhood residents.

Although we find no strong relation between potential support and support actually received, more village residents receive concrete help from their immediate surroundings than city residents. The urbanites who do receive actual help, get it regularly and for different things. The assessment of the network also shows greater variation in the cities, where people tend to be more unsatisfied about the network than villagers. The low assessment can be seen in the large number of urbanites with feelings of loneliness. Although the differences in network scope between urbanites and villagers are not very large, the subjective element does seem to create differentiation.

There are also clear differences in societal participation between city and village dwellers. These differences are not really apparent in the total measure for societal participation though, because different aspects of participation are emphasized in city and village. The degree of activity is about the same for urban and non-urban areas, but in each case involves different societal activities.

The labour participation in cities and villages is nearly the same. There are however major differences in the specification of the unemployed. The number of labour disabled individuals in the cities is considerably higher than in the villages, as is the number of unemployed people. In addition, villages have more residents who name the household as the most important way of spending their time; this applies to families with and without children. In the city we find many more students.

Urbanites and villagers undertake approximately the same amount of volunteer work. There is, however, a large difference in the type of activities. Villagers are involved more often in the organization of social activities in their own neighbourhood, at the church, and with organizations and clubs in their own town.

Among villagers it is very common to provide informal care: most villagers help people outside their own household occasionally with chores, problems, babysitting, care tasks, etc. A significant proportion of them provide this help frequently. This is less common in the cities. Both in the villages and in the cities help is first given to relatives and friends, but the emphasis is different for urbanites and villagers. Villagers give more help to relatives, whereas urbanites tend to support mostly friends. This corresponds with the data over the composition of their respective networks.

Nearly all villagers are members of one or several clubs or associations; they have more memberships in religious organizations, political parties, welfare agencies and neighbourhood organizations than urbanites. This does not affect their social meetings, which are the same for urbanites and villagers. It is interesting to note, however, that urbanites and villagers focus on different groups. Both villagers and urbanites are involved primarily with relatives and friends. In addition, villagers get together more often with people of the same religion, whereas urbanites interact more often with people they know from work or school, and people with the same hobby. Besides meeting at home they also get together in other places; urbanites tend to see each other in cafes or community centres, whereas villagers see each other mostly at the sports club or in church.

Residents of cities and villages go regularly to places of entertainment, but there are large differences in the frequency; villagers (especially youth under thirty) attend museums, concerts, the theatre, movies, cafes and dance locales less often than urbanites. Villagers spend more time on sports and matters related to the church.

Urbanites make more frequent use of facilities like district nursing services, social work and social services. This corresponds with the fact that there are more urbanites who have to manage without support from their social network.

Another aspect we examined about the urban and non-urban areas is the social environment. There is a clear relation between urbanization and neighbourly contacts. Although most of the respondents find a pleasant vicinity important, the social aspects of the living environment are more important for villagers than for urbanites Villagers consider it more important to live close to their family and friends, they have more contact with fellow residents and find these contacts very important. The contacts tend to be more intensive than the neighbourly contacts of urbanites; they visit each other more often and go out together more. Urbanites tend to have more negative experiences with fellow residents. Still, many urbanites would like to have more neighbourly contacts. It appears to be more difficult to realize such contacts in the city. This can be explained partially by the large homogeneity in the villages. Villagers have more similar views and lifestyles, and experience less nuisance from each other than urbanites. They are consequently much more satisfied about their living environment than urbanites. Whereas most villagers want to spend their old age in their current town, urbanites tend to have more serious moving plans.

When we look at all these aspects together, we see that villagers have a much stronger orientation towards the local society than urbanites. At the same time, we see that people with a strong local social orientation often belong among the socially competent, whereas people with a moderate or weak orientation towards the local community tend to belong to the other contact groups; as the local social orientation wanes, we see more socially inhibited, lonely and socially isolated individuals.

Although all kinds of social developments in society have also influenced the social structure in the villages, villagers seem to have a stronger bond with their town than urbanites. Population composition plays an important role here; villages host more people with similar characteristics than cities, allowing for an easier establishment of enduring social contacts with each other than in the cities, where there is more of a variety of lifestyles and etiquette. This heterogeneity raises the chances of social isolation in the cities compared with the villages. The orientation towards the local society also seems to be a protective factor for social isolation. Because of this, local social orientation can be seen as a good indicator of social cohesion and social integration.

At the same time, we must conclude that the large variation in the cities is not entirely negative. Many urbanites do well in the social and societal fronts, whereas others are worse off in all respects.

11 Social isolation
A combined analysis

Ludwien Meeuwesen

11.1 Introduction

The aim of this study is to provide information on the nature and scope of social isolation in modern western society, and to offer insight into its backgrounds, manifestation forms, causes and eventual consequences. With this study we also wish to contribute to the establishing of theories on social isolation, and formulate a new policy philosophy. To realize this, we have chosen a wide approach in which both individual and societal aspects of social isolation are focused on extensively. The following research questions were formulated:

1. What is the scope and nature of social isolation?
2. What individual and societal causes account for this?
3. What consequences does social isolation have for the individual and societal well-being of persons?
4. What significance do the insights of this study have for theories on social isolation?
5. What consequences do these insights have for policy regarding social isolation?

In this chapter we will review the main findings of our study: the starting points, the typology of social contacts, the relation with individual, social-environmental and societal themes. In Section 12.4 we will inter-relate the possible causes for social isolation by means of a multinomial regression analysis in which combinations of the most important variables are used. This will allow us insight into the relative importance of individual and societal factors for social isolation. Section 12.5 discusses specifically the consequences of social isolation for someone's personal, social-environmental and societal well-being. Research questions 4 and 5 will be discussed in the Chapters 13 and 14.

11.2 The typology of social contacts

To have a better understanding of the nature and scope of social isolation, a typology of social contacts was developed, based on a combined use of an objective criterion, the scope of someone's network, and a subjective one, the degree of feelings of loneliness. The basic premise was that an important characteristic of social isolation is the lack of meaningful social contacts. Determining the scope of the social network was done with what is known as the exchange method (Fischer, 1982). The quality of the network was measured from the presence or absence of feelings of loneliness (De Jong-Gierveld and Kamphuis, 1985). Based on these two criteria, a social typology was developed and empirically tested by analysing data of some 2,400 interviews. The typology consists of four groups: the socially competent, the socially inhibited, the lonely and the socially isolated. About two-thirds of the respondents can be considered to be socially competent, a group of people that have many contacts and do not feel lonely. At the same time, it is also the case that 8 per cent of the respondents say they have a small network but are nonetheless not bothered by feelings of loneliness. These 'socially inhibited' people are in a sense vulnerable, because they depend on a small group of other persons. A risk for social isolation arises when one or two people withdraw from this network, for whatever reason. Although an extensive personal network can improve a person's well-being, this is not self-evident. Despite large networks, 22 per cent of the respondents feel lonely. At 6 per cent, the socially isolated are the worst-off, as they have small networks *and* feel lonely.

The network approach of Fischer (1982) deals with someone's potential social support. Besides we have also asked for actual social support. We have mapped out the potential social support of the typology, as well as the actual social support and the balance in giving and receiving social support. With regard to the potential social support, the groups we distinguished differ greatly, which makes sense given that network size is behind this. The socially competent and the lonely have considerably more people whom they can appeal to for support than the socially inhibited; the socially isolated are the worst-off. The socially isolated, and to a lesser degree also the socially inhibited, more often lack all types of support (emotional, companionship, practical) than persons in other groups. The same pattern can be observed in the actual support received: the socially competent actually receive the most support, the socially isolated the least.

The balance between giving and receiving social support differs greatly among the four groups. The socially competent differ here essentially from the other three groups: they indicate giving more help than they receive. The socially isolated show an opposite pattern: they claim to receive more support than they give. The same can be said of the socially inhibited and the lonely, although the differences are less pronounced.

The typology shows a clear relation with most analytical measures, in the sense that the seriousness of the problems in the four groups distinguished runs a more or less linear course. The socially competent are in most aspects the best-off, and the socially isolated the worst-off. The socially inhibited and the lonely take an intermediate position in which the socially inhibited are generally better off than the lonely, albeit not always. The competent are the most balanced, socially speaking. Each of the two intermediate groups runs its own particular risk of social isolation. The socially inhibited tend to be moderately satisfied and give a stable impression, but have relatively few networks, for which reason they are dependent on a small group of people. Any disturbance to this pattern makes this group vulnerable. The lonely have a wide network, but do not seem to manage on their own: they experience a clear discrepancy between ideal and reality. The isolated do not make it on either count, as they seem to be focusing mainly on surviving. They are also the group least satisfied with their social relationships, and feel less protected against loneliness than persons from other groups.

We can conclude that network scope and subjective feelings of loneliness are essential components for the study of meaningful social contacts and social isolation. The subjective elements weigh more than the objective factors. Applying a combination of both criteria produced a clear added value though (Schrameijer, 1990; Lincoln, 2000; Meeuwesen et al., 2001). Although reality is of course much more complex than our model, the social contacts typology offers a productive starting point for research into social isolation.

11.3 Summary of the research results

This section contains a summary of the main findings on the topics life events, personal competences, health, formal and informal support, societal participation, social environment and urban and rural areas.

Life events

With regard to life events, people mention more negative than positive events that they are still dealing with. Contrary to the positive events, negative events have an effect on the typology. As the risk of isolation grows, we see an increase in the number of negative events that respondents are still dealing with. What it comes down to is that the socially isolated are still considerably worse-off than the socially competent. The socially inhibited and the lonely take an intermediate position here. This also applies to major personal and societal events, which can in turn be subclassified into events that are just part of life (like disease and death) and events that are not as self-evident, (like traumatic violent experiences). Next to life events, which can be clearly identified, daily things such as hassles and uplifts play an important role.

People's perception and the experience of the event are much more decisive than network scope to how long and how intensively they carry the burden of negative events with themselves. This network scope does, however, play a role with regard to daily experienced hassles and uplifts. These daily occurrences are seen as important mediating factors towards the perception and experience of major events.

When we review the background variables, it appears that married people mention slightly fewer negative events, and people with lower educational levels mention more negative events than those with a mid- or higher-level education. But it is mostly personal and socialization factors which seem to play a role in terms of handling and processing life events. People are less bothered by major events if they can look back at a happy youth and loving parents, if they are healthier, and if they are well-equipped with personal competences. Early youth and parental support seem to be quite determinant for the way in which someone processes life events later in life. Individuals with higher educational levels and married people process such events slightly better.

Personal competences

As we have discussed, someone's personal competences (like self-confidence, problem-solving capacities and social skills) form a more solid buffer against the consequences of negative events, next to a happy youth. We see once again a clear relation with the social contacts typology. The vast majority of respondents consider themselves competent in a personal sense. The lonely, and especially the socially isolated, feel less able than the socially competent. The lonely and the socially inhibited indicate having more competences than the isolated, but not to the same degree as the socially competent. The lonely are on average a little more socially skilled, and the socially inhibited have slightly more self-confidence and problem-solving skills. It is remarkable, however, that the lion's share of the respondents indicates having a lot of self-confidence and sufficient problem-solving skills, but that only 60 per cent find themselves equipped, socially speaking. It is precisely with regard to social skills that people feel they have shortcomings. Further, the ability to look back at a happy youth forms a solid basis for the degree to which people consider themselves competent. We have also observed that as people have fewer personal competences, they have considerably more chances of becoming lonely after a dramatic event.

People generally like to help others. They are more able to do so the higher their self-confidence is and the more social and problem-solving skills they have. The personal competences are acquired not only for one's own personal benefit but also to assist others. We see once again that the ratio between giving and receiving help is the most balanced among the socially competent.

Individual variables also play a much larger role than background variables when it comes to personal competences. As the respondents mention fewer negative personal life events, have more protective factors, are healthier, and have had a happier youth, they have more self-confidence, more social skills and greater problem-solving capacities.

In addition, people who do not live alone and are employed tend to be slightly more competent than people who live alone and are not employed.

This last situation applies, incidentally, only with respect to the aspect of problem-solving and social skills, but not with respect to self-confidence. Remarkably enough, self-confidence does not lend itself to be trapped in sociological categories. It is a basic feeling that indicates the essence of how someone faces life, something often shaped in early youth.

A lack of personal competences lead to loneliness and isolation, but the opposite is also true: loneliness and isolation can cause a deterioration of self-confidence. There is usually a vicious circle.

Health

On average, the respondents of this study rate their health with a very generous satisfactory mark. The higher the risk of isolation, the less healthy people experience themselves to be. The percentage of isolated people who rate their health as unsatisfactory is four times larger than that among the socially competent. A poorer health assessment is substantially accompanied by stronger feelings of loneliness as well as with a smaller network (albeit to a much more limited degree). Regarding the smaller network, especially the potential for companionship support is lacking.

With regard to the general assessment of health, we see that the pallet of factors playing a role is broader than with personal competences. Both individual and background factors are important. Older people feel less healthy, as do individuals who live alone. Working people, on the other hand, feel healthier; people who feel well-protected, individually and societally speaking, are healthier, and personal competences increase the assessment of one's health. The more negative personal experiences the respondents mention, the less healthy they feel. Having effective problem-solving skills and a social support potential contribute to better health; the other way around, good health leads to more effective problem solving and a greater potential for social support. Here we find an indication for the existence of buffer effects against stressful events: when a person's well-being is threatened by stressful events, an appeal to social resources can limit the damage (Tijhuis, 1996). With respect to depression too, individual factors and background variables play a role, albeit to a lesser degree than in the general assessment of health. Having a lower educational level entails a risk for depression, and older people are depressed more often, just as are single individuals compared to married ones. The healthier one feels, the lower the chances of becoming depressed. Here too we see that personal competences form a buffer against the emergence of a depression.

Formal and informal support

We have seen that people have an informal network at their disposal for all kinds of support. There are also formal support facilities, like family physicians, home care services, meal services, social work, hotlines, the Social

Services Department, and Municipal Credit Banks for people who are physically, mentally or financially vulnerable and for whom their informal network alone is not enough. In general, most people do not use these specific facilities, except for the family physician. The use of such facilities varies from 1 per cent (hotlines) to 9 per cent (home care). Users tend to be seniors and/or people with poor health or with a disadvantageous societal position, like lone parents and immigrants. The fewer types of support, especially practical support, people have in their own circle, the sooner an appeal will be made to professional help. A person may have sufficient sources of support at his disposal, but still appeal to professional help because he does not consider the quality of his network up to par. In this sense too, the quality of someone's network is more decisive than its scope.

The analyses of Chapter 7 show that persons who are physically, mentally and/or financially vulnerable have to manage much more often without a supportive network than the less vulnerable. They have less support from their immediate surroundings, and experience their network considerably more negatively than the non-vulnerable. This means that they have a greater need for support, whereas they can expect less from their social network. In that sense, it is particularly the very vulnerable who find themselves in an unfavourable position.

Especially the lonely and the isolated vulnerable appeal extensively to formal facilities. The lonely vulnerable use specific facilities, whereas the socially isolated generally resort to all types of professional help, regardless of their degree of vulnerability.

The socially inhibited and the socially competent also appeal to formal facilities when necessary, but they do not experience this as a deficiency in their own social network. They appear to deliberately choose to set up their lives that way. However, the lonely and the socially isolated experience a greater discrepancy between the desired and the actual support they receive from their network. They usually are not at ease with the fact that they have had to seek help in the professional circuit. This means that those who rely the most on professional institutions appreciate dependency on such bodies the least.

Societal participation

In the present study we formulated a broad measure for societal participation, in which next to paid labour and study attention is also given to club life, informal care, volunteer work, attendance of sports and cultural events, and participation in all sorts of informal contexts. We consequently formulated four successive categories of societal participation: (i) the socially very passive (5 per cent); (ii) the passive (26 per cent); (iii) the active (39 per cent); and (iv) the very active (30 per cent). On this basis we can also speak more justifiably of societal isolation, namely when people are rarely or not in touch with these facets of societal life. This 'objective' factual measure does not correspond, however, with its evaluation by those involved. The satisfaction with societal well-being is nearly the same among the passive and the active. There is also little difference in the degree to which the groups feel excluded. If they already felt excluded, it has more to do with individual factors. The degree of societal participation is not related to life events. Still, people who are more competent in the personal sphere are also slightly more active societally (this only applies for the subscale of social skills, and not for self-confidence or problem-solving).

We see that as people are younger, have a higher educational level, have more income at their disposal, and are married, their societal participation increases. Having or lacking paid work does not seem to play a role, but of course we know that the younger, more educated, etc. people are, the greater their chances are of having paid work. We can conclude that a number of background variables have an effect on the degree of a person's societal participation. Other societal factors, like degree of dependency on facilities, feelings of exclusion, or feeling societally useless, are not related to societal participation.

With regard to the typology of social contacts, we can say that the more societally active people are, the more competent they are too ($r = -0.18$). At the same time, a substantial percentage of the very passive is competent in a social sense, whereas there also seem to be socially very active people who have a poorly functioning social network. This will be elaborated on in Chapter 12, which focuses on subgroup profiling.

Social environment

Next to social networks and degree of societal integration, attention has also been paid to the meaning of the respondents' social environment. On the basis of this study, we arrive at the conclusion that it is not that community feelings, the degree to which residents identify with their neighbourhood, or the social meaning of the living environment have decreased, as much of the literature claims – they have acquired a different content (Hortulanus, 1995a, 1995b). A 'we' feeling based on factual relationships and activities has made room for a 'we' feeling whose core are shared values, customs and visible behaviour.

With regard to the social environment, the theme of spatial isolation and the degree of homogeneity in relation to lifestyle views and behaviour were examined. We distinguished three forms of spatial isolation: discrepancy between need for neighbourly contacts and actual contacts, absence of a support network within walking distance, and negative neighbourhood identification. The analyses show the following: first, 4 per cent of all residents indicate being socially-spatially isolated, needing social contacts in the neighbourhood but not actually having them. Second, 9 per cent of all respondents have no support network within walking distance of their home. And third, 11 per cent of all residents assess their neighbourhood negatively. These three forms of spatial isolation are inter-related. Residents who can actually fulfil their need for neighbourly contacts have a support network within walking distance more often, and identify more positively with their neighbourhood. As residents assess their neighbourhood more negatively, they are also annoyed much more often about things like noise, feel less safe and have more negative bonds with fellow residents.

It seems that the forms of spatial isolation we distinguished can be partially derived from residents' varying lifestyle and/or personal preferences, but that they can also be the result of a socially more heterogeneous living environment. The degree of homogeneity of lifestyle views also plays a role when it comes to spatial isolation. Residents of homogeneous neighbourhoods, for example, almost always have a support network within walking distance. And as attractive as heterogeneous neighbourhoods can be in terms of other physical/spatial features, chances of low assessment of such neighbourhoods appear to be many times greater than that of a neighbourhood with homogeneous lifestyle views and behaviour. All three forms of spatial isolation we distinguished are more common in heterogeneous neighbourhoods than in homogeneous neighbourhoods.

Spatial isolation is not the same as social isolation. Most people who are isolated in a spatial sense are not necessarily socially isolated. Still, there is a certain relation between spatial and social isolation, and the degree of homogeneity plays an important role in it. Especially in heterogeneous neighbourhoods, there is a higher-than-average number of socially isolated individuals among the spatially isolated. This is not the case in homogeneous neighbourhoods.

With regard to the background variables we used, there is hardly an effect on spatial isolation. The only finding here is that people who live in rural areas are less spatially isolated than urbanites.

Urban and rural areas

The socially competent are encountered considerably more often in rural communities than in cities (75 per cent versus 54 per cent). The lonely are found both in the city and in the countryside, while the other two contact groups are seen more often in cities, where, for example, the number of socially isolated individuals is five times larger than in the countryside (10 per cent versus 2 per cent). The differences in network scope between urbanites and villagers are not conspicuous, but urbanites tend to be more dissatisfied over their network than villagers. This is due partially to differences in population composition. In urban areas we find more younger people, singles and divorced people. Immigrants are also found primarily in cities.

The degree of societal participation does not differ between urbanites and villagers, but these two groups do differ clearly in types of activities. The disabled and the unemployed are more common in cities, whereas in villages household work is mentioned much more often as a main way of spending time. Volunteer work is done in both settings, but the nature of the activities is different among urbanites than among villagers.

The quality of the social environment is observed to be stronger for villagers than for city dwellers. Villagers maintain more contacts with neighbours, and find these contacts important. In cities it is usually more difficult to realize such contacts. This can be due partially to the fact that there is a greater homogeneity in life perspectives and lifestyles in villages than in urban areas. Villagers are also much more strongly oriented towards the local society than urbanites. Such an orientation is often accompanied by social competence too. We also saw earlier that more socially competent people are found in rural communities than in cities. Local social orientation can thus be seen as a good indicator of social cohesion and social integration.

All these findings should be somewhat nuanced: although in several aspects ratings for urban areas are not as rosy, we should realize that the variation in urban areas is much greater than in the countryside. Many city dwellers have a good life, socially and societally speaking, whereas others are worse-off in many ways.

11.4 Effects of individual, social-environmental, societal and background factors on the social contacts typology

In this section, the second research question – *What individual and societal causes account for this?* – is examined. This involves the relative importance of several individual, social-spatial and societal factors with respect to the social contacts typology. To this end, a multinomial regression analysis was done of a combined data set from the first and second phases (N = 460). This reduction of data is dictated by the fact that a number of important variables – the individual factors – only came up in the second interview round. Because not all data was available from all the respondents, we worked with averages, adding the missing data on that basis.

As previous chapters have shown, the four contact groups are partially classified on a hierarchical basis (the competent and the isolated), but not entirely, or at least not per se (the intermediate groups of the socially inhibited and the lonely). Accordingly, the values of the dependent variable (the social contacts typology) do not lie at an interval level. A multinomial logistic regression analysis therefore remains the best way to gain proper insight into the factors that play a role in the classification of the social contacts typology. A criterion group is used (here the socially competent) and the effects of the various independent variables are compared for the three risk groups separately. In this way, a good picture is obtained of the relevant factors with regard to the social contacts typology. It also gives an indication of the percentage of explained variance. Hence in the following analyses we keep comparing each of the three risk groups with the group of the socially competent. This was done successively on the basis of the four groups of independent variables – demographic, personal, social-environmental and societal. Finally, we analysed the effect of all the relevant factors together.

Table 11.1 Multinomial logistic regression (for the social contacts typology) (N = 460), with eight background factors

	Socially inhibited; small network, not lonely (0/1) Coeff (SE)	Lonely; large network, lonely (1/0) Coeff (SE)	Socially isolated; small network, lonely (0/0) Coeff (SE)
Age	0.028 (0.01)**	−0.003 (0.01)	0.012 (0.02)
Gender	0.16 (0.29)	−0.20 (0.25)	−0.11 (0.39)
Civil Status	−0.30 (0.20)	0.26 (0.17)	0.04 (0.25)
Education	−0.37 (0.20)*	−0.26 (0.17)	−0.64 (0.31)**
Income	−0.14 (0.20)	−0.17 (0.17)	−0.46 (0.27)*
Urbanization degree	−1.62 (0.34)****	0.24 (0.27)	−1.29 (0.43)***
Work situation	0.11 (0.38)	−0.16 (0.32)	−0.65 (0.54)
Ethnicity	0.46 (0.43)	−0.41 (0.36)	−0.34 (0.50)
Intercept	0.60 (0.99)	−0.29 (0.82)	1.67 (1.26)

Notes
Reference group: 1/1, the socially competent (large network, not lonely), pseudo R2 (Nagelkerke) = 0.16.
*<0.10, **<0.05, ***<0.01, ****<0.001.

Demographic factors

Table 11.1 shows that of the eight background factors used, only degree of urbanization and educational level have a significant effect on the social contacts typology (all factors together, significant or not, explain 16 per cent of the variance). The socially inhibited and the isolated are more common in cities compared with the competent, and as a group also have a lower educational level. The socially inhibited may be older than the competent, but given the very small regression coefficient this difference is considered indeed significant yet not relevant. The lonely and the competent do not differ from each other that much in demographic factors.

Personal factors

In the personal sphere we see that all the high-risk groups have fewer personal competences than the socially competent (Table 11.2). For the socially isolated, also an unhappier youth, fewer protective factors, generational isolation and a network with few relatives do play a role. The lonely are less healthy than the competent. This model explains 20 per cent of the variance.

Social-environmental factors

The socially isolated are also considerably more isolated, spatially speaking, than the socially competent (Table 11.3). Among the socially inhibited and the lonely we also see a more negative evaluation of the living situation in

Table 11.2 Multinomial logistic regression (for the social contacts typology) (N = 460), with eight personal factors

	Socially inhibited; small network, not lonely (0/1) Coeff (SE)	Lonely; large network, lonely (1/0) Coeff (SE)	Socially isolated; small network, lonely (0/0) Coeff (SE)
Happy youth	−0.86 (0.83)	−1.02 (0.69)	2.26 (1.07)**
Parental love	0.68 (0.62)	0.61 (0.47)	0.35 (0.65)
Health	−0.03 (0.11)	−0.21 (0.09)**	−0.17 (0.14)
Life events	−0.06 (0.05)	0.05 (0.04)	0.09 (0.06)
Protection	−0.09 (0.05)*	−0.07 (0.05)	−0.17 (0.07)**
Personal competences	−0.16 (0.05)***	−0.17 (0.05)****	−0.27 (0.07)****
Generational isolation	−0.37 (0.33)	−0.25 (0.27)	1.01 (0.42)***
Familial network	0.25 (0.25)	0.24 (0.22)	0.73 (0.34)**
Intercept	2.42 (1.81)	3.92 (1.52)***	−8.89 (2.38)

Notes
Reference group: 1/1, the socially competent (large network, not lonely), pseudo R2 (Nagelkerke) = 0.20.
*<0.10, **<0.05, ***0.01, ****0.001.

Table 11.3 Multinomial logistic regression (for the social contacts typology) (N = 460), with eight social-environmental factors

	Socially inhibited; small network, not lonely (0/1) Coeff (SE)	Lonely; large network, lonely (1/0) Coeff (SE)	Socially isolated; small network, lonely (0/0) Coeff (SE)
Report mark on neighbourhood	−0.40 (0.14)***	−0.37 (0.12)***	−0.20 (0.18)
Annoyances in neighbourhood	0.05 (0.04)	0.04 (0.03)	0.05 (0.05)
Spatial isolation	−0.44 (0.28)*	−0.39 (0.25)	−1.07 (0.30)****
Homogeneity score	0.21 (0.16)	0.18 (0.14)	−0.08 (0.22)
Local orientation	0.13 (0.28)	−0.17 (0.23)	0.03 (0.38)
Neighbourhood network	−0.85 (0.43)**	−0.05 (0.44)	−1.34 (0.48)
Neighbourhood negative bonding	0.39 (0.21)*	−0.03 (0.19)	0.09 (0.28)
Social-spatial segregation	0.53 (0.36)	0.46 (0.31)	0.25 (0.45)

Notes
Reference group: 1/1, the socially competent (large network, not lonely), pseudo R2 (Nagelkerke) = 0.12.
*<0.10, **<0.05, ***<0.01, ****<0.001.

their neighbourhood. Especially the socially inhibited seem to have small networks in the neighbourhood, which they evaluate negative. They feel a discrepancy between actual contacts and the desire for contacts. The above model explains 12 per cent of the variance.

Societal factors

Societally speaking, the three risk groups are considerably more passive than the competent, and also indicate feeling considerably more useless in society (Table 11.4). In addition, the isolated feel more strongly excluded, and together with the lonely experience the burden of societal life events more intensely. In contrast, the socially inhibited feel a bit more protected by some degree of societal success. The above model explains 25 per cent of the variance.

Joint effects

In summary, the effect of various groups of factors on the social contacts typology has been examined. Several relevant factors become manifest, such as education, urbanization degree, youth, personal competences, societal participation, report mark on neighbourhood, and spatial isolation.

The last step is to merge all the relevant factors that came out of the four partial analyses into a model. Which factors combined together play a decisive role in the end?

Compared with the competent, the socially isolated have lower educational levels, tend to live in the city, have had an unhappier youth, feel less

Table 11.4 Multinomial logistic regression (for the social contacts typology) (N = 460), with seven societal factors

	Socially inhibited; small network, not lonely (0/1) Coeff (SE)	Lonely; large network, lonely (1/0) Coeff (SE)	Socially isolated; small network, lonely (0/0) Coeff (SE)
Societal success protects	0.65 (0.30)**	−0.06 (0.27)	−0.06 (0.46)
Societal participation	−0.39 (0.17)**	−0.30 (0.15)**	−0.88 (0.24)****
Dependency on facilities	−0.12 (0.27)	0.25 (0.22)	−0.23 (0.39)
Societally not useful	1.81 (0.48)****	2.26 (0.43)****	2.63 (0.56)****
Exclusion	0.07 (0.14)	0.06 (0.13)	0.18 (0.15)**
Life events (societal)	0.14 (0.18)	0.43 (0.15)***	0.45 (0.21)**
Structurally no work	−0.22 (0.16)	−0.16 (0.15)	−0.30 (0.19)
Intercept	−0.03 (0.75)	−0.17 (0.67)	−0.49 (0.89)

Notes
Reference group: 1/1, the socially competent (large network, not lonely), pseudo R2 (Nagelkerke) = 0.25.
<0.05, *<0.01, ****<0.001.

Table 11.5 Multinomial logistic regression (for the social contacts typology) (N = 460), with all the relevant factors (demographic, personal, societal and social-spatial)

	Socially inhibited; small network, not lonely (0/1) Coeff (SE)	Lonely; large network, lonely (1/0) Coeff (SE)	Socially isolated; small network, lonely (0/0) Coeff (SE)
Education	−0.38 (0.21)*	−0.30 (0.20)	−0.76 (0.37)**
Urbanization degree	−0.85 (0.37)**	1.05 (0.33)***	−0.86 (0.54)*
Happy youth	0.19 (0.90)	−0.68 (0.77)	3.76 (1.25)***
Health	0.08 (0.13)	0.06 (0.10)	−0.16 (0.16)
Protection	−0.17 (0.07)**	−0.10 (0.06)*	−0.25 (0.10)***
Personal competences	−0.14 (0.06)**	−0.14 (0.05)***	−0.21 (0.09)***
Generational isolation	−0.14 (0.35)	−0.29 (0.31)	1.37 (0.48)***
Familial network	0.43 (0.27)	0.14 (0.25)	0.86 (0.39)**
Report mark neighbourhood	−0.26 (0.12)**	−0.41 (0.12)****	−0.04 (0.18)
Spatial isolation	−0.14 (0.30)	−0.08 (0.28)	−0.84 (0.38)**
Neighbourhood network	−0.96 (0.47)**	−0.32 (0.50)	−1.33 (0.59)**
Societal success protects	1.20 (0.38)***	0.43 (0.33)	1.11 (0.59)*
Societal participation	−0.38 (0.19)**	−0.14 (0.17)	−0.63 (0.28)**
Societally not useful	1.82 (0.53)***	2.64 (0.46)****	2.69 (0.47)****
Exclusion	−0.05 (0.14)	−0.15 (0.13)	−0.11 (0.18)
Life events (societal)	−0.07 (0.19)	0.43 (0.16)***	0.26 (0.25)
Intercept	7.50 (2.27)***	5.45 (2.05)***	5.77 (3.09)*

Notes
Reference group: 1/1, the socially competent (large network, not lonely), pseudo R2 (Nagelkerke) = 0.44.
*<0.10, **<0.05, ***<0.01, ****<0.001.

protected, are personally less competent, their network tends to be exclusively familial and previous generations dealt with isolation too (Table 11.5). Further, they are more prone to be spatially isolated and their neighbourhood network is small. They are societally passive and in that sense do not feel useful. They have this last aspect in common with the socially inhibited and the lonely. The three risk groups also share a poor development of personal competences and a lack of protective factors. The above model shows that a combination of the four groups of relevant factors together explains 44 per cent of the variance. Demographic, individual, social-environmental and societal factors play a role here. This analysis also shows that many of the decisive factors are of an individual nature, whereas there is also a substantial number of them societal and social-environmental in nature. What actually happens is that we see an accumulation of different factors, which turn out to be negative for the socially isolated. Some of them, the personal competences and the societal participation will be elaborated further on.

Therefore, Chapter 12 offers a more qualitative analysis of the research results in the form of a subgroup profiling. We give an additional description for each of the four social contact groups, which we sub classify even further in terms of personal competences and societal participation.

11.5 Consequences of social isolation

In the previous section we focused mainly on causes of social isolation, and carried out an analysis in which social isolation, or more broadly speaking the social contacts typology, is always considered as a dependent variable. This allows us some insight into the variables that really matter, and the degree to which they matter.

In the various chapters we have repeatedly pointed to the fact that social isolation also has consequences for numerous aspects we have involved in our research. In Section 3.10 already, when discussing the changes in someone's network over the last five years, we discussed that more lonely and socially isolated people saw their networks decrease instead of increase (compared to the socially competent and the socially inhibited). From this we can deduce that when there already are feelings of loneliness to some degree, under certain conditions this can form a hindrance for making and maintaining social contacts. If a person already has a small network, things only get more difficult. The opposite seems to be true for the socially competent. Whereas the socially competent seem to be creative in making social situations work for them, even when there are problems, among the socially isolated we see strong decreases in contacts, both in familial situations and with all kinds of other groups. This can be explained partially as a consequence of divorce or death of a partner, and by age: networks of ageing people shrink gradually as the partner and age peers pass away. It also seems that network changes do not take place randomly, but that changes in their scope and composition can be understood in the light of events in the course of someone's life. In Chapter 4 we looked at these negative life events, observing that the reasons for social isolation can be very different and that there is generally an interaction between the isolated position and the impact of such events. In particular, high-risk groups indicate having become lonely after an important event, whereas they did not feel that way before. Hence the events could be the cause. Especially the isolated also indicated having needed support at that moment but that it was unavailable. They had no one, or didn't know how to mobilize people in their surroundings. We saw that the less personal competences they had, the danger of the situation worsening grew.

What will cross a person's path is never clear. Still, we see that the competent feel the most protected in numerous ways and have the most personal and societal stock, unlike the socially isolated. In Chapter 5 we saw a vicious circle in that sense: people are equipped on a personal level in such a way that chances of isolation decrease, or precisely increase. The other way around, isolation leads to the weakening of several competences, which in turn contributes to increase isolation, and so on. The same is observed with regard to the scope of the networks, their quality, the potential support they provide, etc.

In Chapter 8 we discussed the consequences of social isolation for societal participation. It turned out that the socially isolated feel more often that they are not societally useful and that they feel excluded more often than people with a well-functioning social network. Our reasoning behind the health theme – that lifestyles and living conditions influence health (causative explanation), and the other way around, that health has a selective effect on lifestyle and living conditions (selective explanation) – applies *mutatis mutandis* to social isolation too. It is not one approach or the other, but precisely a combination of both approaches which is considered the most productive. This study will propel the first attempt to contemplate the consequences of social isolation.

When, by way of summarizing, we aim exclusively at the meaning of social contacts, two important aspects can be mentioned: they form a source of social support, and they are a precondition for reaching societal goals. For an analysis of consequences it is important to get an idea of the evaluation of the respondents on these angles. To this end, we will not offer advanced analyses or model development, but a brief description of a number of selected variables that reasonably approach the above-mentioned aspects and observe the eloquence when asking about the consequences of social isolation.

First we will look at social contacts as a source of social support. In general, it is assumed that we need other people in order to be able to enjoy life. For this reason we have focused here on a measure for individual well-being, namely 'I can really enjoy life'. We see that this measure shows a relation with the social contacts typology of $r = -0.27$ (Section 4.4). The more competent people are, the more they can enjoy life; if they are more isolated, they will experience less enjoyment. We have also selected a number of concrete aspects of life: yearly recurring events like Christmas and birthdays. We also asked in general terms about being alone and evaluating it. Finally, we looked at whether the respondents have people in their surroundings who can offer comfort if they are hurting or having problems.

The data of this study show that there is a positive correlation of the social contacts typology with 'being alone during Christmas and disliking it' of $r = 0.20$ as well as 'being alone on one's birthday and disliking it' of $r = 0.28$. Chances of the socially isolated lacking sources of comfort are larger than among other groups ($r = -0.18$), and the social contacts typology also shows a correlation with the chances of 'becoming lonely after an important event' ($r = 0.17$). There is a strong correlation with 'being actually alone and disliking it' ($r = 0.38$). This relation can also be observed in the general assessment of contacts, at $r = -0.35$ (Chapter 3). The higher the risk of social isolation, the lower the general assessment of social contacts, expressed in a report mark, appears. The socially isolated have a clearly lower assessment of the quality of their social contacts than the socially competent and the socially inhibited. The more miserable the situation, the worse those involved evaluate it.

We also looked at social contacts as a societal resource. With respect to attaining societal goals, a measure for societal well-being is a good variable. To this end, we asked respondents questions about satisfaction with their education, work situation, income, living situation and free-time activities (see Section 8.2). The measure for societal well-being constructed on this basis shows a link of $r = 0.24$ with our social contacts typology: societal well-being increases as people are more competent.

This brief sketch of respondent evaluations on the degree to which network scope and quality form a source of social support and are a precondition for the attainment of societal goals leads to the conclusion that an approach that looks at the causes of social isolation as well as its consequences is the most productive: there are more than enough indications that an interaction exists between both.

12 The social contact typology
A further subgroup profiling

Roelof Hortulanus

12.1 Personal competences and societal participation as causes of social isolation

The basic social contact typology developed in Chapter 3 has been analysed in the previous chapters largely in terms of a type of continuum in which the socially competent have the most meaningful social contacts, better than the socially inhibited and the lonely, followed by the socially isolated, who when it comes to social contacts are the worst off. In these chapters we have also mentioned regularly that a further specification of the basic typology of social contacts formulated in Chapter 3 is desirable. We therefore ask ourselves whether it is possible to distinguish new subcategories with specific characteristics within the four basic types. This exposes the measure of social contacts constructed by the researchers, because we now look for categories with an autonomous meaning, which are recognizable and confirmed in the eyes of those involved, and which are probably linked to all kinds of other factors in their own unique way.

In this section we will make such a subgroup profiling through a more qualitative process, establishing additional distinctions within the four social-contact typology groups used up to now. We will pay specific attention to the relation between the four categories of the social contacts typology and the measures for *personal competency* and *societal participation*. These two factors play a significant role in the combined analysis of Chapter 11. Common sense also provides us with both explanations for social isolation: one measure refers to certain character and personality characteristics or to a lack of social skills, the other to non-participation or discontinued participation in society. We therefore distinguish within each group of the social contacts typology those with many and with limited personal competences, and those with extensive and with little societal participation. We make this distinction for the socially competent, the socially inhibited, the lonely and the socially isolated. To keep track of these classifications, the measures for personal competencies and societal participation are dichotomized here. The criterion for many or limited personal competencies is established in this chapter at 12–13 on a scale of 17 (see also Section 5.4). The very passive and the passive are designated as *passive* in this chapter, and the active and very active as *active* (see also Section 8.2).

Tables 12.1 and 12.2 clearly show that a further subgroup profiling on personal competencies and societal participation is worthwhile: all further distinguished subgroups seem to appear to a substantial degree. We then found out statistically to what degree each distinguished subcategory (i.e. for an active socially competent, a passive socially competent, an active socially inhibited, a passive socially inhibited, etc.) deviates from the average of all the categories together in a series of factors used in the research. This involves, for example, the repercussions of life events, health, feelings of social exclusion, environmental isolation, the degree of problem accumulation, life attitude, the significance of informal support, dependency on formal support and of course factors such as age, education and marital status. On the basis of these data we can sketch a sort of profile of each subcategory in the following sections.

Table 12.1 Further profiling of the social typology according to personal competencies, in percentages (N = 436)

Personal competencies	Social contact typology			
	Socially competent	Socially inhibited	Lonely	Socially isolated
Many	66	52	42	34
Limited	34	48	58	66
Total	100	100	100	100

Notes
$Chi^2 = 25.158$; $P < 0.000$.

Table 12.2 Further profiling of the social typology according to societal participation, in percentages (N = 426)

Societal participation	Social contact typology			
	Socially competent	Socially inhibited	Lonely	Socially isolated
Active	70	56	59	44
Passive	30	44	41	56
Total	100	100	100	100

Notes
$Chi^2 = 25.568$; $P < 0.000$.

12.1.1 *Subgroup profiling according to personal competencies*

There is a clear relation between the social typology and the personal competencies of our respondents. The percentages of Table 12.1 show that the socially competent and the socially isolated are each other's mirror in this respect. Among the competent, 66 per cent have many personal competencies, compared with the socially isolated, 66 per cent of whom have limited competencies. There are interesting subgroups nonetheless: one-third of the socially competent have limited personal competencies, whereas one-third of the socially isolated have many personal competencies. Among the socially inhibited and the lonely there are also people with limited as well as with many personal competencies.

Let us first see whether we can sketch a picture of that portion of the socially isolated respondents who – probably against expectations – have many personal competencies. Social isolation need not necessarily mean that people have no self-confidence, problem-solving capacities or social skills. These people are just not capable of initiating contacts that fulfil their need for intimacy and closeness. Hence they miss emotional support, are unsatisfied with the way they spend their leisure time with others, and often miss practical support of people in their direct environment. In that sense, their problem-solving capacity is indeed unsatisfactory and it is clear that such a shortage cannot be met by all kinds of social contacts of a more superficial or functional nature, because the socially isolated with many personal competencies do have such contacts. In fact, we must say that the differences between the socially isolated with many and with limited personal competencies are surprisingly substantial.

The *socially isolated with many personal competencies* feel more protected by their social success and their health, and tend to have to cope with their negative life events more succesfully. They are much less dependent on support facilities or professionals, and societally speaking are very active. It even seems that with all these societal activities they compensate for their inability to enter into and maintain more intimate contacts. *Socially isolated respondents with limited personal competencies* have had many hard hits in their lives and seem resigned to this. All kinds of life events play a negative role in their lives: they have had an unhappy youth, they feel depressive and less healthy, and in the middle of all of this they are unable to fall back on other factors that offer protection. Not only do they feel abandoned, they also experience an emptiness around them and feel excluded in many ways (societally speaking too) and not belonging. Socially isolated individuals who have limited personal competencies are very resigned and passive. If we realize that most of them are single and on average have a lower educational level and income, this subgroup invokes an image of a marginalized existence in many aspects, geared at surviving.

We have identified an unhappy youth and feelings of exclusion as two factors that are characteristic of the subgroup of the socially isolated with limited personal competencies. These are factors that apparently have much to do with poor personal competencies, because in the categories of the lonely and the socially inhibited they are also characteristic of those respondents with poor personal competencies. The differences between the *lonely with limited and those with many personal competencies* seem less pronounced than among the previously discussed socially isolated subgroups. In both subgroups of lonely people, negative life events and the corresponding depressive feelings play a major role, except that the lonely with limited personal competencies are more affected by such events. They feel more abandoned and value their health less than the lonely with many personal competencies.

Two groups can be more clearly distinguished among the socially inhibited. The group of the *socially inhibited with many personal competencies* is a societally active subgroup that is very much oriented towards being societally successful and has not had experience (yet) with negative life events, but does indicate knowing few people who can give them emotional support. This socially inhibited group does not (yet) seem to want to deploy their social skills to form such a personal network. However, among the *socially inhibited with limited personal competencies* it is clear that they simply miss this type of social skills. For them, life events and other problems do play a role in life, but the few people who have a meaning in their life still ensure that they do not yet encounter feelings of loneliness and social isolation. In contrast to the other groups, we see that age plays a role here to some degree. The socially inhibited with many personal competencies are on average ten years younger than the socially inhibited with limited personal competencies (respectively ages 46 and 56). We also saw in Section 6.4 that the socially inhibited as a group have slightly more self-confidence and problem-solving capacities than the lonely as a group, whereas the latter are in turn slightly more socially skilful. Hence among the group of the socially inhibited with limited personal competencies this difference manifests itself in an enhanced form.

Upon closer analysis, the transition between social inhibition and social isolation seems to be more supple than that between loneliness and social isolation. Just like their socially isolated counterparts, socially inhibited respondents with many personal competencies feel protected by their societal functioning and their health. What's more, both hardly appeal to facilities and professionals. Socially inhibited respondents with limited personal competencies have as few protective factors as their socially isolated counterparts. Both groups are less active in society, and are quite closed-off from contact with neighbourhood residents. The significant network of the socially inhibited is not very extended, which makes them vulnerable. Reducing such a network will not bring about changes for them. The lonely know already their vulnerability despite their great network.

Distinguishing subgroups in our social typology on the basis of the personal competencies of respondents produces interesting typifications; these are presented briefly in Table 12.3. It is important to remark that factors

Table 12.3 Further subgroup typification of the social contact typology and personal competencies

	Socially competent	Socially inhibited	Lonely	Socially isolated
Many personal competencies	Balanced people	Ambitious	Misunderstood	Problem concealers
Limited personal competencies	Sheltered	Socially unhandy	Disappointed	Defeated

such as age, sex, ethnicity or living in desirable or undesirable neighbourhoods play no role of significance in this subgroup typification.

The typifications are based, among other things, on the idea that social competency is related to a good balance between individual independence and solidarity with people. We therefore label the socially competent with many personal competencies as *balanced people*. The social network of the socially competent with limited personal competencies offers effective support: people are *sheltered*, even when the individual coping ability is under attack. The socially inhibited with many personal competencies seem to deploy them mainly to satisfy their *ambitions*. They do not emphasize close social relationships – probably temporarily. When the socially inhibited have limited personal competencies, their *lack of social skills* is more noticeable. They are dependent on a small social network that offers a limited degree of solidarity. For the lonely, the balance between independence and solidarity is disrupted in a different manner. For them it is not so much about the number of people with whom they feel a bond – they will gravitate much more towards feeling misunderstood or disappointed. The lonely with many personal competencies feel *misunderstood* because they are affected by experiences of emotional loss. The lonely with limited personal competencies are very *disappointed* in other people, because they cannot lessen their feelings of dependency and limited solidarity. The socially isolated with many personal competencies experience a strong discrepancy. They are capable of a lot and can even manage in more or less functional social environments. They can therefore *hide their problems* to enter into and maintain closer personal relationships. The socially isolated with limited competencies do not have much more to hang on to. They are dependent on and not close to the people around them, and feel *defeated*; they are thus the counterparts of the socially competent with many personal competencies.

12.1.2 Subgroup profiling according to societal participation

In Table 12.2 we see extensive subcategories of the societally active and passive within each of the four categories of our social typology. If we review a series of variables for all eight subcategories, one of the first things to be noticed when distinguishing between societally active and passive respondents is that – not surprisingly – age plays a major role: societally passive respondents are on average older. It makes no difference whether they are socially competent, socially inhibited, lonely or socially isolated. The difference between, for example, the socially inhibited with extensive or with little societal participation amounts to twenty-four years (respectively ages forty and sixty-four). In Section 5.8 we saw that there was no relation between life events and societal participation, but if we examine the four groups from the social typology more specifically on this aspect, differences do appear among the socially inhibited and the lonely. There are fewer negative events among both passive and active socially competent respondents. The opposite occurs among the socially isolated: both the active and the passive subgroups have endured many negative life events. Among the socially inhibited we only notice that the passive subgroup has undergone more negative events of a societal nature. The passive lonely are also confronted with such negative life events. However, what is most noticeable among the lonely is that the societally active ones have endured not only negative societal life experiences but also many more negative personal life experiences. The passive lonely are the only subcategory to actually feel very dependent on professional support, which certainly has to do with their strong feelings of depression. Among societally passive socially inhibited respondents, feelings of exclusion play a large role and they participate less in neighbourhood activities. By contrast, the active socially inhibited feel protected by their societal success. The societally active lonely also have feelings of exclusion, whereas the societally passive lonely deal more with physical health problems.

Active socially isolated people distinguish themselves from the passive socially isolated on the aspect of better physical health and the absence of feelings of depression. They have to care more often for a sick partner. The passive socially isolated present a by now familiar picture: all kinds of negative life events, an unhappy youth, worse health, depression, a lack of protective factors, feelings of exclusion, lower income, etc.

The typifications in Table 12.4 are based chiefly on the way in which societal functioning and personal social contacts are embedded in the life of those involved. Societally active socially competent respondents are *satisfied*: their societal and social functioning go well together. The *passive socially competent* exemplify par excellence that societal passivity does not have to have consequences for the personal social life of people. The societally active socially inhibited are societally successful, but miss some emotional support and are also very *critical* of their social environment. The societally passive socially inhibited are confronted in their lives with societal setbacks, but are *resigned* to this. The societally active lonely have undergone societal as well as personal setbacks, all of which are accompanied by the feeling of being *excluded*. The societally passive lonely have undergone the same societal and personal setbacks, have also had an unhappy youth and do not feel as

Table 12.4 Further subgroup typification of the social contact typology and societal participation

	Socially competent	Socially inhibited	Lonely	Socially isolated
Societally active	Satisfied active	Critically successful	Excluded	Compensators
Societally passive	Competent passive	Resigned	Dependent	Marginalized

healthy; hence they are very *dependent* on all kinds of professional support. The societally active socially isolated have also had societal and personal setbacks and problems in their youth. They are very critical about their social environment but also very active in it, and seem to *compensate* in this way for their setbacks and problems. The societally passive socially isolated have problems on all kinds of fronts: they have undergone societal and personal setbacks, feel unhealthy and excluded, and have little emotional support. Their lives are all in all quite *marginalized*.

12.1.3 Social contacts typology, personal competencies and societal participation

Table 12.5 shows all sixteen combinations possible when we relate the social contacts typology and personal competencies to societal participation. What becomes clear is that among the categories of the socially competent and the lonely the degree of societal participation does not differ, regardless of whether they have many or limited personal competencies. The opposite applies to the socially inhibited and the socially isolated. Particularly the socially inhibited with limited personal competencies tend to be more societally passive. The same goes for the socially isolated with limited personal competencies. Among the socially isolated with many personal competencies, a small majority is societally active.

There are two subcategories in which the majority is societally passive: the socially inhibited with limited personal competencies and the socially isolated with limited personal competencies. Among the socially isolated with many personal competencies, the majority is societally active. The difference between the socially isolated with limited and with many personal competencies is thus larger than the difference between the societally active and passive socially isolated. Specific to the socially isolated with many personal competencies are societal success and health, the absence of negative life events, strong participation in neighbourhood activities, and the clear lack of dependence on facilities and professionals. For them, the main problem is feeling socially connected to others. They miss people to fall back on, a friend or girlfriend – in short, all aspects of emotional and companionship support.

Table 12.5 Social contact typology and personal competencies with societal participation, in percentages (N = 411)

	SC and low pc	SC and high pc	SIN and low pc	SIN and high pc	L and low pc	L and high pc	SI and low pc	SI and high pc	Total
Societally passive	33	27	55	35	39	42	59	46	36
Societally active	67	73	45	66	61	59	41	55	64
Total	100	100	100	100	100	100	100	100	100

Notes
SC = socially competent; SIN = socially inhibited; L = lonely; SI = socially isolated; pc = personal competencies.

Characteristic of the socially inhibited and the socially isolated with limited personal competencies are their passive life attitude and severe dependence on professional support. These are the only two subcategories that end up much more often in a situation of environmental isolation. The average for all subcategories is 22 per cent. However, of the socially inhibited with limited personal competencies 46 per cent are environmentally isolated, against as many as 72 per cent of the socially isolated with limited personal competencies. The degree of societal activity or passivity is irrelevant here.

12.2 Societal and individual well-being as products of social isolation

Until now we have spoken mainly of factors that contribute to social competence, social inhibition, loneliness or social isolation. In this section we would like to discuss their consequences. These consequences are measured by the satisfaction of the respondents with their societal and individual well-being. Societal well-being involves satisfaction with education, work, income, living situation and leisure time. Individual well-being involves mainly enjoyment of life. In Figures 12.1 to 12.4 we introduce our subcategories in order of dissatisfaction with respectively societal well-being and individual well-being.

12.2.1 Societal well-being

The first things that one notices in Figures 12.1 and 12.2 are the very large differences between the subcategories with the least and the most dissatisfaction over societal well-being. The combination of the social contacts

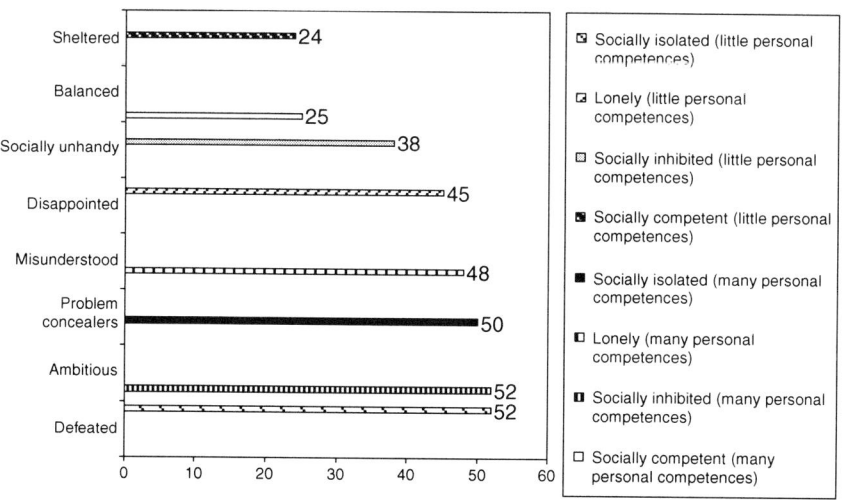

Figure 12.1 Dissatisfaction with societal well-being according to eight subcategories of personal competences, percentages.

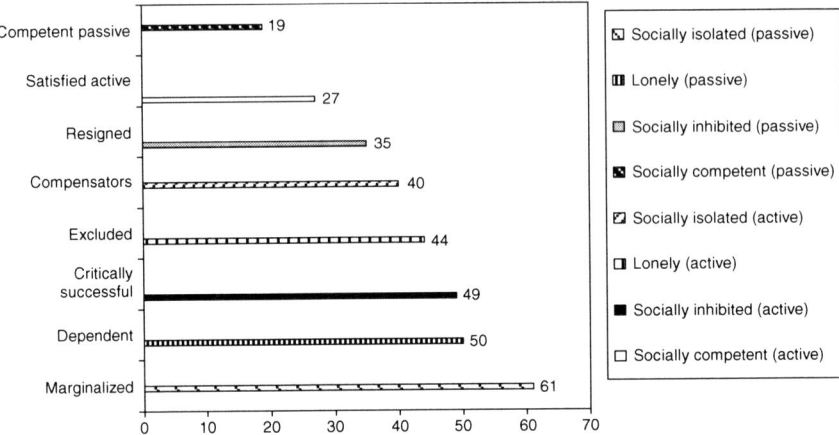

Figure 12.2 Dissatisfaction with societal well-being according to eight subcategories of societal participation, percentages.

typology with personal competencies produces substantial differences. Among the socially competent with limited personal competencies (the sheltered), 24 per cent are dissatisfied with their societal well-being, against 52 per cent among the socially inhibited and the socially isolated with many personal competencies (respectively the ambitious and the defeated). The combination of the social contacts typology with societal participation also produces substantial differences. Among the socially isolated who are societally passive (the marginalized), as many as 61 per cent are dissatisfied with their societal well-being, against 19 per cent among the socially competent who are passive (the passive competent) (Figure 12.2).

The *socially competent*, whether societally active or passive, are most satisfied with their societal well-being. The *socially isolated* who are societally passive are the most dissatisfied. Societally active socially isolated individuals are in fact much more satisfied. Among the *socially inhibited*, what we notice is that those who are societally active are much more dissatisfied with their societal well-being than the societally passive socially inhibited. For societal well-being the degree of societal participation makes no difference among the *lonely*.

We can conclude by stating that being societally passive or active only makes a difference among the socially inhibited and the socially isolated. Among the socially inhibited it is precisely the societally active (the critically successful) who are more often dissatisfied over their societal well-being, whereas the socially isolated in that sense actually benefit from societal activities (the compensators): they are much more satisfied than their socially isolated counterparts.

Just as with the degree of societal participation, for the socially competent it makes no difference either whether they have many or limited personal competencies, at least with respect to their societal well-being, given that they are the least dissatisfied. The lonely and the socially isolated are much more dissatisfied (between 45 per cent and 52 per cent of them), but among them too the degree of personal competency has no influence on their societal well-being. We only see a major difference among the socially inhibited. And just as with the societally active socially inhibited, in this case too those with many personal competencies (the ambitious) are more dissatisfied. In general lines we can say that a difference in societal participation produces slightly more differentiation in terms of dissatisfaction with societal well-being than a difference in personal competencies.

12.2.2 Individual well-being

Although societal well-being and individual well-being are not the same, they obviously influence one another. About one-third of the respondents who are dissatisfied with their societal well-being indicate being unable to enjoy life. Among those respondents who are satisfied with their societal well-being, more than 90 per cent are able to enjoy life. It is therefore interesting to examine whether the data on dissatisfaction with societal well-being presented in Figures 12.1 and 12.2 change if we take individual well-being as criterion. Does personal competency play a much larger role in individual well-being than the degree of societal participation?

At first glance, the differences in Figures 12.3 and 12.4 between the least and the most dissatisfied subcategory are equally large. Among the socially competent with many personal competencies (balanced people) only 3 per

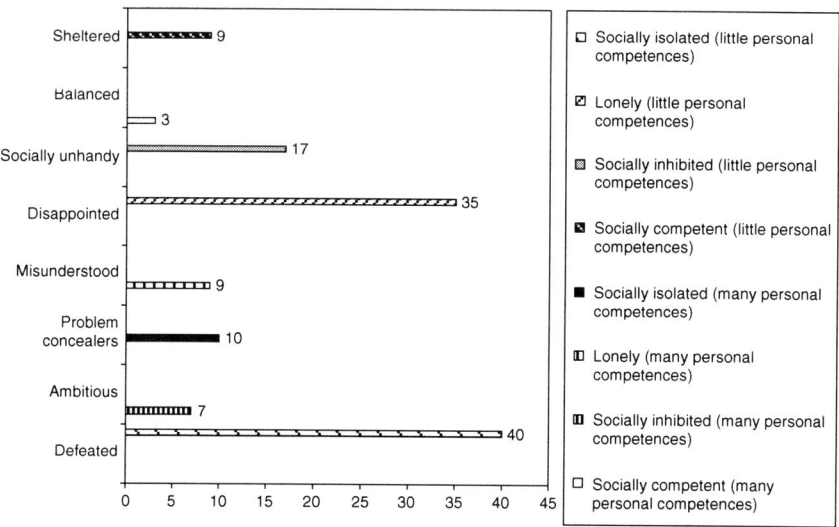

Figure 12.3 Dissatisfaction with individual well-being according to eight subcategories of personal competences, percentages.

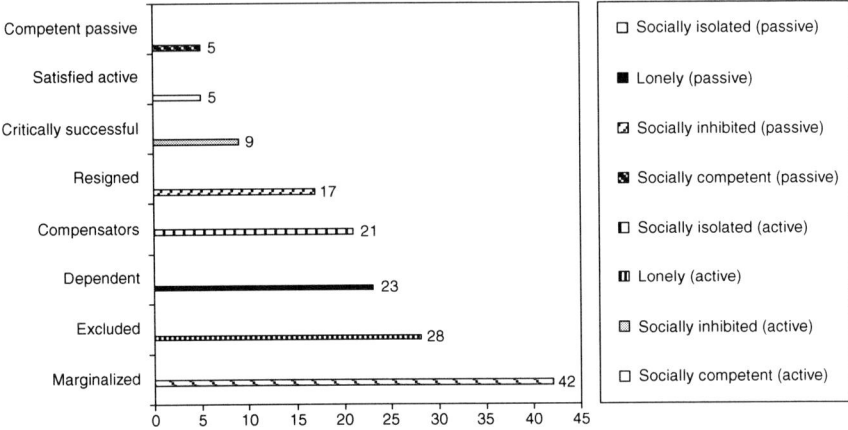

Figure 12.4 Dissatisfaction with individual well-being according to eight subcategories of societal participation, percentages.

cent are dissatisfied, and at 40 per cent the group of the socially isolated with limited personal competencies (the defeated) has the most dissatisfied individuals. We see approximately the same figures for the measure of societal participation: 5 per cent of the passive or active socially competent (respectively the passive competent and the satisfied active) to 42 per cent of the societally passive socially isolated (the marginalized). Personal competency plays nonetheless a more decisive role than societal participation. In Figure 12.3 we see low percentages of respondents dissatisfied with individual well-being (3 per cent to 10 per cent) in all subcategories with many personal competencies (from the socially competent to the socially isolated). Two subcategories with limited personal competencies, the lonely (the disappointed) and the socially isolated (the defeated) are the most dissatisfied with their individual well-being.

In terms of the degree of societal participation, the various subcategories overlap much more (Figure 12.4). For the socially competent and the lonely, being societally active or passive makes no difference to their individual well-being. For them the issue is the very social competence or loneliness. The lonely are of course more dissatisfied. For the socially inhibited and the socially isolated things are different though. The socially passive among them (the redesigned and the marginalized) are clearly the most satisfied. Here too the societally passive socially isolated (the marginalized) are the most dissatisfied with individual well-being.

12.2.3 Relation between societal and individual well-being

The subgroup profiling we presented in Sections 12.1.1, 12.1.2 and 12.1.3 also seems to be relevant if we look at the consequences of social competence, social inhibition, loneliness and social isolation for satisfaction with societal well-being (education, work, income, living and personal interests) and satisfaction with individual well-being (being able to enjoy life).

In Tables 12.3 and 12.4 we labelled the *socially competent* balanced people, sheltered, satisfied active and competent passive. All four subcategories are the most satisfied, with their societal as well as their individual well-being. Apparently their social network contributes so much to their well-being that information over their personal competence or societal participation does not add much to it.

Further distinction into subcategories of the *socially inhibited* produces additional information. The ambitious (the socially active) and the critically successful (those with many personal competencies) tend to be more dissatisfied over their societal well-being: in that sense things tend to be just not good enough for them. This contrasts with their considerable satisfaction with individual well-being. The socially unhandy (limited personal competencies) and the resigned (societally passive) among the socially inhibited are in that respect worse-off: they can apparently accept their societal situation, but lack of social skills and resignation do have adverse effects on their personal well-being.

For the *lonely* (the misunderstood, disappointed, excluded and dependent), in a way the same applies as for the socially competent. Information on their societal participation or personal competency does not produce much more information about their feeling of well-being. This is determined primarily by their feelings of loneliness. Still, there is an important exception. The disappointed (the lonely with limited personal competencies) are less able to enjoy life than the misunderstood.

For the *socially isolated*, being active or passive almost always matters to some extent, the same goes for having many or limited personal competencies. The societally active socially isolated are in our view compensators, just as we have labelled the socially isolated with many personal competencies as problem concealers, but they can in any event enjoy life more than their passive and less personally competent counterparts, who are justly called the marginalized and the defeated. The societally active socially isolated tend to be less dissatisfied with their societal well-being. In that sense, compensation of their poor social network with societal activities pays off.

12.3 Conclusions

It has become clear that our basic social contact typology not only has significance for the typification of the personal network and its quality: it also points towards categories of people who have their own unique standing in life and have different views over all kinds of facets of human existence. The subgroup profiling based on the personal competencies or the societal functioning of people has allowed us a view into this. Still, this is only a first impression. Just the wide gamut of negative factors in the life of, for example, the socially isolated, especially if they also have limited personal competencies or are societally passive, requires a deeper analysis of the living situation of these respondents. Next to the search into the causes and consequences of social isolation in the life of people, it is important to know more about the specific strategies that people have adopted to keep their heads above water and keep functioning more or less autonomously. In that sense, our subgroup profiling just gives the first impulse. Deeper qualitative research will provide more insight into the significance that a specific constellation of factors has in the eyes of those involved (Machielse, 2003).

Part IV
Reflections

13 Research on social isolation into perspective

Ludwien Meeuwesen, Anja Machielse and Roelof Hortulanus

13.1 Introduction

In Chapter 11, the main premises and findings of this study were presented in a rather compressed fashion. We will now examine the research method and the questionnaires used (Section 13.2). We will then discuss the empirical basis of the typology of social contacts we constructed, the generalizability of the results, and the suitability of the measuring instruments used. Some suggestions will also be made for further research into the phenomenon of social isolation. A theoretical view will be offered of the research results (Section 13.3). We will then find out how the research results of this study relate to the existing theories on social networks, and will show the contributions that it can make to an interdisciplinary theory on social isolation.

13.2 Reflection on method

13.2.1 The social contacts typology

This study, which investigates social contacts in general and social isolation in particular, is set up on a large scale. More than 2,400 respondents were interviewed in two urban and two rural locations on the basis of a very wide list of subjects. Half a year later, in a second round, a smaller group was interviewed again, delving more deeply into several personal subjects (such as life events, life attitude and socialization). This second round offered us the chance to penetrate much further into relevant facts of social isolation (see Section 1.7).

The multifaceted analyses of this study have led to several important findings. One important finding of the study is that the social contacts typology we designed and elaborated on was empirically validated. We have seen that to study social isolation, a combined approach of an objective criterion, the network approach (how large is the social network) and a subjective criterion in terms of feelings of loneliness is more productive than using only one of the two criteria (Meeuwesen *et al.*, 2001). The design of the typology is based on reliable and validated methods. Numerous analyses show that the typology differentiates between individual, social-environmental and societal factors. There are mostly light to moderate relations to other factors, but there is no coincidence. We therefore concluded that the social contacts typology is a relatively independent model that cannot be reduced to other factors.

We also make statements over the occurrence in the population of the types we distinguished, the indicated percentages of 64 per cent (the socially competent), 8 per cent (the socially inhibited), 22 per cent (the lonely) and 6 per cent (the socially isolated). These percentages came about by establishing the criterion for a 'small' versus a 'large' network between 4 and 5. No agreement has been found up to now in the literature over a good criterion for a 'small' versus a 'large' network: such a decision is always somewhat arbitrary. The results of our study do correspond with those of other studies. A recent study among medical patients, for example, produced figures of 12 per cent for the group with a small network (Brummett et al., 2001). That percentage corresponds fairly well with our study's finding that 14 per cent has a small network (8 per cent socially inhibited and 6 per cent socially isolated merged together). If we set a classification criterion, for example, between 3 and 4, the percentage of people with a small network would be slightly lower, and 4 per cent of the respondents could be considered to be socially isolated. There is much more of a consensus over the classification criterion regarding loneliness: in many studies, this criterion is validated and chosen for a classification into 'not lonely' (0 and 1) and 'lonely' (from 2), which we have used here.

13.2.2 *Generalizability of the results*

We can make two remarks on the generalizability of these results into the Dutch population. On the one hand, the percentages may be somewhat biased because our classification criterion was used quite widely, which means that the number of socially isolated individuals may lie slightly lower than 6 per cent. We can approach this issue in another way though, and remind ourselves that we opted for a large-scale study among the average population. In other words, we did not search explicitly for the socially isolated. The respondents were selected through a random population sample in the four research locations. We visited homes from among the addresses in the sample, asking people to participate in the study. Large groups of marginalized individuals, like the homeless, prisoners, people in homes, institutions and hospitals were therefore not reached. It is known that relatively many people in these groups are socially isolated (Schnabel, 2000).

Another point is non-response. Although the usual reactions were given in this respect (no time, don't feel like it, not a good moment, moved, etc.), chances of people not opening the door or not wanting to participate in the research are probably greater among the socially isolated than among the other groups of the social contacts typology. This involves those people who speak to no one for days (or weeks) and/or do not leave the house, and find it difficult to receive others in their home. This makes us suspect that the group of the socially isolated is in reality larger than what our study shows.

Taking these comments into consideration, we believe we can make a cautious estimate that, for example, in the Netherlands 600,000 people of the total Dutch population are socially isolated to some degree. The group that risks becoming isolated sooner or later is five times larger. Of course, this doesn't necessarily mean that they will indeed become socially isolated at some point in time, but for some of them it will be the case.

13.2.3 The measuring instruments

With regard to the suitability of the measuring instruments we used, we can say that a number of them are (reasonably) reliable and valid. This involved largely standardized and commonly used lists, like the loneliness scale, the network method, the approach of life events, depression, and – partially – personal competencies. Some questions were asked twice, for instance in open as well as closed form with pre-structured answer categories (as was the case with protective factors against isolation). Some questions (such as those on report marks) were presented to the respondents exactly the same way in the first and second rounds.

We also made partial use of new measures which we ourselves designed, for example, for societal participation and environmental isolation. This involves phenomena over which a strong 'common sense' reigns (such as equalling societal participation with good education and work, or marginalized neighbourhoods with environmental isolation), and which in the context of this study we believe needed a critical approach. Several attempts were made in the present study to that end. The usefulness of a new approach to societal participation and environmental isolation came forth from numerous studied relations with other factors. This does not preclude the need to further validate the measuring instrument designed here. In any event, a start was given to reflection on a useful conceptualization of something such as societal participation and environmental isolation. Similarly, with regard to the concept of health we can observe that although everyone well knows the importance of the concepts of physical health and mental health, few are familiar with a notion such as social health. This study offers countless points of reference to approach health from a social perspective, from someone's social capital.

Extensive attention has been paid in this project to studying statistical relations between the various relevant variables. This offers insights especially into the different relations of relevant direct and indirect factors that play a role with regard to the social contact typology, but on a more abstract level. To get a better idea of the (individual) respondents involved in the study, the typology makes a further distinction into several subgroups: the subgroup profiling according to personal competences and according to societal participation (see Chapter 12). We undertook this exercise in order to form an image of the more concrete world in which the various groups of people live. Of course, such an exercise need not remain limited to personal competences and societal participation, but can also take place in relation to themes like health, neighbourhood cohesion, etc. The same exercise may also be done in relation to the concept of loneliness, which can be split into emotional and social loneliness (Weiss, 1973; Van Baarsen et al., 2001; Dykstra and Fokkema, 2001).

A last point has to be made regarding the combined analysis in Chapter 11. This analysis was based on the smaller dataset, which is not quite representative (see Section 1.7). This means that some of these results may deviate from the results described in the separate chapters. One has to take this into consideration when reading the results of these regression analysis.

13.2.4 Suggestions for further research

The described exercise of subgroup profiling showed that the group of the socially isolated presented quite a varied picture. Many of the socially isolated are inconspicuous, they bother no one. Therefore the wide range of negative factors in the life of the socially isolated, especially if they have limited personal competences or are societally passive, demands a deeper analysis of their living situation. To really understand what their life is like, how it became that way and how they survive, research of a more qualitative nature would be suitable; in that sense, our subgroup profiling only gives an initial impetus (see Chapter 12). Next to the question into the causes and consequences of social isolation in the lives of people, it is important to know more about the specific strategies that people have adopted to keep their heads above water and keep functioning more or less autonomously. The focus can be a certain category of people, and a more specific search can be made for the more extreme forms of social isolation. Large-scale research is less suited for this purpose, while qualitative in-depth interviews are a more obvious choice (Machielse, 2003, 2006).

The observation that large-scale research that is aimed at the average population does not reach certain groups raises the question of how they *can* be reached. If we want to reach less accessible groups in addition to the more accessible ones, methods are required that make it possible to infiltrate or approach certain locations. The theme of social isolation thus demands methods of participating observation, in which locations such as fast-food joints, gambling establishments, and certain streets or squares are explored according to more classical anthropological methods. Key figures such as family doctors, social workers, religious leaders and social services can also fulfil an important role here. The attention could also be directed to the various manifestations of social isolation and their relation with issues like truancy or addictive behaviour.

In this study we have learned much about connections and eventual causes of isolation, but less over its consequences for the individual, for the social environment and for societal cohesion. Although the consequences have been discussed regularly and it has been observed repeatedly that there is also a two-way interaction between various factors, this study does not lend itself so much to making far-reaching pronouncements on the subject. A more longitudinally designed study would be the road to follow here, asking the same respondents about the same themes over a longer period of time and focusing on processes of change. Another obvious option would be to replicate a study such as the present one with a representative sample of other countries of western societies.

Finally, we wish to point to the finding of this study that there is often a difference between the views in the policy world and the experiences of people themselves. A clear example of this is the view that societal participation can prevent the onset of social isolation. This research has shown that respondents often experience this differently. For this reason, it would be interesting to further examine to what degree environmental isolation and societal isolation are related to social isolation in the experience of people themselves.

13.3 Theoretical reflection

What do the research results mean for the existing theories on social isolation? In Chapter 2 we observed that the importance of social relationships in sociological as well as (social-)psychological theory is recognized. In recent years we have also seen an increase in the number of studies into personal networks. Although the lack of such networks is recognized widely in the social sciences, just a few studies focus on the inter-relation between different personal, social and societal factors. Sociologists mostly pay attention to social relationships with a focus on societal cohesion and solidarity. Although the common network approaches do map out the social networks of people in different ways, no attention is paid to the subjective experience of personal relationships or the lack thereof. In (social-)psychology the focus is mainly on subjective feelings of loneliness.

From different theoretical angles there is indeed attention towards certain aspects of social networks, but we have not been able to find a systematic study into social isolation in which all aspects related to this phenomenon are brought together. With this study we have attempted to do this, empirically as well as theoretically. We will now find out to what degree we have succeeded in the theoretical portion.

13.3.1 *An adequate definition of social isolation*

Every theory begins with an adequate definition of the phenomenon to be studied. The same applies to social isolation. Until now, a generally accepted definition of social isolation was not available. There was, however, a consensus over the fact that the lack of *meaningful* personal relationships was an important characteristic of social isolation (De Jong-Gierveld, 1984; Schrameijer, 1990; Sumbadze, 1999; Lincoln, 2000; House, 2001). From this perspective, social isolation cannot be defined in merely objective terms as is the case in the tradition of the network approaches, which equal social isolation to having a personal network with a limited scope or a one-sided composition. The risk of social isolation increases as a personal network becomes smaller, closer or more homogeneous, or when supportive relationships are missing. These relatively objective network approaches do not offer an understanding of the subjective experience of the network, as a result of which they cannot adequately identify the lack of meaningful social contacts. Empirical research shows in fact that emotional aspects play an important role in the assessment of social contacts, and that there is only a weak correlation between this subjective assessment and objective forms of isolation as described in the network approaches.

On the basis of these considerations we have posited that a theory on social isolation should consider not only objective network characteristics but certainly also the subjective experience aspects of the network. We borrowed this subjective criterion from a tradition in which the quality of relationships is central, namely loneliness research. Within this tradition we find various conceptualizations and approaches. A common point of departure is that loneliness is seen as the experiencing of a shortage of personal relationships and consequently cannot be equalled to being 'alone' (objective isolation). The nature of this shortage is described in different ways (Dykstra and Fokkema, 2001). The deficit approach assumes that loneliness ensues when certain types of relationships in the personal network are lacking, so that a number of social needs cannot be satisfied. In this approach a distinction is made between two types of loneliness, in which social loneliness is found mainly among people with a relatively small personal network and emotional loneliness occurs mostly among those who do not have a partner (Weiss, 1973). In this view, the composition of the personal network (the type of relationships that are present) is decisive for its subjective experience. For this reason, we believe this approach is too limited for an adequate definition of social isolation. The cognitive approach to loneliness focuses on psychological processes that are not so much related to an objectively observable lack of relationships, but to the assessment and adequateness of personal relationships. In this approach, loneliness arises as an unacceptable discrepancy between the desired and the realized relationships a person has, and subjectively experienced loneliness is explicitly distinguished from objective isolation (Van Tilburg, 1988; De Jong-Gierveld, 1984). We believe that this cognitive approach to loneliness offers good common points for an adequate theory on social isolation in which not only objective characteristics of the network acquire a place, but also the subjective feelings that people have over the quality of that network.

For this reason, in the situation at hand this *cognitive approach to loneliness* is combined with the *social support approach* that maps out the amount and type of support that people expect from their personal network. The typology of social contacts we developed is based on this combination of a relatively objective and a more subjective criterion. The research results show that both network scope and subjective feelings of loneliness are essential components of the study into meaningful contacts and social isolation, but that the application of a combination of both criteria produces a clear added value. Whereas the network approaches do not consider subjective experience, our model includes it expressly. It also offers more insight than a merely subjective approach. Given that many theoreticians assume that periods of loneliness belong in the normal course of life, measuring only feelings of loneliness is not enough (see, for example, Perlman and Peplau, 1982; Linneman *et al.*, 1990). The model we developed offers a greater understanding of the complex reality than is possible by using just the objective or just the subjective elements. Moreover, using our typology it is not only possible to indicate whether someone has a well-functioning network or is socially isolated – the socially competent compared with the socially isolated – but there is also a possibility of listing two other groups, each at a different risk of ending up in social isolation. Both groups – the socially inhibited and the lonely – are in a sense vulnerable, the first because it depends on a small group of people and the second because despite having a large network it still feels lonely. The data from this study show that the social contacts measure we constructed is important not only in order to typify the personal network and its quality, but that it involves empirically demonstrable categories of people who face life in a certain way and have different views on all kinds of facets of human existence. Through a more qualitative processing it has also been possible to further distinguish between the four groups of the social contacts typology and to obtain an initial insight into the specific way in which certain factors are interconnected in each group.

It is clear that the combination of an objective and a subjective criterion produces a practicable definition of social isolation. Given that this definition could also be operationalized using standardized and commonly-used questionnaires, it proved to be a productive starting point for this research.

13.3.2 A contribution to the social capital theory

This study can also contribute to a broader social sciences theory that is indispensable for a good understanding of the phenomenon of social isolation, namely the social capital theory. We already saw in Chapter 2 that social relationships have been seen traditionally in sociology as elementary building stones for the social cohesion of society (Tönnies, 1887; Durkheim, 1893; Simmel, 1908). Contemporary sociology evidences this in the social capital theory, which points to the meaning of social relationships for the functioning of society. The social capital theory assumes that social interactions between people are important in that they allow cooperation bonds and collective actions within a community or society. Three core elements of social capital are generally mentioned: trust, reciprocity and networks that exist within a group or community (Stolle, 2000; Leeuw, 2001). Most sociologists view social capital as the generalized trust in the norms of reciprocity that are present in a society and which have a positive effect on society as a whole (Putnam, 1993). Social capital thus involves the existence of formal and institutionalized networks, what is known as 'civil society' or clubs, organizations and neighbourly bonds. The amount of social capital within this meaning is seen as an indicator of the mutual involvement between people in society. Others see social capital mainly as a characteristic of individuals, as a resource that contributes to individuals being able to realize certain goals in their lives (Lin, 1982; Bourdieu, 1984). In this approach the emphasis lies not so much on the positive effects of social interactions for society as a whole, but chiefly on the positive consequences for individuals and groups. The presumption is that participation in enduring (relevant) networks is an important achievement or capacity that works to the advantage of individuals (Bourdieu, 1984; Coleman, 1988). There is, however, no certainty as to whether these individual advantages in the end have favourable effects for society as a whole (Stolle, 2001; Field, 2003).

We are of the opinion that the social capital theory has two shortcomings. First, social capital gets more attention at the societal level than at the individual level. Given the increasing level of individualization, social cohesion is high in the agenda, and in recent years much empirical research has been done into the presence of social capital and 'civil society'. Participation in societal activities and formal bonds is central to it, whereas hardly any attention is paid to participation in informal social networks. Second, social capital as a resource at the individual level is conceived in a very limited way. The attention goes primarily to functional and pragmatic bonds within which goal-oriented, rational actions are central, whereas affective and emotional bonds receive hardly any theoretical attention. However, these bonds are certainly as important in the daily lives of people as business relationships, if not more.

This study may provide a more complete picture of social reality than has been the case up to now in social capital theory. In the first place, our study shows that the large emphasis on societal participation in formal contexts requires some nuancing. The great interest in social capital at a societal level is based on the idea that societal participation can contribute to the societal involvement of individuals and consequently to the social cohesion of society. Social life is seen here as a result of the way in which people function in society. Societal participation is considered as an instrument that can prevent social exclusion and social isolation: at a societal level, societal participation ensures mutual involvement and thus societal bonds, whereas at the individual level it constitutes an important source of social contacts that can prevent social isolation and social exclusion. However, the relation between societal participation on the one hand and social isolation and social exclusion on the other is much more complex than social capital theory presumes.

First of all, in our research we have concluded that people's societal participation is not that easily measured. Much empirical research has indeed been done into participation in diverse societal activities, but a measure to typify the total societal activity of people has not been available until now. This is why we have constructed an objective measure for societal activity in which attention is given to six forms of societal participation: participation in work and study, club life, volunteer work, informal care, informal connections and attending recreational facilities or sports events. The advantage of this measure over common approaches (reading societal participation into education and work) is that by using it we can distinguish four categories of people with an increasing degree of societal activity. Although the risk of social isolation increases as someone participates less in societal activities, the degree of societal participation certainly does not appear to be the main cause for social isolation. Definitely as important are personal factors such as the lack of personal competencies, due to which a person is not capable of creating or maintaining a well-functioning personal network. This applies not only to the objectively measured societal participation and involvement, but also to subjective feelings of exclusion (Hortulanus et al., 1992). Feelings of exclusion seem to be much more related to personal than to societal factors. Social exclusion can also occur because people are not part of informal personal networks, and can therefore be seen literally as the expression of people's poorly functioning personal network. This means that the strong emphasis on societal participation with social cohesion in mind is undeserved. This research shows that informal personal relationships constitute a fundamental form of societal participation, which is as important to the social capital at a societal level as social participation in formal and institutional networks.

This brings us automatically to the second lacuna of the social capital theory – the lack of attention towards affective and emotional aspects of social relationships in the private sphere. The instrumental view of social relationships goes together with the emphasis on societal participation and the way in which the concepts of coping and self-efficacy are seen. Social capital theory determines the degree of coping from societal participation and socioeconomic independence. Coping is in fact a societal norm for people's functioning: they must take care of themselves as much as possible, earn their own income and not be dependent on collective facilities. The assumption is that people who participate in society can cope better than people who do not or hardly participate in societal life. From this perspective, social networks are seen primarily as a social resource that favourably benefits things like a person's job mobility or career chances (Granovetter, 1973; Lin, 1982, 2001). The present study shows that this is a very one-sided conception of the ability to cope. People rely on each other not only on a societal level but also in their personal lives. In cases of illness and other types of adversity, it is precisely the affective and emotional aspects of relationships in the private sphere which are important. A close network that can offer social support if necessary is determinant to the degree to which people can take care of themselves in such situations. This study indicates that people who can expect less support from their immediate environment will be quicker to use professional help. This is particularly the case for people who have a specific need for support due to advanced age, poor health or an unfortunate societal position. Participation in a personal network with meaningful relationships is therefore an important form of social capital. The lack of such relationships not only has negative consequences for individuals, but can also have an adverse effect on society as a whole because it increases the pressure on professional facilities. One-sided attention for the functionality and pragmatism of social relationships does not do justice to this societal interest.

We can conclude by stating that this study can confirm in several ways the major meaning of social relationships for the stability and cohesion of society. At the same time it offers sufficient arguments for a broader definition of social capital than has been used up to now. Participation in informal social bonds and the affective function of personal relationships in the personal sphere deserve as much attention as societal participation and the more public and pragmatic function of formal and institutional networks – and consequently a more prominent place in social capital theory.

13.3.3 *A preliminary explanatory model for social isolation*

Although the various network approaches are only oriented towards one single aspect of social relationships (scope, composition or amount of support), they have produced much relevant empirical research material. Using these theories allows us to map out objective characteristics of social networks and to analyse how those characteristics are related with, for instance, demographic and socio-economic factors. In recent years we have seen a flow of studies into the relationships of social networks and background factors of people such as age, sex, living situation, income and education. Research has also been conducted into the changes that affect social networks when there are health problems or important life events such as divorce, death of a partner or prolonged unemployment. There are also countless studies that map out the personal networks of certain population groups – vulnerable groups like the elderly, the divorced, the chronically ill and those who have been long-term unemployed. Some studies have examined the feelings of loneliness of certain vulnerable groups, like the elderly. However, none of these studies has focused explicitly on finding out the causes of social isolation. A systematic study in which the various causes are inter-related and studied within their connection has been missing until now.

This study is the first step towards such systematic research. Several chapters have investigated diverse factors that can play a role in the emergence of social isolation (see Chapters 4 to 11). Personal as well as societal aspects

	Individual	Societal
Temporary	**A** *Life events in personal life* (e.g. loss of partner, divorce, health problems, abuse/threats)	**B** *Life events in societal life* (e.g. job loss/insecure job situation, loss of income, undesirable living situation, education without results)
Structural	**C** *Personal traits and socialization* (e.g. lack of personal competencies, negative socialization, unhappy youth)	**D** *Societal exclusion* (e.g. societal standards regarding coping and (work) productivity, prolonged unemployment, social-environmental segregation, dependency on professional facilities)

Figure 13.1 Explanatory model for the emergence of social isolation.

were discussed. We then examined the relative importance and the inter-relatedness of the various factors (see Chapter 12). It has proven possible to determine some important factors that can explain and predict the emergence of social isolation. What was found is a clear assembly of causes, meaning that different complexes of causes can be identified and inter-related. We have represented this assembly in a (preliminary) explanatory model for the emergence of social isolation (Figure 13.1).

The complexes of causes in boxes A and B need not lead directly to social isolation, but can contribute to it. Factors C and D can be conducive to a temporary situation of social isolation acquiring a structural character. The factors in boxes C and D are in themselves factors that can lead to social isolation anyway: people who cannot cope (such as the ill or disabled) or cannot participate in the culture of (work) productivity have more chances of becoming socially isolated. We will look further into the four boxes of the model.

The causes of social isolation listed in box A can cause a temporary disruption in life. This involves important personal life events that can greatly influence the personal network. These events can have consequences for both the scope and the composition of the existing networks and their quality. Certain relationships can be lost, making the personal network smaller. Social needs can also change: when the existing contacts do not meet the new needs, this can result in strong feelings of loneliness. The factors in box A can also have consequences for societal functioning (B). Important life events can lead, for example, to such changes in someone's work or income situation that participation in societal life becomes more difficult.

In box C we see causes that can give the situation a structural character. While most people pick up and get on with their lives after a while, establishing new meaningful contacts or managing to improve their societal situation, the factors in box C can constitute a hindrance to this. These factors can cause someone to be unable to get over the temporary negative repercussions of negative life events. The factors in box D can also contribute to the problems becoming structural. The more societally-oriented factors listed here can lead to the emergence of a form of structural societal exclusion. In the worst case, people deal with structural factors from box C as well as with factors from box D. Social isolation is then accompanied by a form of societal exclusion, both with a structural character.

The factors in box B also cause temporary disruptions in people's lives. They involve life events which primarily have significant consequences for people's societal functioning. Loss of work, a living environment that is experienced as negative or incomplete schooling can influence a person's life quite negatively and encumber societal functioning. Poor societal participation can become structural if the societal factors from box D also play a role.

Repercussions on the personal network can also be felt due to the factors in box B. Loss of work means that an important source of contacts is no longer there, and a considerable loss of income can lead to financial problems that can hinder interactions with others. This can result in a temporary situation of social isolation. The social need can also change in this context: as people have more free time, the need for contact with others can increase. Just like with factors in box A, after some time most people are able to adjust to the new situation and expand the network that they have maintained or still have, or intensify the existing contacts. When factors from box C are also involved however, social isolation can acquire a structural character. When both personal (box C) and societal factors (box D) play a role, a situation can arise in which there is structural social isolation as well as a structural form of societal exclusion.

Finally, the model makes clear that people who have problems with their societal functioning and are not able to build a supportive network in their private lives end up outside the margins of society, in social as well as societal terms. The model also shows that the various complexes of causes are inter-related, as a result of which problems can be interwoven (one problem enhances the other).

13.3.4 Conclusions

How does this study contribute to theory formation on social isolation? Well, we have been able to produce an adequate definition of social isolation. Whereas up to now there have only been derived definitions – in the network approaches social isolation is defined as the lack of certain characteristics in the personal network – here we see an independent definition of social isolation. This definition is operationalized from two angles, a subjective one and a more objective angle, measurable using reliable questionnaires.

Second, this study focuses attention on societal aspects of social networks as well as on their personal aspects. Whereas (social-)psychological theories tend to deal with the meaning of social relationships for personal well-being, sociological theory approaches social isolation from a societal perspective (the network as a societal resource or as a basis for social cohesion and solidarity). A theory that is explicitly aimed at the importance of social networks is the social capital theory. In this theory the attention goes mainly towards the societal aspects of formal social relationships. This study shows that informal social relationships constitute an equally fundamental form of societal participation that is important for the social capital at a societal level. We also show that the instrumental view of social relationships is closely related to the conception of the ability to cope. When we detect the ability to cope not just from people's societal participation and socio-economic dependency but also from whether they have a supportive network that can offer social support if necessary, aspects such as intimacy, affectivity and involvement acquire importance too. These aspects should therefore earn a more prominent place in a theory over social capital.

Third, we have initiated an explanatory model for the emergence of social isolation, in which societal as well as personal factors are involved. This model also shows that certain factors can ensure that social isolation remains temporary or acquires a structural character, and offers insights into the emergence of interwoven problems.

The study has shown a number of factors that influence the emergence of social isolation. We have made it clear that it is not only societal factors which play a role in the emergence of social isolation, but personal factors also make an important contribution. To further study these personal factors, theories that are oriented explicitly towards social networks and subjective well-being do not suffice. An important contribution to a theory on social isolation can also be made by (social-)psychological theories that are not primarily oriented towards social relationships but do discuss aspects relevant to social isolation, such as coping theories.

14 Towards a new policy vision on social isolation

Roelof Hortulanus

14.1 Introduction

As is the case with many issues, there are all kinds of general notions and views on social isolation, among citizens as well as policymakers. Social isolation is often seen as characteristic of certain *categories of people*, such as the unemployed, seniors, singles, the sick, addicts and the homeless. The assumption is that the non-participation or the living situation of these people strongly increases their chances of social isolation. *Neighbourhood circumstances* are also seen as a breeding ground for social isolation, for example, living in certain neighbourhoods that have a high degree of cultural and ethnic diversity, and different lifestyles and codes of behaviour. Sometimes we link isolation to *personal characteristics and circumstances*. The idea that mental factors can play a significant role has gradually become accepted and in this sense we have become aware of the risks run by overburdened informal carers or lone parents. When governments in western societies formulate policies on social isolation, the focus tends to be on the consequences of unemployment and old age, or living in marginalized neighbourhoods. This underemphasizes social isolation as an independent phenomenon – which can affect everybody – and this is regrettable, because social isolation often manifests itself in a concealed way emerging, for instance, through health problems, deviating behaviour, feelings of uneasiness with living and the avoidance of recreational facilities.

Throughout this book we have gained more insight into the phenomenon of social isolation. First of all we have gained insight into the scope of social isolation and the personal and societal factors that can play a role in its emergence. We have also seen that social isolation has consequences for the individual and societal well-being of people. In fact, social isolation can be seen as a new form of social inequality. This evidences that social isolation should not be seen as a purely personal matter but also as a societal issue. The wide approach of our study has shown that social isolation is not to be found only in certain categories of people or in certain locations: it can be found among the unemployed and the working population, among young and old, singles and cohabitants, the sick and the healthy, urbanites and country folk, and residents of both poor and upscale neighbourhoods. We can conclude by stating that this study has shown that social isolation should not be seen so much as a result of other issues but as an independent phenomenon that can affect everybody and requires explicit attention. This conclusion has major consequences for the premises on which social isolation policy is based and requires further discussion. To start with, we will show that social isolation is a societal issue that requires public attention and involvement (Section 14.2). We will then present the foundations for a new policy vision on social isolation (Section 14.3), and show how these foundations can be shaped into new intervention strategies (Section 14.4). The chapter concludes with a few remarks about the necessary convergence between interventions of professionals and informal support (Section 14.5).

14.2 Social isolation: private problem or societal issue?

A first question we pose here is how we can look at social isolation from a policy perspective. Is social isolation a private problem the government and social institutions should not interfere with, or is there a societal issue that deserves policy attention? In the first case we see social isolation as a personal matter, as a phenomenon that is part of life. We assume that every time period and every type of society has had people who choose to live a withdrawn life, or who are more or less cast out by the society they are part of. From this perspective, governments and social institutions should back off. However, if we see social isolation in this way we observe a peculiar discrepancy with other phenomena, such as poverty or unemployment. In this respect we could also say that these are problems present in every society. But whereas until now social isolation has received little policy attention, the same does not apply to education, labour participation and income. We should probably search for the explanation in the perception of factors that are determinant to our prosperity and well-being, as well as in views on the separation of private and public issues.

To begin with the latter: in our modern society, people's lives are increasingly split into different life domains. On the one hand we see business and functional relations in the public domain within which the government too works. On the other hand there are the affective bonds in the private domain, where public involvement is less self-evident. The way in which people shape their lives and the social contacts they maintain are seen as a purely private matter in which the government does not play a role. We are very reserved when it comes to interfering in the private world, for example, with regard to upbringing, health and social competencies. In contrast, public involvement with education, labour and income is based chiefly on ideas about the ability to cope independently, societal participation and solidarity. The reasoning behind it is as follows: without work and with too low an income it is not possible to build an autonomous life, as a result of which people close themselves off from the society around them and do not contribute to the prosperity of the country and the well-being of their fellow citizens.

These premises are subject to dispute. There are strong indications that our modern society entails new life risks, and that the 'winners' and 'losers' in our society can no longer be defined exclusively in socio-economic terms but also in terms of a lack of social capital (Bourdieu, 1985; Beck, 1992; Schuyt, 1997). Now that people can no longer fall back automatically on family, the church or the local community, they have to deliberately build relationships with others (Giddens, 1991; Castells, 1996). After all, it is an illusion that people can live autonomously – they always have to recur to others. The much-embraced individual ability to cope independently assumes precisely that people are part of adequately functioning social networks (Beck and Beck-Gernsheim, 1994; Van Heerikhuizen, 1997). This modern form of managing requires new competencies and creates new vulnerable people and dropouts. Through policies that strongly emphasize interventions in education, work and income, one misses the importance of the significance of competencies for modern living. What's more, the vulnerable and dropouts are unintentionally further excluded if interventions in the domains of education, work and income are seen as a panacea for the solution of other life problems, like social isolation.

In this study we obtained a great deal of information on social isolation that is relevant to the formulation of policy foundations. In this way we have attained a better insight into the role that social isolation plays in the daily lives of people and into the causes of social isolation. Our analyses have shown specifically that individual factors certainly have as much of an influence on the social network of people as societal factors. Individual factors such as loss of a partner, relationship problems or prolonged caring for a sick relative can bring people into social isolation more quickly than societal factors such as loss of work, poor education or a reduced income. It has also become evident that individual factors of a more structural nature, such as an unhappy youth or a lack of personal competencies, are even more decisive in causing social isolation than societal-structural factors such as prolonged unemployment or a large dependency on welfare-state arrangements. It is therefore not only societal causes which can be identified in the emergence of social isolation: the effects of social isolation lie in the individual as well as in the societal spheres. Persons who become socially isolated attempt to escape their situation or reconcile themselves with it each in their own way: we can observe various survival strategies among the socially isolated (Machielse, 2003, 2006). This does not affect the fact that social isolation generally has negative effects on people's self-confidence and ability to cope, and that it damages their feelings of well-being. It also gives them fewer chances in society and lessens their societal involvement and participation.

The question is, then, why is there reason for public involvement with the phenomenon of social isolation. After all, not every societal issue demands and receives policy attention, just like private life is not always exempted from government interventions. Are the societal repercussions of social isolation such that a problem that is apparently of an exclusively private nature requires policy attention? Let us briefly present the various arguments.

Social problems are always related to major underlying societal issues (Mills, 1951; Schuyt, 1997). If we examine the causes and consequences of social isolation, we not only see individual problems but also important changes in society and developments in the welfare state and the reach of its professional arrangements which affect the social environment of individuals (see also Section 2.3). Our society and our busy lifestyles are increasingly exacting of our social functioning and force us to become more selective in our personal network. Hence institutions and professionals have to deal increasingly with people who have great difficulty in establishing a relationship with their social environment (Van der Lans, 1995; Kunneman, 1998). When they cannot find a connection with the rest of society, doubts arise as to the value of their citizenship and they can start feeling 'superfluous', certainly if the surrounding society distances itself further from them (Beck and Beck-Gernsheim, 1994; Schuyt, 1997). The arrangements of the welfare state are organized in such a way that they appeal to citizens' personal initiative. Furthermore, such arrangements are not made for the – often unarticulated – needs of citizens that are dealing with social isolation, and they are unable to forge new social bonds.

Social isolation touches upon three central goals of the existing social policy: the ability to cope, societal participation and social cohesion. Social isolation is damaging to the individual well-being of people because it affects their mental and physical health as well as their self-esteem (RMO, 1997). Social isolation also sets people behind, societally speaking. From this perspective, social isolation can be seen as a new form of social inequality and isolation from society. In addition, a poor ability to cope and the incapacity to participate in society can be accompanied by the feeling of no longer being part of a system of values and a cultural world shared with others, which can work against the social cohesion of the (local) society as a whole (RMO, 1997). When we approach social isolation as a societal issue, it becomes clear that private matters and societal functioning are intertwined not only in the lives of individual citizens. Seen from a broader societal perspective there is also reason to consider 'private troubles' as 'public worries' (Mills, 1951; Schuyt, 1997): isolation requires attention, from citizens as well as from social institutions and the government.

14.3 A new policy vision

New social relationships require new social and management initiatives and a new legitimation of existing professional interventions (Kuypers and Van der Lans, 1994, Baart, 2001). Having said this, common patterns of thought and action of citizens do not change over night, and this applies equally to dominant ideas in the policy world and embedded intervention strategies of social institutions. These ideas and strategies are often based on deep-seated political convictions, organizational interests and all kinds of other self-evident patterns. The experience some citizens and practising professionals have, does not always penetrate the policy world. As a consequence, the image that politicians and policymakers have of reality can be inadequate towards influencing this reality. We believe such a situation also applies to the phenomenon of social isolation and the significance of social contacts and social networks. Social isolation as policy is not an easy topic. First, it contains a partially hidden phenomenon that involves all kinds of private circumstances. Second, it is a phenomenon that cannot be identified with more familiar social topics at first glance. As a result, social policy can greatly emphasize labour participation of as many people as possible, simultaneously with the need to support those who need support in their own environment. On the one hand, citizens get less time to spend on their social network and social environment, on the other hand they are asked to contribute their bit to support family members, friends, acquaintances and neighbourhood residents.

At the local level, social policy is mainly procedural and less substantially formulated, but the premises are the same as those of national policy (Hortulanus, 2002). The contents of recent local welfare policy have been more oriented towards the creation of conditions for societal participation and economic independence. This is at the expense of its contribution to the everyday social life of individuals through the stimulation of social skills, the organization of informal support and the stimulation of meetings. Professionals in this sector no longer are involved in everyday social life and do not detect signals of social isolation (Baart, 2000). With regard to everyday life, autonomy and the private sphere should be respected as much as possible. This premise fits well with the withdrawal of welfare work into certain accommodations and coordinative activities. Only certain aspects of social isolation are encountered, for instance, when people cause acute nuisance or neglect themselves to an extreme – a problem that tends to involve the police and public health services.

The attention given to existing policies on social contacts and social isolation, can be typified as implicit secondary goals of general social policy. On the foreground are economic independence, societal participation and social cohesion. These goals are expressed mainly through activation measures aimed at labour market participation. Attempts are also made at the local level to express the 'nobody left behind' principle, which must ensure for the societal inclusion of certain categories of citizens that are or risk being excluded, such as addicts, mental patients, the homeless, problem youth and the vulnerable elderly. Finally, social policy has all kinds of measures that are oriented towards the living conditions in certain neighbourhoods and districts.

In recent years, understanding has grown for the relevance of the psychosocial facets of health and the importance of informal support in the form of informal care and volunteer work. Still, none of this has led to a focused policy vision on the meaning of well-functioning personal social networks and the damaging nature of social isolation. The scope of the phenomenon alone should be reason enough to make changes, but other facets of social isolation probably appeal more to policymakers' imagination, such as the strong erosion of individual well-being and the lack of social sources of help. Another argument can be the realization that problems with social contacts play a hidden role in the use of all kinds of professional facilities.

We believe that a new policy vision on the meaning of social contacts and the consequences of social isolation consists of three parts:

1 In terms of *general prevention*, a new standard for social well-being is to be formulated. This standard indicates which factors are part of social well-being. Important here are social competencies and having an informal network for social support. The standard gives a minimum level under which we have to take action. It also indicates how social well-being is to be stimulated.
2 In terms of *risk signalling*, it will indicate how an increased chance of social isolation can be detected and how one can react to it.
3 In terms of *problem reduction*, the 'nobody left behind' principle gets a partially new meaning, so that problems related to social contacts and social support can also lead to specific attention and help.

A new policy vision on the meaning of social contacts and the consequences of social isolation is naturally not only oriented towards government agencies but also towards the individual citizen, informal support networks, private clubs and organizations, and professional social facilities. General prevention, risk signalling and problem reduction entail after all a range of points of interest, from influencing mentality to focused behavioural interventions.

14.3.1 General prevention

A greater emphasis on social contacts, the importance of informal support and social competencies indicates where the government wants to stand in the discussion on the advantages and disadvantages of individualization, the relation between material and immaterial well-being, the importance of the family and the school as socialization systems, and the value of club life and volunteer work for civil society. Governments in western societies do not emphasize social well-being because they cannot already exert a large influence on it, but they do not want to deliberately distance themselves from it either (Reyndorp, 1998). Establishing a standard for social well-being gives all those involved a guideline for evaluating one's situation and actions. From a general prevention perspective, the government emphasizes the following:

1   The advantages and disadvantages of individualization are translated into a new perspective on social inequality. Not only education, paid labour, income and the living situation are part of it, but also health, a meaningful social network, informal support and social competencies (Beck and Beck-Gernsheim, 1994; Ypeij *et al.*, 1999; Hortulanus, 2000).
2   When requesting attention for immaterial well-being, people are placed mainly in relation to each other, presuming a natural combination of individual autonomy and the ability to cope in relation to positive bonds, mutual dependency and frameworks of informal support (Sevenhuysen, 2000). Consequently, much importance is attached to care tasks and volunteer work as self-evident dimensions in the life of each citizen.
3   Social well-being benefits from a broad definition of health, in which next to physical and mental well-being there is also a concentration on social competencies. For this reason, much importance is given to the family and the school as breeding grounds for social competencies. The circumstances in which babies, toddlers and young children grow up are accordingly focused on (Van Dantzig, 1995).
4   All of this uses a broad concept of social participation. Paid labour, care labour and all forms of volunteer work are seen as necessary and active forms of social participation. Informal care, volunteer work and being active in club life should be seen as important elements of the informal social infrastructure people – theoretically – are part of (Hortulanus, 2000; RMO, 2000).

14.3.2 Risk signalling

People can end up in a vulnerable position for all kinds of reasons, including their social network. This can be related to personal characteristics or poor socialization, as well as important life events or a vulnerable social position. Such a vulnerable position can turn into social isolation when there is a lack of own possibilities or external support. In these situations it is important that people from the person's social environment as well as professionals from various social agencies be sensitive to the risks of social isolation, that they signal them and that they do something about it. Risk signalling is thus an important element of a new – local – policy vision to combat social isolation.

This does require boosting a minimal social infrastructure in which informal support and professional interventions supplement one another and merge as a guarantor against slipping down into social isolation. This support and the interventions are intended primarily to help those involved keep a grip on their social life. The policy vision stimulates the personal initiative of citizens and officials, while also indicating what people can fall back on, if they don't know how to proceed.

14.3.3 Problem reduction

The transition between risk signalling and problem reduction is sometimes diffuse, but when there is problem reduction there is already actual social isolation. A new policy vision oriented towards problem reduction requires much insight into the various manifestations of social isolation and its related problems (unemployment, illness, victimization, truancy, addiction, severe social withdrawal behaviour). These problems may constitute specific issues to reduce social isolation. The functioning of the social network of those involved (in a positive as well as a negative sense) and the social competencies and informal support someone has are in any event crucial elements of so called problem entanglement, and at the same time represent specific possibilities for reducing problems in the form of rehabilitation or combating further marginalization.

14.4 New intervention strategies

A good policy vision is not complete with a mere formulation of desirable goals. It must also be aware of possible intervention strategies, in the form of a basic approach to realize policy goals. To this end, a series of questions must be answered: What kind of support exists among citizens towards giving more attention to social isolation? What are the eventual secondary effects of increased attention for social networks and social isolation? How should social isolation be brought to people's attention? Whose responsibility should combating social isolation be primarily? What can be expected in that context from citizens themselves, from their informal social networks and from club life? To what degree is the existing – social – government policy oriented or precisely in conflict with the new policy vision? Are social institutions equipped for and capable of playing a role in the new policy vision? Which social institution is the most adequate party to be involved with social isolation? And if this should involve several parties, who directs everything?

Of course, self-care and the care from one's own informal circuit create the point of departure when thinking of intervention strategies. Social institutions and private organizations provide this self-care and informal help to some degree or other. They do this temporarily until self-care and the informal circuit are properly functioning again, or permanently when support is an enduring condition for an independent life.

Nonetheless, the policy vision formulated to this end will appeal extensively to professional workers – qualitatively as well as quantitatively – in a situation in which there is insufficient support in many fronts already. Question marks should be placed on common practices that are characterized by excessively implemented specialization and methods, too much organizational rationalization, poor financial leadership, and a strong fragmentation of activities and facilities. After all, the discourse on a 'client-centered demand-oriented approach', customer friendliness, an integrated approach, social activation, reintegration and community care, cannot hide the reality that too little money and time is reserved for signalling, intake discussions and for a certain free space to enable professionals to do what is necessary. In other words, for an implementation practice in which the problem definition is precise and the action perspective of the client can be central (Hortulanus, 2001b).

Against this background there should not just be an adjustment to existing intervention strategies, but the design of new strategies that do justice to the significance of social networks and which offer logical ways of action to approach social isolation should also be considered. In light of this formulated policy vision, we must ensure we not only design intervention strategies on three levels but also implement them as well.

14.4.1 General prevention

At the level of general prevention, the first step consists of strategies that underline the importance of good social networks and make citizens as well as professionals alert to social isolation. This can be realized through information aimed at changing citizens' mentality. All kinds of social institutions are made aware of the possibility of paying attention to social competencies, social networks and social support in the context of their regular activities. These can be labour-mediation, social activation and income-support institutions, health agencies, volunteer work and club life, residential organizations, pastoral work, institutions oriented towards education and upbringing, and social-cultural work. The business community should also be made aware of the crucial importance for employees of good social networks and informal support.

Then there are strategies that strengthen personal competencies oriented towards building, maintaining and using social networks. It would then be natural to support programmes for family, school and leisure time – environments that are important for the development of these competencies.

Finally, strategies are to be developed which are oriented towards providing informal support when those involved cannot take care of themselves temporarily. The local government provides a minimal professional social infrastructure and facilitates and stimulates all kinds of local citizens' initiatives aimed at such forms of temporary informal support.

14.4.2 Risk signalling

Risk signalling involves determining the reaction to life events that can damage the social network, and how other risks for social isolation can be signalled and resisted. The intervention strategy is aimed at those involved, as well as at persons from the social environment of those involved, at volunteers and at professionals. For those who are at a high risk of becoming

A new policy vision on social isolation 255

socially isolated, it involves a combination of information together with specific courses and activities to strengthen social competencies. It is very important to stimulate and facilitate informal support networks and citizens' initiatives. That's why this issue constitutes an element of the general preventive strategy. The general preventive information given to all kinds of social institutions should also strengthen their willingness to signal risks and to refer to other organizations. A Local Centre for Signalling, Advice and Support should be established. Such a centre would merge expertise from social work, social-cultural work and community work into a Project Team for Networks and Social Isolation, so that shape can be given to strengthening personal competencies, social contacts and network-building through meetings and activities as well as the organization of information support in one's own social environment. The project team will also have an ombudsman/woman to whom any citizen or official can pass on information about (impending) social isolation. The project team will seek cooperation with other social agencies so that the signalling is strengthened, referral to the centre takes place or there can be concrete cooperation to avoid or reverse social isolation. The most important social agencies with which cooperation will take place are in health care, Municipal Health Services, school physicians, consulting bureaus and mental health services, social relief, education, the Social Services Department, religious groups, local associations and volunteer organizations, the police and the judicial system, and housing corporations. Businesses and commercial institutions such as the catering industry (snackbars, pubs, etc.) can also be made aware of the services of the project team for their employees or clients. What is foremost is that the local centre be seen by individual citizens and residents as a natural and reliable contact service and as a flexible functioning support.

14.4.3 *Problem reduction*

Social isolation is already determined by the time one gets to problem reduction. Through individual case management one determines what kind of support the involved person lacks the most, and what the best way is to reduce or remove social isolation. Of course, the mentioned local centre fulfils its own executive as well as mediating role when tackling existing social isolation. It is important in any event to make a distinction between the backgrounds of social isolation. Is it passed on, as it were, from generation to generation, do specific life events play a role, or is there a form of external societal exclusion? The subjective experience, the combination between the various facets of someone's life (including the social context in which the involved person lives) are essential aspects of an individual-oriented approach. Although in most cases there are individual risks, a category-oriented approach can sometimes be considered, for example, in situations in which a category-oriented approach produces more individual results. This can be the case for certain categories of fellow-sufferers that are closely linked, or when social isolation is so widely connected with another characteristic of people (as is the case with, for example, lone mothers) that attention to the entire category can be the point of departure for the intervention strategy. In a neighbourhood approach what counts is not content but organization, because the neighbourhood or district is a good point of departure for bundling together informal support and professional interventions.

If all of this leads us to conclude that no well thought-out policy or elaborated intervention strategies exist yet, this need not mean that no initiatives have been developed that focus on social isolation. From an instrumental perspective, experiments have already produced important results. Examples are home visits, primary-help networks, volunteers for older people who live on their own, buddy projects for youth, friendship services aimed at companionship and going out, telephone circles, support of informal carers, collective living arrangements, fellow-sufferer contacts, etc. The appeal of these examples is that they come from local initiatives and are driven partially by personal involvement. Weaknesses, however, lie in the fact that they have a limited reach, do not always get going, are very dependent on temporary financial means, and require professional support. While it would not be a good idea to professionalize and create institutional frameworks for such initiatives a much better option would be to stimulate and facilitate them, supplementing them with basic professional support and give them the opportunity to refer to other organizations.

14.5 Conclusions

Social policy can take many shapes. It has a concatenation of policy visions and goals; social reality and the lives of people are influenced in the most contrasting ways through all kinds of professional practices. But if we take the individual lives of people as a point of departure, it becomes immediately clear how important one's own capacities and social environment are when problems arise. This also applies to the problems and risks described in this book, even to an enhanced extent. The paradoxal situation is that having social contacts and patterns of mutual support are found to be so self-evident that we cannot easily imagine how damaging it is when people do not have them. And when people are confronted with it, citizens, politicians and professionals from the social sector are caught in 'may I, can I and shall I' considerations. If citizens are asked under which circumstances of social isolation they would intervene, opinions are divided. Some would intervene if they suspected social isolation, others when social isolation is clearly present, and yet others will only act if those involved ask for it themselves. It goes without saying that people will intervene more quickly with friends than with colleagues, and will be the most reserved when it comes to neighbours. Much reticence can be found among politicians and professionals too. It is not so much about intervening in private lives, because that is also done in the context of social security policies. What's more important is that, up to now, people's social network and social functioning have not been seen as a policy category.

The data presented in this book offer sufficient arguments for change in this area and to recognize the importance of social networks and the damaging nature of social isolation from an individual well-being as well as from a societal perspective. The policy vision presented and the corresponding intervention strategies play a role in these individual and societal interests. At the same time, they constitute prominent examples of the convergence between professional interventions and what people themselves do for each other – in other words, between the formal and the informal infrastructure. This should speak to politicians and administrators, not only because it leads to establishing a clear relation between policy logics and the everyday living environment of citizens, but also because large parts of social policy would be utterly inadequate without the input of the informal networks of citizens.

Appendices

Appendix I Overview of themes in the first questionnaire (N = 2,462)

Background information	Sex
	Age (18–29, 30–44, 45–64, >65)
	Marital status (single/married/divorced/widowed)
	Living situation (single household; partner/no children; partner/children; partner, other; no partner/children; no partner, other; other)
	Degree of urbanization
	Ethnicity (Netherlands/Surinam-Netherlands Antilles/Morocco-Turkey/other; country of birth of father and mother)
	Education (lower/secondary/higher)
	Income (low/average/high)
	Welfare recipient (yes/no)
	Socio-economic status (work situation, education and income)
	Religion
Network information *(Chapter 3)*	Scope of potential support network (instrumental support, emotional support, financial support, social companionship, other persons)
	Composition of network (share of family, friends, neighbours, colleagues or fellow students, fellow members of associations, professionals, volunteers, informal carers, acquaintances)
	Closeness (0–500 m; 500m–5 km; 5km–50 km; >50 km)
	Contact frequency (often, average, little)
	Share of family in network (family-oriented, mixed, not family-oriented)
	Strength of bonds in the network (strong, mixed, weak)
	Changes in network scope five years ago and now
	Changes in network composition five years ago and now
	Reasons for changes in the network
Network experience *(Chapter 3)*	Assessment of social contacts (report mark)
	Need for contacts
	Time spent on network
	Feeling at ease
Loneliness *(Chapter 3)*	Feelings of loneliness
Actual support *(Chapter 3)*	Actual support received
	Actual support given

Health *(Chapter 6)*	Physical problems (last five years) Mental problems (last five years) Assessment of health (report mark)
Hindrances to functioning *(Chapter 7)*	Hindrances to household activities Physical hindrances to freedom of movement Limitations in functioning due to mental problems Financial hindrances to leave home Need to incur debt/use savings
Facilities *(Chapter 7)*	Actual use of facilities Reasons for much/little use Changes in use in the last five years Reason for changes in use Importance for daily functioning View on dependency on facilities
Social participation *(Chapter 8)*	Work situation (works/studies/disabled/retired/job-seeker/other) Volunteer work Informal care outside one's own home (never/occasionally/often) Informal care inside one's own home (never/occasionally/often) Participation in associations and organizations (no participation/passive member/participant/active member) Reasons for little/no participation in associations and organizations Participation in informal groups (excluding family and friends) Visits to recreational facilities Reading the newspaper Activities next to or instead of paid work Changes in social activities in the last five years Reasons for these changes
Views on society *(Chapter 8)*	People who make rules are who benefit from them
Social living environment *(Chapter 9)*	Actual contacts in the neighbourhood (many/few) Need for contacts in the neighbourhood Importance of contacts in the neighbourhood Importance of a welcoming neighbourhood Looks for friends in the neighbourhood Statements about neighbours (doing things together, hates them, fights, too many differences, etc.) Getting along with neighbourhood residents (greeting them, making conversation, visiting) Exchange relations with neighbourhood residents (instrumental help) Participation in neighbourhood activities

260 Appendices

	Reasons for no/little participation in neighbourhood activities
	Use of facilities in the neighbourhood
	Noise in the neighbourhood
	Nuisances
	Feelings of unsafety
	Views on living situation
	Assessment of neighbourhood (report mark)
Neighbourhood cohesion *(Chapter 9)*	Sharing social values
	Participation in informal groups in the neighbourhood
	Orientation towards specific groups
	(Negative) binding with neighbourhood residents
	Assessment/satisfaction with facilities in the neighbourhood
Degree of urbanization *(Chapter 10)*	Degree of urbanization of research locations
Moving plans *(Chapter 10)*	Time lived in current neighbourhood/municipality
	Reason for moving to current neighbourhood/municipality
	Moving plans
	Reason for moving plans
	Reasons not to move
	Activities with neighbourhood residents

Appendix II Overview of themes in the second questionnaire (N = 460)

Protection *(Chapter 3)*	Protection against loneliness and social isolation (experience/estimate)
	Views on a rich social life (open question)
Important life events *(Chapter 4)*	Life events that are still affecting the person (positively/negatively, personally/socially)
	Most important life event still affecting the person
	Reaction to this life event (acceptance/change/repression)
	Help and support (yes/no, friends/professionals)
	Type of support from friends (instrumental/emotional/informative)
	Type of support from professionals (instrumental/emotional/informative)
	Reason for no support from friends
	Reasons for no support from professionals
	Institutions used for professional support

Consequences of important life events *(Chapter 4)*	Changes in the scope of the social network
	Changes in the frequency of contacts
	Changes in social activities
	Changes in feelings of loneliness
Comfort *(Chapter 4)*	Persons
	Other sources of comfort
Uplifts and hassles *(Chapter 4)*	Can enjoy life
	Gets enough compliments
Socialization *(Chapter 5)*	Happy youth (yes/no)
	Unconditional love of parents (yes/no)
	Importance of youth later in life (important/not important)
Personal competencies *(Chapter 5)*	Self-confidence
	Social skills
	Capacity to solve problems (coping)
Life attitude *(Chapter 5)*	Life attitude (shaping it yourself/taking things as they come)
Help with social isolation and loneliness *(Chapter 5)*	Views on doing/not doing something about loneliness or social isolation (friends, neighbours, colleagues, etc.)
	Has given help for social isolation or loneliness (yes/no)
	Type of help (instrumental/emotional/informative/exemplary function)
	Experiences offering help
	Views on sharing responsibilities
	Views on the role of institutions
Health *(Chapter 6)*	Depression
	Assessment of health (report mark)
Social exclusion *(Chapter 8)*	Reasons for feeling of social exclusion
Assessment of different well-being domains	Work situation
	Education
	Financial situation
	Health
	Social contacts
	Neighbourhood
	Recreational activities

Appendix III Comparison of respondents in the first and second research phases with total Dutch population ages 18 and older, in percentages

	First sample N = 2,462	Second sample N = 460	Dutch population aged 18+ (CBS, 1996) N = 12,092,029
Sex			
Men	50	51	49
Women	50	49	51
Age (years)		**	
18–29	22	14	23
30–44	30	26	31
45–64	29	34	30
= >65	18	26	17
Marital status	**	**	
Single	31	28	28
Married	54	54	58
Divorced	7	7	6
Widowed	9	11	7
Living situation	**	**	
Single household	24	27	18[a]
Shared household	64	64	78[a]
Lone parent family	3	4	3[a]
Other	9	5	1[a]
Respondent's country of birth			
Netherlands	89	89	90
Surinam/Antilles	2	1	2
Morocco/Turkey	4	4	2
Other	5	6	6
Education			
Low	55	54	40[b]
Average	28	25	39[b]
High	18	21	20[b]

Notes
**$P < 0.01$ (Chi^2-test for total respondents group and Dutch population).
a Only persons in private households, N = 11,890,000.
b Working population ages 15–64.
CBS, 1996.

Appendix IV Ratio received support and given support, in percentages (N = 1,758)

Type of support		Socially competent	Socially inhibited	Lonely	Socially isolated	Total
Picked up or brought home	R***	70	63##	68###	51###	68#
	G***	71ᵗ	48	51	26	62
Things borrowed or lent (e.g. car, utensil, sugar)	R***	57	46	43	23	51
	G***	66###	53	53##	31#	60###
Providing care for a child or pet	R***	47	26	40	15	42
	G***	46	24	41	18	41
Assistance filling out formsG***	R	41##	38##	46###	40###	41###
		29	22	26	12	27
Providing care in case of illnessG	Rᵗ	28	30	36#	32	30
		29	30	28	23	29
Name of a good doctor or babysitter	R	17	17ᵗ	16	14	17
	G*	19#	11	19	12	18#
Introduction to a club, association, board, etc.	R	14	15	17	13ᵗ	15
	G**	18###	17	14	6	17###
Assistance finding a job	R**	14	13	10	8	13
	G**	20##	16	17#	8	19###
Mediation in problems with agencies or other persons	R**	11	12	16	19#	12
	G**	19###	12	15	7	17###

Notes

Comparison of rows:

R = received support; G = given support (Chi²-test,*P ≤ 0.05, **P ≤ 0.01, ***P ≤ 0.001).

Differences between receiving and giving, comparisons for each cell (paired t-test, ᵗP < 0.1, #P < 0.05, ##P < 0.01).

The most frequently mentioned support situations included being picked up or taken home (68 per cent), borrowing things (51 per cent), taking care of a child or pet (42 per cent), and helping to complete forms (41 per cent). In almost all the situations, subjects with large networks received the most support, except 'mediation in problems'. Generally speaking, lonely and isolated people received this kind of support the most (16 per cent and 19 per cent). In general, the socially competent received support most frequently, as opposed to the socially isolated. The patterns of the socially competent and lonely were similar − although the first group was better off. The patterns of the socially isolated and socially inhibited were also similar. The socially isolated were the worst off in almost all cases.

Relatives, friends and neighbours provided by far the most support; for support of a caring nature, the subjects mainly appealed to relatives and friends; instrumental support was also asked of neighbours. Professionals mainly assisted in filling out forms and mediating in problems and, to a lesser extent, in cases of illness, and finding a job.

Not just receiving support, but giving support also constitutes an essential part of the network approach. The table also shows that support given was mainly instrumental, followed by caring support. A relatively small percentage referred to support in relation to different agencies. Here again there was a difference between the subjects with large and small networks. The group with extensive networks gave support most frequently, being the highest for the socially competent. People with small networks gave by far the least support to others, and this was strongest for the socially isolated. Mostly, the percentage of socially isolated who state they gave support was half the mean percentage of the whole sample. In general, the socially isolated receive and give by far the least support, the socially competent the most, and the two other groups in between.

Across the board, the subjects indicated they gave help more often than they received it; paired t-tests show that the scale has turned in favour of giving support. However, a closer look at the four distinct types of social contacts reveals quite a different picture. The results show that this general image only holds true for the socially competent (the largest group, 64 per cent). The observation for the socially isolated was completely the opposite: on all the issues they claimed they received more support than they offered. The same can be said of the socially inhibited and the lonely, although the differences were less pronounced.

Appendix V Correlations of the four health measures with background factors and mediating factors

	Report mark on health	Physical vulnerability	Mental vulnerability	Depression
Loneliness	**−0.28**	**0.21**	**0.66**	**0.42**
Network scope:	0.084	−0.10	−0.13	−0.14
Social support	0.12	−0.13	−0.12	−0.16
Practical support	0.03	−0.08	−0.07	−0.15
Emotional support	0.02	−0.05	−0.06	−0.06
Disappointed in others	**0.18**	−0.14	**−0.39**	**−0.28**
A burden to others	0.16	−0.02	**−0.23**	−0.13
Changes	0.13	−0.13	−0.12	−0.15
Total life events	−0.12	0.02	0.11	0.01
Negative events	**−0.31**	0.13	**0.26**	0.17
Percentage of negative events	**−0.29**	**0.18**	0.17	**0.25**
Positive events	0.11	−0.06	−0.08	−0.16
Percentage of positive events	0.18	−0.14	−0.18	−0.18
Lonely after important life event	−0.17	0.14	**0.26**	
Annoyances	−0.13	0.06	0.15	0.10
Enjoyment	**0.36**	**−0.22**	**−0.38**	−0.05
Compliments	0.14	−0.06	−0.18	−0.05
Life attitude	−0.01	0.01	−0.00	0.15
Happy youth	0.18	−0.07	−0.17	−0.15
Parental love	**0.22**	−0.08	−0.12	0.02
Importance of youth in life	0.14	−0.16	−0.03	−0.14
Protective sources:	0.15	−0.10	−0.17	**−0.25**
Experience	**0.25**	−0.16	**−0.25**	**−0.34**
Relativizing for comfort	0.12	−0.15	−0.06	**−0.22**
Personal competencies:	**0.25**	−0.16	**−0.24**	**−0.38**
Self-confidence	0.16	−0.10	**−0.27**	−0.19
Coping	**0.27**	**−0.20**	**−0.29**	**−0.28**
Social skills	0.15	−0.08	−0.09	**−0.34**
Background variables:				
Age	**−0.24**	**0.29**	0.03	**0.34**
Sex	−0.03	0.05	0.02	0.09
Civil status	−0.13	**0.19**	0.06	**0.21**
Ethnicity	−0.05	0.02	0.10	−0.16
Location	0.05	0.00	−0.15	0.07
Education	0.15	−0.18	−0.10	−0.19
Income	**0.22**	**−0.23**	**−0.20**	**−0.30**
Socio-economic status	**0.28**	**−0.31**	**−0.22**	**−0.35**
Contact typology	**−0.23**	**0.19**	**0.48**	**0.38**

Note
The correlations in bold are statistically significant.

References

Adriaanse, C.C.M. and Hortulanus, R.P. (1997). Social isolement in het Oldambt: Een studie naar sociale contacten van inwoners van een Groningse regio met speciale aandacht voor 50 plussers. Utrecht: Universiteit Utrecht/Faculteit Sociale Weterschappen.

Asendorpf, J.B. and Wilpers, S. (1998). Personality effects on social relationships. *Journal of Personality and Social Psychology*, 74, 6, 1531–1544.

Arts, C.H., Hommel, A.A.C., Felling, A.J.A. and Knipscheer, C.P.M. (1989). *Ouderen geprofileerd: Meetinstrument ten behoeve van het gemeentelijk ouderenbeleid*. Amsterdam: Vrije Universiteit/Vakgroep Sociologie.

Baarsen, B. van, Snijders, T.A.B., Smit, J.H. and Duijn, M.A.J. van (2001). Lonely but not alone: Emotional isolation and social isolation as two distinct dimensions of loneliness in older people. *Educational and Psychological Measurement*, 61, 119–135.

Baart, A. (2000). Zich afstemmen op de onafgestemden: Hoe professionals marginalen kunnen bereiken. *Sociale Interventie*, 1, 4–21.

Baart, A. (2001). Een theorie van de presentie. Utrecht: Lemma.

Badr, H., Acitelli, L., Duck, S. and Carl, W.J. (2001). Weaving social support and relationships together. In: B. Sarason and S. Duck (eds), *Personal relationships: Implications for clinical and community psychology* (pp. 1–14). Chichester: Wiley.

Bakker, K. (*et al.*) (eds) (1999). *Kwetsbaar en competent*. Utrecht: NIZW.

Bandura, A. (1997). *Self-efficacy: The exercise of control*. New York: Freeman.

Bauman, Z. (2001). *The individualized society*. Cambridge: Polity Press.

Beck, U. (1992 [1986]). *Risk society. Towards a modern society*. London: Sage.

Beck, U. and Beck-Gernsheim, E. (1990). *Das ganz normale Chaos der Liebe*. Frankfurt am Main: Suhrkamp.

Beck, U. and Beck-Gernsheim, E. (1994). Individualisierung in modernen Gesellschaften. Perspektiven und Kontroversen einer subjectorientierten Soziologie. In: U. Beck and E. Beck-Gernsheim, *Riskante Freiheiten. Individualisierung in modernen Gesellschaften*. Frankfurt.

Beck, U. and Beck-Gernsheim, E. (2002). *Individualization. Institutionalized individualism and its social and political consequences*. London: Sage Publications.

Becker, G.S. (1993) [1964]). *Human capital*. Chicago: University of Chicago Press.

Berkel, R. van and Horneman-Møller, I. (2002). *Active social policies in the EU*. Bristol: Polity Press.

Berkman, L.F. and Syme, S.L. (1979). Social networks, host resistance, and mortality: A nine-year follow-up study of Alameda country residents. *American Journal of Epidemiology*, 109, 186–204.

Billington, R., Hockey, J. and Strawbridge, S. (1998). *Exploring self and society*. Hampshire/London: Macmillan Press.
Blum-Kulka, S. (1990). You don't touch lettuce with your fingers: Parental politeness in family discourse. *Journal of Pragmatics*, 14, 259–288.
Boer, A. de (1990). *Leefsituatie en sociale steun bij chronisch zieken in vergelijking met gezonden: Een secundaire analyse*. Bilthoven: RIVM.
Boer, A.H.D. de (1994). *Informele zorg: Een verkenning van huidige en toekomstige ontwikkelingen*. Rijswijk: Sociaal en Cultureel Planbureau.
Boomkens, R. (*et al.*) (1997). *Stad zonder horizon: Stadspolitiek en stedelijke ontwikkeling in Nederland*. Amsterdam: Van Gennep.
Bourdieu, P. (1984). *Distinction: A social critique of the judgment of taste*. London: Routledge.
Bovens, M. and Hemerijck, A. (eds) (1996). *Het verhaal van de moraal: Een empirisch onderzoek naar de sociale bedding van morele bindingen*. Amsterdam/Meppel: Boom.
Bowlby, J. (1983). Attachment and loss: Retrospect and prospect. *Annual Progress in Child Psychiatry and Child Development*, 29–47.
Bowman, C.C. (1955). Loneliness and social change. *American Journal of Psychiatry*, 112, 194–198.
Boxman, E.A.W., Flap, H.D. and Weesie, H.M. (1992). Informeel zoeken op de arbeidsmarkt. In: W. jansen and G.H.L. van den Witteboer, *Sociale netwerken en hun invloed* (pp. 39–56). Amsterdam/Meppel: Boom.
Broese van Groenou, M.I. (1990). *Gescheiden netwerken: De relaties met vrienden en verwanten na echtscheiding*. Utrecht/Groningen: RUG/RUU/ The Interuniversity Center for Sociological Theory and Methodology.
Broese van Groenou, M.I. and Bussbach, J.T. van (1991). De gevolgen van belangrijke levensgebeurtenissen voor de omvang van persoonlijke netwerken. *Gezin*, 3, 162–174.
Brown, J.D. (1991). Accuracy and bias in self-knowledge. Can knowing the truth be hazardous to your health? In: C.R. Snyder and D.F. Forsyth (eds), *Handbook of social and clinical psychology: The health perspective*. New York: Pergamon Press.
Brown, G.W. and Harris, T.O. (1989). *Life events and illness*. Londen: Unwin Hyman.
Brummett, B.H. (*et al.*) (2001). Characteristics of socially isolated patients with coronary artery disease who are at elevated risk for mortality. *Psychosomatic Medicine*, 63, 267–272.
Burt, R.S. (1990). *Tertius gaudens, a study of structural holes as social capital and entrepreneurial opportunity*. New York: Columbia University.
Busschbach, J.T. van (1992). Investeren in relaties: Verschillende visies op sociaal kapitaal als verklaring voor veranderingen in het persoonlijke netwerk. In: W. Jansen and G.L.H. van den Witteboer (1992). *Sociale netwerken en hun invloed* (pp. 57–71). Amsterdam/Meppel: Boom.
Buunk, B.P. and Schaufeli, W.B. (1999). Reciprocity in interpersonal realionships. An evolutionary perspective an its importance for health and well-being. In: W. Stroebe and M. Hewstone (eds), *European review of social psychology*, vol. 10 (pp. 259–291). Chichester: Wiley.
Buunk, B.P. and Schaufeli, W. (2001). Het belang van wederkerigheid in interpersoonlijke relaties voor gezondheid en welbevinden: Een evolutionair perspectief. *Nederlands Tijdschrift voor de Psychologie*, 56, 41–56.
Castells, M. (1996). *The rise of the network society*. Cambridge: Blackwell.

CBS (1992). Een nieuwe maatstaf voor stedelijkheid: De omgevingsadressendichtheid. *Maandstatistiek Bevolking*, 7, 14–18.
CBS (1996). *Bevolking der gemeenten van Nederland op 1 januari 1996.* Voorburg/Heerlen: CBS.
Cobb, S. (1976). Social support as a moderator of life stress. *Psychosomatic Medicine*, 38, 300–314.
Cohen, J. (1999). Trust. Voluntary association and workable democracy. The contemporary American discourse of civil society. In: M.E. Warren (ed.), *Democracy and trust* (pp. 208–248). Cambridge: Cambridge University Press.
Cohen, S. and Syme, S.L. (eds) (1985). *Social support and health.* Orlando: Academic.
Cohen, S. and Wills, T. (1985). Stress, social support and the buffering hypothesis. *Psychological Bulletin*, 98, 310–356.
Coleman, J.S. (1988). Social capital in the creation of human capital. *American Journal of Sociology*, 94, 95–120.
Commissie-Albeda (2001). *Sociaal-economische gezondheidsverschillen verkleinen. Eindrapportage en beleidsaanbevelingen van de Programmacommissie Sociaal-Economische Gezondheidsverschillen-tweede fase.* Den Haag: ZorgOnderzoek Nederland.
Dalgard, O.S., Bjørk, S. and Tambs, K. (1995). Social support, negative life events and mental health. *British Journal of Psychiatry*, 166, 29–34.
Dam, J. ten (1997). *Gezonde stadsgezichten. Een studie naar gezondheidsverschillen en stedelijk gezondheidsbeleid* [Dissertatie]. Amsterdam: Thesis.
Dantzig, A. van (1995). *Is alles geoorloofd als God niet bestaat? Over geestelijke gezondheidszorg en maatschappij.* Amsterdam: Boom.
Dasgupta, P. (1988). Trust as a commodity. In: D. Gambetta (ed.), *Trust. Making and breaking cooperative relations* (pp. 49–72).
DeLongis, A., Coyne, J.C., Dakof, G., Folkman, S. and Lazarus, R.S. (1982). Relationship of daily hassles, uplifts, and major life events to health status. *Health Psychology*, 1, 119–136.
Dignum, K. (1997). *Senior en stad: De betekenis van stedelijke woonmilieus voor de sociale netwerken van minder draagkrachtige ouderen.* Amsterdam: AME/Amsterdam Study Centre for the Metropolitan Environment.
Dijkstra, P. (1974). De zelfbeoordelingsschaal voor depressie van Zung. In: H.M. van Praag and H.G.M. Rooymans (eds), *Stemming en ontstemming. Theorie en praktijk bij de diagnostiek en de behandeling van depressies* (pp. 98–120). Amsterdam: De Erven Bohn.
Draijer, N. (1990). *Seksuele traumatisering in de jeugd. Lange termijn gevolgen van seksueel misbruik van meisjes door verwanten.* Amsterdam: SUA.
Durkheim, E. (1964 [1893]). *The division of labor in society.* New York: The Free Press.
Duyvendak, J.W. and Hortulanus, R.P. (1999). *De gedroomde wijk. Methoden, mythen en misvattingen in de nieuwe wijkaanpak.* Utrecht: Forum.
Dykstra, P.A. (1990). *Next of (non)kin: The importance of primary relationships for older adults' well-being.* Amsterdam/Lisse: Swets and Zeitlinger.
Dykstra, P.A. (2001). Netwerken van informele steun en sociaal-demografische veranderingen. In J.C. Vrooman (red.), *Netwerken en sociaal kapitaal* (pp. 63–81). Amsterdam: Siswo/NSV.
Dykstra, P.A. and Jong-Gierveld, J. de (1999). Differentiële kansen op eenzaamheid onder ouderen: De betekenis van type partnerrelatie, partnergeschiedenis, gezond-

heid, sociaal-economische positie en sociale relaties. *Tijdschrift voor Gerontologie en Geriatrie*, 30, 212–225.

Dykstra, P.A. and Fokkema, T. (2001). Emotionele en sociale eenzaamheid onder gescheiden en gehuwde mannen en vrouwen: de deficiet- en cognitieve benaderingen vergeleken. *Nederlands Tijdschrift voor de Psychologie*, 56, 177–190.

Engbersen, G., Vrooman, J.C. and Snel, E. (1998). *Effecten van armoede: Derde jaarrapport armoede en sociale uitsluiting*. Amsterdam: Amsterdam University Press.

Engel, G.L. (1971). Sudden and rapid death during psychological stress. *Annals of Internal Medicine*, 74, 771–782.

Esping-Andersen, G. (1990). *The three worlds of welfare capitalism*. Cambridge: Polity Press.

Etzioni, A. (1988). *The moral dimension. Toward a new economics*. New York: Free Press.

Feldman, S.S. and Elliott, G.R. (1990). *At the threshold: The developing adolescent*. Cambridge: Harvard University Press.

Felling, A.J.A., Fieselier, A.A. and van der Poel, M.G.M. (1991). *Primaire relaties en sociale steun: Achtergronden van de behoefte aan steun, de aard en omvang van informele steunverlening en daarbij opgedane ervaringen*. Nijmegen: Instituut voor Toegepaste Sociale Wetenschappen.

Field, J. (2003). *Social capital*. London: Routledge.

Fischer, A.H. and Manstead, A.S.R. (1998). Emotionele intelligentie: De kunst om gelukkig en gezond door het leven te gaan. *Psychologie en Maatschappij*, 85, 22, 373–383.

Fischer, C. (1982). *To dwell among friends: Personal networks in town and city*. Chicago: University of Chicago Press.

Fischer, C.S. and Phillips, S.L. (1982). Who is alone? Social characteristics of people with small networks. In: L.A. Peplau and D. Perlman, *Loneliness: A sourcebook of current theory, research and therapy* (pp. 21–33). New York: Wiley.

Flap, H.D. (1987). De theorie van het sociaal kapitaal. *Antropologische Verkenningen*, 6, 14–27.

Flap, H.D. and Tazelaar, F. (1988). De rol van informele sociale netwerken op de arbeidsmarkt: Flexibilisering en uitsluiting. In: H.D. Flap and W. Arts, *De flexibele arbeidsmarkt: Theorie en praktijk* (pp. 48–64). Deventer: Van Loghum Slaterus.

Flap, H. and Völker, B. (eds) (2004). *Creation and returns of social capital. A new research program*. London/New York: Routledge.

Fromm, E. (1941). *Escape from freedom*. New York: Rinehart.

Fromm-Reichmann, F. (1959). Loneliness. *Psychiatry*, 22, 1–15.

Fukuyama, F. (1995). *Trust. The social virtues and the creation of prosperity*. London: Hamish Hamilton.

Gersons, B.P.R. (1995). *Acute psychiatrie*. Houten: Bohn Stafleu Van Loghum.

Giddens, A. (1990). *The consequences of modernity*. Stanford: Stanford University Press.

Giddens, A. (1991). *Modernity and self-identity: Self and society in the late modern age*. Cambridge: Polity Press.

Giddens, A. (1992). *The transformation of intimacy: Sexuality, love and eroticism in modern societies*. Cambridge: Polity Press.

Gorter, K.A. and Winants, B.A.C. (1993). *Gehandicapt en vrouw: Gegevens over de positie van lichamelijk gehandicapte vrouwen op het gebied van onderwijs, arbeid, sociale zekerheid, seksualiteit, primaire relaties, gezondheid en hulpverlening*. Den Haag: Nederlands Instituut voor Maatschappelijk Werk Onderzoek (NIMAWO).

Gouldner, A.W. (1960). The norm of reciprocity: A preliminary statement. *American Sociological Review*, 25, 161–178.
Granovetter, M.S. (1973). The strength of weak ties. *American Journal of Sociology*, 78, 1360–1380.
Granovetter, M. (1974). *Getting a job: A study of contacts and careers*. Chicago: University of Chicago Press.
Habermas, J. (1981). Justice and solidarity. *The Philosophical Forum*, XXI, 1–2.
Hall, A. and Wellman, B. (1985). Social networks and social support. In: S. Cohen and S.L. Syme (eds), *Social support and health* (pp. 23–41). Harcourt, Orlando: Academic Press.
Harris, J.R. (1998). *The nurture assumption: Why children turn out the way they do*. New York: Free Press.
Hechter, M. (1987). *Principles of group solidarity*. Berkeley: University of California.
Heerikhuizen, B. van (1997). Figuraties van zelfredzaamheid. In: K. Schuyt (red.), *Het sociaal tekort: Veertien sociale problemen in Nederland* (pp. 184–193). Amsterdam: De Balie.
Heider, F. (1958). *The psychology of interpersonal relations*. New York: Wiley.
Heller, K. and Rook, K.S. (2001). Distinguishing the theoretical functions of social ties: implications for support interventions. In: B. Sarason and S. Duck, *Personal relationships: Implications for clinical and community psychology* (pp. 119–139). New York: John Wiley.
Helman, C.G. (1994). *Culture, health and illness* (3rd edn). Oxford: Butterworth-Heinemann.
Hess, B.B. and Waring, J.M. (1978). Changing patterns of aging and family bonds in later life. *The Family Coordinator*, 27, 303–314.
Hills, J., Le Grand J. and Agulnik, P. (eds) (2002). *Understanding social exclusion*. Oxford: Oxford University Press.
Hirschman, A.O. (1975). *Exit, voice, and loyalty: Responses to decline in firms, organizations, and states*. Cambridge, Mass.: Harvard University Press.
Hobsbawm, E. (1994). *The age of extremes: A history of the world, 1914–1991*. New York: Vintage Books.
Hooley, J.M. and Hiller, J.B. (2000). Personality and psychiatric illness: From empirical data to clinical practice. *Journal of Abnormal Psychology*, 109, 40–44.
Hortulanus, R.P. (1995a). Sociaal isolement in Nederland. In: P. Driest and R. Zoutman (red.), *Het verbroken contact hersteld: Gemeentelijk welzijnsbeleid en sociaal isolement* (pp. 11–24). Utrecht: NIZW.
Hortulanus, R.P. (1995b). *Stadsbuurten: Een studie over bewoners en beheerders in buurten met uiteenlopende reputaties*. [Dissertatie]. Den Haag: VUGA.
Hortulanus, R.P. (2000). Aandacht voor informele solidariteit. In: R.P. Hortulanus and J.E.M. Machielse (eds), *Wie is mijn naaste, Het Sociaal Debat, deel 2* (pp. 7–22). Den Haag: Elsevier.
Hortulanus, R.P. (2001a). Leefomgeving en sociaal beleid. In: R.P. Hortulanus and J.E.M. Machielse (eds), *Op het snijvlak van de fysieke en sociale leefomgeving* (pp. 7–22). Het Sociaal Debat, deel 3. Den Haag: Elsevier.
Hortulanus, R.P. (2001b). Tijd voor aandacht. In: M. van der Linde (red.), *Van stoplap tot veelkleurige bril: Methodische verkenningen rond maatschappelijk werk* (pp. 33–39). Driebergen: Hogeschool De Horst.
Hortulanus, R.P. (2002). De betekenis van ontspanning, ontmoeting en ontplooiing

in het sociaal beleid. In: R.P. Hortulanus and J.E.M. Machielse (eds), *Ontspanning, ontmoeting en ontplooiing*. Het Sociaal Debat, deel 8 (pp. 7–25). Den Haag: Elsevier.
Hortulanus, R.P., Adriaanse, C.C.M. and Wardt, J.W. van der (1997). *Sociale integratie en segregatie in Amsterdam Oud-West en de Spaarndammerbuurt: Een onderzoek naar zelfredzaamheid, maatschappelijke participatie en sociale cohesie*. Utrecht: Universiteit Utrecht/Faculteit der Sociale Wetenschappen.
Hortulanus, R.P., Kunst, M. and Snel, F.G. (1996). *Welzijn tussen vraag en aanbod: Een wijkanalyse van Utrecht-Noord*. Utrecht. Universiteit Utrecht/Faculteit der Sociale Wetenschappen.
Hortulanus, R.P., Liem, P.P.N. and Sprinkhuizen, A.A.M. (1992). *Domeinen van welzijn: Welzijnsbeleving en welzijnsbeleid in de jaren '90*. 's-Gravenhage: VUGA.
Hortulanus, R., Machielse, A. and Meeuwesen, L. (2003). *Sociaal isolement: Een studie over sociale contacten en sociaal isolement in Nederland*. Den Haag: Elsevier Overheid.
House, J.S. (1981). *Work, stress and social support*. Reading: Addison-Wesley.
House, J.S. (2001). Social isolation kills, but how and why? *Psychosomatic Medicine*, 63, 273–274.
House, J.S. and Kahn, R.L. (1985). Measures and concepts of social support. In: S. Cohen and S.L. Syme (eds), *Social support and health* (pp. 83–108). Orlando: Academic.
House, J.S., Landis, K.R. and Umberson, D. (1988). Social relationships and health. *Science*, 241, 540–545.
House, J.S., Robbins, C. and Metzner, H.L. (1982). The association of social relationships and activities with morality: Prospective evidence from the Tecumseh community health study. *American Journal of Epidemiology*, 116, 123–140.
Hoynck van Papendrecht, B. and Sas, O't (1997). *Gewonde vogels: Een onderzoek naar de situatie van 'lijmsnuivers', de hulpverlening en jeugdprostitutie in Managua*. Utrecht: Universiteit Utrecht, Doctoraalscriptie Culturele Antropologie.
Hughes, M. and Gove, W.R. (1981). Living alone, social integration, and mental health. *American Journal of Sociology*, 87, 48–74.
Hymes, D.H. (1972). On communicative competence. In: J.B. Pride and J. Holmes (eds), *Sociolinguistics* (pp. 269–293). Harmondsworth: Penguin Books.
Janssen, M. (1992). *Personal networks of chronic patients*. Maastricht: Datawyse.
Jehoel-Gijsbers, G.J.M. (2004). *Sociale uitsluiting in Nederland*. Den Haag. Sociaal en Cultureel Planbureau.
Jong-Gierveld, J. de (1984). *Eenzaamheid: Een meersporig onderzoek*. Deventer: Van Loghum Slaterus.
Jong-Gierveld, J. de and Kamphuis, F. (1985). The development of a Rasch-type loneliness scale. *Applied Psychological Measurement*, 9, 289–299.
Jong-Gierveld, J. de and Raadschelders, J. (1982). Types of loneliness. In: L.A. Peplau and D. Perlman, *Loneliness: A sourcebook of current theory, research and therapy* (pp. 105–119). New York: Wiley.
Jong-Gierveld, J. de and Tilburg, T. van (1990). *Manual of the loneliness scale*. Amsterdam: Vrije Universiteit, Department of Social Research Methodology.
Jong-Gierveld, J. de and Tilburg, T. van (1995). Social relationships, integration and loneliness. In: C.P.M. Knipscheer (ed.), *Living arrangements and social networks of older adults* (pp. 155–172). Amsterdam: VU University Press.
Jordan, W. (1996). *Rethinking welfare*. Oxford: Blackwell.
Kal, D. (2001). *Kwartiermaken: Werken aan ruimte voor mensen met een psychiatrische achtergrond*. Amsterdam: Boom.

Kasarda, J.D. and Janowitz, M. (1974). Community attachment in mass society. *American Sociological Review*, 39, pp. 328–339.

Knorr-Cetina, K. (2001). Postsocial relations: theorizing sociality in a postsocial environment. In G. Ritzer and B. Smart, *Handbook of social theory* (pp. 520–537). London: Sage Publications.

Komter, A.E. (1996). Reciprocity as a principle of exclusion: Gift giving in the Netherlands. *Sociology*, 30, 299–316.

Komter, A. and Schuyt, C. (1993). Geschenken en relaties. *Beleid en Maatschappij*, 20, 277–185.

Komter, A.E., Burgers, J. and Engbersen, G. (2000). *Het cement van de samenleving: Een verkennende studie naar solidariteit en cohesie*. Amsterdam: Amsterdam University Press.

Kunneman, H. (1996). *Van theemutscultuur maar walkman-ego: Contouren van een postmoderne individualiteit*. Meppel: Boom.

Kuypers, P. and Lans, J. van der (1994). *Naar een modern paternalisme: over de noodzaak van sociaal beleid. Pamflet*. Amsterdam: De Balie.

Lans, J. van der (1995). *De onzichtbare samenleving: Beschouwingen over publieke moraal*. Utrecht: NIZW.

Lasch, C. (1979). *The culture of narcissism: American life in an age of diminishing expectations*. New York: Warner.

Lazarus, R.S. (1966). *Psychological stress and the coping process*. New York: McGraw-Hill.

Lazarus, R.S. and Folkman, S. (1984). *Stress, appraisal and coping*. New York: Springer.

Leeuw, F.L. (2001). Over de praktische betekenis van sociaal kapitaal. In: J.C. Vrooman (red.), *Netwerken en sociaal kapitaal* (pp. 7–21). Amsterdam: SISWO/NSV.

Lin, N. (1982). Social resources and instrumental action. In: P.V. Marsden and N. Lin (eds), *Social structure and network analyses* (pp. 217–238). Beverly Hills: Sage.

Lin, N. (2001). *Social capital. A theory of social structure and action*. Cambridge: Cambridge University Press.

Linas, A. and Bieliauskas, P. (1982). *Stress and it relationship to health and illness*. Boulder: Westview Press.

Lincoln, K.D. (2000). Social support, negative social interactions, and psychological well-being. *Social Service Review*, June, 231–252.

Linneman, M., Leene, G., Bettink, K., Schram, M. and Voermans, J. (1990). *Uit eenzaamheid: Over hulpverlening bij ouderen*. Houten/Antwerpen: Bohn Stafleu Van Loghum.

Lofland, L.H. (1989). Private lifestyles, changing neighbourhoods and public life: A problem in organized community. *Tijdschrift voor Economische en Sociale Geografie*, 80, 2, 89–96.

Loo, H. van der (1996). Moderniteit en stedelijke identiteit. In: J. van Hoof and J. van Ruysseveldt (eds), *Sociologie en de moderne samenleving: Maatschappelijke veranderingen van de industriële revolutie tot in de 21ste eeuw* (pp. 373–392). Amsterdam/Meppel: Boom.

Loury, G. (1977). A dynamic theory of racial income differences. In: P.A. Wallace and A. Le Mund (eds), *Women, minorities and employment* (pp. 153–186). Lexington: Lexington Books.

Luteijn, F., Starren, J. and Dijk, H. van (1985). *Handleiding bij de Nederlandse Persoonlijkheids Vragenlijst (NPV)*. Lisse: Swets en Zeitlinger.
Machielse, A. (2003). *Niets doen, niemand kennen: De leefwereld van sociaal geïsoleerde mensen*. 's-Gravenhage: Elsevier Overheid.
Machielse, A. (2006). Onkundig en onrangepast: Een theoretisch perspectiff op sociaal isolement. Utrecht: Jan van Arkel.
Mackenbach, J.P. (1994). *Ongezonde verschillen: Over sociale stratificatie en gezondheid in Nederland*. Assen: Van Gorcum.
Mallinckrodt, B. (2001). Interpersonal processes, attachment, and development of social competencies in individual and group psychotherapy. In: B. Sarason and S. Duck (eds), *Personal relationships: Implications for clinical and community psychology*, (pp. 89–118). Chichester: Wiley.
Marsden, P.V. (1988). Homogeneity in confiding relations. *Social Networks*, 10, 57–76.
Mayhew, L. (1971). *Society: Institutions and activity*. New York: Columbia University Press.
Meeuwesen, L., Hortulanus, R. and Machielse, A. (2001). Social contacts and social isolation: A typology. *The Netherlands' Journal of Social Sciences*, 37, 132–154.
Michelson, W. (1977). *Environmental choice, human behavior and residential satisfaction*. New York: Oxford University Press.
Mills, C.W. (1951). *White collar: The American middle class*. New York: Oxford University Press.
Mol, S., Dinant, G., Metsemakers, J. and Knottnerus, J. (1999). Incidentieverschillen van (gewelddadige) ingrijpende gebeurtenissen in landelijke registratiesystemen, enquêtes in de bevolking en onderzoek onder huisartsen: Een literatuuroverzicht. *Nederlands Tijdschrift voor Geneeskunde*, 143, 1308–1314.
Mook, J., Kleijn, W. and Ploeg, H. van der (1989). Depressiviteit als dispositie gemeten met de Zung-schaal: Interne structuur en relaties met angst, boosheid, coping en sociale steun. *Nederlands Tijdschrift voor de Psychologie*, 44, 328–340.
Moos, R.H. (1990). *Coping Responses Inventory Manual*. Palo Alto: Stanford University and Veterans' Administration Medical Centers, Social Ecology Laboratory, Dept. Psychiatry and Behavioural Sciences.
Myers, D.G. (1999). *Social psychology* (6th edn). New York: McGraw-Hill College.
Nolen-Hoeksema, S. (1991). Responses to depression and their effects on the duration of depressive episodes. *Journal of Abnormal Psychology*, 100, 569–582.
Oorschot, W. van (2000). Te nemen of te laten: Over niet gebruik van inkomensondersteunende regelingen. In: R.P. Hortulanus and J.E.M. Machielse (eds), *In de marge: Het sociaal debat, deel 1* (pp. 103–114). 's-Gravenhage: Elsevier.
Orbach, S. (1998). People in distress. In: J. Franklin (ed.), *The politics of risk society* (pp. 90–98). Cambridge/Oxford: Polity Press.
Pearson, C. (1998). *Beyond the welfare state?* Cambridge: Polity Press.
Peplau. L.A. and Perlman, D. (eds) (1982). *Loneliness: A sourcebook of current theory, research and therapy*. New York: John Wiley.
Perlman, D. and Peplau, L.A. (1981). Toward a social psychology of loneliness. In: R. Gilmour and S. Duck (eds), *Personal relationships in disorder* (pp. 31–56). London: Academic Press.
Perlman, D. and Peplau, L.A. (1982). Theoretical approaches to loneliness. In: L.A. Peplau and D. Perlman, *Loneliness: A sourcebook of current theory, research and therapy* (pp. 123–134). New York: Wiley.
Pescosolido, B.A. and Levy, J.A. (2002). The role of social networks in health,

illness, disease and healing: the accepting present, the forgotten past, and the dangerous potential for a complacent future. In: J.A. Levy and B.A. Pescosolido (eds), *Social networks and health* (pp. 3–25). Amsterdam: JAI/Elsevier Science.

Pierce, G.R., Sarason, I.G. and Sarason, B.R. (1996). Coping and social support. In: M. Zeidner and N.S. Endler (eds), *Handbook of coping. Theory, research, applications* (pp. 434/451). New York: John Wiley.

Planalp, S. and Garvin-Doxas, K. (1994). Using mutual knowledge in conversation: Friends as experts on each other. In: S. Duck (ed.), *Dynamics of relationships* (pp. 1–26). Thousand Oaks: Sage.

Ploeg, H. van der, Buuren, E.T. van, Wöstmann, M., Huisman, S., Kleijn, W. and Stoffels, M. (1985). *Psychologisch onderzoek naar (het ontbreken van) de hulpvraag van slachtoffers van geweld. Deel II: Gevolgen, hulpvraag en hulpverlening.* Lisse: Swets en Zeitlinger.

Poel, M. van der (1993a). Delineating personal support networks. *Social Networks*, 15, 49–70.

Poel, M. van der (1993b). *Personal networks: A rational choice explanation of their size and composition.* Lisse: Swets & Zeitlinger.

Portes, A. (1998). Social capital: Its origins and applications in modern sociology. *Annual Review of Sociology*, 24, 1–24.

Putnam, R.D. (1993). *Making democracy work. Civic traditions in modern Italy.* Princeton: Princeton University Press.

Putnam, R.D. (1995). Bowling alone. America's declining social capital. *Journal of Democracy*, 6, 65–78.

Putnam, R.D. (2000). *Bowling alone. The collapse and revival of American community.* New York: Simon & Schuster.

Raub, W. (1997). *Samenwerking in duurzame relaties en sociale cohesie.* Amsterdam; Thesis/Thela.

Reijndorp, A. (1998). *Buitenwijk: Stedelijkheid op afstand.* Rotterdam: NAi.

Rice, L.P. (1987). *Stress and health: Principles and practice for coping and wellness.* Monterey: Brooks.

Ridder, D. de (1988). *Determinanten van psychische gezondheid. Een verkenning van de literatuur.* Utrecht: NcGv/Nederlands centrum Geestelijke volksgezondheid.

Ridder, D. de (1994). *Onderzoek naar de determinanten van psychische geonzdheid: Een verkenning van de literatuur.* Utrecht: NcGv/Nederlands centrum Geestelijke Volksgezondheid.

Riesman, D. (2001/1961). *The lonely crowd: A study of the changing American character.* New Haven/London: Yale University Press.

Rigers, S. and Lakravas, P.J. (1981). Community ties: Patterns of attachment and social interaction in urban neighbourhoods. *American Journal of Community Psychology*, 9, 1, 55–66.

RMO (1997). *Vereenzaming in de samenleving.* Rijswijk: Raad voor Maatschappelijke Ontwikkeling (RMO).

RMO (2000). *Ongekende aankopingspunten. Strategieën voor de aanpassing van de sociale infrastructuur.* Rijswijk: Raad voor Maatschappelijke Ontwikkeling.

RMO (2001). *Kwetsbaar in kwadraat: Krachtige steun aan kwetsbare mensen.* Rijswijk: Raad voor Maatschappelijke Ontwikkeling (RMO).

Room, G. (1997). Sociale uitsluiting en sociale rechten. In: J. Vranken, D. Geldof and G. van Menxel (red.), *Armoede en sociale uitsluiting jaarboek* (pp. 221–231). Leuven/Amersfoort: Acco.

Ros, W.J.G. (1990). *Sociale steun bij kankerpatienten.* Amsterdam: Thesis Publishers.

Rosenthal, R. (1966). *Experimenter effects in behavioral research.* New York: Appleton Century Crofts.
Rubin, L. (1996). *The transcendent child.* New York: Basic Books.
Rusbult, C.E. and Buunk, B.P. (1993). Commitment process in close relationships. An interdependence analysis. *Journal of Social and Personal Realtionships,* 10, 175–204.
Sarason, B.R., Sarason, I.G., Hacker, T.A. and Basham, R.B. (1985). Concomitants of social support. Social skills, physical attractiveness and gender. *Journal of Personality and Social Psychology,* 49, 469–480.
Sarason, B.R., Pierce, G.R. and Sarason, I.G. (1990). Social support: Sense of acceptance and the role of relationships. In: B.R. Sarason, I.G. Sarason and G.R. Pierce (eds), *Social support: An interactional view* (pp. 97–128). New York: John Wiley.
Sarason, I,G., Sarason, B.G. and Pierce, G.R. (1994). Social support: Global and relationship-based levels of analysis. *Journal of Social and Personal Relationships,* 11, 295–312.
Sarason, B.R., Sarason, I.G. and Gurung, R.A.R. (2001). Close personal relationships and health outcomes: A key to the role of social support. In: B. Sarason and S. Duck (eds), *Personal relationships: Implications for clinical and community psychology* (pp. 15–41). New York: John Wiley.
Sarason, B.R., Sarason, I.G. and Pierce, G.R. (1990). *Social support: An interactional view.* New York: Wiley.
Scheepers, P. and Janssen, J. (2001). Informele aspecten van sociaal kapitaal: Ontwikkelingen in Nederland 1970–1998. *Mens en Maatschappij,* 76, 3.
Schnabel, P. (2000). Vergroting van de maatschappelijke cohesie door versterking van de sociale infrastructuur. In: R.P. Hortulanus and J.E.M. Machielse (eds), *In de marge, Het sociaal debat* (pp. 21–34). 's-Gravenhage: Elsevier Bedrijfsinformatie.
Schrameijer, F. (1990). *Sociale steun: Analyse van een paradigma* [Dissertatie]. Utrecht: NcGv.
Schreurs, P.J.G. (*et al.*) (1993). *De Utrechtse Copinglijst ULC: Omgaan met problemen en gebeurtenissen.* Utrecht: Van Doorn.
Schuller, T., Baron, S. and Field, J. (2000). Social capital: a review and critique. In: S. Baron, J. Field and T. Schuller, *Social capital. Critical perspectives* (pp. 1–38). Oxford: Oxford University Press.
Schuyt, K. (1997). *Sociale cohesie en sociaal beleid: Drie publiekscolleges in De Balie.* Amsterdam: De Balie.
Scott, J. (1991). *Social network analysis: A handbook.* London: Sage.
Seligman, M.E.P (1975). *Helplessness: On depression, development and death.* San Francisco: Freeman.
Serraro Pascual, A. (ed.) (2004). *Are activation policies converging in Europe.* Brussels: ETUI.
Sevenhuijsen. S. (2000). De plaats van zorg: Over de relevantie van zorgethiek voor sociaal beleid. Utrecht: Universiteit Utrecht: Faculteit Sociale Wetenschappen.
Shadid, W.A. (1998). *Grondslagen van interculturele communicatie: Studieveld en werkterrein.* Houten/Diegem: Bohn, Stafleu Van Loghum.
Simmel, G. (1996 [1908]). Faithfulness and gratitude. In: A.E. Komter (ed.), *The gift: An interdisciplinary perspective* (pp. 39–48). Amsterdam: Amsterdam University Press.
Slater, P. (1976). *The pursuit of loneliness.* Boston: Beacon Press.

Smith, E.R., Murphy, J. and Coats, S. (1999). Attachment to groups: Theory and measurement. *Journal of Personality and Social Psychology*, 77, 94–110.

Smith, S.M. and Petty, R.E. (1995). Personality moderators of mood congruency effects on cognition: The role of self-esteem and negative mood regulation. *Journal of Personality and Social Psychology*, 68, 1092–1107.

Snijders, T.A.B. (2001). Methoden van netwerkanalyse. In: J.C. Vrooman (red.), *Netwerken en sociaal kapitaal* (pp. 23–41). Amsterdam: SISWO/NSV.

Sonderen, E. van (1995). Sociale steun en sociale netwerken. In: R. Sonderman, C.M.H. Hosman and M. Mulder (eds), *Het meten van determinanten van gezondheid: Een overzicht van beschikbare meetinstrumenten* (pp. 162–184). Assen: Van Gorcum.

Steenbergen, B. van (1996). De toekomst vanuit het onderbouwperspectief. In: J. van Hoof and J. van Ruysseveldt (eds), *Sociologie en de moderne samenleving: Maatschappelijke veranderingen van de industriële revolutie tot in de 21ste eeuw*, 2nd edn (pp. 461–494). Amsterdam/Meppel: Boom.

Stolle, D. (2000). Onderzoek naar sociaal kapitaal: Naar een attitudinale benadering. In: M. Hooghe (red.), *Sociaal kapitaal en democratie: Verenigingsleven, sociaal kapitaal en politieke cultuur* (pp. 25–59). Leuven/Leusden: Acco.

Sullivan, H.S. (1953). *The interpersonal theory of psychiatry*. New York: Norton.

Sumbadze, N. (1999). *The social web: Friendships of adult men and women*. Leiden: DSWO Press, University of Leiden.

Swaan, A. de (1979). Uitgaansbeperkingen en uitgaansangst. *De Gids*, 8, 5–31.

Swaan, A. de (1996). *De mensenmaatschappij: Een inleiding*. Amsterdam: Bert Bakker.

Taylor, S.E. (1986). *Health psychology*. New York: Random House.

Thoits, P.A. (1985). Self-labelling processes in mental illnesses: The role of emotional deviance. *American Journal of Sociology*, 1, 221–249.

Thoits, P.A. (1986). Social support as coping assistance. *Journal of Consulting and Clinical Psychology*, 54, 416–423.

Tijhuis, M. (1994). *Social networks and health* [Dissertatie]. Utrecht: NIVEL.

Tijhuis, M. (1996). Kenmerken van sociale netwerken en gezondheid: Theorie en empirie. *Tijdschrift voor Sociale Gezondheidszorg*, 74(2), 23–28.

Tijhuis, M., Flap, H.D., Foets, M. and Groenewegen, P.P. (1992). Netwerken in Nederland: Een onderzoek naar persoonlijke netwerken van Nederlanders. In: W. Jansen and G. van den Wittenboer (red.), *Sociale netwerken en hun invloed* (pp. 2–38). Meppel: Boom.

Tilburg, T.G. van (1988). *Verkregen en gewenste ondersteuning in het licht van eenzaamheidservaringen*. Utrecht: Elinkwijk.

Tönnies, F. (1887). *Gemeinschaf und Gesellschaft: Grundbegriffe der reinen Soziologie*. Leipzig: Reisland.

Turkenburg, M. and Hortulanus, R.P. (1996). *Een sociale visie op Binnenmaas*. Utrecht: Universiteit Utrecht/Faculteit der Sociale Wetenschappen.

Umberson, D. (1987). Family status and health behaviors: Social control as a dimension of social integration. *Journal of Health and Social Behavior*, 28, 306–319.

Unger, D.G. and Wandersman, A. (1985). The importance of neighbors: the social, cognitive and affective components of neigboring. *American Journal of Community Psychology*, 13, 2, 139–169.

Vaarwerk, M. te and Ridder, D. de (1994). *Onder druk van de omstandigheden: Persoons- en situatiespecifieke determinanten van coping*. Utrecht: NcGv.

Vaux, A. (1988). *Social support: Theory, research, and intervention*. New York: Praeger.

Verhaak, P. (1995). *Mental disorder in the community and in general practice: Doctors' views and patients' demands.* Aldershot: Avebury.
Warren, R. (1978). Exploration in neigbourhoods differentation. *Sociological Quarterly*, 19, 310–331.
Webber, M.M. (1968). Order in diversity: Community without propinquity. In: L. Wingo (ed.), *Cities and space.* Baltimore: Johns Hopkins Press.
Weber, M. (1988 [1920]). *Gesammelte Aufsätze zur Religionssoziologie I-III.* Tübingen: Mohr.
Weiss, R.S. (1973). *Loneliness: The experience of emotional and social isolation.* Cambridge Mass.: MIT Press.
Weiss, R.S. (1974). Loneliness: The provision of social relationships. In: Z. Rubin (ed.), *Doing unto others* (pp. 17–36). Englewood Cliffs: Prentice-Hall.
Wel, F. van, and Hortulanus, R. (2002). *De sociale staat van Utrecht: Naar een integrale analyse van de sociale infrastructuur.* Utrecht: Universiteit Utrecht.
Wellman, B. and Hall, A. (1985). Social networks and social support: Implications for later life. In: V. Marshall (ed.), *Later life: The social psychology of aging* (pp. 191–223). London: Sage.
Wellman, B. and Leighton, B. (1979). Networks, neighbourhoods and communities: Approaches to the study of the community question. *Urban Affairs Quarterly*, 14, 3, 363–390.
Willige, G. van de, Schreurs, P. Tellegen, B. and Zwart, F. (1985). Het meten van life-events: De Vragenlijst Recent Meegemaakte Gebeurtenissen (VRMG). *Nederlands Tijdschrift voor de Psychologie*, 40, 1–19.
Wilson, W.J.W. (1987). *The truly disadvantaged: The inner city, the underclass, and public policy.* Chicago/London: University of Chicago Press.
Wirth, L. (1938). Urbanism as a way of life. *American Journal of Sociology*, 44, 1–24.
Wuthnow, R. (1997). *The role of trust in civic renewal.* Working Paper No. 1. The National Commission on Civic Renewal. University of Maryland.
Ypeij, A., Snel, E. and G. Engbersen (1999). *Armoede in Amsterdam-Noord.* Rotterdam: Risbo/Erasmus Universiteit Rotterdam.
Zilboorg, C. (1938). Loneliness. *Atlantic Monthly*, January, 45–54.
Zoll, R. (1990). Modern individualisme en alledaagse solidariteit. *Tijdschrift voor Arbeid en Bewustzijn*, 3.
Zung, W. (1965). A self-rating depression scale. *Archives of General Psychiatry*, 13, 508–515.

Author index

Adriaanse, C.C.M. 9
Arts, C.H. 31
Asendorpf, J.B. 28

Baarsen, B. van 33, 58, 236
Baart, A. 249, 250
Badr, H. 17, 39
Bakker, K. 29
Bandura, A. 88
Bauman, Z. 22
Beck, U. 5, 22, 25, 248, 249, 252
Beck-Gernsheim, E. 22, 25, 248, 249, 252
Becker, G.S. 19
Berkel, R. van 137
Berkman, L.F. 16, 28, 29, 30, 146
Bieliauskas, P. 101, 102
Billington, R. 14, 18, 23, 25
Blum-Kulka, S. 84
Boer, A.H.D. de 27, 101, 116
Boomkens, R. 157
Bourdieu, P. 19, 20, 21, 240, 248
Bovens, M. 24
Bowlby, J. 28, 33, 84
Bowman, C.C. 21, 32
Boxman, E.A.W. 21
Broese van Groenou, M.I. 27
Brown, G.W. 101
Brown, J.D. 83
Brummett, B.H. 37, 38, 39, 42, 55, 57, 58
Burt, R.S. 20
Busschbach, J.T. van 27
Buunk, B.P. 21, 39

Castells, M. 22, 248

Cobb, S. 15, 16
Cohen, J. 20
Cohen, S. 15, 17, 31, 104
Coleman, J.S. 19, 20, 240

Dalgard, O.S. 27, 65, 103
Dam, J. ten 101, 102
Dantzig, A. van 252
Dasgupta, P. 20
DeLongis, A. 63, 64
Dignum, K. 29
Dijkstra, P. 10, 105
Draijer, N. 27
Durkheim, E. 17, 18, 22, 24, 239
Duyvendak, J.W. 157
Dykstra, P.A. 16, 17, 27, 28, 30, 31, 33, 34, 55, 236, 238

Elliott, G.R. 84
Engbersen, G. 116
Engel, G.L. 28, 64
Esping-Andersen, G. 4
Etzioni, A. 24

Feldman, S.S. 84
Felling, A.J.A. 31
Field, J. 19, 240
Fischer, A.H. 86
Fischer, C.S. 9, 13, 16, 18, 26, 27, 29, 30, 38, 41, 42, 58, 115, 146, 202
Flap, H.D. 19, 21, 26, 27
Fokkema, T. 33, 34, 236, 238.
Folkman, S. 28, 85, 101, 102, 103
Fromm, E. 18
Fromm-Reichmann, F. 32
Fukuyama, F. 20

Garvin-Doxas, K. 87
Gersons, B.P.R. 27, 64
Giddens, A. 22, 23, 25, 248
Gorter, K.A. 27
Gouldner, A.W. 24, 39
Gove, W.R. 16, 37
Granovetter, M.S. 20, 21, 241

Habermas, J. 23
Hall, A. 16, 30, 156, 157
Harris, J.R. 84
Harris, T.O. 101
Hechter, M. 24
Heerikhuizen, B. van 248
Heider, F. 92
Heller, K. 14, 15, 16, 17, 31
Helman, C.G. 104
Hemerijck, A. 24
Hess, B.B. 27
Hiller, J.B. 101
Hills, J.J. 26
Hirschman, A.O. 26
Hobsbawm, E. 24
Homans, G.C. 19
Hooley, J.M. 101
Horneman-Møller, I. 137
Hortulanus, R.P. 5, 6, 9, 14, 29, 31, 37, 39, 55, 82, 83, 100, 118, 137, 156, 157, 207, 241, 250, 252, 254
House, J.S. 15, 28, 29, 30, 32, 37, 238
Hoynck van Papendrecht, B. 82
Hughes, M. 16, 37
Hymes, D.H. 87

Janowitz, M. 157
Janssen, J. 19
Janssen, M. 27
Jehoel-Gijsbers 14, 26, 27, 74, 100
Jong-Gierveld, J. de 10, 27, 31, 32, 33, 34, 37, 38, 42, 43, 55, 57, 109, 202, 238
Jordan, W. 137

Kahn, R.L. 15, 30
Kal, D. 27
Kamphuis, F. 42, 202
Kasarda, J.D. 157
Knorr-Cetina, K. 5
Komter, A.E. 21, 26, 37, 39, 58, 116

Kunneman, H. 25, 249
Kuypers, P. 249

Lakravas, P.J. 156
Lans, J. van der 249
Lazarus, R.S. 28, 82, 85, 101, 102, 103
Leeuw, F.L. 20, 240
Leighton, B. 156, 157
Levy, J.A. 14, 16, 27
Lin, N. 20, 240, 241
Linas, A. 101, 102
Lincoln, K.D. 17, 31, 37, 38, 39, 41, 58, 203, 238
Linneman, M. 28, 239
Lofland, L.H. 23, 156, 157
Loo, H. van der 180
Loury, G. 19
Luteijn, F. 82, 87

Machielse, A. 9, 29, 230, 236, 248
Mackenbach, J.P. 100
Mallinckrodt, B. 27, 39, 81
Manstead, A.S.R. 86
Marsden, P.V. 27
Maslow, A. 63
Mayhew, L. 24
Meeuwesen, L. 9, 203, 233
Michelson, W. 156
Mills, C.W. 26, 249
Mol, S. 64, 79
Mook, J. 109, 110
Moos, R.H. 101
Myers, D.G. 13, 15, 17, 18, 19, 83

Nolen-Hoeksema, S. 86

Oorschot, W. van 74
Orbach, S. 5

Pearson, C. 137
Peplau, L.A. 25, 28, 32, 33, 37, 38, 239
Perlman, D. 25, 28, 32, 33, 37, 38, 239
Pescosolido, B.A. 14, 16, 27
Petty, R.E. 83
Pierce, G.R. 28
Phillips, S.L. 18, 26, 29, 42, 146
Planalp, S. 87
Ploeg, H. van der 79

Author index

Poel, M. van der 13, 16, 31, 38, 41, 57, 116
Portes, A. 21
Putnam, R.D. 19, 20, 24, 240

Raadschelders, J. 33
Raub, W. 24
Reijndorp, A. 29, 251
Rice, L.P. 103
Ridder, D. de 28, 102, 104
Riesman, D. 32
Rigers, S. 156
Rogers, C. 63
Rook, K.S. 14, 15, 16, 17, 31
Room, G. 137
Ros, W.J.G. 28
Rosenthal, R. 84
Rubin, L. 81, 82
Rusbult, C.E. 21

Sarason, B.R. 14, 15, 21, 31, 38, 39, 81, 82, 100, 116
Sarason, I.G. 16
Sas, O. 't 82
Schaufeli, W. 21, 39
Scheepers, P. 19
Schnabel, P. 234
Schrameÿer, F. 17, 21, 37, 38, 58, 203, 238
Schreurs, P.J.G. 102
Schuller, T. S. 19
Schuyt, C. 18, 19, 26, 248, 249
Scott, J. 30
Seligman, M.E.P. 86, 102
Serraro Pascual, A. 137
Sevenhuijsen, S. 252
Shadid, W.A. 82, 87
Simmel, G. 17, 239
Slater, P. 32
Smith, E.R. 28
Smith, S.M. 83
Snijders, T.A.B. 30
Sonderen, E. van 38, 41, 58

Steenbergen, B. van 22

Stolle, D. 19, 20, 28, 240
Sullivan, H.S. 32
Sumbadze, N. 32, 37, 38, 39, 238
Swaan, A. de 22, 23, 25, 85
Syme, S.L. 15, 16, 28, 29, 30, 31, 146

Taylor, S.E. 28, 64, 80, 103
Tazelaar, F. 26, 27
Thoits, P.A. 15
Tijhuis, M. 14, 16, 31, 38, 42, 57, 58, 100, 101, 103, 104, 114, 116, 205
Tilburg, T. van 10, 27, 28, 32, 33, 34, 37, 38, 57, 238
Tönnies, F. 17, 24, 179, 180, 239
Turkenburg, M. 9

Umberson, D. 16
Unger, D.G. 156

Vaarwerk, M. te 102
Vaux, A. 17
Verhaak, P. 79
Völker, B. 19

Wandersman, A. 156
Waring, J.M. 27
Warren, R. 156
Webber, M.M. 157
Weber, M. 22
Weiss, R.S. 15, 33, 236, 238
Wel, F. van 55
Wellman, B. 16, 30, 156, 157
Willige, G. van de 65
Wills, T. 17, 104
Wilpers, S. 28
Wilson, W.J.W. 26
Winants, B.A.C. 27
Wirth, L. 24, 180
Wuthnow, R. 28

Ypeij, A. 252

Zilboorg, C. 32
Zoll, R. 25
Zung, W. 10, 105, 109, *110*, *111*

Subject index

age 44; and depression 112–13; and health 113–14; and life events 77; and mental vulnerability 109; and network size 44; and personal competences 97, 99; and physical vulnerability 108; and report mark on health 107; and social typology 56, 57; and societal participation 152–3
attachment 84
attribution processes 91

background factors *see* demographics
buffer effects: health and 104, 114
buffering hypothesis, 17
bureaucratization 23

causes of social isolation 27–9, 201–14; demographics 27, *210*, 242; an explanatory model 242–4, 245; health (problems) 27, 100, 205, 242; individual factors 209; (in)formal support 205–6; joint effects 212–14; life events 27, 203–4, 242; living environment 29; personal competences 204–5; personal factors 27, *210*, *211*; personality 28; problem-solving capacities 28; social environment 170–4, 207–8, 210, *211*; societal factors 209, *211*; societal participation 28–9, 146–7, 206–7; urban and rural areas 208–9
CBS (Centraal Bureau voor de Statistiek) 16, 180
childhood: and life events 77–8
city: and social isolation 179–200

civil society 35, 240
club life: and urbanization 189–90, 199
cohesion *see* social cohesion
comfort 261
communicative competences 87
contacts *see* social contacts
coping 28, 80, 101–2, 241; coping assistance 15; and health 102–4, 114; and life events 93; social coping styles 28; strategies 85, *86*, 87, 102; and stress 85; *see also* personal competences
country side: and social isolation 179–200
cultural facilities use of 190–1, 199

demographics 43–4; and depression 112–13; and life events 77; and loneliness 45; and network size 44; and personal competences 97; and physical vulnerability 108; and urbanization 182–4
dependency on professional facilities 132–4; and vulnerability 133–5
depression 37, 102, 109–12; and demographics 113; and general health assessment 112; and loneliness 109, 112; and mental status 112; and negative events 112–31; and network scope 109, 112; and personal competences 112–13; and physical status 112; and positive events 112; and religion 112; self-evaluation scale 10; and social typology *110*; and socialization 112; Zung depression scale 105, 109–12

depressiveness 105
differentiation 22
disintegration 24

education 44; and network size 38, 41, 44, 57; and social typology 56; and societal participation 140–3
emotions 86
entertainment: and urbanization 190–1, 199
environment: social living 259
environmental isolation 156–76; as absence of support network 160, 162–3; and homogeneous beliefs about neighbourhood life and behaviour 166–70; measure of 181; and mental health 166; as mismatch between factual and preferred social contacts 160–3; as negative identification with neighbourhood 160, 163–5; and social isolation 170–5; and urbanization 193–4
ethnicity 44; and loneliness 45; and network size 44; and physical vulnerability 108; and social typology 56, 57
events: stressful 101
exclusion *see* social exclusion

facilities 119–22, 259; dependency on 132–4; and informal support 129–32; and social typology 128–9; use of 119–20; and vulnerability 122–5
families: single parent 101
family-bounded contacts: and urbanization 185–6, 198
financial vulnerability 117–18, 125, 128–9; *see also* vulnerability
formal care *see* professional care
formal facilities *see* professional facilities
formal networks *see* institutionalized networks
formal support *see* professional support

Gemeinschaft 179–80
gender 44; and depression 112; and health report mark 107; and life events 77; and mental vulnerability 109; and network support 47; and physical vulnerability 108; and social typology 56
generalizability of the results 10–11, 234–5
Gesellschaft 179–80
giving help: attitude towards 94, 95
globalization 22, 24

hassles: daily 64, 71, 78, 102, 261
health 100–14, 259, 261; and buffer effects 104, 114; and companionship support 114; and coping 114; and demographics 113–14; and depression 109–12; explanatory models for 101–2; indicators 104, 114; and life events 113; and life style 101; and loneliness scale 114; measures 265; mental 108–9; and negative events 113, 114; and personal competences 113; and personal network 14–17, 100; physical 100; and problem solving 114; report mark on 105, 106–7; selection by 101; and significant others 113; social 100; and social environment 101; and social isolation 100–14; and social resources 103–4; and social support 103–4; and social typology *107*, *108*, 113, 114; and stressful events 101; *see also* mental vulnerability
help: with social isolation 261
helplessness 102; and depression 86
hindrances to functioning 259
homeless 101
homogeneity: and environmental isolation 166–70; and neighbourhood 166–70, 173, 174; and social relationships 15, 18; and social typology 173–4; and urbanization 194–6, 200

identity 83
immigrants 101; and social typology 57
important events *see* life events
income 44; and social typology 56
individual well-being 225–9; and personal competences 227; and social

typology subgroup profiling 227–8; and societal participation 228
individualization 22; and loneliness 32; risks 5; and social relationships 4–5, 25–6, 35; societal consequences 4–5, 24
informal care 115–16; and urbanization 188–9, 199
informal groups: and urbanization 189–90, 199
informal help 115–16
informal network *see* personal network
informal relationships *see* personal network
informal support 115–16, 120–1; potential 117, 120; received 117, 120; and use of professional facilities 129–32; and vulnerability 125–6, 135
institutionalized networks 20, 21, 240
intervention strategy 253–6; general prevention 254; and informal support 256–7; problem reduction 255–6; and professional support 256–7; and professional workers 253–4; risk signalling 254–5; and self care 253
intimacy: transformation of 23
isolation *see* social isolation; socially isolated

knowledge: shared 87; and loneliness 87

labour participation: and social exclusion 137; and societal isolation 137; and societal participation 138–9; and urbanization, 187–8, 199
life attitude 93–4, 261
life events 63–4, 101, 102; and changes in network size 51; and childhood 77, 78; consequences of 261; and consolation 75–6; and coping 93; definitions 63–5; and demographics 77; and depression 112–13; effects 74; and health 113, 114; and loneliness 76; negative 63–4, 66, 68, 69, 78, 101; and network size 76; normal 64; personal 69–71, 70; and personal competences 77, 79, 92–3, 97; positive 63, 64, 66, 67, 78; and protection 75–6; and report mark on health 77, 106; risk factors 76–8; and social isolation 63–80; and social support 72–4; and social typology 65–71, 66; social welfare policy 79–80; societal 69–71, 70; and societal participation 77; traumatic 64, 68; *see also* minor events
local social orientation: measure of 181–2; and social typology 197, 200; and urbanization 196–8, 200
location 44; and report mark on health 107; and social typology 56, 57
locus of control: internal 85; external 86
loneliness 39, 42–3, 45, 57, 87, 258; and demographics 45; and depression 103, 109, 112; emotional 33; and life events 76; and network size 45; and personal competences 97; social 33
loneliness research 14, 32–4, 238; cognitive approach 32–3, 238; deficit approach 32–3, 238; interactionist explanations 32; psychodynamic explanations 32; sociological explanations 32
loneliness scale 10, 105; and depression 114; and health 114; *see also* mental vulnerability
'lonely', the 40, 46, 57–59; and depression 109; and individual well-being 227–8; and mental vulnerability 108–9; and personal competences 219–21, 223–5; and physical vulnerability 107; and report mark on health 106–7; and religion 47; and societal activeness 223; and societal participation 221–3; and societal passiveness 223; and societal well-being 225–7

major events *see* life events
marginalization 26
marital status 44; and loneliness 45; and social typology 56
mental status: and depression 112; *see also* health
mental vulnerability 105, 117–18, 125, 128–9; and demographics 109; and personal competences 109; *see also* health; vulnerability

Subject index

minor events 64; daily hassles 64, 71, 78 102; uplifts 64, 71–2, 78; *see also* life events
modern poverty 137
modernization process 22–4, 34–5; and social environment 179–80; and social relationships 25–6
moving plans: and urbanization 192–3, 200
multinomial regression 209–14

negative events 63–4, 66, 68, 69, 78, 101; *see also* life events
neighbourhood 217–29; and activities 159; and facilities 159; homogeneous beliefs about 166–70; identification with 163–5; and support network 158–9; *see also* social environment
neighbourly contacts 158; function of 158; and urbanization 193–4, 199–200
network research 29–31
network (size) 38, 41, 44, 51, 57; changes in 43, 50–2, 51; *see also* personal network
network support, 15; *see also* social support
non-events 64; *see also* life events

objective isolation 33
openness 87

participation in society *see* societal participation
personal competences 81–99, 85–7, 86, 261; demographics 97, 99; and depression 112–13; evaluative reports 97; and health 113; and homogeneity 173–4; and individual well-being 227; and life events 77, 79, 92–3, 97; and loneliness 97; measures 87–8; and network size 97; participation in society 97; problem solving skills 87; risk factors 97–8; self confidence 87, 88; and social balance 99; and social isolation 81–99, 88–91; social skills 87, 88; and social support 98; and social typology 217–29; and socially competent 219–21; and socially inhibited, 219–21; and socially isolated 219–22; and societal participation 217–29; and societal well-being 225–7; and subgroup profiling of social typology 221; and well-being 99; *see also* coping
personal identity *see* identity
personality traits 81
personal network 8, 240; average scope 184; composition 147–8; demographics 44; and depression 109, 112; exchange approach 41; experience 258; features (type of relationship, distance) 46, 51; functionality 21; functions 15–17; and health 14–17, 100; and identity 15; information 258; and life events 51, 76; loneliness 45; negative consequences 17; and personal competences 97; quality of 38, 186, 198; and religion 47; research on 13, 14, 29–34, 238, 242; as social capital 19–21; and social integration 16; and social typology 50–2; and urbanization 184, 186, 198; and vulnerability 128, 135; and well-being 14–17; *see also* network (size)
personal well-being: and social isolation 25–6; and social relationships 6; and social support 15, 16, 34
philantropic particularism 116
physical status: and depression 112; *see also* health
physical vulnerability 105, 107–8, 117–18, 125, 128–9; demographics 108; *see also* health; vulnerability
policy (vision) 249–53; general prevention 251–2; and life events 79–80; problem reduction 253; risk signalling 252
positive events *see* life events
problem accumulation 123–5, 125; and use of professional facilities 123–5
problem solving 82, 85, 102; attitude towards 94; and health 114; skills 87, 88, 102; *see also* coping
professional care 116
professional facilities 118; dependency on 129, 132–4; importance for daily

Subject index 285

life 132–4; and informal support 120–1, 129–32; non-use 125; and quality of the personal social network 121; and vulnerability 122–5, 128–9, 135
professional support 113, 116; intervention strategy 256–7
protection 53–4, 260; and life events 75–6; protective factors 43; sources of 53
public involvement 248

quality of life 100

rationalization 22
received support: and degree of urbanization 185, 198
reciprocity 19, 20, 39, 240
reflexive self 23
religion 47; and comfort 76; and the lonely 47; and network size 47; and protection 53; and social typology 47
research 8–12; aim 8–9; comparison of respondents 261; measuring instruments 235–6; method 9–11, 234–6; (non) response 234–5; selection of respondents 234–5; see also generalizability of the results
residential history: and urbanization 192
risk factors see demographic variables
RMO (Raad voor Maatschappelijke Ontwikkeling) 102, 249, 252
rural society 180

self-confidence 82, 87, 98; and personal competences 87, 88
self-disclosure 87
self-esteem 37, 82, 84
self-respect 82
social balance 39, 52; and personal competences 99; and social typology 58
social bonds 101
social capital 19–21, 34, 98; definitions of 20–1; on different levels 19
social capital theory 239–42; shortcomings 240, 241–2
social change 4–5, 22–4; and social relationships 25–6

social climate: and urbanization 180, 194–6
social cohesion 7, 17, 18, 24, 25–6, 35, 39, 240, 242
social competences: and government policy 8
social contacts: decreasing 149–51; increasing 149–51; need for 46; quality of 58, 117; satisfaction with 43; as a societal resource 216; as a source of social support 215
social contacts typology see social typology
social contexts 23
social control 16, 17–18
social environment 217–29; changes in 6, 22–4, 179–80; and environmental isolation 160–6; functions 158–9; and health 101; and homogeneity 166–70; and social isolation 170–4; and urbanization 192–6, 199–200; see also neighbourhood
social exclusion 26, 35, 100, 137, 240–1, 244, 261; labour participation 137
social facilities: use of 190–1, 199
social identity see identity
social inequality 7
social integration 7, 16, 17, 18–19, 24; negative effects 19; network research 30
social isolation: and certain population groups 242; consequences of 214–16, 237; definition 35–6, 37–40, 237–9, 244–5; and environmental isolation 170–4; and health 100–14; and homogeneity 173–4; as independent phenomenon 246–7; as individual structural factor 248; and individual well-being 227–8; intervention strategy 253–6; as issue for sociale sciences, 24–7; and life events 63–80; manifestations 3–4; as modern life risk 248; objective criteria for 38–9, 58–9; and personal competences 81–99, 217–29; policy vision 249–53; and prevention 251–2, 254; as private problem 6, 246–7; and problem reduction 253, 255–6;

social isolation *continued*
as public issue 6, 26, 35; risk factors 4, 5–6; and risk signalling 252, 254–5; and social capital 248; and (social) cohesion 25–6; and social environment 6, 156–75; and social networks 37, 38; social policy 7, 247–9; and societal isolation 137–55; as societal issue 246–7; and societal participation 28–9, 137–55, 146–7, 217–29, 240–1; as societal structural factor 248; and societal well-being 225–7; and solidarity 25–6; and subgroup profiling 221–5; subjective criteria for 38–40, 58–9; and survival strategy 229, 248; and urbanization 6; and well-being 25–6; *see also* causes of social isolation; health; life events; personal competences; social capital; urbanization

social network *see* personal network
social network approach 38
social orientation *see* local social orientation
social relationships: definition of 13; emotional aspects 241–2; increased importance of 5; as social capital 19–21; and social change 25–6, 35; and social cohesion 7; and societal participation 6–7
social skills 87, 88; *see also* personal competences
social support 242; actual 38–9, 43, 258; appreciation 15; and coping strategies 104; emotional 16, 41–2, 47, 48; functions 47, 48; given 43, 49, 49–50, 95, 96; and health 16, 100, 103–4, 114; instrumental 16, 42, 47, 48; and life events 72–74; and network research 30–1; and personal competences 98; and personal networks 103; potential support 16, 38; practical support 16; received 43, 49, 49–50, 263; social companionship 16, 42, 47, 48, 114; social typology 47, 48, 49, 50; and stress 16–17; and well-being 15, 16, 34; *see also* support network
social typology 39–40, 45–7, 46, 117,
181, 217–29; and changes in network size 50–2; and degree of urbanization 186, 197; and demographics 55–7, 56; and depression *110*; empirical basis 233, 239; and feeling at ease 46; and health 113–14; and homogeneity 173–4; and life events 66, 65–71; and loneliness 39–40; meaningful approach 38–59; and mental status *108*; and need for social contacts 46; and network size 39–40; and network support functions 47; and personal competences 221; and physical status *107*; and prevention 251–2, 254; and problem reduction 253, 255–6; and protection 53, 54; and religion 47; and rich social life 54, 55; and risk signalling 252, 254–5; and social balance 58; and social environment 156–75; and social exclusion 147; and social policy 246–57; and socialization 91–2; and societal participation 137–55, 222–3; and subgroup profiling 217–29; and support 49, 50; and time spend on contacts 46; and use of professional facilities 119–20, 121–2, 134–5; and vulnerability 122–5, 126–8, 128–32, 132–5

socialization 18, 28, 34, 81, 84–5, 261; and depression 112; and report mark on health 106; and social typology 91–2

'*socially competent*', the 40, 46, 57–9; and depression 109; and individual well-being 227–8; and mental vulnerability 108–9; and personal competencies 219–21, 223–5; and physical vulnerability 107; and report mark on health 106–7; and societal activeness 223; and societal participation 221–23; and societal passiveness 223; and societal well-being 225–7; *see also* social typology

'*socially inhibited*' the 40, 46, 57–9; and dependence of professional support 225; depression 109; and environmental isolation 225; and individual well-being 227–8; and mental vulnerability 108–9; and passive life attitude 225; and personal competencies 219–21, 223–5; and physical vulnerability 107; and report mark on health 106–7; and societal activeness 223; and societal participation 221–3; and societal passiveness 223; and societal well-being 225; *see also* social typology

'socially isolated', the 40, 46, 57–9; and dependence of professional support 225; and depression 109; and individual well-being 227–8; and mental vulnerability 108–9; and passive life attitude 223; and personal competences 219–22, 223–5; and physical vulnerability 107; and report mark on health 106–7; and societal activeness 223; and societal participation 221–3; and societal passiveness 223; and societal well-being 225–7; *see also* social typology

social resources 103–4; and health 37
social responsibility 93
social skills 87; *see also* personal competences
societal isolation: and labour participation 138–9, 199; modern poverty 137; and social exclusion 137; and social isolation 137–55
societal participation 137–55, 259; and age 152–3; and composition personal network 147–8; and individual well-being 227–8; and informal support 147–8; and labour participation 187–8, 199; and life events 77; and the 'lonely' 221–3; and marital status 153–4; measure of 140–2, 190–1; operationalizations 138–44; and personal competences 97; and social capital 240; and social exclusion 144–6; and social isolation 28–9, 146–7, 240–1; and social typology 217–29; and the 'socially competent' 221–3; and the 'socially inhibited' 221–3; and the 'socially isolated' 221–3; and subgroup profiling 222–3; and urbanization 187–92, 198–9
societal well-being 225–9; personal competences 225–6; social typology subgroup profiling 25–8; societal participation 226
society: views on 259
socio-economic status 44; depression 112–13; life events 77; loneliness 45; mental vulnerability 109; personal competences 97, 99; physical vulnerability 108; report mark on health 107; social typology 56, 57; societal participation 142–3
solidarity 7, 17, 18, 24, 25–6, 35
stress 102, 114
stressful situations 28
strong bonds 113
subgroup profiling 217–29, *221*, *223*; and independence and solidarity 221; and individual well-being 227–8; and personal competences 221; of social typology 219–23; and societal functioning and personal contacts 222; and societal participation 222; and societal well-being 225–7
support network: average scope 184; and degree of urbanization 184–5; as neighbourhood function 158–9

trust: generalized 20, 240; mutual 20, 87

understanding: shared 87
unemployed 101
uplifts 64, 71–2, 78, 261
urban society 179–80
urbanization 44, 260; and club life 189–90, 199; and cultural facilities 190, 199; and demographic factors 182–3, 198; and entertainment 190, 199; and environmental isolation 193–4; and homogeneity 194–6, 200; and informal care 188–9, 199; and informal groups 189–90, 199; and labour participation 187–8, 199; and local social orientation 196–8, 200; and loneliness 45; measure of 180; and neighbourly contacts 193–4, 198–9; and network size 44; and personal networks 184, 198; and received support 185, 198;

urbanization *continued*
  and social climate 180, 194–6; and social contacts typology 186; and social environment 192–6, 199–200; and social facilities 190, 199; and societal participation 187–92, 198–9; and socio-economic factors 183–4; and support network 184, 198; and volunteer work 188, 199

volunteer work: and urbanization, 188, 199
vulnerability 122–32; and dependency of professional facilities 132–4; and informal support 125–6, 135; and problem accumulation 123–5; and quality of the personal network 126; and received support 126; and use of professional facilities 122–5, 130–2; *see also* financial vulnerability; mental vulnerability; physical vulnerability

weak bonds 20, 113
well-being: domains 261; and personal competences 99; subjective 38; *see also* individual well-being; personal well-being; societal well-being
WHO (World Health Organization) 100

youth 91; socialization 91; happy 91, 98

Lightning Source UK Ltd.
Milton Keynes UK
UKOW03f0525070114

224094UK00003B/76/P